FEMALE BRANDO

THE LEGEND OF KIM STANLEY

JON KRAMPNER

BACK STAGE BOOKS
An imprint of Watson-Guptill Publications/New York

Senior Editor: Mark Glubke
Editor: Michelle Bredeson
Cover Design: Mark van Bronkhorst, MVB Design
Interior Design: Leah Lococo
Production Manager: Hector Campbell

First published in 2006 by Back Stage Books, an imprint of Watson-Guptill
Publications, a division of VNU Business Media, Inc.,
770 Broadway, New York, NY 10003
www.wgpub.com

Library of Congress Cataloging-in-Publication Data

Krampner, Jon, 1952-
  Female Brando : the legend of Kim Stanley / Jon Krampner.
     p. cm.
  Includes bibliographical references and index.
  ISBN-13: 978-0-8230-8847-8 (alk. paper)
  ISBN-10: 0-8230-8847-2 (alk. paper)
  1. Stanley, Kim. 2. Actors—United States—Biography. I. Title.
  PN2287.S668K73 2006
  792.02'8092—dc22   2005036270

Excerpt from "Daddy," from *Ariel* by Sylvia Plath, copyright © 1963 by Ted Hughes.
Reprinted by permission of HarperCollins Publishers.

Excerpt from "mehitabel's song," from *archy and mehitabel* by Don Marquis, copyright
© 1927 by Doubleday, a division of Random House, Inc. Used by permission of Doubleday,
a division of Random House, Inc.

Cover photograph © John Springer Collection/CORBIS

Still photos from the film *Seance on a Wet Afternoon* are from the private collection of
Bryan Forbes, copyright, and are not to be reproduced unless accompanying reviews.

Photograph of Kim Stanley, Jack Lord, and Brook Seawell from *The Traveling Lady* by
Fred Fehl, courtesy of Gabriel Pinski/www.FredFehl.com and of the Billy Rose Theatre
Collection, the New York Public Library for the Performing Arts, Astor, Lenox and Tilden
Foundations.

Printed in the United States

First printing, 2006

1 2 3 4 5 6 7 8 9 / 14 13 12 11 10 09 08 07 06

To the Honorable Henry Waxman,
the Honorable John Conyers Jr.,
Ambassador Joseph Wilson IV . . .

and other American patriots

You stand at the blackboard, daddy,
In the picture I have of you,
A cleft in your chin instead of your foot
But no less a devil for that . . .

—Sylvia Plath, "Daddy"

the things that I had not ought to
i do because i ve gotto
wotthehell wotthehell
and i end with my favorite motto
toujours gai toujours gai

—Don Marquis, "the song of mehitabel"

CONTENTS

ACKNOWLEDGMENTS

My thanks to Veronica Mesias, who was helpful even when she didn't realize it.

Mark Glubke, my editor at Back Stage Books, believed in this project when no one else did, and was a genuine pleasure to work with. Thanks to Mark Dawidziak for directing me to him and to Michelle Bredeson, who braved the midwinter cold of transit-stricken Manhattan to copy-edit the manuscript.

Roger O. Hirson told me to look at the obits page of the *New York Times*. Eli Wallach let me know about Kim's memorial service at the Actors Studio, Delbert Mann pushed me to attend it, and Lou Goth consoled me when I had a miserable time at it.

My crack research team consisted of my father, Robert Krampner, and cousin John Krampner in New York City; the inimitable Lacquie Campbell in Albuquerque (say hi to Pat Robertson, Laquie!); Ward Harrison in Louisville; Ann Holmes and Beverly Bellot in Houston; Jeff Jackson, Sharon Ivy and Beth Parsley in rural Texas; Ellen Bailey at the Pasadena Playhouse; and my mother, Dr. Bernice Elkin.

Local guide services were provided by Joe Wittenburg in Mills County, Texas; Wandah Mayben Alexander in Lampasas County, Texas; Karen Lerner in Tularosa, New Mexico; Nancy Dunn in Artesia, New Mexico; Robert Nott in Santa Fe; and Nita Murphy in Taos. Thanks to Betsy Norton Barrios for her Cooks Tour of Rockland County.

Help in tracking down elusive sources came from Miranda Eastham at the University of New Mexico Alumni Office, Mary Mercier, Gareth May of Actors Equity, Johnny Friedkin, Doris Blum at Whitehead-Stevens, Jackson McGarry, Robert Ellerman, Ti Piper, and Kathy Finley of the Albuquerque High School Alumni Association.

Among the family members most helpful to me were Kim's brother Justin Reid, her daughter Dr. Rachel Zahn, and her cousin-in-law Dorthy Miller.

Credits to the craft of librarianship include Christine Karatnytsky and Jeremy Megraw in the Billy Rose Theatre Collection of the New York Library for the Performing Arts, John Vittal of the Albuquerque Public Library, Helene Mochedlover of the Los Angeles Public Library, Evelyn

Ward of the Cleveland Public Library, Allison Morris of the Ann Arbor District Library, Dace Taub at the USC Regional History Center, Ned Comstock at the USC Cinema/TV Library, Rosemary Hane, Fred Bauman and Alice Birney at the Library of Congress, Barbara Hall and Stacy Behlmer at the Margaret Herrick Library of the Academy of Motion Picture Arts and Sciences, and Harold Miller at the State Historical Society of Wisconsin.

Thanks also to Cinema/TV archivists Dan Einstein and Mark Quigley at the UCLA Film and Television Archive and Maxine Fleckner Ducey and Dorinda Hartmann at the Wisconsin Center for Film and Theater Research.

Especially helpful interviews were provided by Randy Bennett, Henry Denker, Mitch Erickson, Ashley Feinstein, Horton Foote, Sir Peter Hall, Martin Landau, Arthur Laurents, Dorthy Miller, Elissa Myers, Vivian Nathan, Katherine Norris, Rietta Netter Oppenheim, Carl Palusci, Justin Reid, Lucile Reid Brock, Wayne Sabato, Craig Strong, John Weckesser, the late Robert Whitehead, Elizabeth Wilson, Dr. Rachel Zahn, and Paul Zindel.

My stellar but unassuming computer expert David Farber saw me through several high-tech crises. Anita Fore of the Authors Guild helped me through the contract negotiation process with her legal-eagle skills.

Ann Rosenberg served as muse, correspondent, and guide to the cultural history of Philadelphia.

A special thanks to Gerhard Clausing of the department of German at USC for translating a review of *Yes Is for a Very Young Man* from the *New Yorker Staats-Zeitung*.

Delbert Mann, Tad Mosel, David Garfield, Jinx Witherspoon Rodger, Roger O. Hirson, John Weckesser, Dorothy Land Fitzgerald, and Jackson McGarry were all kind enough to read draft chapters.

Thanks to Stephen Kroll for granting me access to the Lucy Kroll papers in the Library of Congress.

Not to be forgotten are Iris Berl, Jim Mentel, Karen Amsterdam, Lydia Sharp, Shaun Considine, Stephen Everett, Richard Stoddard, Phil from Kent, and Guy Strickland of the BBC.

Finally, I owe a posthumous debt of gratitude to Fred Coe, the subject of my first book. With the possible exception of his grandson Sam, I am the last in a long line of writers to benefit from dealing with him, and I miss both him and his wife, Alice.

PREFACE

For several years after finishing my biography of live TV drama produc-er Fred Coe, I searched in vain for the subject of my next book. During the summer of 2001, I was in New York. While there, I called Roger O. Hirson, who had written several shows for Coe. "Did you see the *New York Times* this morning?" he asked. "Kim Stanley died." Many people I had interviewed about Coe had shared a sense of awe and magic about Kim, who starred in many of Coe's productions, and I was intrigued. Although she was one of the greatest stage actresses of the twentieth century, I came to this book out of my interest in live television drama.

Kim Stanley was not an easy person, and neither was writing about her. She was secretive and had a complex, shape-shifting personality, encrusted over with several layers of self-mythologizing. Getting to the heart of that was no easy matter: Sometimes she seemed less a person-ality than a loosely affiliated collection of primal impulses.

Many of her colleagues had died, had Alzheimer's, had pickled their brains in alcohol, or didn't want to talk about her for reasons ranging from still-simmering anger to protectiveness. Family members would cooperate one day and then, with no explanation, not be on speaking terms with me the next. Her worshipful students regarded me as the intellectual equivalent of a grave robber.

But many people did speak to me, many resources on Kim were available, and gradually she came into focus. Still, the whole story is not here. In writing this book, I've aspired to the *Venus de Milo* standard: I hope people will find beauty in it, but important parts are missing.

While Kim was remarkably complex, it's easy to delineate the three things she was best at: acting, teaching acting, and self-destruction. The first is why I wrote this book; the third is why it's so sad.

As part of my efforts to understand Kim, I submitted samples of her handwriting to Lydia Sharp, a certified graphoanalyst. She found many good qualities, including intelligence, generosity, and enthusiasm. But, she added, "Being an actress, she could probably put up a front. Nobody knew this woman." Least of all, I finally concluded, Kim herself.

PART ONE

THE EARLY YEARS

CHAPTER 1

DADDY DEAREST

(1925–1941)

KIM STANLEY, BORN PATRICIA BETH REID, told three different stories about her origins. In the rural Texas version, she has a hardscrabble farm youth outside of Lometa, a small town in the hill country of Texas. Her muffled free spirit labors under the yoke of a hardshell Baptist family for whom the church is the center of society, with movies, dancing, and even the radio forbidden as instruments of the Devil.

This version has a permissive variant: No stern Baptist parents block the picture-show box office, dance-hall doorway, or radio dial. The bright, sensitive young girl even gets a special pass to the adult section of the library and checks out Henry Miller. ("My, my," says the kindly, gray-haired librarian date-stamping *Tropic of Capricorn* for the eager blonde moppet, "aren't *we* a precocious young lady!")

In the urban Texas version, Kim grows up in San Antonio, just beyond the shadows of the Alamo. This version also has several variants, usually Dallas and Houston.

The third version places Kim in colorless, bourgeois Albuquerque, New Mexico, the daughter of a stern, unloving father and his sympathetic but frustrated wife. Sometimes the father is a professor of adult education at the University of New Mexico; at other times, of philosophy.

Kim would mix and match these versions, varying and improvising upon them with the same versatility she would one day use to dazzle Broadway audiences. For all their differences, though, Kim's stories of her origins always have several things in common: She was a daydreaming loner, angry without knowing why, and eager to get out of town and discover the wide world beyond the cramped confines of her girlhood. When her father is in adult education, the third version is true, although the first was her favorite.

"Acting was my ticket out of Texas," she often said. But Kim, while Texan by heritage, was not by experience. She was as authentically New Mexican as the Zia sun symbol or pastel blue and pink colors of the Santa Fe style. Like a good New Mexican, she was even born in an adobe house.

As a state of mind, though, Texas was a place Kim longed to get back to. She had a love-hate relationship with the mythical Texas she hailed from, just as she did with her father, railing against their oppressive Baptist strictures, yet magnetically drawn to their spirited and larger-than-life cowboy qualities. J.T. Reid cast a long shadow over his daughter's life, and any effort to understand the complex and vibrant Kim Stanley must begin with him.

J ESSE TAYLOR "J.T." REID, of Scotch-Irish stock, was born in 1889 on his family's ranch near Gonzales, in a fertile area of South Texas between San Antonio and Houston. The third of eight children of Charles Lafayette "Big Red" Reid and the former Nan Pauline Knowles, J.T. lived a frontier life. His family's ranch was on rich bottomland along the Guadalupe River, with rattlesnakes and panthers living in the nearby woods. When floods led to an explosion of mosquitoes whose bites gave most family members malaria, the Reids moved to a ranch on higher ground. There, J.T. happily spent the years of his early adolescence as a young cowboy, riding the pastures with his older brothers, doctoring calves for screwworms and bulldogging them in the corral for branding, marking, and castrating. As evidence of the Reids' growing status and success, they had a surrey with fringe on top pulled by two bay horses, Bob and Kim.

In addition to Big Red, his wife, and their eight children, the family consisted of Big Red's father, J.T. Reid (for whom Big Red's third son was named), and his wife Ellendea. Although a native of Alabama, the elder J.T. Reid had been a captain in the Fiftieth Tennessee Infantry, which fought in the Civil War at Vicksburg and Chickamauga. He lost his left arm in the war and, in later years, was known to rub his stump and mutter, "Those damn Yankees!" Despite this injury, he lived to be ninety-five. Longevity was a trait of the Reid men: Big Red would live to be ninety-seven, Kim's father ninety-two.

In 1904, when young J.T. was fifteen, his family moved northwest to Lampasas County, in the Texas hill country. While the land was not as fertile as in Gonzales County, Charles Lafayette Reid had more of it to ranch, farm, and accommodate his growing family. His 1,400-acre ranch was on the western edge of Lampasas County near Chadwick's Mill, several miles west of Lometa. Big Red was a Baptist cowboy who eschewed cow-camp coffee for milk, which he sometimes obtained by roping a wild cow and milking it. He was a man's man, once telling his sons, "I'm not raising my boys to be soda-jerking sissies or mama-boys. They are he-Texans, aren't you, fellers?"

The Millers and Stanleys, Kim's ancestors on her mother's side, were well-established in Lampasas County by the time the Reids arrived, the Millers having come from South Carolina and the Stanleys from Tennessee. Milton Miller, Kim's maternal grandfather, and his wife, the former Sarah Ann Stanley, farmed and ranched in the Atherton community a few miles east of Lometa. Self-educated, he was a former schoolteacher, handsome and good-natured, with prematurely white hair. He was a dedicated Baptist who had lost an eye in his youth when a mesquite thorn stuck in it while he was riding the range.

Kim's maternal grandmother, Sarah Ann Miller, was known as Annie. She had been an affectionate young woman whose illustrious ancestors included several Earls of Derby in England; John Stanley, a North Carolina shipbuilder who was a friend of George Washington, and (no source of pride in a Southern family) Nancy Hanks, the mother of Abraham Lincoln. As a young bride, Annie Miller wrote humorous letters about the travails of being a farm wife and sweeping dust and chickens off her front porch. But as she became older, she became more formidable and temperamental, possibly due to a goiter or other thyroid problem.

One cousin of Kim's remembers Annie always kissing him affectionately. But to Kim's brother Justin, their maternal grandmother was fearsome.

"She was a fairly angry human being," he recalls. "It may have come from some kind of physical pain. She seemed to have a lot of resentment. I was afraid of her, because she was always demanding stuff of us." Although eulogized in the local paper when she died as "a consecrated Christian character," she had several non-Baptist habits, among them dipping snuff and taking medicine for her thyroid problem that may have included, and addicted her to, cocaine.

Milton and Annie Miller had seven children. The youngest was Kim's mother, Rubyann, who was born in 1896. One of Rubyann's cousins was Stanley Walker, later an author and city editor of the *New York Herald-Tribune*. In an early showing of his cultural sophistication, he once found a bed of reddish-blue clay at the edge of a dry stream and used it to model busts of Homer, Virgil, Sitting Bull, and other notables. "In this project, I sometimes had the help of my pretty first cousin, Miss Ruby Miller, who lived up School Creek about twelve miles," he later wrote. "Ruby, like me, had a streak of the rebel and the dreamer in her."

Lampasas County has one foot in the American South, with the other in the West. Stanley Walker noted that on the drive up from Austin to Lampasas, farmland gives way to rangeland, with buildings in the county seat a mixture of unadorned stone evocative of early cattle days, and graceful, two-story mansions reminiscent of the plantation South. The rolling hills of Lampasas County feature woods of live oak and juniper, but also patches of prickly pear cactus and yucca. Lampasas County is on the ill-defined fault line between the South and the West; it's a fault line that ran through Kim as well.

It isn't clear how J.T. Reid met Rubyann Miller: A cousin of Kim's thinks they met in Brownwood, Texas, at Howard Payne, a Baptist college where both studied. Kim's brother Justin thinks they met in church in Lometa. Or they may have met at a revival meeting, as the youthful J.T. played guitar for a local tent-revival leader. In any case, the young cowboy and the pretty dreamer took to each other, and on Thanksgiving Day of 1915, they were married on the farm of Milton and Annie Miller.

Like his father, and his father's father before him, J.T. Reid was a patriarch. "Everybody listened and did exactly what he said," says Lynn White, Kim's brother-in-law. "Everybody was scared to death of him. His opinion was the final opinion. He was a big man, a brilliant man, and all of his kids were brilliant. They just had peculiarities."

Kim's father would become renowned as a teacher, professor, administrator, and author. Although his career was in the classroom and the administrator's office, J.T.'s heart was always in the great outdoors, especially if fishing was involved. His writing about it could be clichéd ("Let the big bad Indians come! Big Red and Uncle Cheat could whip the whole passel of Redskins, by grabs!") or more lyrical, as in this passage about the New Mexico desert:

> Our deserts are truly enchanting . . . They broil by day and shiver by night. Beneath their parched sands lie relics of bygone splendor, both natural and human, with voices of the past singing on the eternal winds, gossiping through the wail of the coyote and the screech of the little owl.

J.T. was a versatile and resourceful outdoorsman. One time he was fishing along the Rio Grande near Albuquerque when a young fisherman came running along, yelling for help: A novice, he had gotten a fishhook embedded in his hand by careless handling of the trigger on an automatic fly reel. J.T. calmly forced the point of the hook through his skin, snipped the eye off the hook with a pair of pliers, pulled the hook out, then disinfected the wound with iodine and applied a bandage. On another occasion, he was fishing at Elephant Butte Reservoir in southern New Mexico on the opening day of deer season. Seeing a deer on the bank, he pulled his boat over, shot the deer, got back in the boat, and caught his limit of bass.

Those who recall J.T. fondly say he was calm and easygoing, as you would expect of an avid fisherman, and an accomplished storyteller. J.T. became a community leader in Albuquerque, where he spent much of his life. "He was a well-liked, beloved gentleman throughout the community," says his friend Bob Lalicker, "a dignified and gracious gentleman and a dedicated husband and father."

His fathering had its limits, though. Kim's brother Justin says J.T. had a hard time being close and expressing feelings, something common for men of his era. Paula Reid, Justin's third wife, says, "I got a sense J.T. was from that Southern Baptist background, which is kind of uptight. I don't think he spared the rod much, from what I heard."

He certainly didn't in his professional life: While superintendent of schools in Tularosa, New Mexico, where Kim was born, he announced at the first teachers' meeting, "You have been chosen because you are well-qualified. The janitor will provide a paddle, God has provided a place for its use. Put the fear of God in their hearts and teach them something."

There was another limit to J.T.'s fathering: He didn't know what to make of girls. "He couldn't have understood Kim if they put a gun to his head," says Patricia Frye, the second wife of Kim's brother Justin. "Those were different times—they were just coming out of the Victorian days. What Kim really wanted was a father's love, instead of being dismissed as a child, a woman, and a talent." But she got more dismissal than love. Kim later said, "My father always thought acting was very silly, and I wanted his approval. To him, acting was not a serious occupation. I think he still regards fishing as more important." (J.T.'s son Justin later acknowledged, "He was proud of Kim's acting, and I think a little regretful that he pooh-poohed it when she first started out.")

In their hunting and fishing, J.T. and his three sons would fan out from Albuquerque around the state, going south to the mountains near Carlsbad and north to the mountains around Taos. They fished for trout and bass and hunted deer, doves, quail, pheasant, and wild turkey. Justin never had a store-bought turkey for Thanksgiving until he was twenty-one. "Kim felt left out of these things and none of us really cared whether she felt that or not," he says somewhat ruefully.

J.T.'s attitude toward women was dismissive: Talking about his father's trying to find a mate in "Big Texas Family," his unpublished chronicle of the Reid family, he writes, "Big Red . . . moved along the boardwalk . . . sweeping his eyes over the milling throng as if in search of blue-blooded livestock, preferably she-stuff. Big Red was looking for a wife." And, as an old man, he recalled a youthful evening swim outdoors. "It was awfully nice and cool," he said. "No mosquitoes, no girls, no nothing." Patricia Frye later recalled Kim imitating her father: "There'll be no women-folk talk at the table!" J.T. was a staunch Baptist, and perhaps if there had been a commandment that said "Thou Shalt Love Thy Daughter as Thy Son," he would have, but there wasn't, and he didn't.

Where J.T. left a good legacy for his daughter was as an entertainer: He had a singing cowboy act in which he came onstage dressed as a cowboy, telling stories, singing songs (accompanying himself on guitar as he had done at tent revivals) and demonstrating a cowboy's equipment. His entertaining talent came from his mother, Nan Pauline, who had had a vaudeville-style comedy act with two of her sisters in turn-of-the-century Gonzales, Texas.

The only time Kim ever referred to her paternal grandmother was to proudly claim she had been a full-blooded Cherokee. But except for a cryptic reference in "Big Texas Family" to there being "mixed blood" in his family, J.T. never suggested there was any truth to Kim's assertion. The closest Kim came to being Cherokee is that several years before she was born, her parents and two older brothers lived briefly in Cherokee County, Texas. But writer JP Miller, who was part Cherokee, always believed Kim was too. Similarly, playwright Horton Foote, a native Texan, thought Kim a native Texan as well. And actor Pat Hingle, who attended the University of Texas, believed Kim had been a co-ed there. All three mistaken beliefs about Kim are testimonies to her acting ability.

Kim's tortured relationship with her father would bring trouble to her relations with men: She would marry four times and have countless affairs. "She had a bad father problem," says writer Roger O. Hirson. "Her men problem may have been a function of her father problem." Janice Rule, who acted with Kim in *Picnic,* later became a psychotherapist. She published an article in a professional journal implicitly touching on Kim's father problem, here identifying her as "Françoise":

> Each time Françoise began work on a new play, it seemed that her personal life was suddenly in chaos . . . At first I thought it was bad luck and bad choice of husband or lovers. How could they be so cruel as to fight with Françoise and cause her such pain just at the time when she needed kindness and peace of

mind to deal with the difficulties of building a new character . . . [But] it finally became clear that Françoise felt she needed this climate of real personal chaos to produce those great emotional scenes on the stage . . . This was an example of [her] severe conflicts. I would guess that she was unable to deal with the painful feelings of broken relationships in her past, probably dating back to her childhood. She then had to create new rejections that she could control and use.

Rather than realizing her father was a sexist tyrant who didn't have much use for girls, Patty Reid may have thought that if she worked harder and achieved as her father wanted, he would love her. Kim had to excel and she had to perform. In time, she would come to excel at performing, but at a cost. "In order to meet the perfectionist's standards and deadlines, we adopt striving behaviors to counter all obstacles," writes Cynthia Curnan, a psychotherapist and expert on perfectionism. "These striving behaviors override self-care needs and sooner or later result in a collapse of some kind."

The father felt most at home in the great outdoors, the daughter, probing psychological interiors. "She wanted to please him and yet she was rebelling against him," Kim's brother-in-law Lynn White says. "He was a hard one to please." Choosing Stanley, the maiden name of her mother's mother, as her stage name, may have been part of that rebellion.

In some ways, J.T. Reid and Rubyann Miller were a study in opposites. He was inflexible and unyielding; she was capricious and whimsical. He was tall (six feet isn't that tall now, but it was then); she was short, perhaps only four feet eleven inches, although, as her son Justin says, "She was small but mighty." Sometimes erratic, she was courageous, imaginative, helpful, and affectionate. She was also shapely and attractive, which may have made her, in twenty-six-year-old J.T. Reid's eyes, blue-blooded livestock of the she-stuff variety.

"She was a sweet, very intelligent, and very emotional woman whose insights were very deep and accurate," Justin says. "She didn't get fooled by much." As a young woman, she had dreams of acting herself, but had to put them behind her when, having just turned nineteen, she became

J.T.'s wife. She never lost her hill-country accent, something Kim adapted for roles such as Cheri, the Southern torch singer in *Bus Stop*. "Kim used to say (imitating Rubyann), 'Patty Beth Reid! What're you doin'?'" recalls Meredith Alexander, who studied acting with Kim in the 1970s.

One day as a college student, Kim's mother helped herself to clothes belonging to her sister Lena, with whom she was rooming. "Ruby roomed with Lena one year at Baylor," says Katherine Norris, a second cousin of Kim's on her mother's side. "She told me a story about having one good dress she was saving for a special occasion. When she went to put it on, she discovered that Ruby was out and about on campus, flirting and wearing her dress." Rubyann never entirely lost this flirtatious quality. "She was sassy and cute, tart, with a very strong Texas sense of humor," says Paula Reid. "Coy and flirtatious. She always had that kind of flirtatious aspect with her, even in her eighties, cracking jokes and everything."

Rubyann was a giving person: Toward the end of her father's life, she helped care for him while living in San Antonio with Kim and Justin. A quarter of a century later, she would help Kim raise her children in New York, and they remember her to this day with abiding fondness. But among the Millers, she was something of an outcast, as was her talented daughter.

"Kim was kind of the black sheep of the family," says Catherine Hynson, another second cousin of Kim's on the Miller side. "Her mother was kind of 'out there,' too. The rest of the family was farmers and oil money, kind of conservative." Juanita Nanninga, a girlhood friend of Kim's from Albuquerque, remembers raised eyebrows over Rubyann (who operated a beauty parlor) coloring her own hair. "She stood out just a little bit," she says. "It was a staid university community."

Rubyann was also regarded by her family as capricious. "She kind of went and did what she wanted to when she wanted to do it," says Herbert F. Miller, a first cousin of Kim's. "She was (always) jumpin' from one thing to another. She didn't start with one thing and stick with it. She seemed to be interested in findin' out what was going on everywhere. There wasn't anything wrong with her heart—it just didn't know which way it wanted to go sometimes."

At several points in her life, Rubyann developed severe emotional problems. "She kind of assumed roles that were grand and then nothing came of it," Kim's brother Justin says. "She had a lot of (emotional) crashes in her life. But she was very strong about it and maintained herself all the way through. She was a real strength unto herself and had great confidence." Some family members say Rubyann was a paranoid schizophrenic. While this condition was overdiagnosed between the 1960s and '80s, several of Rubyann's relatives are psychotherapists. And Justin does not dispute the diagnosis. "As she got older, she was much more difficult to be around," he says. "She dominated all conversations and had a lot of paranoia."

For Kim, her mother was the only family member who supported her dream of acting when she was young. "My mother was the only one who encouraged me to think about acting," she said. "She was very helpful to me always. But I don't think she took my acting terribly seriously." According to an in-law, though, Rubyann took it too seriously.

"Ruby aspired to be an actress and instead turned out to be a schoolteacher's wife and always felt she had been cheated in life," says Lucile Reid Brock, the first wife of Kim's brother Howard. "So she showered all her affection on Patty. She lived her life through Patty." Dorthy Miller, who married Kim's cousin Marvin, agrees. "Ruby seemed possessive of Patty, didn't want anyone to get too close to her," she says. "She seemed jealous of other people being friends with her."

For all their differences, J.T. Reid and Rubyann Miller had much in common: They were vital, strong-willed hill-country Baptists from high-achieving, hard-driving families with a high incidence of drinking and emotional problems. "It was a dysfunctional family, and yet a family of overachievers," says Lucile Reid Brock.

Both the Millers and Reids had deep Baptist roots. The Reids strongly opposed alcohol, tobacco, and gambling. The Millers regularly worshipped at the Sims Creek Baptist Church, where Milton F. Miller served as secretary and which he had helped to build. Among the Christian denominations, Baptists have a reputation of being somewhat conventional and stodgy. "If Christianity covers the world like Sherwin-Williams, Baptists cover Texas like a wet blanket," writes Baptist philosopher Raymond Flynn. "As a Baptist, you can do almost anything as long as you don't enjoy it, drink it in public, do it to music, or continue it after 10 P.M."

Although her parents were not always as stern as Kim implied—no one had to go to church on Sunday, for example, if they didn't want to—they did take their Baptist faith seriously, and some of Kim's wilder excesses may be seen as a reaction against it: She would chain-smoke, drink excessively, and, as a Broadway star, have a prolific extramarital sex life. But while Kim's lovers would recall her as vibrant and alive in bed, she was ultimately as bleak and compulsive in asserting her sexuality as Puritans are in denying theirs.

Rietta Netter, a lifelong friend of Kim's, visited her family in Taos in 1941. Netter was struck by the emotionally buttoned-down style of the Reids. "Some families are very close, show their emotions, and are demonstrative," she says. "But the Reids were kind of far away from each other. I come from a very close-knit family, and I'm used to seeing hugs and kisses and emotions showing, but when they were together, they didn't have too much of that."

In a classic study of mental illness in disorganized rural communities, a researcher wrote, "There were houses there and paths outside the houses, but there were no paths leading from one house to another." Perhaps because there were so few paths among members of Kim's family, there was a lot of mental illness. Kim was emotionally erratic, and would suffer a career-ending nervous breakdown in 1965. Her oldest brother, Howard, deserted his family in the late 1950s in what his then-wife Lucile describes as an episode of mental illness. Kim's brother Justin, after the failure of his third marriage, went to Big Sur where he considered jumping off a cliff before participating in group work at the Esalen Institute. Justin's daughter Dana died in the early 1980s under ambiguous circumstances, which Justin believes to have been suicide. Carol White, J.T.'s daughter by his second marriage, served as student body president at Highland High School in Albuquerque, married, and became a popular middle-school teacher before being diagnosed as psychotic.

Just as there was much mental illness in the family, so was there much interest in understanding it. Kim's brother Howard became a psychiatrist, as did one of his sons. One of Justin's sons became a neo-Jungian psychotherapist; Kim's daughter Lisa trained as a psychiatric social worker; and Katherine Norris, a second cousin of Kim's, is licensed as a professional counselor and marriage and family therapist.

Its Baptist roots notwithstanding, there were drinking problems in the family. Rubyann's cousin Stanley Walker noted that his uncle Jim "was known to have taken nips from the snake-bite bottle in his earlier days, though when he became older, he was firm in his denunciation of the stuff," while his uncle John was "a sometime schoolteacher [and] politician . . . it was said that his drinking held him back from what might have been a notable career." Kim's brother Justin and maternal cousin Rubalee Hankamer, among others, would have drinking problems as well.

With these dark strains in the family came a tendency to be emotionally opaque. "There was a quirk in all of them, an air of mystery," says Dorthy Miller, who married into the family. "If they don't want you to know something, honeychile, you're not going to get it out of them, because they just close it off and change the subject." While there are exceptions, both Reids and Millers maintain a reluctance to open up more commonly associated with certain Sicilian clans. "There are a lot of secrets in that family [the Millers] we won't ever know," says Robert Ball, "because my grandmother [Rubyann's sister Lena] was the queen of propriety."

One of the family's colorful quirks was its members' tendency to change their names: Kim's mother was born Rubyann, but at various times shortened it to Ruby or Ann. Her sister Lena, irritated at being told she had the same name as Lena Horne, changed her name to Linda late in life and refused to speak with friends who wouldn't call her by her new name. Kim's brother Justin Truman was known as Truman as a youth, Justin as a man. And her daughter Laurie Rachel, feeling it was the name of a diminutive person, dropped the "Laurie" in college.

W HEN J.T. AND RUBYANN UNITED the Reid and Miller families, he was working as a schoolteacher in Goldthwaite, Texas, where their first son, Howard, was born in 1916. Their second son, Kenneth, was born in 1918, when J.T. was teaching at a community college in Rusk, Texas. (Ironically, Kenneth, who would die while training to be a World War II fighter pilot, was born on Veteran's Day.) After several teaching and administrative jobs in Texas, J.T. became superintendent of schools for

Tularosa, a small southern New Mexico town of 800 people, in the fall of 1922. As regional historian C.L. Sonnichsen notes, it's an inhospitable land:

> The Tularosa country is a parched desert where everything, from cactus to cowman, carries a weapon of some sort, and the only creatures who sleep with both eyes closed are dead. In all the sun-scorched and sand-blasted reaches of the Southwest there is no grimmer region. Only the fierce and the rugged can live here—prickly pear and mesquite; rattlesnake and tarantula. True, Texas cattlemen made the cow a native of the region seventy-five years ago, but she would have voted against the step if she had been asked.

And, in an observation that could apply to J.T. as well, Sonnichsen wrote, "If it has no tenderness, it has strength and a kind of magnificence."

In Tularosa, the Reids lived in the Clayton house, which still stands. There were two additions to the Reid family there: Justin Truman was born in a hospital in nearby Alamogordo in 1923, and on February 11, 1925, the day *The Emperor Jones,* starring Paul Robeson, opened on Broadway, Patty Beth Reid was born.

Kim was not born in the hospital like her brother, but in the Clayton house, a fifteen-room, two-story adobe at 600 Eighth Street. It isn't clear why she didn't have a hospital birth. (Perhaps, as was often the case during Kim's life, she was in a hurry for a change of scene.) Oddly, the house is also the birthplace of another actress, Jan Clayton, who played the mother on the *Lassie* TV series. It's a remarkable coincidence that one house in a small southwestern town is the birthplace for two such different actresses, one a post–World War II icon of maternal domesticity, the other a vital but haunted tragedienne with a no-holds-barred approach to life.

Kim once told the Associated Press she had her first artistic stirrings in Tularosa. "A tot in love with make-believe, she started 'running' shows by borrowing the ballet costumes of playmates," the AP noted. This story has to be viewed skeptically, though: Kim was no more than six months old when J.T. Reid left Tularosa in the summer of 1925 to become superintendent of schools in nearby Artesia, New Mexico.

Kim acknowledged Tularosa as her birthplace, but never mentioned her three years of infancy in Artesia. Perhaps she thought doing so would undermine her image as a native Texan, although Artesia, by virtue of proximity, its flat, uninflected landscape, and the presence of oil, has a Texan feel to it. There was an oil boom underway when J.T. Reid and his family moved there: After the Illinois No. 3 oil well became the area's first gusher, the population increased by 50 percent between 1924 and 1926 (although it was still just 2,800 people), and the scent of crude oil was as pervasive as salt air at the beach.

As in Tularosa, J.T. Reid was highly regarded. "It is a matter of pride that the public schools here are in a splendid condition," the *Artesia Advocate* wrote in an article about Reid, "[with] modern buildings, up-to-date equipment and an efficient faculty." In October 1927, the high school football team, the Artesia Bulldogs, lost 18–6 to the Roswell Coyotes. Even this was regarded as a plus for Reid, though, as it was the first time Artesia had crossed Roswell's goal line since 1916.

J.T. Reid was a rising star and, while in Artesia, was elected vice president of the New Mexico Educational Association, earning a front-page headline in the *Advocate*. At the 1928 graduation exercises for Artesia's elementary and high school, he got J.F. Zimmerman, president of the University of New Mexico, to serve as commencement speaker. This was only fair, as Zimmerman had just hired Reid away from Artesia to serve as founding director of UNM's adult education program.

In the fall of 1928, when the Reids moved to Albuquerque, it was a city of 35,000 people with fewer than 40 miles of paved roads. Clyde Tingley, a Southwestern version of Chicago's Richard J. Daley, was mayor, and work was just beginning on the airfield that eventually became Albuquerque International Sunport. New Mexico's largest city had just gotten its first radio station, KGGM, with studios in the Franciscan Hotel.

Local author Erna Fergusson would remark upon the lack of tall buildings, calling Albuquerque "a one-story town." "Even in its busiest districts, as in all the Southwest, the sky predominates," she wrote. But she acknowledged it could be drab. "Downtown looks best at night," she added. "Stores have gone all out for neon signs; Central Avenue glows in many colors. By day, not so good. One [person] said: 'Any building that was ever built in Albuquerque is still here.'" And, Fergusson observed, it was "a town that seems to have ways in, but none out," a sentiment Kim would agree with.

Fergusson acknowledged that Albuquerque's placid history did not compare with the romance and drama of Santa Fe, but pointed with pride to its spirit of racial tolerance and noted that "Anglo" was not a synonym for "white." "Three cultures [Anglo, Hispanic, and Indian] have flourished here and none has died," she said. "In New Mexico, Anglo . . . connotes citizens of . . . any heritage other than Spanish. This is carried so far that a Negro bootblack, asked what was being offered for votes, replied, 'I dunno, boss, they ain't got round to us Anglos yet.'"

Kim grew up along Route 66 where it passed through the University Heights section of Albuquerque in the form of Central Avenue, "a gangling kid with loose blonde hair and a fringe of white lashes veiling her lively glance," according to one article. She and her brothers would be baptized in a church near Albuquerque High School. Anabel Everett, who dated Kim's brother Kenneth at the University of New Mexico, says Kim was quiet and didn't talk much.

Behind Kim's lively glance was a lively imagination. Her brother Justin remembers watching her play with dolls. "I thought of her as being unsatisfied with her life in reality and capable of playing a role from early on," he says. "She didn't get much attention from her father and needed to be somebody herself, so she cast herself in all kinds of roles." A 1963 profile of Kim in *Show Magazine* notes:

> As a child and teenager, Patty Beth is remembered by her contemporaries as a busy, assertive kid, trailing after her brothers, less adept than they at the hunting, fishing and riding that enthralled her father . . . But she had something uniquely her own: a rich and potent fancy that transmuted even the simplest conversation into drama. "With Patty Beth," says a neighbor, "you could never be sure who it was you were meeting. She had a way of changing shape from day to day."

There is beauty in Albuquerque, in the sun rising over the craggy

Sandia Crest at dawn, in nearby Indian petroglyphs, and the splash of waterfowl in the woods along the Rio Grande. But to Kim, Albuquerque was sterile, drab, and arid. "I lived," she later said, "in a state of continual frustration. I could not shake the feeling that there was outside Albuquerque a world larger than the world I knew. I wrote turgid poetry that started with apostrophes, like 'You men sitting in the dark corners . . .'—but most of the time I simply counted. I counted everything: leaves on trees, pickets on fences, cracks in pavements, in a kind of contained rage. I did it in anger and out loud to hear my voice, to be sure that I was real."

Kim fluctuated between a desire to be an artist or poet and the desire to be popular and the May Queen. She was a great fan of Bette Davis, saw Laurence Olivier and Merle Oberon in *Wuthering Heights* as many as twenty-five times, and continued to love the film as an adult.

Patty Beth Reid had markedly different relations with each of her three brothers. She loathed her oldest brother, Howard, as a bully and an emotional carbon copy of their father. When she was eight, Howard took her to see her first movie, *King Kong.* "My brother snuck me out of the house and snuck me in to see it," she later said, "'cause he knew when King Kong stepped on the pygmies I would just go crazy. I went to the bathroom and vomited and he had to take me home." Justin adds, "Howard was a strong Leo personality who thought he knew everything. He had a penchant for practical jokes, and I think of him as a certifiable sadist." So did Kim. "Kim really disliked him and made it clear to us," says her daughter Rachel. "I was raised thinking, 'You really don't want to have anything to do with this guy, because he's a nutcake.' Kim thought it was incredibly ironic that the guy was a psychiatrist."

Kenneth, a year younger than Howard, was his opposite: good-natured and emotionally generous. "Kenneth was my hero," says Justin. "He was a kind human, and the only close male in my life who I could say really loved me." Anabel Everett recalls him as extremely intelligent, with dark red hair, fluent in Spanish, and somewhat sarcastic. "He sounds like a real bright spirit among the siblings," adds Paula Reid.

Justin says that as a child, he was "fat, dumb, and happy." Although his initials were J.T., he was the closest of the brothers to Kim in age and temperament. He adds, though, "she would accuse me of being like Pa whenever she wanted to stick me with the skewer." But Paula Reid says Justin did have the patriarchal streak that ran through the Reids, and that his tendency toward command and control would doom their marriage, his third. Both Justin Truman and Patty Beth would have artistic aspirations and drinking problems: As Kim Stanley, Patty Beth would fulfill her artistic aspirations, unlike Justin. But unlike his sister, Justin would beat his drinking problems.

The family had a solid, middle-class life, insulated from the Depression by J.T.'s job as head of the extension (adult education) division at the University of New Mexico. After eighteen years, though, his marriage to Rubyann was under strain. "Pop tended to dominate, although Annie did express herself," Justin says. "I remember a kind of feeling of tension. They just didn't get along well."

In 1933, when Kim was eight, Rubyann divorced J.T. on the grounds of adultery. Depending upon your point of view, this was either a courageous or a foolhardy thing for a woman who had no career to do during the Depression. A good hairdresser, although she didn't enjoy it, Rubyann opened a series of beauty parlors and also received sixty dollars a week alimony from J.T. The children went back and forth between the parents.

Ironically, although Rubyann left the marriage because of J.T.'s infidelity, it was J.T. who would settle down to an enduring second marriage, while Rubyann went from one man to another. In 1933, J.T. married Florence Isaacs, a descendant of a Mayflower family, who was one of his graduate students at the University of New Mexico. They would have one daughter, Carol Ann. Rubyann would marry at least once more and have several live-in relationships, usually with men in the arts. One was artist Carl von Hassler, who supervised the painting of the murals in the lobby of Albuquerque's Franciscan Hotel. Family lore holds that they were married, but the state of New Mexico has no record of that. In all likelihood, they lived together without benefit of clergy, something as unusual in 1930s Albuquerque as coloring your hair.

When Kim was a ninth grader at Lincoln Junior High School, she appeared in a play she later recalled as "New-Mown Hay." "It was all about new-mown hay and a young man haying, and I was the ten-year-old ingenue in it [she was thirteen at the time]," Kim told Lillian Ross of the *New Yorker*: "I can clearly remember the experience, doing something up there on the stage, and getting a feeling that was powerful and special, unlike anything else I had ever felt."

The play may have been *Stebinses' Gulch: An Xmas Fantasy,* a pastoral about life on the Stebins family farm written and directed by Patty Reid's English teacher, Violet Moore, which was staged in the school auditorium on the afternoon of December 22, 1938. Kim's romantic lead was Edwin Johnson, now a retired engineer in Albuquerque.

"The only reason I was in that play was that my father said, 'Either you go out for dramatics or you don't play basketball,'" Johnson says. "I was scared to death the whole time. She was relaxed." According to *Show Magazine,* Kim also played an intense Calpurnia in a Violet Moore–directed *Julius Caesar* and a mythological animal in another play.

Violet Moore later recalled Kim as a gifted, hard-working actress, even as a novice. "Patty was the most responsive child I ever worked with," she said. "I figured if any of my drama students was going to make a success of acting, it would be Patty." On another occasion, she added, "I shall never forget Patty. She was a perfectionist, and never tired of rehearsals." Moore also remembered Kim as a straight-A student with character and personality, modest, kind, and considerate of others.

In her 1961 *New Yorker* interview, Kim described Moore as "a lovely, warm, kind lady" and gave her credit for starting her in acting. Kim rarely acknowledged those who helped her up the ladder, such as Edwin Snapp and Ellen Crowe, her directors when she was a drama major at the University of New Mexico. She spoke little of the Pasadena Playhouse, where she went after UNM, and when she did, it was only with scorn. She never mentioned Bill Hodapp's Bluegrass Theatre in Louisville, her next stop, and eventually turned on Lee Strasberg. But as Kim went back and forth between her parents ("I dreaded the feeling of coming home to an empty apartment"), sometimes Violet Moore would take her home and give her milk and cookies, a kindness Kim never forgot.

A s KIM STANLEY, Patty Reid would be the most important dramatic actress to come out of Albuquerque, a city better known for TV sitcom stars such as Vivian Vance *(I Love Lucy),* Neil Patrick Harris

(Doogie Howser, M.D.), and Bill Daily *(I Dream of Jeannie)*. But at the end of Kim's sophomore year at Albuquerque High School, her mother took her and Justin Truman away to Texas. Rubyann may have wanted to escape the beauty-shop grind and fulfill her own artistic aspirations. "My mother was trying to find a good place to be. She needed help from her family," Justin says. "I think she wanted to settle in San Antonio, then Houston, then Galveston, but it just didn't work out."

In San Antonio, Rubyann and her two youngest children lived near her sister Novella, who had married an attorney. Rubyann helped to care for her ailing father and married an ex-convict named Bill Decker who helped her try to set up an interior-decorating and furniture-making business. Neither Rubyann's business nor her marriage was successful. But Kim had an epiphany in San Antonio.

In 1940, *The Philadelphia Story* was released. The film starred Katharine Hepburn as spoiled heiress Tracy Lord, with Cary Grant as the ex-husband scheming to win her back on the eve of her second marriage, and James Stewart as the cynical tabloid reporter assigned to cover her society wedding. Hepburn had played the role on Broadway, where it was produced by the Theater Guild. Loyal to the play and the Guild, Hepburn agreed to do a national tour of the play after the movie was released.

On January 8, 1941, *The Philadelphia Story* was staged at the Texas Theatre in San Antonio, with Joseph Cotten in the Cary Grant role and Van Johnson in the James Stewart role. Rubyann was in the audience with her daughter. "I was overcome. I was transfixed," Kim later said. "The impact of Katharine Hepburn's personality was fantastic. It was a comedy, but after the curtain came down I sat there and cried, because I wanted it to go on all night."

When San Antonio didn't work out, Rubyann took her two youngest to Houston, where they lived with her sister Lena and Lena's husband, oilman Earl Hankamer (Glen McCarthy, the subject of Edna Ferber's *Giant,* had been a junior partner on one of Earl's ventures). Rubyann always felt her devout Baptist sister disapproved of her—and her daughter Patty Beth. "I think my mother (Earl and Lena's daughter Rubalee) found Kim headstrong and rather too free-spirited for her taste," says Kim's second cousin Robert Ball. "I gather from remarks made by my mother and grandmother that they had had some kind of falling-out when Kim lived with them. She just wasn't willing to knuckle under to my grandmother's very puritanical rules."

As a concession to Lena, Justin and Kim were rebaptized in Houston. Even so, Rubyann and her children did not fit comfortably under the Hankamers' roof and were sent to live in the Hankamers' vacation home on the mainland side of Galveston Bay. But Rubyann couldn't earn a living there. Her friends and life were in Albuquerque, as was her ex-husband. His job at the University of New Mexico may have meant sharply reduced tuition costs for Kim and Justin, who would soon begin college. Albuquerque is called the Duke City for its namesake, the Duke of Alburquerque, but to Kim, it would always be the Dad City, and associated with her love-denying father. Now she was heading back to it and to him.

"The secret lies with the father," Pulitzer prize–winning playwright Paul Zindel said of Kim. "It's also the secret to her anger, her disappointment in life. It's the secret to her power. When you explore it, I think you're going to find that she could never please her father, that more than anything she wanted to be her father. This was the power that hung over her and made her demons all focus and go wild and come out. I think it was the secret of her talent and what made Kim Stanley what she was."

Having failed to make it in Texas, Rubyann returned to Albuquerque with Justin and Patty in tow.

CHAPTER 2

THE YELLOW ROSE OF NEW MEXICO

(1941–1946)

S HORTLY AFTER RETURNING TO ALBUQUERQUE, Patty Reid went up to Taos to live with J.T., who was running the Taos County Project, a multi-agency effort spearheaded by the University of New Mexico to improve Third World living conditions in pre–jet set Taos. The average annual income of farming families in Taos County was then less than two hundred dollars, and it had the highest infant mortality rate of any county in the U.S. The Taos Project, ably directed by Reid, was making considerable headway against these and other social problems before it was curtailed in 1943 by World War II.

Patty lived with J.T. in furnished apartments at the Harwood Foundation on Ranchitos Road. In her 1961 *New Yorker* interview, Kim told Lillian Ross, "[F]or my senior year in Taos, where my father was working . . . I spent that whole year with him, and I was one of three non-Mexican pupils in the school."

Kim made it sound like it was just her and her father, but, in reality, she and J.T. had a lot of company at Harwood. J.T.'s second wife, Florence, whom Kim never liked, was there. So was Kim's brother Howard, the head of the New Deal's National Youth Administration for northern New Mexico. Howard's wife Lucile was there, as were visitors such as Rietta Netter, Lucile's cousin from Mississippi, who became a lifelong friend of Kim's.

Kim didn't spend the whole year with J.T. in Taos, as she graduated in the spring of 1942 from Albuquerque High School. There, she appeared in the senior class play, *Once and for All,* a gangster comedy by Sidney Duvall, playing the role of Linda Webb. In Kim's memory, however, she prolonged her stay with J.T. and airbrushed out the others, so she could have, if only in her imagination, quality time with her father. In reality, there was excellent trout fishing on the Rio Grande near Taos at the bottom of a vertiginous canyon known by locals as "The Box," and odds are J.T. spent more time there than he did getting to know his daughter.

Patty enrolled as a freshman at the University of New Mexico in August of 1942. The wartime UNM was much smaller than today's—one classmate of Kim's remembers its enrollment being less than that of Albuquerque High School. Patty spent two and a half exciting years at the university as a drama major and frequent performer in student productions at Rodey Hall. She made important early strides in honing her craft, then left without a degree in December of 1944. But that's not the story she later told.

Kim usually said she attended the University of Texas. In a tribute to Kim's supposed Texas roots, columnist Earl Wilson once called her "purtier than an oil well." But as Professor Lyman says of one of his ex-wives in *Bus Stop:* "She was Southern—or pretended to be." Sometimes Kim said she split her college days between the University of New Mexico and UT, graduating from the University of Texas in 1945 or '46. But there is no evidence she went there. Several of Kim's obituaries say she went to Texas State at Waco, but there's no such institution. Baylor, where Kim's mother Rubyann attended, is in Waco, but Patty Reid never went there either.

Kim also spun yarns about what she majored in. Columnist Sidney Fields wrote, "At the University of Texas, Kim was intent on being a psychologist and was quite bright at it." "Did me more good at that age than any dramatic work," she told him. Kim sometimes claimed she had been pre-med. "After two years at the University of New Mexico, she switched to the state university in Texas, a psychology major and a pre-medical student and was graduated in 1946," one article noted. "She withdrew hurriedly upon being confronted with a cadaver." Another indicated, "She agreed to study pre-medical courses and turned to dramatics only as an extracurricular activity."

Despite this just-fell-off-the-turnip-truck pose, Patty Reid had a steely determination to succeed as an actress. "She said, 'I'm going to get to the top some day, you just wait and see,'" recalls Falba Murphy, a sorority sister of Kim's at UNM. "She had the guts to pursue it, too."

(Kim's comptetitiveness would manifest itself in other areas as well: Her sister-in-law Patricia Frye recalls Kim liking her potato salad and asking for the recipe, which Frye gave her. Frye in turn asked for Kim's recipe for chili. "The next time I saw her, she said, 'Did you leave anything out? It just didn't taste the same.' I hadn't left anything out," Frye recalls. "Then I remembered that her chili recipe didn't taste the same. *She* had left something out. I think the reason she accused me of leaving something out was because she had. Nobody was going to top her chili recipe. Nobody was going to beat her.")

As an undergraduate at UNM, Patty wore plaid, pleated skirts, long, baggy sweaters, and saddle shoes—the collegiate look of the time. But Jinx Witherspoon, a sorority sister of hers adds, "She always dressed better than anyone else. Her mother spoiled her and kept her in beautiful clothes." As a hairdresser, Rubyann couldn't afford an expensive wardrobe for her daughter, but may have passed along a strategy from her own undergraduate days. "[Patty] lived at the sorority house for a while," Falba Murphy later said. "I remember everybody complaining about her. She was always just walking into people's closets and taking clothes out that she wanted to wear. When they wanted to find their clothes, they had to go in her closet and look for them."

The sorority Patty Reid belonged to was Kappa Kappa Gamma, the most prestigious on campus. She was an active member, helping to initiate new members and, in the fall of 1942, serving as the sorority's candidate for "Sweetheart of Sigma Chi." In interviews, she never acknowledged her sorority ties. Kim Stanley smoked too much, drank too much, and had a wild personal life, but no skeleton from her past is more extraordinary than the fact that this hard-driving, fast-living Bohemian had once been an active sorority girl. It makes sense, though, when one considers how much she must have hungered for female companionship in the patriarchal confines of her home.

Dorothy Land, a fellow drama major, recalls her as a happy young woman. One day they were shopping in the Old Town section of Albuquerque when they got the giggles. "We were laughing so hard, we were falling down. And we were in a busy area in Old Town," Land says. "People were walking around us—'Let's get away from these kids.' We were young and just having a good time."

But Jinx Witherspoon says, "Somehow, there was a sadness about her." That's how Falba Murphy recalls Patty Reid as well. "She used to come and spend the night, two or three nights with me. My parents liked her a lot," she says. "I remember my father feeling kind of sorry for her. Her mother and father were divorced. Her father had remarried and she didn't like his wife—never did. Her mother was kind of a strange woman—she had several husbands, and just wasn't a very stable person, as I remember. [Patty] was tossed back and forth between the parents. She had kind of a hard-up life."

Early warning signs of Kim's drinking problem appeared at UNM. "The first time I ever had gin in my life was with Patty," Jinx Witherspoon later recalled. "We were somewhere and she said, 'I must talk to you.' Then she said, 'I must have a drink.' Now, I'd never had a drink before. My father was a Presbyterian minister, and I remember I was slightly shocked. I think she said, 'Well, I have to have this, because I'm depressed and upset.' I never really got to the crux of it, but I know she had various love affairs."

Her primary love affair, though, was with the theater, where her ability and hard work made her the leading lady of the UNM drama department. "It was just so apparent that she was head and shoulders above the rest of us," says Kathryn Lou McIntosh, a fellow drama student. Patty Reid also worked on costume and tech crew for shows and was a member of the Dramatic Club and Theta Alpha Phi, a national honor society for drama students.

Patty's first appearance onstage at UNM was in *Thunder Rock*. Written by Robert Ardrey and directed by drama professor Edwin Snapp, it was performed in Rodey Hall in October of 1942. Ardrey's 1939 play was an early version of *Casablanca:* An idealist grown cynical withdraws from the world, but finds his idealism renewed and prepares to battle the forces of darkness sweeping over Europe. John Conwell played Charleston, the lighthouse keeper in Lake Superior who serves as a link between the living and the dead. Patty, in a supporting role, played Melanie, the ghost of a young Viennese woman who had perished in a Great Lakes shipwreck.

Of all her UNM productions, *Thunder Rock* was the only one Kim ever mentioned in interviews. "My first real acting experience was in 1942, when I was a sophomore [she was a freshman, actually] at the University of New Mexico," Kim told Lillian Ross of the *New Yorker.* "Although I really did feel something about this girl I played, I wasn't thinking seriously about an acting career." But "play acting was not a matter of 'playing' with Kim, even then," the *Albuquerque Journal* noted in 1954, while director Edwin Snapp later told the *Albuquerque Tribune* that Patty had worked hard both as an actress and backstage.

One of Melanie's more moving speeches comes during a romantic scene with Charleston in which she tells him that she envies the flesh-and-blood woman he will one day fall in love with. "I envy all the living, in your times and all times, their right to love, and to smile, and to lift up their eyes to the sky," she says. Although Patty Reid had no way of knowing it, this *carpe diem* speech would be sadly appropriate for her brother Kenneth, who died one month later while training to be a pilot in the Army Air Force.

J UST BEFORE 8 P.M. ON TUESDAY, NOVEMBER 3, 1942, a week before he was scheduled to graduate from Lubbock Army Flying School in Texas, twenty-five-year-old Kenneth Reid was piloting a Cessna T-50 Bobcat trainer (the plane used on the 1950s TV series *Sky King*) along with William Phillippe, another aviation cadet. They took off as part of a formation out for a routine evening flight; it was cool and partly cloudy, with good visibility and a southwesterly breeze of 10 miles per hour.

Shortly after the planes took off, Reid and Phillippe fell behind. Aviation cadets in the other planes noticed their cabin lights were on, suggesting that the plane had developed engine trouble and Reid and Phillippe were trying to fix it. The plane dropped out of sight, and shortly afterwards, a huge ball of flame lit the night sky 20 miles southwest of Lubbock. Kenneth's body was completely eviscerated, with third-degree burns all over. "He had so much promise," says Anabel Everett, who dated Kenneth at UNM, "so much to offer." After Kenneth's funeral, Patty and her brother Justin made several tearful pilgrimages to Kenneth's gravesite in Albuquerque's Fairview Cemetery. The horror of her brother's violent and untimely death would stay with her for the rest of her life.

Patty Reid's next show at Rodey Hall was *Double Door* in February of 1943. She played Caroline Van Bret, the dominated younger sister of family matriarch Victoria Van Bret in a turn-of-the-century aristocratic New York family. John Conwell had a supporting role. Director Edwin Snapp had been drafted, so the Rodey Hall productions now had a new director: Ellen Crowe from New York, whose flaming red hair caused the students to affectionately call her "Red El."

"She had a wonderful background in the theater and had been onstage in New York," Jinx Witherspoon recalls. "Ellen Crowe had a great influence on Patty and helped her enormously on presentation, on stage presence, on speech, on getting rid of her New Mexico accent. She took Patty in hand, and I have a feeling that Patty to her was her own daughter." The effects of Ellen Crowe's coaching may be seen in Patty's first review in the Albuquerque press. "Patricia Reid, who played the cowed younger sister, provided effective contrast to the decisive Victoria," the *Albuquerque Tribune* noted. "Her shoulders drooped. Her meek voice [and] faltering gestures were never far from the shrill hysteria provoked by her sister's cold rages." Patty's last freshman-year production was Lillian Hellman's *Watch on the Rhine* in April of 1943. She played Martha de Brancois, the unhappy wife of a Romanian count. John Conwell starred as Kurt Muller, a member of the German underground. It was his last UNM performance before he was drafted. In addition to being the drama department's leading man, Conwell was also Patty

Reid's—they became engaged during her freshman year, and a sorority sister remembers the large diamond ring he gave her. He took her to visit his family in an affluent suburb of Chicago, but his being drafted ended their engagement.

In January of her sophomore year, Patty appeared in *Babushka,* a one-act Russian Christmas play, in the role of Olga, a disillusioned young girl. The next month she made her only appearance with the Albuquerque Little Theatre, a community theater founded by Broadway actress Kathryn Kennedy O'Connor. "I remember a nervously sensitive young girl listed as Patty Reid on our program of *Lady in the Dark,*" O'Connor later wrote. "Her graceful young talent was quite apparent."

Patty Reid's next UNM show was *The Campus Wash, or: I Lost It in the Laundry.* Staged in April of 1944, it was a series of skits about life on campus written and produced by UNM students and, according to the *Lobo,* the student newspaper, "This production requires intimate knowledge of campus figures and local jokes." Patty starred as Annie, a UNM coed. The show got mixed reviews: The *Albuquerque Journal* called it "very funny in spots," while adding, "the script lags embarrassingly in others." The *Albuquerque Tribune,* however, singled out Patty Reid for praise. "Miss Reid's performance was excellent," it said. "She took the part of the flirt whose ambition was to collect as many tokens of affection as possible with a subtlety remarkable in an amateur actress."

The next month Patty directed *Soladeras,* a one-act play by Josephine Niggli about the brave women who set up camp and cooked for soldiers during the Mexican Revolution and fought alongside them. The final performance of her sophomore year came in June with her starring role in *Mrs. Moonlight,* a British drama about Sarah Moonlight, a young married Englishwoman whose wish to never grow old is granted, turning her into an outcast from her family. Critics from both Albuquerque papers praised Patty Reid. "Patty's youth and beauty carried her through most of the play but in the intense last act, she really came forward with a genuine, emotional interpretation," said the *Albuquerque Journal.* And the *Albuquerque Tribune* added, "Miss Reid's interpretation of several difficult scenes . . . had the restraint and complete naturalness rarely found in amateur players." Patty's sorority sister and fellow drama major Jinx Witherspoon agreed. "She was perfect in that, enchanting," she says. "It was a nickname I gave her in my own thoughts. If I think of her today, I remember her only as she was in *Mrs. Moonlight*."

Witherspoon recalls Rubyann as a stage mother who pushed her daughter forward, always wanting her to be a star. And at UNM, she was. "Patty was the queen of the university," she says. "She had sort of an aura about her. She was not only lovely to look at, she dressed better than anybody else. She had a sort of stature, something that was slightly mysterious." That mystery, Witherspoon adds, may have been her reluctance to acknowledge she was a child of divorce, something that was still unusual.

In the fall of 1944, Ellen Crowe took a semester off as director of Rodey Hall productions at UNM. Her replacement, John Kerr, was from Seattle; in December, he was slated to become a director at the Pasadena Playhouse in Southern California. In September, he directed Pirandello's *Right You Are If You Think You Are* at Rodey, with Patty Reid playing Amalia, the wife of Mayor Agazzi. The next month, she appeared in *Helen's Husband,* a student-directed one-act play. Apparently a comedy with a Trojan War setting, it was her last performance at the University of New Mexico.

It appears that John Kerr and his wife, Virginia, encouraged Patty to follow them to the Pasadena Playhouse, and, in December of 1944, midway through her junior year, Patty Reid left the University. In later years, she would say a director (sometimes *the* director) from the Playhouse just happened to be in town, saw her perform, and planted in her head the notion, which had never previously occurred, that she might become a professional actress. Often she told the story vaguely enough to imply the town was Austin, Waco, or somewhere out on the plains of Texas. In reality, she followed one of her UNM professors to the Coast.

The night before she left for the Pasadena Playhouse, Patty Reid was having dinner at the Alvarado Hotel in downtown Albuquerque with Rubyann and J.T. Across the hotel dining room, she saw Violet Moore, the junior high school teacher who had given her her first taste of acting. Patty jumped up, ran across the room, put her arms around Moore, and told her how much she had inspired her to seek a stage career. The next morning Patty and Rubyann were on the train to Southern California.

THE PASADENA PLAYHOUSE was founded in 1917. It took off as an acting school in the 1920s, during the transition from silent films to talkies, when Hollywood studios sent actors there to learn how to speak on camera. Its alumni would eventually include Horton Foote, Dustin Hoffman, Gene Hackman, Lee J. Cobb, Frances Farmer, and James Arness of *Gunsmoke*. When Patty arrived there in January of 1945, the Playhouse was beginning a period of explosive growth fueled by passage of the GI Bill.

Patty and Rubyann shared an apartment in Pasadena. Kim later told an interviewer that everyone in her family except her mother opposed her going there. But while staunchly Baptist Aunt Lena may have looked askance at acting, she paid for the bulk of Kim's tuition at the Playhouse and outfitted her with a wardrobe. "Kim was so positive that she wanted to be an actress that Aunt Linda [a name Lena later assumed] helped her get some training," says Flo Miller Shields, who was married to an uncle of Kim's. "She said, 'If you're going to be an actor, you've got to be educated in it.'" Kim told interviewers she was able to go to the Playhouse because of a scholarship. While she may have obtained one, it appears Aunt Lena paid most of her bills.

Although the Playhouse offered a two-year program, Patty would stay for only one year, leaving early as she had done at UNM. Remarkably, she appeared in no plays there, as it was Playhouse tradition for first-year students to focus on their classwork. They weren't going to make an exception just because one of their students would someday be Kim Stanley, and that restriction chafed on Patty Reid. "Pasadena turned out to be like a glorified junior college," she told an interviewer, "and I quit after one year because I was ready to take on life in a less diluted form." She rarely named the Playhouse in interviews and usually trashed it when she did. "Patty Beth was never too happy at the Playhouse," says Dabbs Greer, a classmate of hers. "She was a very independent kind of person, and the regimentation that has to go on at any school—I think she wanted more artistic freedom."

Because she never went onstage at the Playhouse, Kim made little impression on fellow students like Barbara Turner. "I was talking to a friend from my class at the Playhouse years after and said, 'You know, nobody in our class ever amounted to a hill of beans as far as the theater is concerned.' She said, 'Well, there's Kim Stanley.' And I said, 'Kim Stanley wasn't in our class.' She said, 'Yes, she was, Barbara! Patty Beth Reid!' I simply did not connect the two people. There was a metamorphosis there."

Part of that metamorphosis, she says, was in Patty Reid's personality. "She was decidedly mousey. I can't recall that she ever read for anything. She was never cast in anything, which is incredible, when you think about it," she says. "Here she had this enormous talent, and she's not making any impression on anybody, so I think she thought everybody was a bunch of clods, and they probably were."

But another part of Kim's metamorphosis, Turner adds, was physical. "The reason I never connected her with Kim Stanley is that Kim Stanley was always quite voluptuous, and Patty Beth Reid had a figure like an ironing board. She was very collegiate-looking. She used to wear long plaid skirts with stitched-down pleats, which you can't wear if you have any hips at all."

Patty did impress at least one member of the Playhouse staff, though: Jack Harris, a director and production coordinator, who may have seen her in some class exercises. "She had something that was a little different from the other students," he says. "I knew that she was going to be somebody. I saw her in some student things there. She was just so outstanding in them that you could tell she was going to do things with her life if she wanted to."

Among Patty Reid's classmates was Pat Reid of Pasadena. In an effort to distinguish herself, Patty Reid of Albuquerque took the stage name Patricia Stanley. She later claimed this was because Pat Reid had already joined Actors Equity, although she never did.

In the summer of 1945, Edward Balcomb, a boyfriend of Patty's at UNM, visited her and Rubyann in Pasadena. He slept on their living room sofa and, when their car developed trouble, replaced its spark plugs. On July 16, about the time of Balcomb's visit, the United States exploded the world's first nuclear bomb at the Trinity Site, 100 miles south of Albuquerque. Guests in south-facing rooms in Albuquerque's Hilton Hotel who were awakened by the blast saw a fearsome red glow fill the sky. Patty Reid was connected to this event by her father: He had developed an adult-education program at the Los Alamos Laboratory where the bomb was created.

"J.T. set up the adult ed. classes in Los Alamos during the war," says Lynn White, Kim's brother-in-law. "He had security clearance to go up there. He would talk about the blockades, the checkpoints every two miles on the way up there. You only had so much time to get from one checkpoint to another."

Back in Pasadena, Patty's behavior was setting off shockwaves among her family. Katherine Norris, a second cousin on the Miller side, was at Lena Hankamer's house as a child when Lena got a phone call from Rubyann in Pasadena. "My grandmother turned to my grandfather and said, 'Patty has run away on the train with some man. She'll never make anything of herself now,'" Norris recalls.

The man in question appears to have been Bruce Hall. A handsome, talented actor six years older than Patty Reid, he had starred in many Playhouse productions a few years earlier and had already done several national tours of Broadway shows. He was, in the words of one friend, "a lady-killer." Although romantically involved at the time with a young actress in New York named Patricia Neal, Hall returned to the Playhouse in December of 1945 to star in *Night Must Fall,* and it was about this time Patty Reid went absent without leave from Pasadena.

Kim later said she tried to get into the movies while at the Pasadena Playhouse, although the evidence is inconclusive. "Warner Brothers signed her to a movie contract, but it took only three months for Kim to decide that Hollywood was not her dish. She walked out on the contract, without any violent opposition from the brothers Warner," says a 1949 article in *Theatre Arts* magazine. But if there ever was such a contract, no evidence of it remains. Another article says "[She] flunked a Warner Bros. screen test," while Kim told interviewer John Kobal, "I went in to see Michael Curtiz . . . He said I had too many photographic problems." Lacking an active imagination, though, was never one of her problems.

Unknown to Patty Reid, several people who would play important roles in her future incarnation as Kim Stanley were then nearby in Hollywood. Lucy Kroll, who would become her agent and mother hen, was a literary analyst at Warner Bros. in 1945. Lee Strasberg, her Actors Studio mentor and father figure, was directing screen tests at Twentieth-Century Fox. And Alfred Ryder, her third husband, had a one-year contract with Paramount in 1946.

SOMETIME BETWEEN DECEMBER OF 1945 AND APRIL OF 1946, Patty Reid left the Pasadena Playhouse and went to Louisville, Kentucky. Deek Kelley, a classmate at the Pasadena Playhouse, was performing in Louisville with Bill Hodapp's Bluegrass Theatre. She told Patty they needed some actresses to fill walk-on roles in their season of winter stock at the National Theater, a fading former burlesque house in downtown Louisville. Patty lived in a rooming house which, like the National Theater, had seen better days.

Under the stage name Patricia Stanley, Patty appeared as Peggy, a movie producer's secretary in Sam and Bella Spewack's *Boy Meets Girl*, which began its run at the Bluegrass Theatre on April 30, 1946. Her first line as a professional actress came when Benson, a screenwriter, asks if she's seen any of the films made by the studio's aging cowboy star. "Don't ask me anything, Mr. Benson," she says. "I've got the damndest toothache." Kim later described the role as a walk-on, but it was more of a walk-off: She delivered six lines, then got up and exited.

On May 7, the Bluegrass Players staged *Lady Honey*, the first play of acclaimed author MacKinlay Kantor. Focusing on an aristocratic young Englishwoman who opens her home to allied servicemen during World War II, the play took a critical pasting from the theater critic of the *Louisville Courier-Journal*, who said, "[It] did nothing to establish a dramatic interest, sustain it, or carry it to any sort of climax worthy of the term." Billed as the play's world premiere, this also appears to have been the last time the hapless work was performed anywhere.

Appearing in the minor role of Colonel Gracie Lumpkin was the actress known only a week before as Patricia Stanley. But now she was Kim Stanley, the role she would play for the rest of her life. It's unusual to choose one's stage name in stages, but in Louisville, Kim completed the shedding of her birth name she had begun in Pasadena.

Kim was not long for Louisville, either: By late May, the Bluegrass Theatre had folded. Edward Balcomb, now on leave from the Navy, visited her in Louisville. "They were holding the Kentucky Derby," he recalls. "I was still on active duty in the Navy. I went up there and looked her up. She told me one evening the troupe was breaking up—it just wasn't making it. She said, 'I'm headed to New York.' She went to New York with whatever pennies she had in her pocket."

Bill Corwin, who was dating the daughter of the man who bankrolled the Bluegrass Theatre, remembers that Kim went on to New York with Deek Kelley, although Kim always said she came to New York alone. A month before Kim left Louisville, the cover of the *Saturday Evening Post* featured a Norman Rockwell drawing of two cleaning ladies in a Broadway theater. The curtain has gone down, the audience has left, and the house is quiet. Taking a break from their chores, the cleaning ladies look through the playbill of the show just concluded. But for Kim, the curtain was about to go up. Either by herself (as she said) or with Deek Kelley (as Bill Corwin remembers) she boarded a Greyhound bus and headed for New York.

The Playwrights' Company
Presents

KIM STANLEY
IN
"The Traveling Lady"

A New Play by HORTON F.

JACK LORD   LONN
KATHERINE SQUIRE   KAT
Calvin Thomas Helen Carew Mo

Directed by VINCEN
Setting, Lighting and Costumes

PART TWO

ON THE NEW YORK STAGE

CHAPTER 3

"YES" IS FOR A VERY YOUNG WOMAN

(1946–1949)

ON JUNE 20, 1945, the *Queen Mary*, still painted gray from wartime service, steamed into New York harbor, carrying nearly 15,000 American servicemen from World War II. Those on board beheld an exuberant city: Crowds gathered along the waterfront and the towers of Manhattan gleamed in the afternoon sunlight. Unscarred by war, New York was proud, self-confident, and profoundly optimistic. "It was the town of all towns," writes author Jan Morris, "and this was a culminating moment in its history."

One year later, the newly self-christened Kim Stanley, a twenty-one-year-old golden blonde, arrived by bus from Louisville. The young Kim was a combination of paradoxes: driven and intense, yet gentle and sensitive; shy and quiet, yet vibrant and flirtatious. At dusk one rainy spring evening, her bus pulled into the Port Authority Bus Terminal on Forty-second Street. No longer supported by her Aunt Lena, she had only (or said she had only) twenty-one dollars to her name.

Although she always claimed to have come in 1947, contrary evidence, much of it from her, places Kim in New York in the spring of 1946.

That was when she left Louisville, and several plays she reports having seen, including *Antigone* with Katharine Cornell and *The Glass Menagerie* with Laurette Taylor, closed in the spring and summer of '46. She was not impressed with Cornell, but Taylor was a revelation.

"The first week I was in New York, somebody I met while waiting on tables said, 'You better go and see *The Glass Menagerie,*'" she later said. "I didn't see anything [on Broadway] that looked like my vision of theater. Then I saw Laurette Taylor in *The Glass Menagerie* and I said, 'Oh, that's what I mean.' Laurette Taylor turned the page for me." Taylor was legendary for her ability to not only play a role but become it, and eventually Paddy Chayefsky, Helen Hayes, and Harold Clurman would compare Kim to her.

Kim later said she didn't know anyone in the city when she arrived, but that isn't so: There was Bruce Hall from the Pasadena Playhouse, soon to become her first husband; Ellen Crowe, her director from the University of New Mexico; and Jinx Witherspoon, her UNM sorority sister. "I came to New York in 1944," Witherspoon later recalled. "We kept in touch. And I always said, 'If you come to New York, I've got an apartment.'" Kim also had a list of movers and shakers in the theater that was compiled by Stanley Walker, former city editor of the *New York Herald-Tribune* and Rubyann's first cousin.

As Kim later told the story, she took a room at a cheap rooming house in the West Thirties with a bedbug-ridden bed for a month and a half, sleeping on the floor instead. (Jinx Witherspoon thinks Kim stayed with her upon arrival, but isn't sure.) "I went up to Kermit Bloomgarden's office straight off the bus, and told him he would have to replace [Barbara] Bel Geddes in *Deep Are the Roots,*" Kim later said. Supposedly, Bloomgarden and other producers such as Russell Crouse told her to go back to Texas, a state to which she was native by ancestry, if not birth or experience.

Although she later developed a disdain for Shakespeare because she felt he didn't write good parts for women, Kim recited portions of his work as she made the rounds of producers and agents. "I sat everybody down and made them listen to me do Shakespeare—very badly," she later said. Auditioning is the bane of the actor's existence, and for Kim, it was more difficult than most. Her account of auditioning throws light on the difficulties she later had going on stage.

"Making the rounds is like trying to sell yourself, as if you were something on the hoof," she said. "I would get paralyzed, once in an office, and would be unable to remember the name of the play I was trying to get a job in. I hated the whole procedure. It was humiliating. They'd ask me what I had done on Broadway, and I couldn't speak. Emotionally, I couldn't take it. My hands would start sweating. I would feel like a cipher. Nothing was worth that."

FORTUNATELY, KIM WAS ABLE TO FIND WORK in the theater soon after arriving in New York. Unfortunately, it would prove short-lived and be her last acting work for two years. The Pompton Lakes Summer Theater in northern New Jersey, near Paterson, put on a series of light comedies in the auditorium of the local high school. Kim was hired as part of the troupe.

The actor Mitchell Kowal ran the company that summer along with his brother. Kowal, whose screen credits include *Cass Timberlane* and *Abbott and Costello Meet the Mummy*, sensed Kim's talent and hired her, although many of his associates thought little of this young woman with no New York theater experience. According to Kowal, it was at Pompton Lakes that Kim got her first Actors Equity card. She played Corliss Archer, the boy-crazy fifteen-year-old in *Kiss and Tell* and Prudence in *The Pursuit of Happiness.*

Shortly afterwards, though, she was fired, later giving two explanations. In one, she left because the assistant producer had a "yen" for her. In another, there was no implication of sexual harrassment, and she was fired for unspecified causes. "It didn't make me feel that I couldn't act, but it came as a terrible blow." Producer Kowal had a different story: After *Kiss and Tell*, Kim's next play was going to be *The Bishop Misbehaves.* "When this girl did not show up for rehearsals, I asked her why and she said, 'I don't feel like working this week,' so I fired her."

Kim returned to New York—exactly where she lived is unclear. She was always a restless spirit, and trying to figure out where she lived, especially during this period when she was obscure and on the move, is no easy matter. Over the next three years, she stayed several times with Jinx Witherspoon at her second-floor apartment in a brownstone at 44 West Eighty-fifth Street, a few blocks north of the Museum of Natural History (her mother Rubyann sometimes stayed there with her). Kim roomed with another young actress, Janet Shannon, on the Upper West Side. There was also an apartment in the East Twenties.

Also lost in the haze of Kim's early years in New York are many of the details of her brief marriage to Bruce Hall. Apparently in the fall of 1946, Kim and Bruce, whom she had met at the Pasadena Playhouse almost a year earlier, were married, probably in New York. Hall had grown up in Rye, an affluent Westchester County suburb. He was one of three children of Glenn Hall, an antiques dealer who had a brief career as a tenor at the Metropolitan Opera, and the former Germaine Ames, whose father had been a top executive of the Marshall Field department store in Chicago.

A handsome blond with a fine speaking voice, Bruce was a talented actor. He was also a prodigious drinker. Despite his wealthy background, he and Kim lived in a run-down cold-water flat on Third Avenue. Kim later said it was on either Thirty-second or Thirty-sixth Street, in Murray Hill, but Bill Corwin, a friend from Louisville, places it about ten blocks north, closer to Turtle Bay. Regardless, the small apartment, which Kim and Bruce shared with a young black actor Corwin only knew as "Shadow," was a dump.

"This was a trashy area," Corwin recalls. "Trust me, it was really rough. I would never park my car on that street." The elevated subway, or "El," still ran along Third Avenue, and since Kim and Bruce's apartment was on the second or third floor, it was perfectly situated to absorb the full squawk and screech from passing subway cars. "When the train went by, you didn't talk," Corwin says. "You just shut up and let it go by. I guess this was about the bottom for her."

In a professional sense, Kim was the junior partner in their marriage: Bruce had done ten shows at the Pasadena Playhouse; she had done none. In 1946, he appeared on Broadway in *Joan of Lorraine,* which gave Kim the chance to meet the play's star, Ingrid Bergman. (On a less agreeable note for Kim, Hall suggested they meet his ex-girlfriend Patricia Neal one day for tea; Kim spent much of the time glaring at her.)

But Kim became disillusioned with his drinking. "She wasn't a heavy drinker, but Bruce was," Corwin remembers. "He was bombed most of the time I saw him. So apparently she just had her fill of it and said 'Bye-bye.'" The marriage lasted no more than a year or two.

Hall's subsequent credits include *Playhouse 90* and *Camera Three* on television and extensive work in regional theater. But his star never rose, something he accepted with an equanimity his friend Cliff Robertson recalls, by way of Tennessee Williams, as displaying "the charm of the defeated." Most of his colleagues lost track of him and little remains to mark his passing. Asked what became of him, veteran television executive Ethel Winant quips, "I don't know. I imagine he's still looking for work in New York."

To support herself, Kim turned to modeling, working as a dress model in the fashion house of Herbert Sondheim, whose son Stephen would later become a theater legend in his own right. "I was hired as an outdoor-girl type model—four showings a day for fifty-six dollars a week," Kim recalled. "It was deadly work. I couldn't take it for very long, because I was afraid my whole life would revolve around things like 'Do I look better with my eyebrows heavy or light?'"

Kim later told Lillian Ross of the *New Yorker* that one of her jobs during this period was touring Southern towns, modeling dresses by designers such as Balenciaga and Fath. She never mentioned this in other interviews, though, and no one who knew her during this period recalls her doing it either.

Then she went to work as a cocktail waitress at the Sheraton Hotel at Lexington Avenue and Thirty-seventh Street. "I thought I'd save more money if I gave up modeling and went to work in the cocktail lounge of the Sheraton," Kim later said. "On good weeks, I'd average ninety dollars a week in tips. I wore high-heeled shoes and a transparent skirt, and ads for the lounge would show a picture of me with the heading 'I'm at the Sheraton Lounge. Where are you?'" Speaking of the indignity of having to wear a transparent skirt, she later reflected, "It was the only time I hated people and the last chance I gave myself to hate." Kim gave another account of this experience that made her sound less like a victim of the oppressive patriarchy: "I was one of that famous crew of waitresses at the Sheraton Hotel. Our trademark was those transparent outer skirts. That should have made us a target for wolves, but it didn't. The place catered to a family-type crowd." Apparently, nothing lured families from the suburbs like waitresses in transparent skirts.

WHILE KIM WAS STRUGGLING to find a foothold, another actor to whom she would often be compared had found his breakout role: Marlon Brando as Stanley Kowalski in *A Streetcar Named Desire,* which opened on Broadway on December 3, 1947. Brando's gritty, intense, and galvanizing performance heralded the arrival of Method acting.

In addition to their both being Method actors who trained at the Actors Studio, Kim and Brando had a lot in common: They both had strict, authoritarian fathers married to mothers who had unsuccessfully aspired to be actresses; they both rebelled against the conventionality and boredom of their middle-American childhoods; and they both hated to audition. They both projected unrefined sexual energy onstage and were casual about engaging in sex offstage. And they were the best. "She and Marlon were the top of the profession, of that style of acting, to those of us who came up in the '50s," says Georgann Johnson, who played Tony Randall's wife in the live sitcom *Mr. Peepers.*

But in 1947, this kind of acclaim was nowhere in sight for Kim, and the struggle to achieve it was taking a toll. "She had taken to drinking too much," Jinx Witherspoon recalls. "Ellen Crowe [one of Kim's directors at the University of New Mexico] said it worried her terribly. And her mother said, 'I'm worried about Patty. She goes through these depressing times, and sometimes takes to the bottle a bit.'"

Nikki Tachias, a roommate of Witherspoon's during this period, says, "It all seemed to work okay (between Kim and Rubyann). The mother was very supportive." But relations between Kim and her mother were strained. "Her mother was bugging her for reasons I don't remember exactly," says screenwriter Lorenzo Semple Jr., one of Kim's lovers during this period. And actor and director Gene Saks says, "I think she bothered Kim a great deal. It was a stormy mother-daughter relationship."

Kim and Rubyann were at odds. Kim was drinking and her acting career, which held all of Rubyann's hopes, was going nowhere. Money was tight, and Rubyann's temperament, like her daughter's, was mercurial. It took a sharp downdraft in the fall of 1947, when Rubyann had a nervous breakdown. Her nephew Marvin Miller, along with Kim's brother Howard, had to come up to New York to get her. They took Rubyann back to Texas, where she convalesced at the home of her brother Melvin and his wife. Their return to Texas was by train rather than flying, as Rubyann had a fear of flying, a phobia her daughter would inherit.

After two years of wandering in the wilderness, though, Kim was about to get her break. In the summer of 1948, she joined the Interplayers, one of several semi-professional theater groups that rented small Greenwich Village theaters for the summer and put on plays. When the Interplayers moved into the Provincetown Playhouse on MacDougal Street near Washington Square Park, they found a gift from the past: a poured concrete cyclorama. The inward-curving backdrop had been used by the original Provincetown Players for special lighting effects in their 1920 world premiere of Eugene O'Neill's *The Emperor Jones*.

As *Theatre Arts* magazine noted, all of these summer groups—composed of young, dedicated, and idealistic theater people—had their own statements of ideals, "always of a frighteningly high-minded sort." The Interplayers were no exception: The program for e.e. cummings's *him*, which they did that summer, earnestly proclaimed its faith in "the democratic principle of diversity in the marketplace of ideas." This wasn't just a statement in the program, either. "We had philosophical discussions such as 'Is Democracy Acceptable, Permissible, or Workable in a Theater Company?'" recalls press agent and Interplayers publicist Merle Debuskey. "We were very serious about all that."

Summer theater groups in the Village were not luxury operations. Members of the Interplayers received no salaries and worked as a cooperative with no chore too menial for any member: Kim took her turn cleaning out the men's room. She also sold lemonade during intermissions. "Very embarrassing," she later recalled. "Me, about to be an Eleanora Duse, yelling, 'Lemonade. Get your lemonade.'" To try and beat the New York City summer heat, they rigged up a primitive air-conditioning system consisting of trays of ice and a fan, which was supposed to blow cool air from the melting ice onto audience members. Sometimes, it just wound up splashing them.

After a show, some of the Interplayers would head uptown. "We would go to Forty-second Street and watch two movies for the price of one," Merle Debuskey recalls. "If it was too hot, we would go up to Central Park and, on occasion, sleep in the park." Legendary author E.B. White wrote about such nights in his 1948 book *Here Is New York,* with its description of concerts at the Central Park band shell:

> In the trees, the night wind stirs . . . The electric lights illuminate the green branches from the under side . . . The cornetist steps forward for a solo . . . then from the [Hudson] River another horn solo begins—the *Queen Mary* . . . In the warm grass beyond the fence, forms wriggle in the shadows, and the skirts of the girls approaching on the mall are ballooned by the breeze, and their bare shoulders catch the lamplight.

Perhaps those were Kim's shoulders catching the lamplight: They certainly had a great effect upon the men of the company.

"She was not a classic beauty, but collectively, she was extremely attractive," Merle Debuskey says. "And she knew it, and she knew how to use it. Kim became the golden fleece. From Day One at the Interplayers, every male was in pursuit." This engendered a somewhat practical attitude on her part. "She could be very charming if she wished, but she was very selective in the use of that charm," Debuskey adds. "If she was interested in you or what you were doing or could do for her, she was charming. But that was subject to review."

The Interplayers staged *him,* e.e. cummings's wildly experimental play, on the twentieth anniversary of its world premiere on the stage of the Provincetown Playhouse. Gene Saks starred as "him," a playwright having trouble with his girlfriend and the play he's trying to write; Janet Shannon co-starred as "me," the girlfriend. The play is an unwieldy but enjoyable amalgam of surrealism, Dada, Expressionism, and stream of consciousness, festooned with puns and other forms of wordplay. There are twenty-one scenes with seventy-two roles. Among the play's other unusual aspects:

• In some scenes, "him" talks about scenes he plans to write; they are acted out in the scenes that follow.

• One set reappears intermittently throughout the play, each time rotated by 90 degrees, until it has made a full circle.

• In another scene, there is no set—the curtain goes up on an unadorned backstage area.

• Long before the advent of the Living Theater, actors pop up from the audience and run through it.

Reflecting the play's offbeat spirit, cummings wrote in program notes to the 1928 version, "Don't try to despise it, let it try to despise you. Don't try to enjoy it, let it try to enjoy you. Don't try to understand it, let it try to understand you." Actors in the original version who wanted to understand it, though, could go to cummings, who lived in the Village, and ask for help. This was not a courtesy cummings extended to the Interplayers—he sometimes walked past the Provincetown Playhouse while rehearsals were in session, but never went in.

Kim was not in the cast on opening night, but joined the production during its run, playing one of the Three Wierds, harpy-like figures who serve as the play's Greek chorus. "She was a very attractive blonde who looked like an Ivy League coed, very Greenwich [Connecticut]–looking," Gene Saks recalls. "Girls who looked like that looked as if they should be in the society pages of the *New York Times* getting married." Saks also remembers her as very quiet, smart, and idealistic.

Despite reviews of the "A for effort" variety from the *New York Post* and the *Telegraph,* the show did well, running for sixteen weeks to capacity audiences until the group's theater lease expired. That winter, the Interplayers performed W.H. Auden's *The Dog Beneath the Skin* at the Carnegie Recital Hall; Kim played Iris Crewe of Honeypot Hall and the Queen of Ostnia. Internal frictions led to a split, though, and the next summer, a breakaway faction of the Interplayers, including Kim, reconstituted itself as Off-Broadway, Inc. (OBI).

In March, 1949, Kim received her first New York press exposure: a full-page photo spread in *Theatre Arts* magazine of her reading for producer Kermit Bloomgarden. It was part of a series called "Theatre Arts

Introduces . . . ," in which the magazine purported to introduce aspiring young actors to Broadway heavy hitters. Speaking on behalf of small, experimental off-Broadway groups, Kim said, "I know it must sound pompous, but how the hell can an actress develop if she's lucky to get one Broadway part a year?" In the photo, a young and slender Kim wears what appears to be Bruce Hall's wedding ring, although she was now separated from him. It was a remarkable publicity windfall for an actress with only two small off-Broadway roles to her credit, and it's unclear whether Lorenzo Semple's romantic interest in Kim helped to bring it about (he was then a staff writer at *Theatre Arts*).

When the summer theater season of 1949 arrived in Greenwich Village, Kim was a leading member of Off-Broadway, Inc., which operated out of the Cherry Lane Theatre on Commerce Street in Greenwich Village. Of the Village scene then, *Theatre Arts* magazine noted, "It is virtually impossible for any off-Broadway company, no matter how wretchedly mismanaged, to lose money over a full summer season; such is the charm of the Village that in addition to the seriously theatre-minded, there are always enough casual strollers to fill a good part of the house."

The Village summer season of '49 was notable for two things: its stupefying heat and cultural vitality. *Theatre Arts* called it "New York's hottest summer on record," but added that things were hot culturally as well, declaring it the most important since the Provincetown Players had staged the premieres of works by Eugene O'Neill and Theodore Dreiser. The magazine noted the profusion of theater groups (five), the amount of interest they had drawn from uptown critics, and the fact that they had banded together into a trade association to secure an Equity-waiver agreement, allowing established performers to appear at below-scale rates.

For an ephemeral, semi-pro acting group, Off-Broadway, Inc., had an astonishing array of talent: In addition to Kim, there were actors Gene Saks, Bea Arthur (soon to marry Saks), Michael Gazzo, Nehemiah Persoff, and Tony Franciosa, directors Lamont Johnson and Curt Conway, scenic designer Ed Wittstein, and press agent Merle Debuskey. They did two plays that summer: *Yes Is for a Very Young Man* by Gertrude Stein and *Too Many Thumbs* by Robert Hivnor.

In addition to being a production company, OBI also functioned informally as a school: Kim taught acting and diction, and Michael Gazzo taught acting. It was the first time Kim encountered the teachings of Stanislavski. "It was my first brush with the so-called Method," she later said. "There are times in your life when you suddenly have insight, and this was one of those times for me."

Bea Arthur was impressed, and not only with Kim's acting. "She was so beautiful. And my God, what a stage presence. What talent. She was extraordinary. I just felt out of her league." That beauty, however, would cause dissension within OBI. "Kim had gotten involved with several people on a very intimate level," Tony Franciosa recalls. "It seemed to me that it caused a lot of friction within the company."

Kim was involved with Michael Gazzo. "Kim and he had been lovers in the days of the Cherry Lane Playhouse," recalls Ben Gazzara, who met Gazzo in 1955. "And Mike couldn't get her out of his mind." Kim and Merle Debuskey were also an item. Asked if he had been romantically involved with Kim, he says, "Oh my goodness gracious. Uh—yes. We had our moments." And, although he wasn't a member of the group, Lorenzo Semple Jr. was another of Kim's lovers. "Many afternoons, we sat drinking stingers at a bar called the Thistle Inn on West Fifty-fourth Street," he says. "I was completely enchanted by her—this smart, open, good-looking Texas girl with the wonderfully husky laugh, so different from the preppie types I had grown up with. We talked about the theater and life and I often wound up going boozily downtown with her and spending the night. What added, in my eyes, even more luster to Kim than her theater aspirations was her claim that she'd been the lover of one of the legendary Cardinal ballplayers, I think Enos Slaughter."

Yes Is for a Very Young Man was the first of OBI's two shows that summer. The Gertrude Stein play shows the fissures that develop in a French family and community under Nazi occupation. Husband Henri (Gazzo) is a member of the French Resistance. His wife, Denise (Kim), is a royalist who supports Marshal Petain's Vichy government (the Nazi puppet regime in France during World War II), and her brother Ferdinand (Franciosa) is a kid still trying to figure things out. Their neighbor Constance (Bea Arthur) is an American woman, much like Gertrude Stein, superficially neutral but a tacit supporter of the

Resistance. Gene Saks had a small role as a German soldier.

Kim's character, Denise, comes by her traditionalism honestly: According to her husband, Henri, her mother is a direct descendant of Joan of Arc. She also has a temper, telling Henri at one point, "You beast, if you were not my husband and going to be the father of my child, I would kill you." One newspaper review noted Kim's aptness for this aspect of her role, saying, "[Denise] is played very well by Kim Stanley, using a temperament that flared up impetuously and subsided equally rapidly." Courtesy of Gertrude Stein, Denise and all the characters in the play have an oddly Cubist way of talking, operating on the premise that if something is worth saying, it's worth saying three or four times. Angered in one scene, Henri says, "Let everybody shut up, let everybody shut up, shut up, shut up."

Lamont Johnson remembers OBI as a lively, talented group. "They were very dynamic," he says. "All of them. Wonderful, budding young actors and excitable temperaments. Extremely opinionated and talented." And in no area were they more opinionated than acting theory.

"We were all studying with various offshoots of Method teachers, and when we got into rehearsal, we spent most of our time arguing about the Method. That was wretched," he says. "I was a Sandy Meisner person, but there were Stella Adler ones, Lee Strasberg ones, and Berghof–Uta Hagen ones. Everyone had different positions and held to his or her position."

This internecine ideological warfare led to Johnson's dismissal from the show. "Mike Gazzo took me out on the fourteenth-floor fire escape landing of the Actors Studio and said I had to go—there was too much dissension," Johnson says. "If I'd been deeply moved by that, I would have jumped." Gazzo took over the play's direction, and things went from bad to worse.

A week before *Yes* was scheduled to open on June 6, 1949, Johnson got a call from Gene Saks. "He said, 'Lamont, we're in worse trouble than ever. Would you come back?' And I said, 'Only on one condition—that everybody shut up!'" (But Johnson did not say, "Let everybody shut up, let everybody shut up, shut up, shut up.")

Kim was not only a performer, but one of the show's producers, the only time in her career she would play this role. "Kim was really uptight, the last-minute details of getting everything together, knowing her own role, and getting the theater ready," says Nikki Tachias, one of her roommates at this time. "She seemed to be in charge of a lot of stuff. The hope was that they would get the uptown critics downtown. So she put a lot into it—herself and, I think, all the funds she had." She also threw her living space into the pot: Several rehearsals of *Yes* were held in the second-floor apartment at 44 West Eighty-fifth Street she shared with Tachias and Jinx Witherspoon.

This production was not the world premiere of *Yes Is for a Very Young Man* (which was done at the Pasadena Playhouse in March of 1946), nor was it the American premiere (ditto) or even the East Coast premiere (Princeton University Players, July 1948). It was, however, the New York City premiere, and to New Yorkers, that's always a big deal.

"Nobody paid much attention to off-Broadway," Merle Debuskey recalls. "But because it was Gertrude Stein, all the first-line critics came down to the Cherry Lane Theatre. It was really quite remarkable—Commerce Street was lined with limos. Everybody came, and everybody wanted to get to Kim." Nikki Tachias recalls that she, Kim, Rubyann, and Jinx Witherspoon stayed up late after coming home to anxiously wait for early editions of the next morning's newspapers to hit the streets.

Reviews for the play were mixed, ranging from the applause of the *Christian Science Monitor* ("It makes the little Cherry Lane Theatre seem bright indeed these days") to the jeers of *Women's Wear Daily* ("When Miss Stein writes with a semblance of clarity, the illusion of profundity is stripped away . . . a comparatively shallow play"). Lamont Johnson was generally praised for his effective direction; all of the actors received mixed reviews. Except for Kim.

"The most interesting member of the cast is Kim Stanley, who brings humor, credibility, and charm to the role," wrote Richard Watts Jr. of the *New York Post*. William Hawkins of the *World-Telegram* said that Kim was the most successful member of the cast, handling a varied and emotional role effectively. Brooks Atkinson of the *New York Times* wrote, "In Kim Stanley, as a young French mother, the Off Broadway people have a talented actress with temperament, craft, and, if there is any justice on Broadway, a future." Her notices from the *New York Journal-American, Christian Science Monitor,* and other publications were similar.

Although *Yes* is an ensemble piece, and Merle Debuskey sent out press kits with photos of various cast members, only one photo accompanied reviews: a young Kim with a dreamy, sensuous, slightly haunted look. "The superb notices lifted Kim Stanley out of obscurity," author Stuart W. Little wrote in his 1974 book, *Off-Broadway: The Prophetic Theater.* "Never again would she appear on a stage anywhere without a sense of excitement and anticipation."

Scheduled to play for only four weeks, *Yes* ran for eight. *Theatre Arts* said receipts from *Yes* plunged unexpectedly, causing the Cherry Lane Theatre to go dark for a week. But Merle Debuskey remembers it differently. "In our naïveté, we thought it was our responsibility to encourage new playwrights," he says. "We had this hit, we were sold out, and we closed it down to put on something called *Too Many Thumbs.*"

One of 200 scripts submitted to OBI by World War II GIs, *Too Many Thumbs* is the story of a super-chimpanzee in a lab that quickly evolves into a man and then a saint-like figure. It was written by Robert Hivnor, an English professor at the University of Minnesota. Michael Gazzo was chosen to direct. Nehemiah Persoff gamely played the quickly evolving chimp, named Too Many Thumbs; Gene Saks was G.E. Macklebee, a professor of religion who hopes to make a good Christian out of the rapidly evolving chimp; Dick Robbins was starchy anthropologist Arthur Smith; and Kim played Jenny Macklebee, the professor's daughter—girlfriend first of Smith, then of the chimp in his humanoid phase.

"The play had its weaknesses," Persoff says diplomatically, "but Kim didn't give up. She really was a trouper—she worked hard in it. There were many difficult passages to go through, and she was supportive all the way." Tony Franciosa also remembers Kim working hard. "I was stage-managing it, and she was waiting to go on," he recalls. "She put her head on my shoulder, just laid it there for several seconds and said, 'Oh God, I'm so fucking tired.' I looked at her and I don't know what I said, but I will never forget that moment. It was quiet, tender, and lovely."

She was not just tired, though: Kim was pushing herself into a state of exhaustion. "I don't think she took care of herself," Merle Debuskey says. "She passed out onstage twice. Once I think we rushed her to a Catholic hospital on the East Side. Another time, I took her home and called a friend of mine who was a physician. I remember putting her to bed and piling everything on top of her to keep her warm. She was shaking and her teeth were chattering."

Kim was also having trouble with the play's director, her lover Michael Gazzo. "The rehearsals started the demise of the theater," Tony Franciosa recalls. "Mike Gazzo was going out with Kim and having personal problems with her. He left the production for personal or artistic reasons." Nehemiah Persoff knew Curt Conway, an actor who was doing some directing, and OBI brought him in to replace Gazzo.

A thirty-six-year-old Irish Catholic from Boston, Conway had debuted on Broadway as an actor in 1935's *The Young Go First.* Good-natured, feisty, independent, and politically committed, he was a highly regarded acting teacher (and something of a drinker) who had been a member of the Group Theatre in the '30s, studying with Harold Clurman, Elia Kazan, and Lee Strasberg.

"I first became aware of Kim when she tried to cut my salary because the budget was low," Conway later said. "I was immediately intrigued with her, but I absolutely refused to take a salary cut to salvage their investment." One of the first things Conway had to do was figure out how to salvage the play, which was not going well in rehearsal. "We got to the end of the play, where the man was evolving, and we really didn't know which way to go," Nehemiah Persoff recalls.

Conway proposed radical surgery. "Curt was asked to look at a rehearsal," Tony Franciosa says. "He said, 'I know what the problem is.' I said, 'Really? What?' He said, 'Cut out the third act.' Hivnor was there and just sank into his seat and got smaller and smaller." But it was a canny decision on Conway's part: The second act concludes with an anguished, powerful speech by Too Many Thumbs about his ambivalence at evolving into a human. The third act consists of a lot of cockamamie philosophizing, such as this oddball and ungrammatical speech:

PROFESSOR MACKLEBEE: Soon all the people of our time, born in one vast tomb of the Gods, can come out now into the fields where beauty and oxygen is, and the only manna which has ever fallen will cover the earth—meaning.

One can't fault OBI for staging such a play—it's exactly what you should do when you're young, idealistic, and pretentious. "We thought that was wonderful—the real stuff," Kim later said. "None of us had the slightest idea what it was about."

After the play opened on July 27, it did get some good reviews: Richard Watts Jr. of the *New York Post* wrote, "It has the rare gift of freshness and imagination," while *Variety* said it started weakly, although it built into an amusing and fanciful comedy. But the *Daily Compass* said it was confusing and plagued by "too many themes," and *Women's Wear Daily* complained it was cluttered with as trite an assortment of personalities as had ever been gathered for one show. While the *World-Telegram* said Kim and Dick Robbins were convincing as lovers, *Variety* said Kim had little to do but lend charm to the proceedings.

In a life-changing event for Kim, Conway gave her a good review of his own. "He took a shine to Kim," Nehemiah Persoff recalls. "But there was never any feeling that there was anything going on until opening night. He went in [to her dressing room] to congratulate her, and I think they came out lovers."

After the close of *Too Many Thumbs*, Off-Broadway, Inc., went the way of most small, idealistic, underfunded theater groups, and Tony Franciosa says Kim's golden-fleece status may have played a role. "There was a lot of sexual intrigue around her," he says, "and the resultant friction contributed to the demise of the company."

Three weeks after Kim and Curt met, he told her he was going to marry her. "She later told me that my approach intrigued her, that she loved my being so positive," Conway later recalled. Kim went on to study with Conway at the American Theater Wing, where another one of the students was Jack Klugman.

"The first day in class, Curt would throw objects at people, like a comb or a key ring. And he'd say, 'Personalize it. Tell a story about it,'" Klugman recalls. "He threw Kim a cigarette lighter, I believe. She started to talk about her brother in Texas—I don't know if this is real or not—who died in the war. And she had us all in tears. I knew this was a great talent."

Another place Kim got to hone that talent was in the fledgling medium of television. During Kim's early days in New York, television ran a distant second to radio as America's premier electronic medium. Network radio was at its peak in the fall of 1946, while in the first six months of that year, only 225 television sets were produced in the U.S. There were a few small commercial TV stations in cities of the Northeast, and people who watched boxing matches or baseball games on them usually did so in bars rather than at home.

Kim appeared on *Hollywood Screen Test,* a show in which newcomers performed scenes with well-known actors. She was also on *The Bigelow Show,* a variety show featuring ventriloquist Paul Winchell and his smart-aleck dummy, Jerry Mahoney, in one segment and mental telepathist Joseph Dunninger in another. And in the fall of 1949, Kim appeared on an episode of *Boris Karloff Mystery Playhouse.* Compared to radio, television was still in its infancy, but the June 8, 1948, premiere of Milton Berle's *Texaco Star Theater* paved the way for TV to become America's dominant broadcast medium.

Kim's next off-Broadway play was not in Greenwich Village, but on Manhattan's Upper West Side. Having played a descendant of Joan of Arc in *Yes Is for a Very Young Man,* Kim now played the Maid of Orleans herself in George Bernard Shaw's massive *Saint Joan.* It was staged in the fall of 1949 by the Equity Library Theater, established by Actors Equity to provide work for its members, at the Lenox Hill Playhouse on West 103rd Street.

Saint Joan was directed by Philip Robinson. In addition to Kim, the cast included two future notables: film director George Roy Hill, who played the Earl of Warwick, the English nobleman who is Joan's chief tormentor; and Jack Klugman, who played Captain de la Hire, a French officer sympathetic to Joan. As Klugman recalls it, he was hired less as an actor than as an enforcer for Kim.

"She really didn't like confrontation," Klugman says. "Curt [Conway] begged me to do the play, so I would be the buffer between her and the director. He and Kim said they wanted me to do de la Hire. I said, 'Christ, I can't even pronounce it.' But I adored her, and Curt was the best acting teacher I ever had, so I did it." Kim would tell Klugman which director's notes she didn't want to take, and Klugman would pass her wishes along to Robinson. "He would say, 'Well, why didn't she tell me?' And I said, 'Because if she tells you, she'll quit.'"

The role of Joan fit Kim well. When Joan is given command of the French army, Shaw's stage direction indicates she is radiant and falls on her knees in thanksgiving; "radiant" is a word often applied to Kim's stage presence. And Joan's line to her military aide about going into battle could also apply to Kim's difficulty going onstage: "I am frightened beyond words before a battle; but it is so dull afterwards when there is no danger."

Klugman, impressed with Kim's performance, could see her growing as an actress. "She was wonderful. She was developing," he says. "She wasn't the consummate actress that she became. But her ability to concentrate—her concentration was enveloping. When I would do a scene with her, she was able to bring me into the reality that she created."

Actor Walt Witcover, who had a small role in the production, was similarly impressed. "I've seen many Saint Joans—Uta Hagen, Siobhan McKenna, Diana Sands—but Kim was the best I've ever seen," he says. "I was sitting there as one of her inquisitors, thinking she was a witch to be condemned, and she moved me to tears in rehearsal."

Witcover also remembers that Kim's offstage life wasn't lacking in drama, either: He socialized with her and Curt Conway, observing several violent quarrels between them. "Sometimes it was uncomfortable, because they wouldn't hold back. Both were free and volatile and weren't careful in thinking twice about what to say." On one occasion, Witcover invited Conway and Kim to a party at his place. "She was having some fuss with Curt and went into the bathroom, locked the door, and threatened to slit her wrists," he says. "Luckily, she didn't. But she was very passionate."

One night, Curt Conway came to watch Kim perform in *Saint Joan.* It was a revelation for him. He went out during intermission, smoked a cigarette, and decided to shift his career focus from acting to teaching and directing: He knew he would never be half as good an actor as she was. The play had an impact on Kim's career as well, as producer Kermit Bloomgarden saw her performance. His next Broadway show was already cast, but Kim made an impression on him, and it wasn't that she should go back to Texas.

CHAPTER 4

METHOD TO HER MADNESS

(1949–1952)

YEARS AFTER KIM HAD ACHIEVED STARDOM, Paul Zindel tried to recruit her for his play *And Miss Reardon Drinks a Little,* hoping to entice her with the fact that Julie Harris was in the cast. But Kim gave that as a reason for not signing, decrying Harris's tendency to show up for the first rehearsal with the play all worked out in her head and no room for the growth and improvisation Kim favored.

But however much Kim disliked Harris's approach, it was Harris she would have to thank for her Broadway debut. When *Montserrat,* the Emmanuel Robles play directed and adapted by Lillian Hellman, opened at the Fulton Theatre on October 29, 1949, Julie Harris appeared in a small supporting part. Midway through the play's brief run, however, Harris left the show to take the juicier starring role of Frankie in Carson McCullers's *The Member of the Wedding.* Producer Kermit Bloomgarden then tapped Kim to replace her.

Felisa, Kim's role, was a courageous Indian maiden in Spanish colonial Venezuela. She stiffens the resolve of Montserrat (William Redfield), a principled Spanish officer, not to betray liberator Simon Bolivar to the harsh, sadistic Spanish commandant Izquierdo (Emlyn Williams), even though it will cost her her life. In later years, Kim rarely spoke about the part, which had only twenty-five lines and one good speech, and flippantly at that ("The little Indian girl who goes out to be killed. There's a lot of laughs in that, right?"). But when she joined the case in late November, it was her first Broadway role.

Montserrat is set in Venezuela in 1812. Montserrat refuses to tell Colonel Izquierdo where Bolivar is hiding. To get him to talk, Izquierdo rounds up a group of innocent civilians from a nearby marketplace and has them executed one by one, hoping Montserrat will crack in order to spare their lives. Just when he's about to weaken, Felisa gives a speech ("Stay with what you believe . . . [D]eath is death, no better for one than another") that puts carbon in his spine, although it means that she and Mathilde (a young mother played by Vivian Nathan) will be the last of six hostages to be shot in cold blood.

All that shooting made an impact not only on the audience at the Fulton, but next door at the Morosco, where Arthur Miller's *Death of a Salesman* was playing. Early in the show, several characters worry about the suicidal tendencies of Willy Loman, played by Lee J. Cobb. When the first hostage in *Montserrat* was executed every evening, playgoers at the Morosco thought Loman had killed himself offstage. Noting that a lot of gunpowder was expended in dispatching the hostages, one journalist reported, "'There goes Willy' is the remark heard lately in the audience at the Morosco."

Reviews for *Montserrat* were mixed. John Chapman of the *Daily News* said, "Lillian Hellman . . . has found a play to her liking—and mine—in *Montserrat*. Its demand upon the audience's reserves of pity and anger is so insistent that in comparison *Death of a Salesman* is recalled as a jolly prank." And William Hawkins of the *New York World-Telegram* noted that on opening night "after a dozen curtain calls, nearly all the audience sat and continued clapping."

But Brooks Atkinson of the *New York Times* was less impressed, noting, "In view of the harrowing theme it has to unfold, *Montserrat* ought to be completely devastating . . . [but] the effects it achieves are mechanical."

One problem was that in *Montserrat*, the villain is a lot more fun than the hero, who is wretchedly sincere and earnest to a fault. Richard Watts Jr., in the *New York Post,* said of Emlyn Williams, "This enormously powerful British actor makes the sardonic soldier so compelling and interesting a figure that by comparison William Redfield's tortured young idealist seems pallid and ineffectual." (Williams also adversely affected director Lillian Hellman, who later admitted she felt intimidated by him.)

One night, perhaps nervous at making her Broadway debut, Kim went on stage and stood in the wrong place. Staying in character, Vivian Nathan calmly went over and, while the action continued, led her to where she was supposed to be. Although Mathilde (Vivian Nathan's character) hates Felisa (Kim's), in real life, Vivian and Kim would form a fifty-year friendship.

"She had a terrific sense of humor," Nathan says of Kim. "Her laugh was full-throated, loud, and infectious. She was very polite. But don't get her angry. There was a volatility there, which helped in her acting. The temper flared quickly, and just as quickly died down."

Through the years, Nathan would also get a close look at Kim's dark side. As she had done onstage, Nathan would try to steer Kim in the right direction offstage, but would find this more difficult. "She was a more vulnerable person than most of us," she says. "And as a result of that vulnerability, she drank. She drank to kill her inability to cope. That made her another sort of person. She was Jekyll and Hyde."

Like Kim's temper, *Montserrat* also died down quickly, closing after sixty-five performances. She had appeared in about half of them. The final performance came on Christmas eve of 1949.

But on the heels of *Montserrat*'s closing, there was a happier development: Curt Conway had been pressing Kim to marry him, and in January of 1950, she agreed. Ironically, in light of Gene Saks's observation that Kim looked like an Ivy League coed from Greenwich, Kim and Curt were married in Greenwich, Connecticut, on January 28. He was thirty-six, she was twenty-four; it was the second marriage for both (Conway, a Catholic, had gotten his first marriage annulled).

Kim married Conway under the hybrid name "Patricia Kimberly Stanley," a combination of her birth name, her imaginary name (despite what she said in some interviews, "Kimberly" was not her middle name), and her stage name. The name she chose to marry under suggests how fluid her identity was, and how much difficulty she may have had locating its core.

Following a wedding reception in Manhattan, they settled down to married life in an apartment at 47 Morton Street, on a tree-shaded block in Greenwich Village. In addition to becoming a noted director and acting teacher, Conway's acting credits would come to include the Gregory Peck film *Gentleman's Agreement,* the world stage premiere of William Saroyan's *The Time of Your Life,* and a memorable episode of *The Twilight Zone* in which he plays a shadowy figure who encourages neo-Nazi Dennis Hopper and who turns out to be Adolf Hitler.

Conway was a man of strong political convictions: After Elia Kazan "named names" before the House Un-American Activities Committee in 1952, Conway crossed the street one day in midtown Manhattan to avoid greeting him. And neither did he take any guff from another former Group Theatre mentor of his, Lee Strasberg.

"He quit the Actors Studio," Lonny Chapman recalls. "He walked out on a Lee Strasberg session. Curt wanted to talk about something. Strasberg said, 'I don't want to hear from you.' He said, 'You don't want to hear from me? I'm leaving.'"

BUT KIM WAS JUST STARTING at the Actors Studio with Lee Strasberg, and it would prove to be a period of remarkable creative growth for her. Shortly after her marriage to Curt, she auditioned for membership in the Actors Studio. The late 1940s and the 1950s were the peak years of the Studio, and winning admission was not easy: Between the fall of 1948 and the spring of 1951, more than 2,000 performers auditioned; only thirty, including Kim, were accepted.

The Actors Studio was founded in October 1947 by Elia Kazan, Robert Lewis, and Cheryl Crawford, all veterans of the Group Theatre. As director Harold Clurman observed, the Studio was a place where already-trained actors could pursue "post-graduate" work. In many of its personnel and in its devotion to Method acting, the Actors Studio was a lineal descendant of the Group Theatre of the '30s and '40s, although the focus of the Studio was actor training rather than production.

In turn, the Group Theatre had been heavily influenced by the Moscow Art Theater, founded in 1896 by Constantin Stanislavski. Stanislavski, along with several of his colleagues, originated the Method (called "the system" by Stanislavski), the most influential movement in acting since the Elizabethan period. Several members of the Group studied with members of Stanislavski's troupe who came to America in the '30s, providing a direct link between the Moscow Art Theater and the Actors Studio.

When Kim joined the Studio, it was located on the fourteenth floor of 1697 Broadway, in the building that would later house the Ed Sullivan Theater. As Actors Studio historian David Garfield notes, Studio actors would become known for their distinctive brand of emotionally volatile acting, a style which was unconventional, deeply felt, and psychologically detailed, more impulsive than calculated, and more openly emotional than intellectual. While Harold Clurman acknowledged that most members of the Studio were "quite sane about their activities," he noted that there is always a tendency in such organizations toward clannishness and cultishness.

For Kim, the Actors Studio became the focus of her professional activities during this period, and she would hear no criticism of it. "It was like coming home," she said of joining the Studio. "It can't be understood by people who have never been to the Actors Studio."

She felt the same way about Lee Strasberg, who joined the Studio in 1948, and became its sole teacher in the fall of 1951. Once at the Studio, Strasberg devoted himself to it so unceasingly that his name became synonymous with the Studio. A brilliant, controversial figure, Strasberg was erudite, insightful (one colleague said he had "a jeweler's eye" for talent), a tireless advocate for actors, and a man who made enormous contributions to the acting profession. "Along with Stanislavski and Brecht, he was one of the major names in twentieth-century theater," said actress Viveca Lindfors. "Olivier is great, but he hasn't made an original contribution the way Strasberg has."

To his detractors, however, Strasberg was vain, smug, pedantic, and brutally critical. "James Dean did a scene," director Jack Garfein later recalled. "Strasberg absolutely slashed him, and he never did a scene again." He was also remarkably passive-aggressive. On one occasion, Franchot Tone, an actor who had also been a member of the Group Theatre, went to Strasberg's home to consult with him. He entered the study and greeted him. Strasberg looked up, nodded, turned back to the book he was reading, and continued listening to the stereo. An hour and a half later, when Strasberg still hadn't turned down the stereo, Tone said, "Good night, Lee," and left.

For the first few months Kim was at the Studio, Strasberg had her working only on comedy, much to her discomfort, as she was drawn to serious dramatic roles. She worked on a scene from *Red Peppers* with Nehemiah Persoff and played Gwendolyn in the garden scene from *The Importance of Being Earnest.* The value of Strasberg's pushing Kim in this direction would become apparent several years later when she soared to stardom in comic roles in *Picnic* and *Bus Stop.*

Kim also worked under the tutelage of Elia Kazan. In one project, Kazan oversaw the staging of three different versions of the first act of Ibsen's *Hedda Gabler* at the Studio. One, directed by Marlon Brando, placed Hedda in a decadent Southern environment. The second, directed by Steven Hill, featured Jo Van Fleet and attributed Hedda's behavior to sexual frustration. The third, starring Kim, was directed by Bert Conway, Curt Conway's younger brother. It placed her in a militaristic environment, with Hedda's behavior based on "the psychological factor that her father had wanted a boy when she was born."

As an approach, the Method became identified with actors such as Brando and their visceral style of acting. But as Kim put it, "Wearing a leather jacket does not make you a Method actor, and Method actors do NOT mumble. [Some who observed Kim in rehearsal would not necessarily agree with this.] The Method simply makes you as free as possible."

The Method provides a series of techniques by which an actor can fully engage his imagination in the role he is playing. "The purpose of the Stanislavski Method," wrote Harold Clurman, "is to teach the actor to put the whole gamut of his physical and emotional being into the service of the dramatist's meaning." That includes not only immersing oneself in the character's life in the play, but imagining what it was like before the curtain rose.

As an approach to acting, the Method is not inherently proletarian. "Since the Method is a technique, not a style, there is no necessary connection between realism and the Method," Clurman said, while Robert Lewis made fun of the idea that "the Method is useful only in 'family plays about the Bronx.'"

One of the best-known Method exercises, emphasized by Lee Strasberg, is affective memory, in which an actor recalls all the sensory details—sights, sounds, and smells—of a real-life incident that evoked a strong, specific emotion in order to display that emotion on stage.

Although Strasberg considered affective memory and improvisation his two most useful research and teaching tools, at least one of his Actors Studio colleagues did not share his enthusiasm. "[Elia] Kazan . . . had always had reservations about some aspects of Strasberg's teaching—especially about the emphasis put on the actor's personal experience as tapped by means of affective-memory exercises," Studio historian David Garfield notes. (But Shelley Winters would call it "the most powerful tool I ever learned to use in acting.")

Kim was also a great admirer of Strasberg, who became a kind of father figure to her. "Strasberg is the greatest man in the theatre today—a completely dedicated man," she said in 1961. "He made it possible for the whole world to open up with me." Kim felt Strasberg was brilliant, a conclusion Strasberg would almost certainly have agreed with.

Through a combination of her own native abilities and intelligence and Strasberg's tutelage, Kim would become the dominant young dramatic actress of the Broadway stage in the 1950s. Studio historian Foster Hirsch calls her "the First Lady of the Studio," adding, "Like Brando, the ultimate actor's actor, she commands enormous respect among theater professionals. Virtually every Studio member I talked to cited Stanley as the finest actress he or she knew of. The impact of her style on Studio actresses has been as keen as Brando's on Studio actors." And director Arthur Penn would call her the American equivalent of Eleanora Duse, the great Italian actress famed for riveting performances in which she didn't just interpret characters but seemed to embody them.

Kim would remain active at the Studio through 1952. Once she caught fire in *Picnic,* the combination of her increasingly busy professional and family lives would limit her time there. While she continued to attend the Studio on an occasional basis through the mid-1960s to observe the work of others and be part of the scene, she did little or no scene work herself after this period.

Kim's second Broadway play was *The House of Bernarda Alba,* written by Spanish poet Federico García Lorca, who only fifteen years earlier had been executed by the Fascist government of General Francisco Franco. Produced by the American National Theater and Academy (ANTA), and directed by Boris Tumarin, it opened in Greenwich Village and moved to Broadway's ANTA Playhouse on January 7, 1951.

Bernarda Alba is a classic Spanish autocrat, more Catholic than the Pope, a General Franco in a skirt. When her husband dies, she orders her five daughters sealed up in her house for a long period of mourning. Angustias, the oldest and plainest one, has a boyfriend whom she is expected to marry. But Adela, the youngest and wildest daughter (played by Kim), has a clandestine affair with her older sister's boyfriend. When Bernarda discovers the affair, she tries to shoot the boyfriend, but misses. Adela, mistakenly believing her lover is dead, hangs herself.

The painter Jada Rowland, who played a beggar's child in the production, recalls Kim as amiably maternal. "She was kind and warm to me as a child, and always seemed vaguely distressed in a kind of charming way." But Sylvia Davis, who played Angustias in the show's Greenwich Village incarnation, saw Kim differently: as a powerhouse. "I'll never forget Kim's preparation for her entrance," she says. "She paced back and forth in the small space backstage like a mad stallion trying to break out of his stall. It was electrifying."

The audience felt Kim's intensity. JP Miller, author of *Days of Wine and Roses,* says, "The production was ordinary, but when Kim came on as one of the daughters, you could feel the crowd pick up. I said, 'Who is that gal?' and somebody told me. It was like she had a light within her."

The House of Bernarda Alba lasted for only seventeen performances on Broadway. Howard Barnes of the *Herald-Tribune* praised the show's "breadth, eloquence and cumulative terror," but he was in the minority. "This little dandy is from the oh-the-pain-of-it, or Civic Repertory, school—a form of drama which has always given me the willies," wrote John Chapman of the *Daily News*. And Robert Coleman of the *Daily Mirror* added, "[It's] primarily for students of the European drama. We do not think it will appeal to the average playgoer."

Katrina Paxinou, the play's star, drew mixed reviews. William Hawkins of the *World-Telegram* said that "she dispels such force of character that the strange, remote play becomes entirely believable." But Richard Watts Jr. of the *New York Post* said "there is something about her highly mannered style that seems to me grotesque and extravagant rather than powerful and moving." Although Paxinou didn't realize it, one of her colleagues agreed with Watts. "Oh honey," Kim later said, "she was chewing up all the scenery."

Kim made out better with the critics. "Kim Stanley makes a frightening person of the daughter who steals her older sister's fiancé," Barnes wrote, while Coleman said, "Miss Stanley is particularly outstanding as the youngest and most unfortunate of the Alba daughters. Her performance is well worth the attention of our commercial managers. She has the equipment to be a star."

I N A "LIFE IMITATES ART" IRONY, *Bernarda Alba* is about a passionate affair involving illicit lust and the defying of social norms. Within a year of the play's closing, Kim would begin an affair with Brooks Clift, the brother of Montgomery Clift, and have a child by him in 1953 while still married to Curt Conway. The multiply married Brooks would declare Kim the love of his life, but Conway refused to give her a divorce.

For now, though, it was Conway's turn to be the proud father. On October 9, 1951, Kim gave birth to her first child, a daughter named Lisa Kimberly Conway. Fall is traditionally regarded as the best time to open a Broadway show, and it was the season when Kim would premiere all three of her children. Kim was delighted with her new role as a mother; in fact, she was delighted with babies in general. "She came to see my baby Roberta, when she was born," Anne Jackson recalls. "She took a look at her and said, 'Oh my God, she looks exactly like Merle Oberon.' And I loved that, because Roberta was born when [husband] Eli [Wallach] was doing *Teahouse of the August Moon* and she was slightly jaundiced. She had this wonderful Asian look about her and black hair and brows that looked like Matisse did them."

Shortly before Lisa's birth, Kim's father, J.T., and his second wife, Florence, moved to 602 North Dartmouth Street in the University Heights section of Albuquerque, where they would share an enduring and happy marriage until J.T.'s death in 1982. Kim visited him in the summer of 1951, while pregnant with Lisa.

"She hadn't seen her father since she'd gone away to the Pasadena Playhouse," says playwright Arthur Laurents. "And she was showing. The father didn't even say hello. He pointed to her belly and said, 'If it's a boy, bring him around.'" This astonishing remark would find its way into Laurents's play *Claudia Lazlo*. Kim had based her version of *Hedda Gabler* at the Actors Studio on a militaristic father who had wanted a boy when she was born; it's easy to see where she got the idea.

Although *Bernarda Alba* had a short run, one member of the audience would play a key role in Kim's career: Lillian Valish, the wife of playwright Horton Foote, who was then casting *The Chase*. "I'd never seen Kim, but my wife had been to see *The House of Bernarda Alba*," Foote says. "She said, 'This is one of our great actresses. You HAVE to get her into *The Chase*.' Jose [Ferrer, the play's director] had never heard of her and I'd never seen her, but I bullied my way in and said, 'We've got to use this actress. I think she's terrific.'"

Ferrer was something of a prodigy at the time, having two other plays on Forty-eighth Street, where *The Chase* would appear: *Stalag 17* and *The Shrike*. One critic even suggested renaming Forty-eighth Street "Calle Jose Ferrer." Ferrer assented to Kim's casting, and she appeared in the supporting role of Anna Reeves, estranged wife of convict Bubber Reeves (Murray Hamilton). While Bubber is in prison, she lives with his friend Knub McDermont (Lonny Chapman) and has a tendency to drink when she's under stress.

The Chase pivots on Bubber Reeves's jailbreak and return to the Texas Gulf Coast town of Richmond, where he vows revenge upon Sheriff Hawes (film actor John Hodiak), who sent him away. As citizens of the town become increasingly terrorized by the escaped convict in their midst, they start congealing into a lynch mob, while the belea-guered sheriff and his wife (Kim Hunter) stand for law and order.

The pervasive fear of townspeople in *The Chase* aptly reflected those of Americans during the Cold War spring of 1952: In the summer of 1949, Stalin's Soviet Union had exploded its first nuclear bomb. That fall, Communists seized power in China. In February of 1950, Senator Joseph McCarthy of Wisconsin gave his first "Communists in the State Department" speech in Wheeling, West Virginia. And in June of the same year, the Korean War began as North Korea invaded the South.

Richmond, the fictional setting for the play, was not simply a gener-ic forum for these national anxieties, though: The play has a finely etched sense of place. Writing of his hometown of Wharton, Texas, the model for Richmond, Foote noted,

> [A]t night . . . there is the quietness and then very faintly I begin to hear the tree frogs, the katydids in the pecan trees around the courthouse square, the waltz from a Mexican dance hall, the blues from a negro restaurant, a woman saying good night to a neighbor, [and] a whistle from some mockingbird that mistakes the brightness of night for daylight.

That attention to local color, as well as a gripping sense of drama, is evi-dent throughout *The Chase*.

Lonny Chapman, who played Kim's live-in boyfriend, found it both a delight and a challenge to work with her. "She was just marvelous," he says. "She was just so giving and inventive. To be on the stage with Kim was—it wasn't that she changed blocking or anything, but she never did things quite the same way. She surprised you—you never knew." Foote was similarly impressed. "She was extraordinary in it," he says. "So much so that she almost spoiled other actors for me." Out-of-town critics joined Kim's fan club. In Philadelphia, where *The Chase* had its first try-outs, the critic for the *Philadelphia Bulletin* wrote, "It remains for a young actress named Kim Stanley to carry off honors on the distaff side with a touching, restrained and wholly admirable performance as Bubber's wife."

When *The Chase* opened on Broadway on April 15, 1952, at the Playhouse Theater, however, critical reception was mixed. John Chapman of the *Daily News* called the play "a psychological western," adding, "I enjoyed and admired it." And Jim O'Connor of the *Journal-American* added, "[I]t's a real arouser! . . . There's a feeling of watching, watching . . . waiting, waiting . . . worrying, worrying. The tension is almost like a nightmare . . . One of the best plays of the season."

But Richard Watts Jr. of the *New York Post* said, "*The Chase* suffers from the tendency to repeat itself in the manner of an over-extended one-act play." And the powerful Brooks Atkinson of the *New York Times* was not amused. "Mr. Ferrer's direction is self-conscious and pretentious," he wrote. "Apart from some well-written small scenes, Mr. Foote's drama does not make much impression on the theatre."

Once again, though, Kim garnered accolades from the New York critics. Richard Watts Jr. wrote, "In the small role of the killer's dull, frightened and unfaithful wife, Kim Stanley is particularly believable and understanding." And Jim O'Connor added, "Outstanding in a small role is Kim Stanley as Anna Reeves . . . Her facial expression, gestures, mannerisms all contributed to a well-delineated character. She is a TV actress who studied in those off-Broadway studios and workshops. Mark Kim Stanley as a comer."

But in the short run, the only thing that came was the play's closing notice: Its last performance was on May 10, after only thirty-one performances. Despite the brevity of the show's run, Kim was not in the cast when it closed: On May 3, the *New York Times* reported she was leaving the show, to be replaced by Madeleine Sherwood, so she could enter Doctors Hospital in uptown Manhattan for a medical condition not disclosed in the article. It was an augury of things to come in Kim's Broadway career.

But as a sign that the *Journal-American*'s critic had presciently labeled Kim a comer, she garnered several awards for her performance: the Outer Circle Award, the Daniel Blum Award, and the Theater World award as the one of the most promising theater personalities of 1952.

In addition to being impressed with Kim's acting, Horton Foote also took to her as a person. "She was bright and just marvelous to be with, one of the funniest and wittiest women I've ever known," he says. One example, from Eileen Heckart: "She would always take the opposite point of view, be the devil's advocate, just to make an ass of you. She could talk better than most people I know, talking her way around, in, and out of anything. One night, she was giving one of these great orations, and I said, 'You are so full of shit.' She fell on the floor laughing. 'Of course,' she said. 'But it took you long enough to find out!'"

Kim and Foote soon began to lead parallel lives: Their children were about the same age, and Kim and Horton's wife, Lillian, became close friends. Over the next decade, Kim emerged as one of the foremost interpreters of Foote's work: They would collaborate on another Broadway play, six live TV dramas on two continents, and an acclaimed feature film.

DESPITE KIM'S DEVOTION TO THE THEATER, the critic from the *Journal-American* was justified in calling her a TV actress. During this period, she appeared on half a dozen live TV dramas, plus a variety show, *Cavalcade of Stars,* on the short-lived Dumont Network. On *Cavalcade,* she did a scene from Clifford Odets's *Golden Boy* with John Garfield. Soon caught up in the Red Scare, Garfield would be dead of a heart attack less than two years later at age thirty-nine, shortly after refusing to name names before the House Un-American Activities Committee.

But it was all smiles on June 3, 1950, as Kim and Garfield finished their scene, the last act of that evening's show. Host Jerry Lester called Garfield out in front of the curtain to join the show's other performers in celebrating *Cavalcade*'s first anniversary. Garfield led an obviously delighted Kim out and put a goofy-looking party hat on her as she joined the rest of the cast (which included ventriloquist Paul Winchell and an elegant Jane Withers in her pre–"Josephine the Plumber" days) in singing "Happy Birthday" to *Cavalcade of Stars.*

Five months later, Kim appeared on *Ford Theatre,* an hour-long live dramatic anthology. The *Ford* episode Kim appeared on was *Father, Dear Father,* with Edward Everett Horton as her father. In light of Kim's long-running problems with J.T., the show's title is tantalizing, but, as with many live TV dramas, no known copy of the show survives. Kim also appeared on several live half-hour dramatic anthologies during this period, with melodramatic titles like *The Trap: Sentence of Death* and *Sure as Fate: The Vanishing Lady.*

Kim appeared on another anthology, *Danger*, on June 10, 1952, in an episode called *The System,* about a cigarette girl in a gambling hall who saves a compulsive gambler (Eli Wallach) from getting roughed up when he can't cover his debts. What's notable about the otherwise-unremarkable show is the way Kim instinctively underacts for the cool television cameras, while Wallach, who hasn't gotten the hang of live television yet, performs in a histrionic manner that would have worked well on Broadway, but comes across on television as hyped-up scenery chewing.

As a Method actress, Kim was well-qualified to cope with the harrowing experience of live television, with its high pressures, merciless deadlines, and technical challenges. "The regular Broadway actors who lacked television experience found it frightening as hell. If they went up [forgot their lines], it showed," says veteran Broadway stage manager Porter Van Zandt. "But the Studio actors—whatever happened, they used it. If a cable [from a TV camera] were wrapped around their ankle, pulled them down, and they hit the ground, they would use all of that and keep right on going." In a possibly apocryphal story, Helen Hayes was in the middle of a live show with a young Method actor. "I have to pee," she said. "Use it!" he replied.

Kim found live TV drama, with all of its demands and pressures, a refreshing contrast to the stage. In her long-running stage plays, she would grow weary of repeating herself, even with the variations she introduced into her performances. But a live TV drama was always a one-night stand and never got stale. (Although Kim would sometimes complain it was sad she couldn't repeat a live TV performance and vary it.)

Also, because the TV camera was almost in her face, she didn't have to project to the back of the second balcony. One newspaper article noted that Kim found live television the most relaxing medium for acting. "I never think anybody's watching," she said, "until I go home to Texas, and find out they see everything."

Although Kim wasn't actually from Texas, her cousin Raymond Hankamer and his wife, Camille, who lived in Houston, were. Their son

Ray Jr. recalls, "The family would gather around the Hoffman Easy-Vision TV whenever Kim would appear in one of those live television dramas. There was a little something, sort of exciting, but also slightly disapproving, coming from this hardshell, uncompromising Baptist family."

And it was in Houston where Kim would have her first starring role on the stage since her arrival on Broadway. In September of 1952, only twenty-seven years old, she starred as Blanche DuBois in *A Streetcar Named Desire* at the Playhouse Theater. Houston, on the sweltering Gulf Coast, was not ordinarily where a rising young Broadway actress would choose to perform in the pre–air conditioning summer of 1952. But a decade earlier, Kim had been the poor relative of the faintly disapproving local branch of the family and may have wanted to show them she had come up in the world. Vincent Donehue directed, Bob Stephenson played Stanley Kowalski (the Brando role), and James Gavin played Blanche's suitor, Mitch (the Karl Malden role).

The impression one gets of Kim in this production is of someone who is strong physically but not emotionally. Ann Holmes, who reviewed the show for the *Houston Chronicle,* says, "I remember thinking how fragile she was, like Montgomery Clift. She was well-cast in that." But Bob Traweek, the show's costume designer, says that physically, there was nothing fragile about Kim.

"When Vivien Leigh's Blanche gets off the train [at the start of the film version], you realize she's sick. You immediately feel there's something wrong," he says. "Kim was physically strong, a little sounder when she arrives. When she's destroyed, it's a little different. Here's this almost stable human being who's running from life and then it finally envelops and destroys her."

For the scene where Blanche meets and vamps the newspaper delivery boy, Traweek designed a dress of white chiffon over cream-colored chiffon with a boated neckline and a handkerchief-drop, or serrated, hem. She liked it so much that she took it with her when the production ended. But the emotional intensity of the scene troubled her.

"When she finished that scene with the paperboy every night, she'd have to go in and redo her makeup because she cried so hard," Traweek says. "She was so wrapped up in it, she got to where she couldn't speak to the leading man offstage. That role really got to her. She said, 'I'm going back to New York and I'm going to ask Jessica Tandy [who premiered the role on Broadway] how in the name of God she did this for as long as she did.'"

Another challenge Kim faced was the resistance of an audience that saw Blanche (with a certain amount of justification) as a parasite on the household of her sister and brother-in-law. "It was a terrible situation for Kim," Traweek says, "because the audience took Blanche as a comic role, that she was taking up Stanley Kowalski's time, his place, his home. She really had to work to win the audience, and she did. In her final performance, that was the best Blanche I ever saw in my life."

In the three years since she had arrived on Broadway, Kim had moved from last-minute replacement in a supporting role to leading lady, but all her shows had been short-lived. Kim was due for a break, and in her next show, she would not only get that break, but make it.

CHAPTER 5

A STAR IS BORN

(1952–1956)

IRECTOR JOSH LOGAN had his doubts. Millie Owens, the brainy, angst-ridden kid sister in *Picnic,* was only sixteen. The actress wanting to try out for the part was twenty-seven, twice-married, and a mother. Logan asked her to read for Madge, Millie's beautiful older sister, but Kim demurred, saying she had never been the prettiest girl in town.

"For Millie, an unknown actress in her twenties begged to be allowed to read for me in costume, sure that I would think her too mature if I just interviewed her," Logan later recalled. "I was intrigued. A young boy-girl appeared onstage in blue jeans, a man's shirt with its tails hanging out, and a little Confederate corporal's cap. Her face was scrubbed shiny and she spoke with a slight impediment, as if she were wearing braces. She electrified us all. There was our Millie, with all her various emotional and comic shadings."

Kim appeared to Logan as a boy-girl, but when not trying out for the role of a confused adolescent on the cusp of womanhood, she was all girl. A lovely hazel-eyed ash blonde, five feet five-and-a-half inches tall, she was described by the *New York Daily News* as "lush, blonde and womanly." (To appear less womanly to Logan during her audition, she wrapped a diaper belonging to one-year-old daughter Lisa around her breasts.) Although she could speak in a regal, imposing manner, her voice, when not excited or angry, was soft and whispery, oddly similar to Marilyn Monroe's. Sensitive, intelligent, moody, and temperamental, there was a sadness about her, but also a keen sense of humor.

Feeling he had never really seen Millie until Kim had showed him what was in the part, Logan decided to take a chance on the less vital visual aspects of the role. But he hedged his bets.

"I remember Josh telling her, 'Don't let the audience see your face at the beginning of the play,'" recalls Elizabeth Wilson, who played school-teacher Christine Schoenwalder in *Picnic*. "They staged it so that Kim kept her face way from the audience for a long time. Then when she turned around, there was no problem. It was Millie."

In the fall of 1952, Dwight Eisenhower was elected president. The U.S. exploded the world's first hydrogen bomb, obliterating Eniwetok, an atoll in the Marshall Islands. On the cultural front, Ernest Hemingway published *The Old Man and the Sea* and, that November, Kim Stanley landed the role that would lift her from the ranks of the unknowns.

Picnic got its start when William Inge, fresh from the success of the dark, cloistered *Come Back, Little Sheba*, decided to write a play that took place in the sunshine. An early title was *Women in Summer*, for the women of different moods and characters who sat on front porches on summer evenings during his Kansas boyhood.

Picnic centers on Madge Owens (Janice Rule), a beautiful eighteen-year-old girl living in a small Kansas town with her impoverished mother and not-so-beautiful, intellectual younger sister. (Kim's favorite line as Millie: "When I get out of college, I'm going to New York, and I'll write novels that'll shock people right out of their senses.") Madge is expected to marry her wealthy boyfriend, Alan (Paul Newman, in his Broadway debut), but then Alan's magnetically handsome friend Hal (Ralph Meeker) appears, having hopped a freight train into town.

Hal is dynamic and vital, but also, as he ruefully acknowledges, a bum. He nonetheless manages to stir up Madge, Millie, and Rosemary Owens (Eileen Heckart), an old-maid schoolteacher who boards with them. In the end, Madge rejects Alan and runs off with Hal, despite his limited prospects. "I haven't moralized on these people, nor have I even garnered from their lives anything that might rightly be called a theme," Inge wrote, "unless it possibly is that love and romance cannot always be dictated . . . by one's ideals." Peggy Conklin played Flo Owens, the girls' mother, Arthur O'Connell was Howard Bevans, Eileen Heckart's reluctant suitor, Reta Shaw was schoolteacher Irma Cronkite, and Ruth McDevitt was neighbor Helen Potts.

Picnic, which takes place at the time of the town's Labor Day picnic, would undergo the most protracted of labor pains before reaching Broadway. Its half dozen sets would be reduced to one, its title changed numerous times, and Josh Logan was in, then out, then in as director. But the biggest struggle, pitting Logan and the Theater Guild, which produced the play, against William Inge, was over the play's ending.

Although beautiful, Madge is not very bright ("They had to burn down the schoolhouse to get her out of it," Millie sneers) and works as a salesclerk. After she has a fling with Hal, Inge wanted him to abandon her, forcing her to return in shame to the Five and Ten. But Logan felt this was too depressing and prevailed upon Inge to have Hal and Madge run off together, providing her with at least an ephemeral, illusory ray of hope.

Kim also got Inge to make changes to the script. "During rehearsals, Janice Rule and I worked by ourselves a lot and tried to find moments in the play during which we could reveal some of the inner life of the two girls," she said. "Mr. Inge helped us by changing the script so that instead of always fighting with me, Madge at least had moments when she made a sincere effort to understand my problem." One possible change: In the first scene of act two, Madge tells Millie, desperate for approval, how nice she looks in her dress and counsels her on how to talk to boys.

As Curt Conway knew, Kim's dedication to her role did not end when she left rehearsals. "When I know and understand a character so well that I think about her in terms of 'I,' it's time for my husband to take a vacation," she later said. "When I reached that stage in *Picnic,* he would say, 'For heaven's sake, can't you leave that adolescent at the theater?'"

While this attitude produced riveting performances, one friend and colleague of Kim's said her dedication could get a little over-the-top. "Kim went into characters so completely and so deeply that she lost her own sense of identity," says Anne Jackson. "It's all very well to get into a character and feel their pain, but at some point, you have to be able to separate yourself from your creation, and I don't think she could do that."

In addition to igniting her career, *Picnic* also marked the beginning of Kim's lasting friendship with Janice Rule. "Janice respected Kim very highly. She thought she was the best," says Rule's ex-husband Ben Gazzara. "I think she was a bit envious of her ability."

Although he played the tepid, responsible Alan, Paul Newman also understudied Meeker as the high-octane Hal. Logan later recalled his difficulties getting Newman to loosen up. One day while he watched him rehearse the dance in which Hal and Madge begin their mutual seduction, Logan said, "You dance well, but can't you wiggle your ass a bit?" Already a wise guy but not yet a liberal, Newman retorted, "Please Josh, I'm a Republican."

Even in an era when Broadway shows customarily had out-of-town tryouts, *Picnic* had a remarkably long and expensive pre-Broadway tour, one that would prove as manic-depressive as Logan himself. Columbus, Ohio, the first stop, augured smooth sailing: When the curtain went up opening night, the audience was so impressed with Jo Mielziner's set— the adjoining yards of two weather-beaten Kansas homes—that it spontaneously burst into applause. The cast had five curtain calls, and the *Columbus Citizen* said, "This thrilling creation of a play is headed for New York—and possibly a place in theatrical history."

Inge had worked as a drama critic in St. Louis, the play's second stop, but the reviews there were largely negative, with a group of St. Louis doctors getting into the act. One character in the play said that in Sweden, poor people receive the same quality of medical care as the rich. The *St. Louis County Medical Bulletin* blasted this as support for socialized medicine. Whether to mollify St. Louis doctors or not, the line was dropped.

Picnic then went to Cleveland and Boston, getting mixed reviews in both cities. Part of the problem was Hal, whose swagger and boastfulness alienated audience members. Logan worked at smoothing his rough edges, with one change coming in Boston, courtesy of the city censor. In the last scene of the second act, Madge (Janice Rule) tells Hal (Ralph

Meeker) they have to go to the town picnic. Inge's original line for Hal: "We're not going to any goddamn picnic." Boston censor Walter Milliken told Josh Logan that since profanity was illegal in Boston, the line had to be eliminated. It was replaced with this exchange:

HAL: Do we have to [go to the picnic]?
MADGE: Yes.
HAL: There are other places with not so many people.

This helped to soften Hal and made him more sympathetic. "For this improvement," wrote critic Elliot Norton, "the management is indebted to Boston's city 'censor,' who rarely gets credit for anything."

In a story Kim told on herself, she also ran afoul of a Boston bluenose. Supposedly, cast members were having dinner at a Boston restaurant when an august-looking middle-aged couple came over to them. The wife said to Kim, "You gave a charming performance, my child," then noticed the "child" had a large Manhattan cocktail in front of her. Gasping "Good heavens," she made a hasty retreat, along with her husband, out to "the chaste air" of the Boston Common.

Picnic opened at the Music Box Theatre on February 19, 1953, on a Broadway more receptive to musicals than dramas. Outstanding Broadway musicals of the '50s include *Finian's Rainbow, Brigadoon, South Pacific, Kiss Me, Kate, Guys and Dolls,* and *My Fair Lady. New York Times* critic Brooks Atkinson notes that the drama was then something of a stepchild, writing, "Except for [Tennessee] Williams, [Arthur] Miller, and a few others, the cruel futility of the outside world was catching up with Broadway, which is a holiday promenade not equipped to cope with intellectual problems." Those few others included Inge, Horton Foote, and the late Eugene O'Neill. Except for Miller, Kim would eventually appear in works by all of them.

The 1950s were an era with a great sense of community among theater people. "There was a real theater world," recalls painter Ellen Adler, daughter of legendary acting teacher Stella Adler and stepdaughter of her husband, director Harold Clurman. "People hung out, and there was no big thing about who had money and who didn't. I'm trying to figure out when people stopped buying Fords and Plymouths and started buying Jaguars. Because that simply did not exist then. If you were an actor, you were a Bohemian and you were free."

Broadway critics were enthusiastic about *Picnic*. William Hawkins of the *World-Telegram* wrote, "[It] is one of those rare plays in our theater literature which draws its roots from American soil." In the *New York Times*, Brooks Atkinson wrote, "Memorable though *Come Back, Little Sheba* was three seasons ago, *Picnic* is a notable improvement." And Richard Watts Jr. wrote in the *New York Post*, "It revealed power, insight, compassion, observation and a gift for looking into the human heart that we had all expected of Inge, and I'll be astonished if it isn't a dramatic hit of vast proportions."

The few dissenters focused on Logan, with Walter Kerr of the *Herald-Tribune* questioning why the director had applied a firm, staccato, and rigid style to the play's fragile summer-sunset mood. And Harold Clurman, who had seen Inge's script before the new ending was added, wrote in *The Nation* that lyric realism in the sound 1920s tradition of the prairie novelists was now being offered as the best Broadway corn.

The show was a critical and box-office triumph, Kim's first on Broadway. Co-stars Janice Rule and Ralph Meeker were praised by critics, as were most cast members. But Kim's notices showed that it was a career-making decision for her to fight her way into the role of Millie.

"As a tomboy with brains and artistic gifts, Kim Stanley gives a penetrating performance that conveys the distinction as well as the gaucheries of a disarming young lady," Brooks Atkinson wrote in his opening-night review for the *New York Times*. Several days later, he added, "Kim Stanley gives a stunning performance as the awkward adolescent—crude and boyishly belligerent on the surface but almost preternaturally aware."

William Hawkins of the *World-Telegram* said one of the play's most touching moments was when Kim, as Millie, suddenly grows up and throws away the stick she was going to beat a teasing boy with. And, in the *Saturday Review*, Henry Hewes noted, "Kim Stanley has, in her portrayal of Millie, added her name to an exclusive list of postwar American actresses which includes Barbara Bel Geddes, Julie Harris, Maureen Stapleton, Kim Hunter and Geraldine Page."

Joining these reviewers was Josh Logan. "She has amazing control despite the fact that she works at a very high emotional level," he said. "She makes an immediate impact on the audience and is enormously successful at giving the illusion of the first time at every performance. In addition, she is what I wish all actors were—creative. Almost everything she does in *Picnic* she invented on her own, and all I've had to do is edit a bit."

But Kim had her critics. Criticizing the decision to have the hunky Ralph Meeker stride around without his shirt for a good part of the play, Walter Kerr of the *Herald-Tribune* wrote, "Since Marlon Brando last appeared in these parts, the male is no longer male unless he is stripped to the waist, covered with sweat, and given to communicating by grunts, stammers and the practice of spitting through his teeth," adding that much of Meeker's performance consisted of strutting, chest-thumping, and slack-jawed mumbling.

"Even more astonishing is the imposition of this *Streetcar* style on Kim Stanley," Kerr added, unaware that her choices were her own. "Miss Stanley seems to me one of the most promising young performers on Broadway . . . But her assumption of the nervous-tic mannerisms, the lolling tongue and the sing-song rhythms cuts across and falsifies the independent vision of her performance; it also makes her seem rather more a cretin than a class intellectual."

Harold Clurman, who later directed Kim in *Bus Stop* and *A Touch of the Poet,* wrote in *The Nation,* "The adolescent sister who was a kind of embryo artist waiting to be born has become a comic grotesque who talks as if she suffered from a harelip." Kim later told him she'd been trying to simulate wearing braces with rubber bands, an explanation the amused Clurman said should have gone into the *Playbill* or a few extra lines of dialogue.

A few critical brickbats couldn't dampen Kim's triumph, though. Dorothy Land (now Fitzgerald), her friend from the University of New Mexico, was in New York with her husband, and got a backstage pass from Kim. But when they went backstage to congratulate her, they couldn't get close. "Her dressing room was jammed with people," Fitzgerald recalls. "She was just shining." Also seeing her in *Picnic* and several of her other plays were her uncle Earl and aunt Lena. "Sometimes Kim was friendly and sometimes not," says Katherine Norris, who serves as informal family historian for Kim's mother's side of the family. "They chalked it up to her drinking problem and somewhat unstable personality." In turn, Norris adds, Kim often saw her family members as judgmental.

Offstage, Kim displayed the same preternatural awareness that Brooks Atkinson attributed to her onstage. In one instance, it touched upon the woman who understudied her and Janice Rule: a fledgling actress named Joanne Woodward.

"We'd meet after the show and go and have drinks," a friend of Kim's later recalled. "One night she said, 'I want you to meet my understudy and get your impressions.' The understudy was to join us, a young girl from the South. She came in, and was quite charming. We talked for maybe an hour, then the understudy left." Kim asked her friend for impressions of Woodward.

"I think she's charming," he said.

"Yes, but beyond that, what do you think?" Kim insisted. And she kept digging.

"Let me put it this way," her friend said. "I think that young lady will probably achieve whatever she's going for."

Kim smiled and said, "I think you're right."

"What does that mean?" he asked.

"She's going for Paul Newman."

"But Paul Newman is married, with children," the puzzled friend said.

Kim smiled and left it at that. And, sure enough, Newman later left his wife for Joanne Woodward.

During the spring of 1953, Janice Rule, like Josh Logan, was struck with how hard Kim worked at making every moment on stage in *Picnic* matter. After a few months, most of the actors had gone dead, Rule thought, but not Kim. But although Kim came alive on stage, getting her onto it could be a problem. "She didn't like to act," Eileen Heckart said. "She didn't like to go to the theater, she didn't like to perform. As it got later and later in the afternoon, she would dread going to the theater more and more, and so many times, she just skipped it." This was only an occasional problem on *Picnic,* but it would worsen later.

By June, Kim couldn't go to the theater even if she wanted to: She was pregnant, and had left the show to prepare for the birth of her second child. On May 30, 1953, a few weeks after *Picnic* won the Pulitzer Prize and three and a half months after it opened on Broadway, Kim appeared as Millie for the last time. She was replaced by Betty Lou Holland.

Beginning with *Picnic,* an oddly symmetrical, almost metronomic pattern emerges in Kim's Broadway career: the alternation of hits with flops. It was as if her aversion to going to the theater were such that she didn't want to be in two hit shows in a row.

The public and Kim's husband, Curt Conway, assumed that her second child was his, but they were wrong. Kim was having an affair with Brooks Clift, brother of screen star Montgomery Clift. Brooks was an earthy, moody, and energetic man who had a wide variety of careers, including television director, advertising executive, and producer of TV commercials. He was also prolific in his women, five of whom he married. (The fourth, Eleanor Roeloffs, is now better known as Eleanor Clift, *Newsweek* correspondent and television pundit.) On New Year's Eve of 1953, Kim and Brooks got together on the fourteenth floor of a New York City hotel, and nine months later, they had a son.

The point at which Kim told Curt that the child wasn't his isn't clear, but his response speaks volumes to his character and love for Kim: He helped to raise the child as his own, even after he knew otherwise. For her part, Kim refused to leave Curt or give the child his father's name. When her son was born at Doctors Hospital in uptown Manhattan on September 15, 1953, he was known as Jamie Conway, a name he would keep into his early teens.

"I became emotionally unhinged. I considered murdering her," Brooks later told Montgomery Clift biographer Patricia Bosworth. "She was the most important person in my life. I worshipped her." But Kim would not marry Brooks. "For Brooks, the relationship with Kim was one of the high points of his life," Bosworth says. "It kind of defined him in some ways. He was in love with her. From her point of view, I think he was just a lover and that was it."

If Kim had gotten pregnant a few months earlier, she would have lost the role that ignited her career. When *Picnic* was trying out in Boston, she had supposedly shocked a proper Bostonian by drinking a cocktail; Kim's extramarital activities would have really made that Beacon Hill matron's eyes bug out.

Soon after Kim left *Picnic,* she and Curt moved from their Morton Street apartment in Greenwich Village to Huntington, Long Island. They lived in a small house on Laurel Drive in a wooded area of the town's Centerport section, overlooking a bay leading to Long Island Sound. They may have hoped to find a bucolic idyll there, but just as they drank and fought in Greenwich Village, they would drink and fight in suburbia.

And despite her idealized view of motherhood, Kim was not well-adapted to it. In a home movie from this period, Kim pushes a child in a swing. She only pushes with one hand, and in between pushes, rests her hand on her hip. Her body language says, "I'm not into this." Later in the film, as Lisa and Jamie run around on the back porch, Kim smiles at them, but doesn't interact with them. Nor does she interact much with anyone else who appears in the film.

AT THE SAME TIME Kim was making a splash on Broadway, she also attained stardom in a medium uniquely emblematic of the era: live television drama. Now fed a regular diet of filmed cop shows and "reality" programs, few Americans remember when television dramas were live instead of canned, from New York rather than Los Angeles, and used an anthology format instead of series. An anthology had a different story and characters each week: One show might be a comedy, the next a tragedy, melodrama, historical costume piece, or quasi-documentary.

Live TV was a vibrant medium, with maverick producers such as Fred Coe *(Philco-Goodyear Playhouse),* Worthington Miner, Herbert Brodkin, Felix Jackson *(Studio One),* and Martin Manulis *(Playhouse 90)* battling networks, sponsors, and Red-baiters to turn out moving and compelling shows. A staple of live TV was the "kitchen-sink drama," in which the action took place in the home of a middle-class family.

Although sometimes derided by critics, kitchen-sink drama was necessary because of the technical limitations of the medium. The period's bulky image-orthicon cameras meant remote outdoor shots were out of the question. In small, cramped mid-Manhattan studios, actors had to make quick costume and make-up changes during commercials, avoid tripping over camera cables on the studio floor, and remember their lines. There were no retakes, and if something went wrong, it happened in front of tens of millions of viewers. But out of this chaos, live TV produced classics such as *Marty, The Trip to Bountiful, Twelve Angry Men, Patterns, Requiem for a Heavyweight, Days of Wine and Roses,* and others.

Kim Stanley became the leading lady of live television drama, much as Rod Steiger was its leading man. "She was one of the great actresses of the live television era, kind of the queen bee of the medium," says *Marty* director Delbert Mann. "When she did something, it was a special event."

One of the remarkable facets of Kim's acting, writer JP Miller said, was how she acted big in the theater, where you have to project to the back of the balcony, but small for television, where live cameras made any tendency to overact look foolish. And she never forgot her lines or crumbled under the pressure of live TV. "She had the guts of a thief," writer Roger O. Hirson says. "She was like a rock—you knew nothing was going to go wrong."

Within two weeks of opening on Broadway in *Picnic,* Kim again starred as Joan of Arc, this time in a March 1, 1953, episode of *You Are There,* a show which dramatized historical events. Airing from CBS's studios above Grand Central Station, it was narrated by Walter Cronkite.

"The show was rather ludicrous, because we did it in a studio about the size of my office," recalls director Sidney Lumet. "The smoke from the burning at the stake drifted into Walter Cronkite's booth, so that as he did his final summing-up, he was coughing." But Lumet says there was nothing ludicrous about Kim's performance.

"She was absolutely brilliant," he says. "Kim, in the heart of her acting, always had a tremendous quality of 'little girl lost.' And Joan of Arc is the original little girl lost. It was just an amazing performance."

But it was Kim's next live show that would ignite her television career as *Picnic* had done on Broadway. On Easter Sunday of 1953, she starred in *A Young Lady of Property,* an episode of *Philco-Goodyear Playhouse* written by Horton Foote and directed by Vincent Donehue.

She played Wilma, a fifteen-year-old girl in Harrison, a fictional Texas town near the Gulf Coast, which was featured in much of Foote's work. She bullies her tagalong friend Arabella (Joanne Woodward) to seek a movie career with her in Hollywood, even though both really just want to stay in Harrison, marry, and have families.

Wilma faces a crisis when she learns that her father (Jim Gregory) plans to remarry and sell the house her late mother left to her. Her aunt (Margaret Barker) and Gert, the black housekeeper (Fredye Marshall), spring to her defense, but it's Wilma's intercession with her father's new bride (Kim's friend Vivian Nathan) that saves her house and changes her hostility for her stepmother into affection.

In the show, Kim goes through a wide range of emotions from joy to sorrow and excitement to despair without any flashiness or calling attention to herself. In one scene, Wilma tells Gert she's going to audition for Mr. Delafonte, supposedly a Hollywood director. "Never heard of him," Gert says (for a good reason: he's a con artist). "Well," says Kim in a tone of voice that is the platonic ideal of pouty adolescent condescension, "I wouldn't let anyone know if I was that ignorant."

But Kim could also be moody and elegiac, as in telling the housekeeper what a fifteen-year-old would do with her own house:

> I'll rent out rooms and sit on the front porch and rock and be a lady of mystery, like a lady I read about once that locked herself in her house. Let the vines grow all around. Higher and higher until all light was shut out. She was eighteen when the vines started growing, and when she died and they cut the vines down and found her, she was seventy-three and in all that time she had never put her foot outside once.

While Kim could have no way of knowing how prophetic this would be about her own life, she was already an elusive quantity. As Roger O. Hirson recalls, "She was an incredible person with a lot of mystery."

Variety praised the show, calling it one of the best *Philco-Goodyears*, one of the season's highlights, and "a personal triumph for Miss Stanley, [who] gave a performance that was alternately amusing and moving." Delbert Mann recalls, "All the eccentricities of the actress herself went into that character. It's wonderfully revealing of her." Even Kim, her own severest critic, felt a measure of satisfaction. Several years later, after having starred on Broadway in *Picnic* and *Bus Stop*, she said she had come closer to doing what she wanted in *A Young Lady of Property* than in anything else.

A Young Lady of Property marked another milestone for Kim: It was the first time her own father and stepmother saw her on television. Florence told the *Albuquerque Journal* they were looking forward to watching it. (J.T., who had just retired from the University of New Mexico and taken up a second career as a real estate salesman, had no comment.) But despite Florence's warm remarks, Kim's relations with her stepmother were not as close as Wilma's with hers, according to Kim's brother Justin.

"They did not have anything near a close relationship," he says. "The times I remember, they barely spoke, and certainly not of anything you would expect from a stepmother-stepdaughter relationship." Kim's daughter Rachel remembers it differently though, saying, "Florence was just lovely and really cared for Kim, in spite of, I'm sure, things she had heard from J.T." She recalls them having a warm relationship during the final years of Florence's life.

Kim's next live show, also written by Horton Foote, was *Tears of My Sister,* airing on August 14, 1953. It was an episode of *First Person Playhouse,* an experimental show produced by Fred Coe and directed by Arthur Penn. Using the subjective camera technique, it let the audience see the story unfold from the perspective of the unseen narrator.

On *Tears of My Sister,* the low camera position reflected the point of view of a confused and frightened young girl (voice supplied by Kim), who watches the intrigues in a boarding house where she lives with her eighteen-year-old sister (Lenka Peterson, a Jessica Lange look-alike) and mother (Kathleen Squire), who forces her sister to marry a man she doesn't love for money. Kim's voice pulls us into the point of view of the frightened young girl trying to understand the complex family machinations that swirl around her.

Two months later, Kim was back in front of the camera on *The Death of Cleopatra,* another episode of *You Are There.* Kim would later say it was her worst live show: "A friend of mine said we looked like trick-or-treat." But Marian Seldes, who also appeared on the show, would always remember Kim's impulsive, last-second makeup changes as the show was going on the air:

> As the technicians at the CBS studio . . . raced against the ticking of the relentless electric studio clock, the floor manager's voice boomed into the dressing rooms: "Five minutes to air, company onstage." Kim Stanley—our Cleopatra—dashed back to her dressing room, dissatisfied with her makeup. She pulled the black wig away from her tawny mane of hair, grabbed a pair of manicure scissors, and with ferocity and hurried carelessness, started to cut off her eyebrows and was drawing on Cleopatra's as the urgent voice called, "Places, places, Miss Stanley." Several seconds later, apparently in control of her heartbeat and her talent, the marvelous actress slipped into her place in Egypt and Walter Cronkite's voice set the scene.

Rather than being her worst show, *The Sixth Year,* an episode of *Philco-Goodyear Playhouse* airing on December 2, 1953, was one of her best. Written by Paddy Chayefsky, it's the story of a marriage imperiled when a husband loses his job, and then his nerve, when he has trouble finding work. "Kim Stanley pulled off one of the best of recent dramatic performances," *Variety* said. "Miss Stanley's wild outburst after quietly asking Stevens [Warren Stevens, who played her husband] if he wanted to go to the movies was a piece of art in itself."

Along with her remarkably golden, shiny blonde hair, Kim's zero-to-sixty-in-under-five-seconds emotional expressiveness was on display in *The Scarlet Letter,* which aired on *Kraft Television Theatre* and starred her as Hester Prynne, with Leslie Nielsen as Reverend Dimmesdale and Bramwell Fletcher as Roger Chillingworth. Criticizing Chillingworth for supposedly nursing Reverend Dimmesdale back to health while playing upon his guilt and sapping his spirit, Kim's Hester says evenly, "Better he had died at once." Then suddenly her throat tightens and she makes a gesture with her head toward Chillingworth like a cobra striking as she unleashes her venomous rage: "Hast thou not tortured him enough?"

"There was a sort of explosion that happened," Leslie Nielsen recalls. "All of a sudden, whatever you hold back as an actor or an actress, it surged to the surface. I've often talked about Kim obliquely, saying that you can't be judgmental about acting, because you never know when it's going to happen."

It happened less spectacularly, but just as effectively, in *Paso Doble,* on the Alistair Cooke–hosted *Omnibus* on Valentine's Day of 1954. Written by Budd Schulberg, it's the story of a young American couple from the Midwest (Kim and Arthur Franz) vacationing in Mexico who meet a sensitive but doomed young bullfighter (John Cassavetes), pressured by his father to carry on the family bullfighting tradition. In her role, Kim is the essence of a demure, supportive, conventional, postwar American housewife. When a scene called for industrial-strength emoting, no one could do it better than Kim. But she also excelled at creating scenes and characters that convey the essence of everyday life without flashiness or pyrotechnics.

Surprisingly, Kim was ambivalent about how diverse her television roles were. In the Broadway *Playbill* of *Traveling Lady* she would express gratitude to the medium for the wide range of roles it afforded her, while almost simultaneously telling the Associated Press that her parts on live TV were "usually crazy girls who jump out of windows." Go figure.

Somebody Special, an episode of *Philco-Goodyear Playhouse,* which aired on June 6, 1954, wasn't very special, as its writer, JP Miller, was the first to acknowledge. Written in a rush because another script had fallen through, it's a mundane story about marital discontent between a barber (Harry Townes) in Jackson Heights, Queens, and his wife, Ruthie (Kim). One day Ruthie hears a record and is convinced that new singing sensation Sammy Andrews is really Simi Andrusko, a boy who liked her in high school. Surely there wouldn't be any harm if she looked him up again . . .

Even if it wasn't one of Miller's better efforts, Kim still went all out. "She was fiercely loyal to whatever character she was playing, whether it was a *Philco Playhouse* or a Broadway play," Miller later recalled. "She put just as much time and effort into it. There was no such thing as just walking through a part for Kim." That meant a lot of research.

"She studied those ladies who live in the little crackerbox houses in the suburbs, with a parking strip but no garage and a baby carriage out front on the cracked sidewalk and women standing out there drinking a Coke and smoking and talking to the next-door neighbor, the real New Yorky kind of talking," Miller said. "Every move she made, every glance from her eye had something to do with the character."

That work paid off. Kim's outer-borough accent is flawless and especially impressive if you've just seen her as a Southerner in *A Young Lady of Property*. On one occasion, Ruthie is about to put the Sammy Andrews album on the record player. As she takes it out of its case, Kim licks her upper lip in a lazy, sensual way that contrasts beguilingly with her demure Jackson Heights housedress.

As the record starts to play, she fluidly goes through a rapid sequence of emotions, looking up as if trying to remember her one-time admirer, closing her eyes with mild pleasure, suppressing some intense emotion, registering mild pleasure again, looking down and closing her eyes raptly and thoughtfully, then expressing a kind of pride that Simi has made good as Sammy. After rehearsals, Kim and JP went to Hurley's Bar, a hangout for NBC regulars near the RCA Building. Noting Kim's penchant for drinking, Miller said, "She liked to toss off a few."

IN LATE APRIL AND EARLY MAY, Kim and Lillian Gish did a touring stage version of Horton Foote's *The Trip to Bountiful* in the college towns of Evanston, Illinois (Northwestern University), and Ann Arbor (University of Michigan). Gish reprised her role from live TV and Broadway as Carrie Watts, an elderly woman living in Houston with her shrewish daughter-in-law Jessie Mae (Kim) and henpecked son Ludie (John Conwell), who is determined to revisit her Gulf Coast hometown. Conwell, a Chicago-area native, was no stranger to Kim: He had been her fiancé when they were leading man and lady of the University of New Mexico drama department during World War II.

The *Ann Arbor News* noted that Lillian Gish played her part movingly and skillfully. Of Kim, it said, "Miss Stanley, always in character, delighted the audience with a magnificent portrayal of the tantrum-throwing willful parasite Jessie Mae." There was praise for Frank Overton as the sheriff sent to stop Mrs. Watts from going to Bountiful but who takes her there instead. The only pan was for John Conwell.

"While all other characters . . . gave evidence of a reasonable Texas accent, John Conwell alone failed to do so," it noted. "Otherwise, as Mrs. Watts' weak-willed son, he is little more than adequate." Conwell took that as career advice, becoming a television casting executive. He and Maxine Runyan (whom Kim had briefly pushed aside when she dated Conwell in college) would settle into a long, happy marriage in Santa Barbara.

But Kim's marriage to Curt Conway, on the other hand, was deteriorating. "Their marriage was stormy," says Lonny Chapman, Conway's partner in several acting schools. "But at the same time, it was very good, because they fed off each other theatrically. They got into some pretty good battles. Usually drinking had something to do with it."

By the time Kim was on the road with *Bountiful,* Curt had moved out, renting a room from Nehemiah Persoff and his wife in Manhattan. But Persoff thought highly of Kim as well. "I had signed a movie contract and there was money coming in, but I needed five hundred dollars desperately," he says. "I asked several big stars and they referred me to their financial advisors. Then I turned to Kim. Without any questions, she loaned me the money."

In August of 1954, Kim was scheduled to play in Philadelphia's Playhouse in the Park as Lorna in Clifford Odets's *Golden Boy* and as Sabrina in *Sabrina Fair* by Samuel Taylor. Possibly owing to her marital problems, she withdrew less than three weeks before opening.

The reason Kim's agent, Lucy Kroll, gave for the sudden withdrawal isn't clear, but she had medical ammunition ready if needed: a note from Dr. Sewall Pastor, a Huntington, Long Island, psychiatrist. "This is to certify that Kim Stanley has been under my professional care for some time," he wrote on July 15, 1954. "She has had several attacks of severe Anxiety Neurosis, and I have ordered her to go to the mountains where she can be with her husband and two children. Because of her present state of health it is very important that her family be re-united and remain together at least until her condition improves." (Kim also had a psychiatrist in New York: Eva Klein, an elegant, pleasant, well-tailored woman with a mittel-European accent and an office on Fifth Avenue.)

By October, Kim had patched things up with Curt and was on the road with him, Lisa, and Jamie for her next Broadway play. In four years, she had gone from unreviewed replacement in *Montserrat* to well-reviewed supporting roles to a featured role in *Picnic* and was now on the brink of stardom.

The Traveling Lady again showcased her in a Horton Foote work. Kim played Georgette Thomas, a hardscrabble Texas housewife with a young daughter, Margaret Rose (Brook Seawell), who is let down by her ne'er-do-well ex-con husband, Henry Thomas (Lonny Chapman), but finds her white knight in lawman Slim Murray (Jack Lord, later the star of television's *Hawaii 5-0*). Kim's commitment to the role was evident as early as December 1953, when Lucy Kroll, seeking live TV work for her, said she was waiting until *The Traveling Lady* was ready to produce.

"She was a great champion of my writing, which meant a great deal to me," Foote says. "She understood what I was about, and not many people did in those days. She was vociferous in defense of my work and, when she was in something, wouldn't allow a word to be tampered with."

Lonny Chapman, who played Kim's no-goodnik husband, remembers that in early rehearsals, she observed some well-known Actors Studio traditions. "She liked to work into the role," he says. "The first couple of days of rehearsal, you'd think she was just mumbling. A little bit like Marlon [Brando]. He's mumbling at the first couple of rehearsals, where-as some actors, they got the performance at the first reading, right? But not Kim."

In addition to husband Curt Conway and the kids, Kim brought a nursemaid with her on the road. Backstage, Lisa played dolls with Brook Seawell, who was a few years older than her. Kim sought out her usual entertainment. "Out of town, you couldn't unwind after the show, so we'd go to the bar and talk about theater," says Chapman, who recalls her fondness for vodka martinis. "She loved to do that, except with Jack Lord. She thought he was stiff as an actor. She said no matter what she did on stage, even if she stood on her head, he'd still do the same thing." One of the men in the company Kim liked better was Bruce Hall, her first husband, an understudy on the show. It isn't clear how well he got along with Curt, who seems to have been remarkably forbearing about the men in Kim's life.

In *The Traveling Lady*, Georgette and her daughter, Margaret Rose ("I like verbena too," Georgette says, "but I didn't like the sound of Margaret Verbena"), come to the small Texas town where she believes her husband Henry Thomas will soon be released from prison. But when they arrive, Georgette learns he's already out but hasn't told her, despite her hard work to earn money for the lawyer who obtained his pardon.

Foote's gifts of language and characterization lift the play above the routine "Father, come home from the bar" melodrama. But while it makes a moving point about the ability of some people to weather adversity while others crumple, it's not very dramatic: At the end, everyone is the same as they were at the start, and there's no great clash of ideas or personalities.

At its first stop, in Princeton, New Jersey, *Variety* said Kim did fine in the leading role, but otherwise turned thumbs down: "The heroine is supposed to be a sensitive, misused young mother cursed with a sensitive, misled husband and saved by a sensitive, misunderstood hero," it drily observed. "She also has a sensitive daughter who wants somebody to sing her a hillbilly ballad."

The reviews didn't get any better in Cincinnati: The *Times-Star* said "[it] moves like a tired turtle under a Texas sun," while the *Cincinnati Post* critic listened in on two theatergoers: "Between acts of *The Traveling Lady* last night, a gentleman said, admiringly, 'Chekhov' and a lady promptly riposted 'Procter and Gamble.'" In Cleveland, there was a ray of sunshine from a critic who called the show "a moody and often richly human comedy of life in the Texas cotton country." Otherwise, it was more of the same.

There were more bad omens in Cleveland: On opening night, a man in the audience, later ejected, distracted members of the cast and audience with his loud, inappropriate laughter. It got so bad that at one point Mary Perry, who played the dotty old Mrs. Mavis, improvised the line, "There's that dove again."

Then Kim had a panic attack.

"We had to hold the curtain for her until she got herself together," Horton Foote remembers. "She once said to me jokingly, 'You know, I could kill Geraldine Page—she doesn't have a nerve in her body. She can call the nurse about her children, then go right onstage, while I'm sitting there suffering and worrying about going on.'"

Despite her anxieties, Kim took good care of her onstage daughter. "She was very kind to me, very maternal," Brook Seawell, then seven years old, later recalled about her Broadway debut. "There were other [actresses who played my mother] who were maybe warmer, but this was my first experience, and she made it a very good one." She noted a few quirks, however.

"In our opening scene, we were supposed to have gotten off a long, hot bus ride and walk on stage," Seawell says. "Wardrobe always ironed my little cotton dress and Kim couldn't stand that, because, being a Method actress, she thought we would be very rumpled. So she would spit on my clothes and crumple them in her hands as we were waiting to go on. Wardrobe couldn't stand it, but it did look authentic." Sometimes, though, Kim would miss and spit on Seawell. "It was a little icky for me," she recalls.

The Traveling Lady opened on Broadway at the Playhouse on October 27, 1954. The bonding between Georgette and Margaret Rose was cemented as they jointly faced a near-disaster at a matinee when late for their entrance. "Kim gave my arm a jerk to get me onstage faster, and I tripped," Seawell says. "There was a nailhead on the set, and I fell on my knee onto the nailhead. It went into my knee.

"There was no orchestra pit, and I could see the faces of the little old ladies in the front row," she continues. "They used to hang their canes on the edge of the stage, and I could see their mouths making the shape of an O—this exhalation.

"The blood just spurted out. It was so gory! And it hurt so much. I just sat there on the set holding my knee. Kim, who kept a handkerchief crumpled in her hand all the time, gave me the hanky to stanch the flow.

"And then she said, obviously unscripted, 'Are you alright, baby?' There was this enormous pause. I wanted to wail and run off the stage, but I realized you couldn't do that. I just wiped my tears and looked up and said, 'Ah'm fine, mama, ah'm fine.' And we went on with the show."

But the critics were not impressed. "In the old days of the Palace Theatre and the Orpheum Circuit, *The Traveling Lady* would have been done in twenty minutes—and been the better for it," said John Chapman of the *Daily News.* In the *New York Times,* Brooks Atkinson said, "It is a series of minor characterizations arranged around a major one. It is strung together loosely. It substitutes local color for drama. And, like Georgette, it has trouble in saying anything." Walter Kerr of the *Herald-Tribune* added, "The author has . . . been true to life; but he has also been unforgivably dull."

Reviews were good for Kim's fellow cast members, mixed for director Vincent Donehue. But Kim's notices were as glowing as the play's were disparaging and were often written by the same critics. Brooks Atkinson of the *New York Times* said,

Georgette is an inarticulate, bewildered drudge who does not appear to be very bright. But this is where Miss Stanley comes in. She retains the drab facts of the character—the flat vocal tones, the embarrassed hesitation, the awkward posture, the daze and indecision. But by the time Miss Stanley gets through with her, Georgette is a glowing beauty with a valiant spirit and heroic strength. For Miss Stanley has at last come into her own as an actress who can portray not merely a part but a character and illuminate it beautifully from within. This is a stunning piece of acting.

Walter Kerr, who savaged the play, added:

Toward the end of the evening she manages, in a few fumbling gestures and some broken sentences, to suggest three sorts of life all at once: the life of the child whose shoe she is buckling, the crude pleasure of her own remembered childhood, [and] the violent and wasted life of the man neither of them will ever see again. The performance brims over with hints of hidden, half-understood emotion.

And, in *The Nation,* Harold Clurman compared her to great American actresses of the past:

> Kim Stanley is the youngest addition to that line of American actresses whose emblematic figures are Laurette Taylor and Pauline Lord. They express the inarticulate but eloquent womanhood of those who have never learned to become ladies . . . Kim Stanley has amazing naturalness [and] a genuine connection with whoever is her partner on the stage. She rarely stiffens with false theatrical projection.

The lone exception in praising Kim was William Hawkins of the *World-Telegram,* who said she was occasionally very affecting but lacked the necessary dynamism to make the script come alive.

Soon after the reviews were in, members of the Playwrights Company—Maxwell Anderson, Elmer Rice, Robert Sherwood, Robert Anderson, Roger Stevens, and John Wharton—voted for the first time in the group's sixteen-year history to promote an actor to star billing over the title after a play had already opened.

"Roger Stevens called me one morning and said, 'Would you go with me to see if we can get permission from Kim to put her name over the title?'" Horton Foote recalls. "And I said, 'I surely will.' She and Curt were staying in a very modest hotel [in Manhattan]. Without warning, we went up and knocked on the door. She sleepily heard our news and graciously agreed."

Kim deserved that promotion, Foote says. "She had enormous instincts and intuition. A wonderful sense of truth onstage and great emotional daring," he adds. "She had a concentration onstage that was compelling. She could use stillness, she could use quiet. She could not say anything, and yet there was this compelling thing about her. She changed the whole style of acting in that period for young women. They weren't always good imitations, but she had an enormous influence."

In Albuquerque, J.T. was contacted by a local newspaper about his daughter's new stardom. He came from a time and place when men were taciturn to a fault and proud of it, as his formal response indicates. "We certainly are proud of her," he said. "We think it is a great tribute to a schoolgirl who has fought her way to the top." But many schoolgirls have fought their way to the top; only one happened to be her father.

Kim still pretended that, like her father, she was a Lone Star native. *Traveling Lady* publicist William Fields got *Dallas Morning News* columnist John Rosenfield to write a profile of Kim. Struggling to be both accurate and gallant, Rosenfield wrote, "William Fields thinks Texas should preen itself over Miss Stanley . . . On the other hand, there might be a competitive preen with New Mexico. Miss Stanley first blinked her larcenous eyes in Tularosa, N.M. Her father is on the faculty of state university at Albuquerque. If not 'borned in Texas' she was 'rared in Texas' somewhat . . ."

Trying to pass herself off as the Yellow Rose of Texas was only part of Kim's self-mythologizing, and many of her interviews can be read with a "strange interlude" approach. One sample, from the *Philadelphia Bulletin,* with truth in parentheses: "Miss Stanley, who majored in psychology (she didn't) and minored in literature (she didn't), first at the University of Texas (she wasn't) and later at the University of New Mexico, from which she graduated (she didn't), had not thought about acting in those days (she lived and breathed it)."

It's difficult to put together a unified theory of Kim's fabrications. Ordinarily, self-mythologizing casts the speaker into a background of wealth and privilege or, alternately, heart-rending poverty with Horatio Alger–like struggles to overcome it. But Kim's doesn't conform to a tidy pattern: I'm from Texas . . . I'm part Cherokee . . . I didn't work to become a star. Ultimately, her yarn spinning is similar to her performance in long-running plays, where she maintained a character's essence, but added different tones and colors, variations on a theme that could never exhaust her deep well of creativity and restlessness.

During the run of *Traveling Lady,* Kim was briefly caught up in the Red Scare. She ran as part of a progressive slate of officer candidates for AFTRA (the American Federation of Television and Radio Artists). She lost, but got more votes than other members of the slate. Aware Inc., one of the notorious Red-baiting organizations of the '50s, claimed she was one of the members of the slate who had "significant public records in connection with the Communist-front apparatus," although all it had to say about her was that she had studied at "the left-wing Actors Studio," and was married to Curt Conway, who was indisputably a progressive.

Turning up in the *Aware Bulletin* did no harm to Kim's career. Broadway, Brooks Atkinson noted, was "economic anarchy." As such, Broadway was "not susceptible to domination by rational businessmen," with the result that "hoodlums like McCarthy can never find out who's in charge . . . or where the center of power lies."

Despite its contribution to Kim's career, *The Traveling Lady* closed after only thirty performances on November 20, 1954. J.T. and Florence, who planned to attend the show in the spring, never saw it. Kim, loyal to the role that brought her stardom, performed it twice more on live television: on *Studio One* April 22, 1957, with Steven Hill as Henry Thomas and Robert Loggia as Slim Murray, and in England on ITV's *Armchair Theatre* July 27, 1958, with Denholm Elliott and Ronan O'Casey.

Kim now settled in for as much suburban domesticity as she could manage with Curt, Lisa, and Jamie. "Curt is delighted she's starring in her equally glamorous role as wife and mother," the International News Service reported. "To Kim, at the moment, this is the best kind of critical acclaim." Several years later, after their divorce, Curt reflected on that appraisal. "She is a wonderful mother," he said. "And she has said again and again that stardom means nothing to her, that she would give it all up if it were a choice between career and children. I don't know that she really could. But with her integrity, she'd try."

Kim's next stage show was a one-night stand by design. *The Great Dreamer* played in Madison Square Garden, then at Eighth Avenue between Forty-ninth and Fiftieth streets, on December 23, 1954. Written by Norman Rosten for the Hanukah Festival for Israel, the show was the story of Theodore Herzl, founder of modern Zionism. Dana Andrews played Herzl, Kim his wife. (A few years later, Kim would convert to Judaism, and her participation in this play may have been an early indicator of her interest in it.)

The Bridge, a live television drama Kim did on January 11, 1955, for *The Elgin Hour,* showed her willful streak in fine form. She played a French woman suspected of collaborating with the Nazis during World War II; her hair was then shorn by her fellow townspeople.

"At one point, she said to me, 'This will be the place where I break down and cry,'" director Daniel Petrie recalls. "I said, 'Kim, I think it's wrong for you to break down. The strength is in your behaving with dignity.' So she said, 'Oh, okay. Okay. Okay.' But she didn't like it very much at all.

"This was done live. At the end, where the big emotional moment was, the camera came right in on her. She was solid and strong, but then boom! a tear comes down her cheek. I liked it. It was very good, very moving.

"About a month later, my wife and I had a little party in our apartment at Peter Cooper Village. Kim was there, Horton Foote, I think, maybe Joe Anthony and his wife. We were talking about the show. Kim looked over at me and said, 'He didn't want me to cry at all, but I sneaked a little tear out!'"

K IM THEN ACCEPTED THE LEADING ROLE in her signature stage play. More than a decade earlier, when William Inge was teaching at Stephens College for Women in Columbia, Missouri, he took a bus trip from Columbia to Kansas City. During the ride, which included three stops, he watched with growing distaste as a man picked up one of the women passengers. "It developed into a rather tawdry affair," he later recalled.

Now Inge had written a play that transmuted that experience into something more inspiring. Bo (Jerome Courtland), a young cowboy fresh off the ranch, takes a liking to Cherie (Kim), a singer, or "chanteuse," as she comically describes herself, from a seedy Kansas City nightclub. He kidnaps her and is taking her back to Montana, along with Virgil (Crahan Denton) his sidekick/buddy/mentor. The bus also carries Dr. Lyman (Anthony Ross), an alcoholic, oft-divorced professor with a fondness for underage women, and is marooned for the night in a greasy-spoon diner in a small Kansas town. Rounding out the cast are Elma (Phyllis Love), an innocent young waitress; Grace (Elaine Stritch), the cynical, world-weary woman who owns the diner; Carl (Patrick McVey), a bus driver of ambiguous marital status; and Will (Lou Polan), the wise, no-nonsense sheriff. Inge called the play *Bus Stop*.

Producer Robert Whitehead picked Kim for the part of Cherie, the third-rate torch singer from the Ozarks with a belligerent screech and a heart of gold. "I don't think I ever thought of anyone else for it," he later said. "There may have been one or two other people who went through my mind, but I knew I wanted Kim." So did director Harold Clurman. "I don't know anyone of her age to equal her for sheer basic acting talent," he later said. But he knew about her hobgoblins, adding, "Kim Stanley's idealistic thirst for perfection—impossible of realization—on and off stage, is the source of the intense anguish and anger in her."

Clurman asked Boris Aronson to design a set that would evoke the spirit of Edward Hopper's painting *Nighthawks*—middle-American, mid-century, middle of the night—a hash-house counter viewed from outside, with those seated at it appearing ordinary, although each is as unique and distinctive as his or her own fears and aspirations. Aronson was grateful for the work. As he told Clurman, "I haven't had a call all year, not even a wrong number." Inge was grateful for something else—unlike *Picnic,* his script for *Bus Stop* went into production almost word for word.

For Cherie's Southern/Ozarks accent, Kim turned to Rubyann. "I hardened it a little, but otherwise, it is my mother," she told a reporter, adding innocently, "Perhaps mother won't recognize herself." For her second-act star turn, when she climbs onto a café tabletop in her night-club costume to run "That Old Black Magic" through a musical shredder, she made use of an experience she had had on the road with *The Traveling Lady.*

Although Kim was virtually tone deaf, she modeled her singing on a third-rate singer she saw in Cleveland while out with colleagues after the show. "The naive expression on her face was totally unrelated to the suggestive gestures she used while singing," Kim later recalled. "It was awful." In addition to borrowing from the worst, though, Kim also modeled Cherie's singing on the best, courtesy of Elaine Stritch.

"Clurman told me I could [mentor Kim] and I said, 'Kim, would you like to imitate Frank Sinatra?' and she said 'Sure!,'" Stritch later recalled. "It was one of the most brilliant things I've ever seen on stage."

But, as was often the case, Kim doubted her competence, let alone her brilliance. While the show was on the road, either in Princeton or Philadelphia, she had a panic attack about her ability to do the tabletop rendition of "That Old Black Magic." A local doctor was called in to prescribe something for Kim's nerves, and a call went to Curt Conway, who came down from New York.

"There was a doctor in the room," says Martin Landau, who heard the story from Conway. "I don't know if he was there to prescribe sedatives or what. There was Mr. Clurman, Mr. Hall [Bruce Hall, Kim's first husband, was again an understudy on one of her shows], Mr. Conway, and Miss Stanley. The doctor was befuddled, and it wound up looking like a Moss Hart door-slamming comedy.

'Who is Mr. Clurman?' the doctor asked.

'Mr. Clurman is the director of the play,' one of those present responded.

'Who is Mr. Hall?'

'Mr. Hall is Miss Stanley's ex-husband.'

'But who is this man?'

'This is Mr. Conway, Miss Stanley's current husband.'

"The doctor didn't quite understand who all these people were, none of them being Mr. Stanley."

Her visceral self-doubt notwithstanding, Kim developed insights into Cherie that eluded her creator. One interviewer observed, "Although Inge says Cherie is running away from the cowboy because she is frightened by his roughness, Kim believes she is frightened by other things—by his purity compared to her own hard and loose way of life." This interpretation is supported by the script.

Despite Kim's anxiety on the road, Janice Rule would later observe that the warm and genial spirit of the play had a beneficial effect on Kim's frame of mind while she was in the show. After she became a psychotherapist, Rule published an article in a professional journal in which Kim is disguised as "Françoise":

At one point, she was asked to play in a light comedy. The role was a sweet, dumb, rather sexy, nightclub dancer. It called on Françoise's tenderness, comic imagination, and sense of fun.

There was no pre-rehearsal chaos; she became optimistic, bright, cheery and adorable. These were not the qualities generally attributed to Françoise, the private person; she was stubborn, perceptive, serious, and, in turn, compassionate and cruelly honest with her friends. For as long as I had known her, Françoise had had a weight problem. Yet, without dieting, she enjoyed a slim figure for the entire run of the play.

The first out-of-town tryout for *Bus Stop* was in Princeton, where Kim got into trouble by taking her Stanislavski too seriously. In *An Actor Prepares,* the founder of Method acting writes, "If I ask you, 'Is it cold out today?' before you answer . . . you should, in your imagination, go back onto the street. [Remember] how the people you met were wrapped up, how they turned up their collars, how the snow crunched underfoot." It was early February, with snow on the ground. Kim, who made her *Bus Stop* entrance from a Kansas snowstorm, went for a walk to soak up the necessary sensations. By the time the show hit Philadelphia, she had the flu.

"I said to her, 'You're off your rocker,'" Robert Whitehead later recalled. "'You can't go wandering in the snow in order to get the feeling of cold feet.'" On February 14, when *Bus Stop* opened in Philadelphia, Kim had a fever of 104 degrees. Her face was pale and covered with perspiration. "I never knew how Whitehead did it," company press agent Barry Hyams said. "But he talked to Kim like a Dutch uncle in her hotel suite, got her to the theater, and all but pushed her onstage. She was superb as usual and well enough after the performance to go out with friends."

The next night, however, she was out of the company. A reporter from the *Philadelphia Inquirer* at her sickbed in the Benjamin Franklin Hotel said she looked like a helpless little girl propped up in bed. Robert Whitehead, who later worked with her in *A Touch of the Poet,* was one of her greatest admirers as an actress.

"She constantly did things that took my breath away," he said. "And she constantly did things she might not be sure to do the following night." Whitehead was fond of her, but with a measure of exasperation: In one interview, he used the word "neurotic" seven times to describe her. "Kim had a great gaiety," he said. "She could be very charming and effective in appreciating what was happening around her. She had a sense of humor which pervaded that. And although she was an unhappy person, God knows, she had a sense of the ridiculous that was very attractive."

Out-of-town critics gave *Bus Stop* mixed reviews at best. R.E.P. Sensenderfer of the *Philadelphia Bulletin* called it a moving and richly rewarding play about a group of bus passengers and their lonely lives. And *Bulletin* reporter Laura Lee, in a profile of Kim, said she was responsible for one remarkable piece of silent acting. After rebuffing Bo's advances for two acts, Cherie sits alone at a table in Grace's Diner and for the first time thinks it might not be so bad to marry him after all. "You know before she has said a word that she has reconsidered," Lee wrote. "This bit of silent, motionless acting is as compelling as that of the players who are acting and talking across the room."

But there were just as many bad reviews. The *Philadelphia Inquirer* called it a letdown, saying it was sprawling, extremely conversational, and seldom flared into stirring action. *Bulletin* columnist Earl Selby was harsher. Seeing a limousine with a convoy of motorcycle policemen several days after *Bus Stop* opened, he said he thought it was Inge leaving town under armed guard. Pressed by irate theatergoers to see the show again, an unrepentant Selby added, "We did not mean to say that *Bus Stop* was the world's worst play, all we meant was that it was the worst we've ever seen."

Much of the criticism centered on Jerome Courtland, who played Bo, Cherie's cowboy abductor. "A single major fault," *Variety* noted in Princeton, was that "the character who holds the key to the play and around whom the theme is built is not the character to whom the audience is drawn. It is not the cowboy, played with admirable verve but shallowness by Jerome Courtland, that the audience watches. *Bus Stop* belongs to the cowboy's corn-fed 'chantoosy,' played handsomely by Kim Stanley."

The producers had originally wanted Albert Salmi to play Bo, but Salmi had a run-of-the-play contract for *The Rainmaker,* which was still running on Broadway when *Bus Stop* was cast in December. But on

February 12, two days before *Bus Stop* opened in Philadelphia, *The Rainmaker* closed. Salmi was signed as Bo, Courtland was dismissed, and Salmi was up in the part before the show left Philadelphia. *Bus Stop* casting director Terry Fay recalls that Courtland accepted his replacement with dignity. "It just wasn't working out, and it seemed wiser to make another choice," she says. "And he was so gracious about it. He was just a darling fellow about the whole thing."

Aware of Kim's delicate sensibilities, Robert Whitehead anxiously went to tell her in her room at the Benjamin Franklin that her co-star had been replaced. "I thought she would be shaken and upset," he later recalled, "but she stared up at me for a moment and said, 'I wondered when you'd ever come to that conclusion.'" Elaine Stritch says a key to the success of *Bus Stop* is that every character was perfectly cast for their role. With Salmi as Bo, the missing piece of the puzzle was in place as the show headed to New York.

When she wasn't onstage, Kim tried to integrate her family life with her acting career, something more difficult in the '50s, when the rare professional woman was also expected to be a paragon of domesticity. Although by most accounts Rubyann was delighted her daughter was a success, Kim pretended otherwise, telling one reporter Rubyann was shocked that she continued to act with two children at home. When telling interviewers how she raised her children, whether it involved their sleeping schedule or taking them on the road with her, Kim had a defensive, but understandable, tendency to say, "My pediatrician says . . ." or "My pediatrician agrees . . ." to support her actions.

One professional action Kim claimed to have taken on *Bus Stop* was turning down star billing over the title. "Cherie just isn't a star part," she said, prompting the *New York Post*'s Earl Wilson to observe, "That's not commercial and it's not Texan." In the *New York Times*, Arthur Gelb said she had set a precedent by demoting herself from the stardom she had attained in *The Traveling Lady.*

Years later, Robert Whitehead said that before *Bus Stop*, Kim hadn't really reached the point in her career where she could demand to be billed above the title, or where he felt her name above the title would be a ticket-selling commodity. "I'm sure I never offered her star billing above the title," he said, while *Bus Stop* casting director Terry Fay doesn't remember it either. "I would think she would be thrilled," she smiles. "I don't think she was that modest."

But notes made by Lucy Kroll on January 7, 1955, as contracts were being signed, support Kim's memory. After having spoken with Robert Whitehead, Kroll wrote, "Kim's feeling on billing . . . star solo billing above title wrong, as part does not warrant it . . . ensemble . . . also feels . . . if boy is star name, then can share together . . . if not, [Kim] to take first star billing after title." This is what was done.

Bus Stop arrived on Broadway during an especially fertile theater season: 1955–56 also featured Arthur Miller's *A View From the Bridge, The Diary of Anne Frank, Waiting for Godot, The Lark* (a drama about Joan of Arc starring Julie Harris), *The Chalk Garden, The Matchmaker* (which served as the basis for the musical *Hello, Dolly!*), and *My Fair Lady.*

Bus Stop opened at the Music Box Theatre Wednesday night, March 2, 1955, at 8:40 P.M. It was one of the most important nights of Kim's life. But when this temperamental and high-strung actress arrived at the theater, she got a shock: Robert Whitehead's wife, Virginia, had shortened the skirt for the costume in which Kim gets up on the table and sings "That Old Black Magic." This was done against Kim's wishes (she felt it showed too much leg as it was) and without her knowledge. "She expected her dress to be a little more modest, and Ginny Whitehead shortened it without telling her, which is a mean trick to play on any actress," Elaine Stritch says. "[But] she used that emotion, though, and there were tears in her voice when she sang 'That Old Black Magic.' It was lovely."

Phyllis Love says Virginia Whitehead performed a different kind of surgery on Kim's costume, tearing out some of the rhinestones and leaving holes so Cherie would look more like a cheap girl from the wrong side of the tracks. In either case, Kim was not amused. "When she came to the theater that night and saw that costume, which had become a part of her, she went into a fury! And when she went on stage, she was still furious," Love recalls. "She was so angry that she read every line differently than she had while we were on the road. It was so spectacular that the audience clapped every four or five lines, because it was so true the way she said it. This went on for three acts—it was something I had never seen in the theater. I told her she should pay Virginia Whitehead to rip up her costume every night."

The critics were as enthusiastic as the audience. In the *New York Times*, Brooks Atkinson wrote, "Having written a wonderful play two years ago, Mr. Inge has now written a better [one] . . . His play [has] an artistic and intellectual maturity that was less conspicuous in *Picnic* or *Come Back, Little Sheba.*" Robert Coleman of the *Daily Mirror* compared *Bus Stop* to *The Canterbury Tales* and *The Decameron,* adding, "It has heart, compassion, wisdom and loads of laughs." And William Hawkins of the *World-Telegram* said, "*Bus Stop* has the same irresistible glow about it that makes a fire magnetic to people coming in out of the cold." Of the theater critics at New York's seven daily newspapers, the only dissenter was John Chapman of the *Daily News,* who said, "I just couldn't get myself to care very much about the romance."

Director Harold Clurman came in for praise, as did all members of the cast, with the *Herald-Tribune*'s Walter Kerr saying of Albert Salmi, "Sullenness isn't normally an appealing characteristic in a leading man; Mr. Salmi makes it seem as if it were a virtue to be prized and nourished." Kim's notices were the kind every actor dreams of. Here's how Walter Kerr led off his review:

> Earlier this season, Miss Kim Stanley was made a star and, for the first time saw her name go up in lights over a theater. For her new play, William Inge's *Bus Stop,* she modestly suggested that she be billed along with the other actors beneath the title.
>
> The trouble with that girl is that she can't see herself. When she walks on the stage, the set changes color. When she fumbles in her bag for a lipstick, all life around her seems to stop and stare until the momentous search is completed. When she drawls out a simple, "Well, really!" in her magnificent adenoidal tones, the English language acquires more comic and pathetic overtones than you had ever noticed before. Miss Stanley can bill herself any way she likes. She is the real thing, and word is going to get around.

Brooks Atkinson wrote in the *New York Times,* "As the nightclub singer, Kim Stanley is superb. Still the traveling lady, she gives a glowing performance that is full of amusing detail—cheap, ignorant, bewildered, but also radiant with personality." *Life* magazine said, "She now stands as one of the first ladies of the stage." Even Maurice Zolotow of *Theatre Arts,* who said Kim needed to be careful about substituting tricks for an understanding of character, added, "She owns a perfectly amazing repertoire of facial expressions and optical gleams."

The *New York Times* noted another extraordinary facet of Kim's opening-night performance: Her rendition of "That Old Black Magic" brought down the house. "Show-stopping routines in musicals, revues, or farces are not uncommon," it noted. "But Kim Stanley accomplished [this] rarity . . . in the straight play *Bus Stop* during the second act on opening night." What makes this remarkable, on top of her tone deafness and apoplectic rage about her costume is that she had a fear of heights and some nights had difficulty getting up on the table to sing.

One of the keys to Kim's greatness as an actress was something Walter Kerr noticed about her performance as Cherie: her ability to simultaneously express several conflicting emotions and thus elicit a similarly complex reaction from the audience. "Even as she's ducking out from under [Salmi's] clumsy but confident embrace and screeching at him fiercely to shut him up, she pauses to furrow her forehead and muse, 'Someplace deep inside me I got a funny feeling I'm gonna end up in Montana,'" Kerr wrote in his review. "Miss Stanley not only gets laughter but solid applause with this line; it just goes to show what I mean."

Kim's coworkers were equally laudatory. "Most of my part in *Bus Stop* was listening to Kim, and there wasn't a boring moment," says Elaine Stritch. "She was riveting. You had to be an awfully good actress for the audience not to see a tremendous difference between her reality and your lack of it." Astonishingly, Kim reacted skeptically to all this praise, saying she suspected much of it was simply deferred payment for her performance in the short-lived *Traveling Lady.* That skepticism did not keep her from cashing her checks, which were considerable: Once *Bus Stop* was a hit, she was making $1,300 a week in 1955 dollars.

Although she had a husband and two children at home and faced a

Puritannical and repressive moral and sexual climate, Kim maintained a very active extramarital social life during *Bus Stop*. She was often at Downey's, a Times Square restaurant that was a noted actors' hangout. "We met at Downey's," Ben Gazzara recalls. "She was doing *Bus Stop*, and I was doing *Cat on a Hot Tin Roof* down the street. She was talking to Elaine Stritch. They were a lot of fun. I was especially impressed with how much they could drink. I felt like a piker."

During the run of the show, Kim dated Cliff Robertson. She also had an affair with writer JP Miller. "Kim was very restless, very sensitive, very liberated," Miller later recalled. "I'd go by and pick her up after work. I wasn't even that crazy about jazz, but just because she wanted to go, we went to hear jazz down at some place in the Village. She was in hog heaven." She was also, he added, a woman of mystery. "She was extremely secretive," he said. "We drank quite a bit together, but she never really unloaded her sorrows on me."

Ellen Adler, Harold Clurman's stepdaughter, says Kim also had an affair with Clurman. "I wouldn't be surprised," Robert Whitehead said years later. "I would accept that it's probable. But I can't give you any guarantee." Elaine Stritch is dubious, saying, "Harold was in love with Kim. Kim was not in love with Harold, but she had great respect for him." And Phyllis Love is agnostic. Asked if she saw any evidence that Kim had an affair with Harold Clurman, she responded, "No! No. Ooh— someone did?"

During the run of *Bus Stop* Kim also met fellow actor Alfred Ryder, probably at Downey's. Kim liked to go there, feeling it was less pretentious than Sardi's. "She was very proud of going to Downey's," Ellen Adler says. "She used to say to Harold [Clurman], 'You go to Sardi's and that's really not the place. You don't get it.'" Phyllis Love remembers that when *Bus Stop* opened in New York, Curt Conway was often around. But by the time Kim left the show, her escort was Alfred Ryder.

BORN ALFRED CORN in 1916 to Max Corn, a successful Jewish dentist, and his wife, Zelda, Ryder grew up in Brooklyn, along with his sister, who would become the actress Olive Deering. By the time Kim was born, he was already a child actor, and at age twelve, appeared on

Broadway as Curly, one of the lost boys in Eva LeGalliene's *Peter Pan.* In 1929, at age thirteen, he played son Sammy Goldberg to Gertrude Berg's Molly on the radio version of *The Goldbergs.* He appeared in the Group Theatre's version of *All the Living,* directed by Lee Strasberg, and the Group's world premiere of Clifford Odets's *Awake and Sing.* Among his later film credits are *True Grit* (1969), in which he plays the frontier lawyer who grills John Wayne as Sheriff Rooster Cogburn for his tendency to shoot suspects first and ask questions later.

Actor Pat Hingle remembers Ryder as very gentle and cultured, while Phyllis Love says he was a good match for Kim, very bright and talented. But he was as unpopular with many of Kim's friends and colleagues as the genial Curt Conway was popular. While bright and articulate, he could also be abrasive. He had a long and successful career, but felt he had been meant for greater things. "He was tense. Extremely tense," Ellen Adler recalls. "He had been sort of promised that he would be a great Broadway star, and somehow it never happened. He felt that acutely."

By October of 1955, although still married to Curt, Kim was living with Alfred at 54 Riverside Drive on the Upper West Side of Manhattan. It was the time of the three Kims—Hunter, Novak, and Stanley—and a *New York Times* profile of Kim noted that for a recent spread with glamour photos of the three stars in *Vogue,* Kim had been asked to pose wearing some of her favorite jewelry. The *Times* approvingly noted, "Miss Stanley showed up for the sitting, obligingly wearing her favorite—and only—adornment: a wedding ring."

There was a similar unintended irony in a *New York Mirror* profile of Kim, which observed, "Kim Stanley . . . is the first to admit she's leading a double life. And Kim is the first to insist that these two personalities remain separate and distinct." The two personalities, according to the article, were the actress and the suburban Long Island housewife. "Of the two personalities," the article noted, "Kim puts the latter foremost whenever they conflict." But the actress/housewife was only one face. The sexually adventurous, hard-drinking, self-destructive Bohemian was the other. Her public image was Fannie Farmer, but her private life was Fanny Hill.

During its long run, *Bus Stop* had many repeat visitors, including

Marilyn Monroe, who was set to star in the film version. Josh Logan, who directed the film, sent her to study Kim's southern accent. Robert Whitehead, trying to help Marilyn and perhaps be a shrewd businessman as well, suggested she star in the show's road company. "When we sold the movie rights, I knew they had Marilyn in mind," he later said. "I said, 'To make yourself more effective in the movie, perhaps you should play it on the road.' She didn't do it, though. I think she was scared of going on the stage. She never really did go on the stage."

Although Kim was dedicated to the New York theater and Marilyn was the quintessential Hollywood movie star, Kim was fond of her. "Anyone who had any largeness of spirit loved Marilyn," she said later. "And she won us all, not just the [Actors] Studio, but . . . the intelligentsia, all those people, she won everybody." Later that year, under the wing of Lee Strasberg, Monroe would be at the Actors Studio's first session at its new permanent home in a former church on Forty-fourth Street between Ninth and Tenth Avenues.

As *Bus Stop* continued its long run, Kim increasingly became prey to her jitters about going onstage. At the Thursday matinee on July 14, 1955, midway through the first act, Phyllis Love fainted. Fourteen-year-old Ken Pressman of Cynthiana, Kentucky, was in the audience. "She simply keeled over backwards and plopped to the floor," Pressman recalls. "There was much consternation, and the curtain came down." When it rose again, the play continued with Love's understudy Patricia Fay in the role. "Of the performances I saw Kim do, that was not my favorite, or even close," Pressman says. "Because my feeling was that her concentration was blown."

Given Kim's onstage rapport with Albert Salmi, she probably wasn't happy when, on August 1, Dick York (later co-star of the '60s sitcom *Bewitched*) replaced Salmi, who joined the show's road company. The role of Cherie was played on the road by Peggy Ann Garner, who became Salmi's first wife.

In late June, Kim started missing shows. Robert Whitehead had two backups for her: an understudy (Norma Crane) and a standby (Tammy Grimes). Grimes was taken both with the person and performer. "I remember watching Kim perform from the back of the house and thinking she was rather like silk," Grimes says. "Subtle, very silky. Very feminine . . . There was nothing tough about her whatsoever. She was very vulnerable—one sensed that right away. Rather like a deer, a doe. As opposed to a scruffy dog or cat or a very feline Siamese."

But observing Kim and stepping into her "chanteuse" costume, Grimes learned, were two different things. "I didn't realize what I had to come up to in regards to playing with the other players at their level of performance," she says. "They were used to having Kim there and had their performances already set. Everything was more or less timed out, and they gave strong, very simple, refined performances. They weren't going to not do that just because I was there. I had to catch up with them."

She also had to mollify the audience. Before going on the first time, she was standing backstage when the announcement was made that the part of Cherie would be played by Tammy Grimes. "There was booing," she recalls. "They booed. I remember hearing that and saying, 'Oh, dear. It's difficult to walk out there. But not that difficult.'"

For Kim, though, it was that difficult. In addition to missing seven performances the last week of June, she vacationed from August 23 through September 12. She became ill and only played the first act on October 10. She was out of the show October 11 through 15. Then, after the show of October 25, Anthony Ross, forty-six and apparently in good health, went home after playing Dr. Lyman and died in his sleep of a heart attack. "Kim fell apart," Robert Whitehead later recalled. "She felt she couldn't go on without him. Facing the fact that you go on and live and play it out was not included in her particular neurosis."

Two days after Ross's death, Kim got a doctor's note recommending that she be allowed to leave the show early because her continuing in *Bus Stop* could cause serious damage to her health. The doctor indicated Kim was suffering from paroxysmal tachycardia (a psychosomatic condition characterized by intermittent rapid heartbeat), fibromyositis of the back (muscle aches), viral pneumonia, and anemia.

Kim's witch's brew of symptoms late in the run of *Bus Stop* gave rise to an apocryphal story about her and Elaine Stritch. Supposedly before the curtain went up one day, Stritch came across Kim throwing up, "a frequent prelude to her entrance," a magazine noted. "Honey," Stritch reportedly said, "let's skip that Actors Studio stuff, okay?" The story reflects popular perceptions of the sensitive, brilliant star and the gruff, no-nonsense Stritch, but is false. "I'd never have said such a thing to anybody," Stritch says. "How awful!"

Ever the consummate gentleman, even to his own financial detriment, Robert Whitehead let Kim out of her contract early, and on November 4, the day after the film version of *Guys and Dolls* opened in New York at the Capitol Theater, Kim gave her final performance as Cherie. Norma Crane and Tammy Grimes filled in for her, and on November 21, Barbara Baxley took over the role. "Once you pushed Kim on stage, she'd be brilliant," Whitehead later said. "But you'd almost have to force her onstage because, night after night, she'd be in an emotional state which she said precluded her going on. I don't think it was stage fright. I think it was life fright."

Ironically, neither Kim nor *Bus Stop* would receive a Tony Award. In 1955, plays were eligible for Tonys if they opened before March 1. *Bus Stop* opened on March 2. By the time the Tonys came around in 1956, many original cast members were gone and it was almost a different show.

Another irony about the play is that, while it is profoundly optimistic, the lives of many of its principals hardly justified such an outlook. In what could be called the *Bus Stop* curse, William Inge eventually committed suicide; Albert Salmi murdered his second wife before shooting himself to death; Tony Ross died prematurely during the play; Kim and Elaine Stritch both battled alcoholism; and Phyllis Love's first husband suffered from a debilitating chronic mental illness.

A more amusing postscript to *Bus Stop* comes in the form of scathing remarks Kim made several months after the show about the critics who had praised her so warmly. What was hurting the theater, she told an interviewer, was the shortsightedness of drama critics, whom she categorized as "a bunch of fatheads." Unhappy with the short run of *The Traveling Lady* as well as the tepid reception sometimes accorded serious or edgy plays, she said, "These are the men who keep telling us how eager they are to see the theater do better and finer things. Yet they're the very fellows who are often to blame for a worthy play's failure to do business."

The critics, smitten with Kim, refused to take offense. In the *New York Journal-American,* John McClain wrote:

> What is quite obviously chewing on Miss Stanley is the fact that sandwiched somewhere in between a fistful of rave notices there was the suggestion by someone that she had not achieved stark perfection. A fig for seven pounds of deliriously doting press clippings—it is only human that the actor or actress will fasten upon one phrase or sentence that is condescending and spend a sleepless night plotting revenge on the author. More power to Miss Stanley! Let's all take the fight out into Shubert Alley and belabor each other with old manuscripts until somebody cries "Uncle Vanya."

And Whitney Bolton of the *Morning Telegraph* added with good-natured pedantry, "It is almost impossible to assemble, say, fifteen men anywhere in the world in any art, profession or business and not have some fatheads in the group."

AFTER LEAVING *BUS STOP,* Kim had a miraculously quick recuperation, returning to live TV on December 20, 1955. She appeared in Tad Mosel's *The Waiting Place,* an episode of Fred Coe's new live dramatic anthology, *Playwrights '56.* Having just portrayed a worldly nightclub singer, Kim was again an adolescent, a little girl lost. Seven weeks short of her thirty-first birthday, Kim played a fourteen-year-old girl who has trouble accepting her widower father's desire to remarry. The role of Abby, written by Mosel with Kim in mind, was similar to Wilma in Horton Foote's *A Young Lady of Property,* although set in Mosel's Midwest rather than Foote's Gulf Coast Texas.

Kim was anxious about being so much older than her character, and after producer Fred Coe sent the script to Lucy Kroll, writer Tad Mosel was summoned to Kroll's office.

"Lucy sat at her desk. I sat opposite her," Mosel recalls. "There was only one light in the room, on Lucy's desk. Far off, in the shadows of the room, was Kim, sitting in a corner.

"I could not see her face. She spoke, so I heard her voice. It was just the loveliest voice ever put on a woman, soft, gentle, and very distant.

"Suddenly, I put it all together—Kim didn't want me to see how old she was! Her looks would not have influenced me, because I knew how old she was, for heaven's sake. That was not a big secret. Lucy Kroll was finding out if Kim should do it, and I told her the truth, that I wrote it for Kim." But just like Blanche DuBois in *A Streetcar Named Desire*, Kim avoided the harsh light out of fear a potential suitor would know her true age.

Once Kim went into rehearsal, Mosel recalls, she was unhappy with Louis-Jean Heydt, who played her father. "He was a good, solid movie actor, kind of attractive," Mosel says. "He always played the losing man on the team. When you saw him, you said, 'Oh, he's going to get killed in battle.' Kim was miserable with him. She didn't complain, but she was just fumbling through rehearsals."

Three days before the show was to air, Fred Coe threw a Christmas party at a hotel in midtown Manhattan. When Frank Overton from *The Trip to Bountiful* walked in, Kim threw her arms around him and said, "Oh, I wish you were playing my father!" Mosel reported this to Coe and director Arthur Penn. "Poor Louis-Jean got fired and Frank Overton got hired," Mosel recalls. "He learned the role in one day, went through the camera work and everything. He went on the air and was wonderful."

Although Kim was always a trouper on live TV, even she acknowledged the pressure just before airtime was extraordinary. Making it more so on *The Waiting Place* was the last-minute hovering of several make-up artists trying to decide how to best turn her into the fourteen-year-old Abby. "With only seconds to go, people were standing around me, studying my face from five different angles," she later said. "It was terrible. I was ready to scream."

Variety was ecstatic about the show. "For about the first ten minutes . . . it looked as if producer Fred Coe had flipped his lid. Imagine casting Kim Stanley as a fourteen-year-old," it said. "But after those few minutes, you could have called him Canny Coe, for Miss Stanley delivered one of the stunning virtuoso performances of this or any other season." That performance, it noted, was aided by "a top-notch wardrobe job that flattened out her bulges and a good make-up job that erased her facial lines," but "it was Miss Stanley's pluperfect portrayal of an imaginative and somewhat overpossessive child that was the clincher." It is yet another indicator of Kim's extraordinary versatility as an actress that, three years after successfully portraying the fading Blanche DuBois on the Houston stage, she starred as a fourteen-year-old before the merciless and unsparing live television camera and brought it off without a hitch.

Abby's imaginative nature is best expressed in one of her lines, which applies to Kim as well. "I could be anything," she tells a neighborhood boy. "There's a hundred people inside of me. A whole band of people, just waiting for me to choose one of them to be."

The next person Kim chose to be was a young woman who defies her parents' wishes and runs away from home to marry the man she loves in *Flight,* a Horton Foote drama airing February 28, 1956, on *Playwrights '56.* When she goes to meet her boyfriend in San Antonio, though, she learns he has abandoned her. For all its literary merit, though, *Playwrights '56* was cancelled after one season, the victim of *The $64,000 Question,* harbinger of a wave of quiz shows that helped to bury live TV drama.

Kim's next show, *Joey,* airing March 25 on *Alcoa-Goodyear Playhouse,* featured her and a twenty-three-year-old Anthony Perkins. He played a dishwasher, browbeaten by his father, whose most ambitious activity is feeding pigeons in the park. Kim played a stripper, temporarily working as a dishwasher following repeated run-ins with the law, who puts a spark into Joey. John Crosby of the *Herald-Tribune* liked the performances of Perkins ("I suspect the movies will be calling shortly") and Kim, of whom he said, "She can take a line like, 'So, it's you and the pigeons, huh?' and make it funny and touching and deeply revealing, all at once."

But another reason live TV drama was starting to lose its hold on the public imagination was creeping Marty-ism. (*Marty* was the moving 1953 Paddy Chayefsky drama about the love between an unattractive butcher and a schoolteacher he meets at a dance.) Although, small-scale kitchen-sink dramas played well on live TV, there were too many of them. Crosby said *Joey* was emblematic of an increasingly frequent genre on live TV: "inarticulate drama in which ordinary folk suffer their ordinary dreams in prose of . . . extraordinary ordinariness."

DURING THIS PERIOD, Kim had several flirtations with the movies, but none were consummated. JP Miller has said the movies didn't really want her, but it was really she who didn't want the movies, with one exception: *From Here to Eternity.*

Years later, Kim recalled fighting for the part of Alma, the nightclub hostess, which went to Donna Reed, who won an Oscar as best supporting actress. When asked by interviewer John Kobal in the early '80s if she had wanted to play the Donna Reed girl, Kim responded with self-deprecating humor, "The Donna Reed girl! Just because she got the Academy Award? That's my part!"

Kim told Kobal about going in to see legendary Columbia kingpin Harry Cohn with director Fred Zinnemann. Cohn was a legendary bully who admired Mussolini, even having his office redecorated to resemble Mussolini's. "Staring right at me, not even looking at Mr. Zinnemann, [Cohn] said, 'Why are you bringing me this girlie? She's not even pretty.' Looking straight into my eyes. I mean, I knew I wasn't pretty," she added, "but I wasn't ready for that kind of artillery at that close a range! . . . I did call him a pig or something. And when I looked at Mr. Zinnemann, he was purple—with both rage and embarrassment."

Eli Wallach withdrew from the role of Private Maggio, creating a career break for Frank Sinatra, because Wallach wanted to honor his commitment to appear on Broadway in Tennessee Williams's *Camino Real.* Wallach was close to Kim at the time and says he's never heard the story about Kim and Cohn and doesn't know if it's true.

But although Kim could be an accomplished yarn-spinner, the story may well be true. On November 12, 1952, Kim's agent, Lucy Kroll, wrote to Columbia vice president Jerry Wald, "I am calling your attention to a brilliant new talent. Her name is KIM STANLEY . . . I am having Arthur Willy, Columbia's recently appointed talent head, interview her . . . for the part of Alma in your production of *From Here to Eternity* . . . Her grooming has been completed, her acting is extraordinary, and she is photogenic. [Jose] Ferrer says she is loaded with sex, so what more could you want?"

Three days later, Wald wrote back that Cohn would undoubtedly see Kim when he came to New York the following week. But Cohn wanted to put Donna Reed in the role because she had been under contract at MGM for eight years. He wanted to embarrass Louis B. Mayer, and in February of 1953 offered the part to Reed.

Kim was actively considered for Clara, the female lead in the film version of *Marty,* which went to Betsy Blair. On October 19, 1953, Lucy Kroll wrote to Harold Hecht of Hecht-Hill-Lancaster, saying Kim had decided not to do a screen test because she had just given birth to Jamie and was exhausted. Five days later, Hecht wrote back to Kroll asking Kim to reconsider.

She appears to have done so, because nine months later, in July of 1954, Kroll wrote to Kim, telling her that director Delbert Mann had returned from the Coast and was ready to offer dates for the rehearsal and shooting of the film. In the letter, though, Kroll says she had told Mann that doing *The Traveling Lady* on Broadway was Kim's first priority. That's what won out.

Kim had one more near miss with the movies at this time, with producer Hal Wallis. Just as Kim was withdrawing from *Bus Stop* in November 1955, Lucy Kroll told Wallis that Kim could do a film after January 1. A cynic might question how Kroll could so actively solicit work for Kim while Kim was getting out of *Bus Stop* by telling Robert Whitehead how fragile her health was.

In a memo to Wallis, his assistant Paul Nathan wrote, "I saw Kim Stanley last night and would . . . BEG her to sign pictures with us." Nathan suggested putting her in *Summer and Smoke* with Montgomery Clift (Laurence Harvey did it instead) and several other films. In late December, Wallis requested kinescopes of several of Kim's live TV shows, then wrote to her, saying he was pleased she had agreed to do a screen test using scenes from either *Summer and Smoke* or *The Rainmaker* with director Joseph Anthony. Wallis expressed interest in being present for the test.

In an *Albuquerque Tribune* article on January 11, 1956, Kim said she was going to make both films in Hollywood that summer. She didn't: Katharine Hepburn starred in *The Rainmaker,* and, when *Summer and Smoke* was made five years later, Geraldine Page had the female lead. What may have kept Kim out of these films was the aggressive, take-no-prisoners negotiating style of Lucy Kroll: In a January 1956 memo to Wallis, his assistant Joseph Hazen detailed a copious and nonnegotiable list of Kroll's conditions for Kim's appearing in the films. In the twilight of the studio era, Hazen felt that these conditions (including $75,000 for the two films and Kim's having the right to decide which subsequent films she would appear in for Wallis) were excessive for someone, who, although a Broadway star, had no track record in films. Wallis may have agreed.

Although Kim's movie debut had fallen through, the spring of 1956 marked a milestone in her personal life: Having left her marriage to Curt Conway in fact, she now did so in law, obtaining a Mexican divorce on April 3. And films were at best a secondary interest, with the stage her home. Having just triumphed in a traditional comedy, she would now make a 180-degree turn to star in an experimental drama the likes of which Broadway had never seen.

CHAPTER 6

A SLAP OF THE POET

(1956–1960)

KIM WAS ON TOP OF TWO WORLDS IN 1956: Broadway, where she had just completed three triumphant and increasingly prominent roles, and live television drama, where both the quality and quantity of her performances in a remarkably diverse array of roles were unexcelled. She was also the leading lady of the Actors Studio, although her hectic career and life no longer allowed her to do scene work there. But her unceremonious exit from *Bus Stop* was a warning light of trouble ahead.

On the personal front, she appeared to be settling down. Kim was living with Alfred Ryder, daughter Lisa, and son Jamie in the second-floor apartment at 54 Riverside Drive they had shared since the fall of 1955. She was pregnant with her third child.

Actress Mary Tahmin recalls Ryder as gentlemanly and quiet, but he could also be temperamental. "Alfred was a skyrocket," says Kim's brother Justin Reid. "He had a lot of creative energy that went off like a rocket that goes wild and crazy up in the sky." He could be abrasive and overbearing and, as was the case with Kim's two husbands, he was handsome, intense, and a drinker.

On October 19, 1956, Kim gave birth to a daughter, Laurie Rachel, who was delivered through Caesarean section. She was Ryder's daughter, but her birth certificate didn't reveal it: Her name was listed as "Laurie Rachel Conway." The space for the father's name was left blank. Kim may have done this because she was still legally married to Curt Conway when her younger daughter was conceived.

Why didn't Kim simply list Alfred Ryder as the father? "My answer is that it never fit, as many facts of her life never fit, the very traditional moral script that she still bought into in a bizarre way, even though it was totally in conflict with how she lived her life," says her younger daughter, who, as an adult, would drop the "Laurie" and simply go by Rachel. "But she was always trying to fit her life into this moral script that really [couldn't accommodate it] . . . and it was probably a source of a lot of her pain."

Kim's next play had its genesis while she was working on *Bus Stop*, although it was as far from *Bus Stop* as one play can be from another. About 1955, playwright Arthur Laurents had a vision of a woman running through the woods in a peignoir. Laurents, who had been in psychoanalysis with Judd Marmor, fashioned a play from that image about a young career woman, under stress in her personal and professional life, who retreats to her family's cabin in a forest. She is tormented by a girl and two young women who turn out to be younger versions of herself (played, oldest to youngest, by Joan Loring, Anne Pearson, and Barbara Myers) and also confronts images of her father (Onslow Stevens), ex-husband (Robert Culp), and a lover (Pernell Roberts). Under the weight of all these conflicts, she has a nervous breakdown, but finally comes to terms with herself.

The play was *A Clearing in the Woods*. Kim was not the first choice for Virginia, the play's harried heroine: Laurents had originally hoped for, and had conversations with, Katharine Hepburn. Then there was another unlikely candidate. "I'll tell you who else flirted with it—this is bizarre," says Laurents, with wry amusement. "Mary Martin. With Jerry Robbins directing. That would have been something. Flying through the trees . . ."

Although the play is a deeply introverted exposition of Freudian principles, these great ladies' interest in the role is understandable:

The actress who plays Virginia is offstage for only five minutes during the play and displays a wide range of moods. But once Hepburn and Martin passed on the play, Kim's interest was crucial for *Clearing* to make it to Broadway. "If it wasn't for Kim, the play wouldn't have gotten on," Laurents says. "Roger Stevens [who co-produced the play] adored Kim. When she became interested, then there was the money." While the odds of making money on *Clearing* were long, Stevens believed in the play. So did Kim: In January of 1956, while in negotiations with Hal Wallis about the possibility of making her film debut in *Summer and Smoke,* she made it plain that she would not do the film if its production conflicted with *Clearing.*

Rehearsals for the play began at the end of November, allowing Kim six weeks of postpartum recovery following the birth of Laurie Rachel. For Robert Culp, who played her ex-husband Pete, a once big man on campus who's gone nowhere in life, watching Kim rehearse was a revelation. Three years earlier, he had appeared in *The Prescott Proposals,* a play by Howard Lindsay and Russell Crouse starring Katharine Cornell. It was a traditional Broadway drama, and was traditionally rehearsed.

"You just went in, and most of the rehearsal was about learning the blocking, learning your lines and that was it," Culp says. "Now it was a different world. The Method was in play. On *Clearing,* I remember just standing there in utter awe, watching Miss Stanley work in rehearsals. It was something that, up close and personal, I had never seen before, except in class.

"She appeared to be doing the same thing every night, but she really wasn't," he continues. "She was refining it in her heart, her soul, and her mind, and putting those three together so it would catch fire for her. And there were moments, not every night, where she was transcendant. She—was—beatific. There's just no other way to describe it."

Joseph Anthony, the play's director, was more familiar with the Method than Culp, but was still in awe of his star, calling her "a truly heroic actress [who] releases you from the fears and miseries of your own life." He defined her essential quality as "a faculty for total belief," adding, "It isn't even a faculty that's essentially related to the stage. Kim can sit in the grass, hear birds, feel the wind, and summon up whole worlds."

Laurents was impressed by her immaculate diction and an ear so perfect she could do any accent. "Concentration is one of the real secrets of acting," he adds. "When Kim concentrated, she was totally in the character. And you could see it. You know those watches where you can see the works? With some revered names, you see the works. With Kim, you couldn't."

Laurents saw Kim's vibrant, Rabelaisian side as well, writing, "Her laugh is inimitable . . . hoop-skirted lustiness which makes an audience beam as it reaches for a handkerchief." What did her laugh sound like? "It was a big laugh, loud, boisterous, full and free," he says. "A really hearty laugh." But its counterpoint was Kim's deeply ingrained passive-aggressiveness. She knew there was humor in her character which she hadn't yet brought out, she told Laurents, but asked him to be patient, saying she'd have it in two weeks. She told him this the night before the play opened on Broadway.

When Kim was causing trouble in rehearsal, Laurents called Eva Klein, her psychotherapist. "She said, 'Kim can lick you all with one hand tied behind her back,'" Laurents recalls. "I said 'Thank you.' You know, we thought she was so fragile. She wasn't."

One thing that set Kim on the warpath was her costume, designed by Lucinda Ballard, a lovely, ethereal bluish gown with dark blue-gray underlays. For the second act, when she finds herself, the underlays were of a lighter hue to reflect her lightening spirit. "Kim balked," Laurents says. "She was so literal. She was sure the audience could tell the difference, but they couldn't." Eventually Kim went along with Ballard's concept.

More than forty years later, Laurents would memorialize Kim in his play *Claudia Lazlo* (2001), whose protagonist, Madeline Gray, has a lot of Kim in her. Brilliant but erratic and mercurial, Madeline Gray bestrides the stage like a colossus, sprinkling her conversation with "darling" the way some people put salt on their corn on the cob. Her motto: "I'm entitled to do as I please when I please with whom I please," an attitude Kim displayed at one time or another (and sometimes simultaneously) towards food, sex, and alcohol.

Kim's going from *Bus Stop* to *A Clearing in the Woods* was a bold statement of refusing to be typecast, like Dustin Hoffman doing *Midnight Cowboy* after *The Graduate*. But as a vehicle, *Clearing* would prove no better than the Edsel, the ill-fated automobile introduced to the public just as the play went into rehearsal. And there was another evil omen: This was Kim's first Broadway play in which her character's father appears on stage. Given Kim's parlous relations with J.T., it was a recipe for trouble.

Clearing opened in Philadelphia on December 26, 1956, at the Walnut Theater to mixed reviews. One journalist noted that "the method that playwright Laurents has used in shifting back and forth in time seems to have confused some people and enthralled others." The *Philadelphia Bulletin* was not enthralled, saying, "While the acting is often brilliant individually, it does little to clear the fog of the text." Similarly, the *Philadelphia News* deadpanned, "Miss Stanley has always had our deepest regard as a performer. We can hardly say she seemed mannered last evening, having no idea at all what a young woman might be like when hemmed in by three of her previous selves."

But the play did have its out-of-town supporters. The *Philadelphia Inquirer* called it "beguiling and stimulating," while *Variety* added, "All plays . . . that resort to symbolism or fantasy have limited audience appeal because many playgoers like to have everything spelled out for them in concrete form and resent having to think for themselves."

When the play opened January 10, 1957, at Broadway's Belasco Theatre, the critical chorus again ranged from "A for effort" to outright dismissal. "In a flabby season, at least Playwright Laurents attempted something provocative and at times achieved something striking," noted *Time*. Brooks Atkinson of the *New York Times* called it a superb production and performance, but he added, "Virginia is not an interesting woman . . . She has nothing except her sickness to offer the audience.

"Neurotic characters are valid subjects for dramatic literature," he added, citing Hamlet, Hedda Gabler, and Blanche DuBois. "But we take a personal interest in them because we see them working out their destinies in relation to society rather than in isolation." (Atkinson may have inadvertently encouraged Laurents to give *Clearing* its free-form structure: Reviewing his 1952 play *Time of the Cuckoo,* he said it was "written with grace by a man . . . who can afford to take liberties with conventional forms.")

Tom Donnelly of the *World-Telegram & Sun* began his review, "Something tells me I'm going to have a difficult time conveying a coherent impression of the evening, but I'll do my best . . ." Another critic who found himself flummoxed, although more crankily so, was John Chapman of the *Daily News.* "I can only guess that this is a fantasy with psychoanalytical overtones," he wrote. "There must be hidden meanings in it somewhere—and no doubt some of them are dirty. But because I grew up as a fairly ordinary police reporter and neglected my studies of psychopathia, I am unable to submit a lucid report about last night's goings-on."

Other critics described the play as "arduous," "pretentious," and "an endurance test for the hardy bent on seeing how much they can take under fire and survive." Robert Coleman of the *Daily Mirror* mentioned the scene in which the three younger versions of Kim's character dance around her and, like the witches in *Macbeth,* chanted, "I am Virginia! . . . I am Virginia! . . . I am Virginia!" at which point a member of the audience called out, "I am bored!"

Kim's notices were better than those of the play. In the *Times,* Brooks Atkinson called her performance splendid, saying it was "personally beautiful, plastic in its flow of images, emotionally alive and searching . . . a rich and luminous performance." In a separate article, he added, "[The play] is never monotonous because Miss Stanley has the abundance, the insights and the incandescence of the artist." Similarly, Tom Donnelly called her performance brilliant. Images using intense light to describe Kim's performance would be a hallmark of her theatrical career.

In the damning-by-faint-praise department, Robert Coleman of the *Daily Mirror* wrote, "Kim Stanley wrestles valiantly with the mental midget, Virginia," while John Chapman simply sneered, "Miss Stanley keeps tossing her head as if her scalp itched."

Still, Kim retained her capacity to charm the critics as well as impress them. Toward the end of the play's run, John McClain of the *Journal-American,* who had panned it, went to her dressing room and asked her if she still felt critics were "fatheads." She proceeded to explain why, in light of the lambasting of *Clearing,* they were. But at the end of the article, he amicably wrote, "I don't think Miss Stanley and I settled anything, except that we became quite friendly and I discovered she needs a nurse for her two older kids. Anybody know of a good one?"

The play's technical aspects also got good notices, with *Time* praising Oliver Smith's woodland set, which it called "a sort of field-and-stream of consciousness." The *Saturday Review* praised the lighting effects of Feder (who went by only his first name) for illustrating the state of Virginia's psychopathy.

Unfortunately, there was psychopathy backstage as well. Tom Hatcher, who played a young man who briefly meets Virginia, dryly notes, "It was a very dysfunctional cast." When Kim had been an acting student ten years earlier at the Pasadena Playhouse, Onslow Stevens was already a well-established actor who frequently performed there. According to Arthur Laurents, Kim had a crush on him in Pasadena, and he rejected her.

Nonetheless, Kim suggested Stevens play her father. Once he was in the cast, though, she soured on him. "At first, she was wonderful to him," Laurents recalls. "Then she began subtly to drive him mad. She made his life miserable. She would leave notes scrawled on his dressing-room mirror. Finally, he flipped during a matinee." (Laurents believes this happened at the second matinee; he knows it wasn't the first, because Kim spent it in her dressing room sleeping off a hangover.)

As Laurents remembers it, Stevens got drunk and was locked in his dressing room, but somehow got out. "He went after her with an axe, which they had backstage in case of fire. They came with straitjackets to get him. And at the moment in the play when he was to appear, the stage manager came onstage and Onslow came down the aisle, both saying his lines. Well, the play was rather far-out for that time, and the audience thought it was part of the play. It was bizarre. They nabbed him and took him away."

Tom Hatcher remembers the incident, minus the salient detail of the axe. But that was not the end of Stevens's problems. Possibly goaded on by Kim's aversion to him, Joan Loring and at least one other young actress in the show played a practical joke on him that went horribly awry.

"There was some bad blood between Onslow Stevens, Joan Loring, and some other woman in the cast," Robert Culp recalls. "But Joan Loring was the more spirited of the two or three. They rigged up a bucket of water over a door, and when he opened the door, it fell on his head. It doused him with water, but the weight of the bucket hurt him and put a gash in his head. He called Equity and brought charges. She was barred from the theater for the last two performances." In his dismissive review of *Clearing*, Robert Coleman of the *Daily Mirror* wrote, "Onslow Stevens was probably wishing he were back in Hollywood." Coleman had no idea how true that was.

Owing to its experimental structure and largely humorless, psychologically probing nature, *A Clearing in the Woods* was not a crowd-pleaser. Two days after it opened, there was a notice in the *New York Times* that it would close after four performances. Following a surge of sales in response to that announcement, the producers placed an ad in the *Times* reversing course, and announcing the play would run indefinitely.

Kim fought for the play, talking it up in the press. "I'm notoriously bad at guessing what reviewers will like," she told one interviewer. "But I was sure they'd like it. It has so much for everyone with an emotional problem—and who hasn't one? [The critics] should see the mail that's coming in. Women of all kinds are saying it was the most important emotional experience of their lives." On a more prickly note, she added, "as Shelley Winters predicted on opening night, the critics probably identified themselves with the daddy image and resented it." Kim took a 50 percent pay cut from her $1,500 weekly salary in an effort to keep the play going.

But efforts to keep it open were unavailing, and it closed on February 9, 1957, having run less than a month. After the last show, Robert Culp went to Kim's dressing room to take leave of her. "Alfred Ryder was sitting with her in the dressing room. She seemed wan, drawn, and exhausted, the way it might be for anyone at the end of a run," he recalls. "I simply said goodbye and shook hands with Alfred. He seemed immensely supportive of her, very sweet."

I N ADDITION TO HER BROADWAY STARDOM, Kim was still the leading lady of live television drama. "In the short, flickering history of TV, other actresses may have surpassed Kim Stanley's record of 100 performances," *Newsweek* observed, "but none have equalled her in her consistent quality of performance and her peak portrayals." (Her actual number appears to have been closer to forty, which is still considerable.) In that article, "The Girl on Your Set," Kim talked about why she liked live TV so much.

"On live TV, you can have a wonderful, immediate close contact. You can tell a whole story in a face," she said, causing the article's writer to muse, "Miss Stanley's face is probably as mobile as any on the 21-inch screen, portraying love, perplexity, and anger with the explicit understatement that TV's X-ray eye requires." Critic Ben Gross of the *Daily News* said simply, "Kim Stanley . . . is the greatest actress on television."

Now, when much of television drama is "all cops, all the time," it's hard to remember when TV drama was a more diverse and wide-ranging medium. Kim defended it against those who felt it was inferior to the theater. "I've never understood those actors who feel TV is just a bread-and-butter job and that the real work is on the Broadway stage," she said. "I love the medium to watch, more than the movies and sometimes more than the stage." But Kim's volume of work on live TV was decreasing: Between 1952 and 1956, she did more than twenty live TV dramas; between 1956 and 1960, only six. She had a busy schedule in the theater and would make her first movie during this period, but another reason for the decline in her television productivity was that live New York TV drama was an endangered species: Filmed shows from Hollywood were booming, and during the 1957–58 season, only one dramatic anthology, *Kraft Television Theatre,* would air live from New York.

Two months after *A Clearing in the Woods* closed, Kim was back on live TV for the first time in almost a year. The vehicle for her return was the television adaptation of Horton Foote's *The Traveling Lady,* which aired on *Studio One* April 22, 1957, with Robert Loggia as Henry Thomas, her good-for-nothing ex-con husband, and Steven Hill as Slim Murray, the small-town deputy sheriff and knight in shining armor. Robert Mulligan directed. "It deserved a better fate," Kim said of the play's short 1954 run on Broadway. "I've been interested in redoing the play for some time. It's one of the greatest plays I've ever worked in."

As Georgette Thomas, Kim displays joy and sorrow with equal vividness. In the first act, when her puzzled husband asks how she's gotten into town sooner than he expected, Kim answers, "I just came in on a bus!" Before she speaks, there's a little "huh" of anticipation and eagerness; when she says "on a bus," a rising pitch in her voice conveys pure exultation.

In the second act, though, she learns her husband has gotten into trouble and will have to return to prison. Slim Murray approaches her on the porch of the house where she's been staying to break the bad news. Kim looks worried, then her lips start to quiver in barely suppressed sobs. The corner of her mouth falls and her eyes look downcast. She turns away from Slim, leans on a support post for the porch and takes hold of it with both hands, absentmindedly stroking it, and asks, "What am I gonna do? What in the name of God am I . . ." Her voice breaks, and she's momentarily silent. She starts crying, and it's the real thing—her entire body heaves. While still crying, her face turns to anger and she pounds the post with one hand, cries "God!" turns back and looks imploringly at Slim. This is all seamlessly woven together. *Time* called her performance "sunlit," while *Variety* said it was "a score for Kim Stanley, who repeated . . . with mist-eyed sincerity as the Texas-travelin' wife."

On May 15, Kim starred in *The Glass Wall* on *Kraft Television Theatre*. Adapted by Roger O. Hirson from a novel by Cecile Gilmore, it's the story of a married woman who has been hospitalized with catatonic schizophrenia for eight years. She recovers and is discharged, only to learn that her husband (Richard Kiley) has remarried. She meets his new wife (Mary Fickett), who has bonded with their daughter, and self-sacrificingly withdraws, rather than attempting to re-enter the lives of her husband and daughter.

The *New York Times* said Kim's performance was "magnificently controlled and moving," Sid Shalit of the *Daily News* praised her "restrained pathos," and Marie Torre of the *Herald-Tribune* wrote, "Following Kim Stanley's sensitive portrayal in *The Glass Wall*, it was generally agreed in TV circles that Kim rates a best-actress-in-TV award." Years later, the show's writer added his thoughts. "I didn't think the show was very good," says Hirson, "but Kim made me cry. She was out there, with all her feelings to see."

But while Kim could dominate the stage or TV screen, there were still times when she would relapse into the little girl who wanted daddy to take care of things. In one scene of *The Glass Wall,* her psychiatrist, played by Jack Klugman, is talking with her after she's recovered from the muteness of eight years of catatonic schizophrenia. Neither Kim nor Klugman liked the director's staging of the scene, feeling the psychiatrist was sitting too close to Kim's character. Klugman spoke up, Kim didn't.

"I said to the director, 'I can't do that!'" Klugman recalls. "He said, 'Why?' I said, 'She hasn't spoken in years. I'm not going to crowd her. It's a terrible comment on psychiatry and I won't do it.' He said, 'But I've got a shot that's so beautiful!' I looked at Kim and she wasn't saying anything. Finally, I said, 'Look. You want someone to do it? Get yourself another boy!'

"We were rehearsing [in a studio] on Second Avenue and Sixtieth Street, I think. I walked out. I quit, and the director followed me. Kim stuck her head out the window, watching. We walked about two blocks, and the director said, 'Alright, we'll do it your way.' When I got back, I said, 'Where the hell were you, Kim? Why didn't you say something?' And she said, 'I knew you would take care of it.'"

On June 13, Kim went to Hollywood to appear in Clifford Odets's *Clash by Night,* produced for *Playhouse 90* by Martin Manulis and directed by John Frankenheimer. It was Kim's first TV show in Hollywood and her first time back in Southern California since her unhappy year as a student at the Pasadena Playhouse in 1945. She stayed at the Montecito, an Art Deco–style apartment hotel in the foothills above Hollywood Boulevard.

Ironically, in light of Odets's deep proletarian roots, Kim and the other performers on the show had to sign a loyalty oath. Senator Joseph McCarthy, the noxious Red-baiting Republican senator from Wisconsin, had been discredited as a political force by the Army-McCarthy hearings of 1954. But McCarthyism was still poweful, especially in the corridors of the easily intimidated networks. Before appearing on *Clash,* Kim was sent a form in which she had to certify that she had never participated in scores of organizations deemed subversive by the Attorney General of the United States, among them the Chopin Cultural Center, the Connecticut State Youth Conference, and the Veterans of the Abraham Lincoln Brigade, who had fought against the Fascists in the Spanish Civil War.

On a lighter note, this was still the time of the three Kims, and a Los Angeles journalist asked her if she thought the public had trouble keeping them straight. "Certainly no one is going to confuse me with Kim Novak and I don't think anyone gets me mixed up with Kim Hunter," the former Patricia Beth Reid told Hal Humphrey of the *Los Angeles Mirror-News,* who identified her as "the former Patricia Kimberly Reid." "I am the only one who has a legitimate right to the name anyway," she added, "and I resent the others' using it."

Clash by Night is a romantic triangle, involving Mae and Jerry Wilenski (Kim and E.G. Marshall), a working-class married couple on Staten Island, and Earl Pfeiffer (Lloyd Bridges), Jerry's sexually adventurous friend, who becomes their houseguest and Mae's lover. At first, Jerry refuses to acknowledge the affair, but when confronted with proof, he strangles Earl. Kim's disaffected outer-borough blue-collar housewife (with matching accent) gave her another chance to display her versatility in a period when she would soon portray a falling-apart movie star, a poor Southern country girl, an aging Parisian courtesan, and the willful young daughter of an early nineteenth-century Irish-American tavern owner.

One constant through many of these roles was Kim's unbridled sensuality, clearly on view in *Clash.* When she comes back from an evening at an amusement park with Bridges, she's wearing a floral wreath, which she starts to take off while talking to her hapless husband. It gets caught in her hair, and she langorously lets it remain there. When she finally pulls it out, she makes an openmouthed pout suggestive of sexual release—especially so since we've just seen her and Bridges kiss for the first time.

In the spirit of life imitating art, Kim had an affair with Clifford Odets while working on *Clash.* The play was adapted for TV by F.W. Durkee, a protégé of Odets, but Martin Manulis wasn't satisfied with the script and brought Odets in to write a new scene. Odets's obituary in the *New York*

Times noted, "He moved unobtrusively around Hollywood's social circles, frequently with an attractive girl on his arm." Kim was one of those "girls." Director Lamont Johnson remembers running into Kim and Odets at a party hosted by Roddy McDowall.

"We had a great chat," Johnson recalls. "She seemed to be . . . emotionally very delicate, on the brink of one of her problems. She'd always been a little strange and withdrawn or suddenly, violently demonstrative. There was a sort of manic-depressive quality to her. She was quite drunk. Odets was very attentive, but he would go off and chat with other people, and she would seem to feel—panicked or something. I couldn't quite get to the bottom of it. I thought, 'This gal is much too young and much too successful [to be acting like this].'"

Years later, Kim would say they had come close to marriage. "Clifford was the one I didn't marry," she told an interviewer. "But that was really because he was not good with children. But I loved him a lot. I really loved him," adding, "Clifford had cruelty in him." However, Odets's son, psychologist Walt Odets, doesn't believe things got that far. "I think it was very brief," he says. "I had an impression of who his important girlfriends were. I don't think Kim was an important girlfriend. But he had a lot of respect for her and liked her. They were very close in some ways."

Kim was still close to Curt Conway as well, and in the spring of 1957, they came close to reconciling, despite the fact that she was now living with Alfred Ryder and had had a child by him. A party was held at Franchot Tone's house on the Upper East Side to celebrate their impending reunion. Martin Landau, who was at that party, remembers that the party didn't follow the script. "They had one of the biggest brawls I ever saw, which ended their relationship," he says. "We didn't hear the beginning of the argument. By the time it became vociferous, they were calling each other names. It was like, 'How could I ever think we'd get back together?' and that sort of thing."

A possible fuse for Kim and Curt's blowup: He appears to have learned the truth of Jamie's paternity around this time. "Curt was crazy about Jamie," Landau says. "But he was horrified when he found out it wasn't his kid." Although their marriage and romance was over, Kim and Curt would remain close. And given his reputation for being able to calm her down, the producers of Kim's first film would give him a small part just to avail themselves of his services.

THE FILM WAS *THE GODDESS*, Paddy Chayefsky's first screenplay not adapted from one of his successful live TV dramas. It's the story of Emily Ann Faulkner, a pretty, movie-mad poor white Southern girl who claws her way to the pinnacle of movie stardom as Rita Shawn, but never finds love, happiness, or stability.

Kim and Paddy got off to a good start, with a Lucy Kroll memo from late April indicating that writer and star had had an "excellent" meeting. In one of his first press interviews about the production of the film, Chayefsky raved of Kim, "There's just one in a generation like her. First Laurette Taylor, now this one." Behind the scenes, though, there was friction between Kim and Paddy almost from the start.

"Who the hell do you think she is?" Chayefsky asked Kroll after Kim apparently changed her mind and balked at appearing in the film. "To get an Academy Award is worth the effort. And this," he modestly said, "is the opportunity." Kim, who had unhappy memories of Columbia studio head Harry Cohn from her unsuccessful effort to land the part of Alma in *From Here to Eternity,* was leery of dealing with Columbia again. Chayefsky may have told her he could green-light her appearance in the film, but it then turned out he needed Columbia's approval. "Columbia . . . they lied," Lucy Kroll jotted during a conversation with Kim on June 26, "[Kim] does not want to do the picture under these circumstances. If Paddy had called to tell her he needed Columbia OK, she would have leveled with [him]."

Director John Cromwell also had reservations about Kim, centering around her lack of film experience. In one conversation with Lucy Kroll, he said the film needed "an actress of size," one who already had made an impression on the filmgoing public. In a conversation Kroll had with Kim on June 27, Kroll jotted down that Cromwell said he would not do the movie with Kim. Whether Cromwell actually said this or it just represented Kim's anxieties is unclear. In the same conversation, Kroll noted that Columbia was still hoping to get Marilyn Monroe to do the film, following which, she ironically wrote, "Good luck, go get her."

What would have made Monroe's casting a coup for Columbia is that she was the lightly fictionalized subject of the film. At one time or another, sometimes vehemently, both Kim and Paddy denied this, citing figures such as Rita Hayworth and Jayne Mansfield, or composites of them. The denials aren't convincing, though: The Goddess is a blonde bombshell movie star from a white-trash background whose husband, Frank Rumsie (Lloyd Bridges), is an ex-athlete with traditional values adrift in Hollywood, while her first husband, John Tower (Steven Hill), is a moody intellectual. For the ex-athlete, read "Joe Dimaggio" (Rumsie was originally a baseball player, but was changed to a boxer for legal reasons). For the moody intellectual, read "Arthur Miller," to whom Monroe was married at the time.

Ironically, in light of the fact that John Cromwell wanted "an actress of size," one concern the filmmakers had about Kim was her weight. Milton Perlman, who co-produced the film with Chayefsky, later said she promised to lose weight, but failed to do so. A possible clue as to how much weight comes from notes Lucy Kroll made during a conversation with Kim. "She did not ask for the part," Kroll wrote, cryptically adding "15 lbs."

Instead of shedding 15 pounds, though, Kim gave serious thought to shedding the film. On July 1, three weeks before it was set to begin shooting, she called Lucy Kroll to say Chayefsky had told her the part was hers if she wanted it. But she wasn't sure, saying she wanted until July 7 to decide if she was going to do *The Goddess;* a Horton Foote play, *The Day Emily Married;* a Carson McCullers play, *The Square Root of Wonderful;* or even another movie, which David Susskind was to produce.

Once she chose *The Goddess,* though, Paddy Chayefsky worried about her well-known ambivalence toward publicity. He wanted language in her contract specifying a publicity tour of fifteen or twenty cities. It didn't go in, although a rider was attached to her contract saying that she agreed, subject to reasonable convenience, to make public appearances in connection with publicizing the film. Chayefsky's concerns would turn out to be justified, though, as Kim had an expansive notion of "reasonable convenience."

On July 22, 1957, filming began at a small studio on West Fifty-fourth

Street in Manhattan. "The heat was pushed into the background of conversation by the excitement of a young author and a young star making fresh starts in pictures," wrote a reporter for the *Herald-Tribune*. The first scene to be filmed was an early one: Emily Faulkner, still a high school girl, goes for a ride in the Cadillac of a socially prominent town boy (Burt Brinckerhoff) and puts out because she knows that, given her low social status, it's the only way she can get dates. "As the Cadillac was bounced up and down by a husky young stagehand who took joy in his work [which helped to simulate the motion of the car's going down a country road projected onto a screen behind it], Mr. Chayefsky began circling the set, looking rather like a honeybear nosing out sweets," the reporter added. "Sweat dripped off his brow and his voice raised a New York counterpoint to Miss Stanley's drawl." Although Kim played a sixteen-year-old in this scene, she was a thirty-two-year-old mother of three, causing the *Saturday Review* to observe she was probably the most elderly-looking teenager since Norma Shearer played Juliet.

Two days later, the company moved to Gold Medal–Biograph Studios in the Bronx, where much of the film was made. Chayefsky told a reporter that the film, with a budget of only $600,000, would have been more expensive had it all been done in Hollywood. Plus most of the cast and crew were New Yorkers and liked it there. Somewhat portentously, he discussed his vision of the film.

Chayefsky was unhappy with critics who said he was only the dramatist of "little people," such as "Marty," the lovelorn Bronx butcher who had made him famous. "I've tried to write *The Goddess* as a major work of art," he said. "These are big people. *The Goddess* represents an entire generation that came through the Depression with nothing left but a hope for comfort and security. Their tragedy lies in that they never learned to love either their fellow humans or whatever God they have."

Kim was feeling less expansive. When a reporter asked her what she thought *The Goddess* was all about, she snapped, "Didn't you ask Paddy or the press agent? I assume it's an ironic title. She's never known a love experience and substitutes fantasies about success in Hollywood." This flippant attitude extended to herself: When someone mentioned there was a Kim Stanley salad on the luncheon menu at the Gold Medal–Biograph cafeteria, she quipped "Isn't that jazzy?" with unrestrained sarcasm.

After several days' shooting at Gold Medal–Biograph, cast and crew went to Ellicott City, Maryland, where scenes from the Goddess's impoverished childhood and youth were filmed. (Eleven-year-old Patty Duke, making her film debut, played the Goddess as a child.) Kim, who had avoided movies as long as possible, was already beginning to display her displeasure with the medium.

One Saturday night, key cast and crew members gathered in a hotel bar in Ellicott City. Gerald Hiken, who plays the Goddess's uncle when she's a child, remembers Kim complaining about moviemaking. "They don't care about quality acting," she said. "All they care about is that you know your lines. If you just say your lines right and they can hear you, they say, 'Print it.'"

At this point, someone pointed out to Kim that the company manager was sitting nearby, implying that her popping off might hurt his feelings. "She turned around, and in a fairly loud voice, asked him, 'Did you hear what I just said?'" Hiken recalls. "He said, 'Yes, Kim, I did.' She said, 'Well, print it!'"

On stage and in live television, you did a performance all the way through, giving it an integrity and continuity that the slice-and-dice nature of moviemaking didn't allow for. "I was shocked to learn that movies are a director's medium, not an actor's," Kim told a reporter. "Whatever concept I may have had of a role, if it wasn't similar to the director's, I might as well have been in Chicago." Making films, she said, was like playing poker in the dark. Kim, who had a bawdy sense of humor, would have been delighted that in later years, her quote was transformed in the media echo chamber into "playing poke-in-the-dark."

In addition, there were too many cooks on *The Goddess*. Paddy Chayefsky had wanted to direct his own work, but Columbia didn't like that idea. So Chayefsky hired John Cromwell, a director who was capable, but sufficiently easygoing that Chayefsky could direct the film through him. And Steven Hill had his own ideas and wasn't hesitant about sharing them with Kim.

"Kim needed a strong hand," says Martin Landau. "But she had a director in Cromwell, a director in Paddy, and a director in Steve Hill. It was unsettling . . . I think Kim didn't want to hear it from a three-headed monster. She wanted to hear it from one director with certainty. She needed that father figure to tell her to do it." Betty Lou Holland, who plays Kim's mother in the film, recalls, "In the beginning, she and Steve Hill felt they weren't getting enough direction from John Cromwell, but she ended up loving John Cromwell. Apparently, her gripe was with Paddy."

After several days back at Gold Medal–Biograph in the Bronx, the company went to Hollywood for location shooting. In one scene, Rita Shawn, emotionally distraught, undergoes an intense, but ephemeral, conversion to Christianity by her mother, who was wild as a young woman and has since become a religious fundamentalist. The scene took place in Shawn's home, a large, modernistic house with a sliding roof over the living area, which had once belonged to Noah Dietrich, an associate of Howard Hughes. But it was the New York stage actresses, not the house, that impressed the crew members.

"The religious conversion scene is a fairly long one," Betty Lou Holland recalls. "When we did it the first time, we got applause from the Hollywood crew. We thought it had something to do with our acting. No! It was because we could remember all those lines." Also impressed was columnist Sidney Skolsky. After her brief conversion, Rita Shawn quickly abandons her newfound religion when she learns her mother isn't going to stay with her. Kim proceeds to unleash one of the most fearsome expressions of rage ever seen on camera. Skolsky, on the set, was looking forward to seeing Kim do the scene several times. But she got it perfectly in one take. "What's the movies coming to when an actress does it great on the first try?" he complained.

Kim, of course, was hard on herself. "I felt like an amateur in the movie medium," she told a reporter after principal photography was finished. "It was only in the last week that I began to feel as if I belonged."

Kim disliked Hollywood the place as well as the industry. "Hollywood is like a Hollywood movie," she said. "It's like when you are twelve years old and went to the movies and had fantasies about Hollywood. Well, it's a fantasy place with pink houses and weird architecture. It's charming, all right, but it's only for children." Kim's disdain for Hollywood left openings for other actresses capable of doing the wide-ranging, intense characterizations that were her trademark. Joanne Woodward, poolside on one occasion at the Chateau Marmont, said she was in Hollywood because she did the best Kim Stanley west of the Rockies.

During the film's post-production, Kim did pitch in on publicity. An article in Kim's hometown *Albuquerque Tribune* written by a Columbia publicist allowed her to burnish her personal mythmaking. She had majored in psychology at the University of Texas, she said, graduating in 1946. Even more remarkably, in another article, Kim claimed she was cool as a cucumber about going onstage. "Acting, she said, isn't as taxing to her as it appears to be to other actresses," the article claimed. But her stage phobia was already the stuff of Broadway legend.

The friction between Kim and Paddy, manageable at the film's outset, would worsen during production. "She's the greatest," Chayefsky told a reporter. "Difficult. Wants things her way, but compromises when she realizes her way isn't always best. She's terrific." His opinion would change as, according to Chayefsky biographer Sean Considine, open warfare broke out on the set between star and writer.

A reporter from the *New York Post* observed one scene where Kim was lighting a cigarette. Chayefsky repeatedly insisted, "Now remember, there should be a lot of smoke. I want more smoke." Kim, exasperated, insisted that she wouldn't perform unless he got off the set. Chayefsky left, but just as cameras were about to roll, he called out from a vantage point high above the scenery at Gold Medal–Biograph Studios, "Now remember, more smoke. More smoke!" Arthur Laurents recalls, "Paddy told me she banished him from the set, but he came on anyway, and she would say, 'I know you're there! I can see you—you're hiding. Get out!'"

Kim was not the only temperamental actor in the cast. Late in the film, Steven Hill as John Tower, her first husband, unsuccessfully tries to introduce Rita Shawn to the daughter she hasn't seen in years. "We had about twenty extras, which today sounds like nothing, but for the budget of that film was a big deal," recalls veteran publicist Johnny Friedkin. "Steve had to walk up two steps to a porch. But he wouldn't do it, because he wasn't motivated. Everybody was ready to kill him."

Principal photography on *The Goddess* finished in early September. Kim had a private screening at Columbia of the film's rough cut, arranged by Friedkin, who watched it with her. "She cried through the whole thing. She was such a perfectionist she was disappointed in herself," he says. "At the end, I said, 'Listen, I'm not a con artist. I say what I think. And I think you're great. It's one of the great performances I've seen.' And she was crying all the way through. I was like—how can I get up and crawl out of here?"

Producer Milton Perlman thought she was unhappy because the camera showed, especially when images were projected onto the big screen, that she wasn't a teenager anymore. Elizabeth Wilson, who plays Rita Shawn's assistant, acknowledges that "she was beginning to be a little bit on the heavy side."

Because of Kim's unhappiness, she decided not to help publicize the film. (A notable exception: a glamour spread she did for *McCalls Magazine* called "How to Pose for a Pin-Up Picture," in which she does an uncannily good job of simulating the allure of Marilyn Monroe.) In spite of the rider to her contract specifying she would help publicize *The Goddess,* she not only did not exert much effort to publicize the movie, she wasn't even in the country when it came out.

"Kim Stanley told Columbia Pictures that she 'hates' *The Goddess* and refuses . . . to help in publicizing it, even though it's an odds-on bet to bring her an Academy nomination," Walter Winchell reported. Kim told one reporter that the film looked like it was in its second week of rehearsals. "She doesn't give a damn for publicity," Johnny Friedkin said in an interview. "The whole thing is distasteful to her . . . She won't compromise with her own feelings and convictions."

She did talk briefly about *The Goddess* two months later, though, on November 18, when she gave an interview to Martin Agronsky of *Look Here,* a news-maker interview show airing Sunday afternoons on NBC. Guests on the show included cultural notables Aldous Huxley and Rod Serling, as well as Secretary of State John Foster Dulles, Cuban president Fulgencio Batista, and Senator John F. Kennedy of Massachusetts (then rumored to be interested in the 1960 Democratic Party nomination for President).

The show opens on an empty NBC soundstage. There's a sofa in the foreground; Kim appears from a door at the rear and walks out to meet

Agronsky, waiting for her at the sofa. She removes her coat, and Agronsky, like a gentleman, offers to put it away for her. Kim, in no mood for chivalry, ignores him and drapes the coat over the sofa herself.

She's wearing a blouse with a two-strand pearl necklace, a button-down dirndl skirt, and high heels. She looks a little heavy, is quiet and muted in her manner, somewhat uncomfortable and surprisingly plain: The overall effect is of someone who just stepped out of a secretarial pool. This prompted a writer in the *Albuquerque Tribune* to note, "The *Tribune*'s Howard Bryan interviewed Miss Stanley in Albuquerque recently and came back to the office with the words that she is really a glamorous girl who dresses strikingly. In the black and white Agronsky cameras, however, she doesn't come through that way. Perhaps it's done purposely to keep her in the serious-actress category. We'd like to see her in the Bryan version once."

Explaining to Agronsky how she builds a role, Kim speaks with delightful self-deprecation. "You have some ideas that you discard and are no good and you keep some that are no good that you should have discarded," she says, laughing. Agronsky wants to know about the metamorphosis actors undergo. "How do you become what you are not?" he asks. She thoughtfully replies, "We're not so different. We're all human beings."

But some of her comments are disquieting. "Applause are nice to hear. It's nice to be recognized as a person," she says, as if it were the person being applauded and not the work. She also seems to have trouble distinguishing herself from her characters.

"You are her [the character] to a large degree—or she is you, do you know what I mean?" Her voice drops to a whisper as she adds, "I don't know which—it's hard to tell." And talking about her role in *A Clearing in the Woods,* she says, "This girl tried to commit suicide every night. I mean, I tried to every night because I had to go to the theater every night."

In a premonition of her later disappearance from the stage, she says she doesn't want to go on acting for the rest of her life, because there are other things she wants to do, listing "family things" and reading and painting. Agronsky doesn't ask "And how do you expect to earn a living at these things, Miss Stanley?" but, this being the '50s, he may have assumed her husband would take care of that. The few questions about *The Goddess* had more to do with her breaking into movies than the film itself.

Commenting on the show, *Variety* alluded to the psychologically probing nature of Agronsky's questions. "Reclining on a couch, rather than sitting on one, would have been a more appropriate position for Kim Stanley," it said, adding that she had projected warmth and sincerity. Recalling her well-publicized remark calling theater critics "fatheads," it added with a hint of disappointment, "The result was less spectacular than some of the actress's previous interviews in which she's given legit critics a rough going over."

In mid-December, Kim prepared to sail to England to do the British premiere of *Cat on a Hot Tin Roof* in London's West End. But five days before she was to get on the *Queen Mary*, *The Goddess* rose up to vex her: Some of her lines hadn't come out clearly, and Chayefsky wanted her to redub them. She refused, saying she had to prepare for her trip. Chayefsky had an attorney send Kim a telegram threatening legal action; she responded with a letter, also drafted by a lawyer, politely telling Chayefsky's lawyer to go fly a kite. It appears, however, that Kim did find time to redub the lines before she sailed for England.

On December 17, with all three of her children and their nurse, but without Alfred Ryder, with whom she was apparently feuding, Kim sailed for England. She stayed in the Mayfair home of Alfred Lunt and Lynn Fontanne, although when that proved too expensive (forty pounds a week, no servants included), they moved to another place in South Kensington.

Where they did not stay—or even visit—was with Jinx Witherspoon, Kim's friend and sorority sister from the University of New Mexico, whose Upper West Side apartment had been her refuge when she was struggling off-Broadway. Now living in London, Witherspoon was married to George Rodger, the international photojournalist who cofounded the Magnum photo agency. "There was a big piece in the *Telegraph*," Witherspoon recalls. "I clipped it, wrote her a note, and said, 'I'm living in England. I'd love to see you. Come stay!' But I didn't get a reply." It was a pattern Kim would later repeat with increasing frequency.

Kim had been interested in playing Maggie the Cat since *Cat on a Hot Tin Roof* had opened in New York several weeks after *Bus Stop*, with Barbara Bel Geddes as Maggie. Tennessee Williams's tale of family intrigue on a large plantation in the Mississippi Delta revolved around Big Daddy, the patriarch, dying of cancer but not realizing it; a son, Gooper, and his wife, Mae, almost ready to push Big Daddy into his grave so they can take over; and Brick, the other son, and his wife, Maggie, who are at odds over Brick's alcoholism and homoerotic relationship with his now-dead friend Skipper. "Tennessee Williams was very keen on her and wanted her to do it," Sir Peter Hall, the play's director, recalls. "I met her in New York. We got along and she decided to come over and do it." Like Williams, Hall was impressed with his star.

"She had an enormous range," he says. "She was a very complete stage actress. That's not so common these days. She had a very fine, well-modulated voice. Her equipment was very strong. But she also had an ability to be extremely credible emotionally and let the audience in to what she was doing. She could play bitchy parts, difficult parts, neurotic women and yet break your heart, because you wanted to help her sort out her problems. That was her great achievement, I think, in *Cat.*"

Hall, whose career has spanned two generations and brought him into contact with the cream of British stage and screen actors, says Kim compares well with them. "I've worked with Olivier, Gielgud, Richardson, Evans, Ashcroft, Sellers, and Charles Laughton," he notes. "And I have to say she's one of the greatest actors I worked with of that regal collection." He adds, however, that Kim carried her perfectionism like a cross. "It's not enough to have talent in the theater," he says. "You have to have talent for handling the talent. And she couldn't, in some sense, handle her own talent. If it wasn't perfect, she suffered very much. She didn't accept compromise easily. It distressed her to a very great degree."

Cat also distressed British sensibilities of the late 1950s because it dealt with homosexuality. As a result, it was banned by the Lord Chamberlain's office. According to one unconfirmed report, the Lord Chamberlain had been willing to grant his seal of approval to *Cat* if the script were revised to say that Brick refused to have sex with Maggie because of the broken ankle he incurred while trying to run the high hurdles just before the play opens. No one connected with *Cat* was willing to do this, so it was produced by the New Watergate Theater Club. The club was a shell group set up by Hugh ("Binkie") Beaumont, head of

H.M. Tennent, Ltd., the British equivalent of the Shubert organization. It sold private subscriptions to the show, which technically was then not presented publically.

"The Lord Chamberlain was the head of the Queen's household," Sir Peter Hall explains. "In 1750 or thereabouts, he was also given the power to license plays so they shouldn't be abusive of politicians or immoral or seditious. This corrupt practice of censoring plays continued until 1968, when the Lord Chamberlain was abolished, thank God. I had many run-ins with the office. They were a collection of army and naval officers, retired, with excessively dirty minds. Their job was to find dirt, often where none existed.

"When I put on Samuel Beckett's *Endgame,*" he continues, "the line 'God, the bastard, he doesn't exist' was deleted by the Lord Chamberlain with a note saying he could not tolerate a play in which the legitimacy of the Almighty was called into question. *Cat on a Hot Tin Roof* was banned because it suggested that there might possibly be such a thing as homosexuality."

There were also repercussions for one cast member. Vanessa Petty, a slight-of-stature sixteen-year-old schoolgirl, played Trixie, one of the "no-neck-monster" children of Gooper and Mae who afflict Maggie. The headmistress of her school told her not to return to school if she took the part. (She took it anyway, got home tutoring during the play, and returned when *Cat* ended.) "I don't know what the fuss is all about," the British schoolgirl said in an interview, showing more aplomb than some of her elders. "I don't find the play in the least shocking."

When *Cat* opened at the Comedy Theatre on January 30, 1958, it starred Kim as Maggie the Cat, with twenty-five-year-old Canadian actor Paul Massie as Brick and Leo McKern as Big Daddy. Renee Houston had been scheduled to play Big Mama, but at the last minute decided to do an Alec Guinness film instead and was replaced by Bee Duffell. Daphne Anderson played Mae, and Alan Tilvern was Gooper.

A distinctive aspect of the production was its third act. When *Cat* had its world premiere on Broadway in 1955, director Elia Kazan, unsatisfied with Tennessee Williams's original third act, prevailed upon him to write a new one. As a result, Big Daddy remains onstage to dominate much of the third act, and the play ends on an optimistic note, with Maggie asking Brick just before the curtain comes down, "Nothing's more determined than a cat on a hot tin roof—is there? Is there, baby?" But in the London third act, Big Daddy doesn't reappear, and the play ends with Maggie saying, "I do love you, Brick. I do!" "Wouldn't it be funny if that was true?" he sardonically responds, echoing the same doubt Big Daddy expresses earlier in the play about Big Mama's protestation of her affections for him.

There's a poetic quality to the London third act which the New York third act lacks, and its final scene as performed in London feels like the real one. On the other hand, it's nice to have Big Daddy in the third act, so Maggie can make her announcement to him about supposedly being pregnant. Also, Gooper and Mae are more thoroughly humiliated when Big Daddy himself discovers how eager they are to have him out of the way. Both third acts have their strong points.

Tennessee Williams later wrote, "I had to violate my own intuition by having Big Daddy re-enter the stage in Act Three. I saw nothing for him to do in that act and did not think . . . it was dramatically proper that he should re-enter." Kazan, for his part, wrote, "I thought the third act was by far the weakest of the three . . . I suggested that Big Daddy be brought back, a suggestion that had nothing to do with making the play more commercial."

In New York, the dominant and imposing Kazan prevailed upon Williams, as he frequently tried to do with others. For years, he and fellow Actors Studio cofounder Cheryl Crawford ate lunch at a Greek deli in midtown Manhattan. Crawford always asked him not to order dishes for her with feta cheese; he always did, perhaps thinking he could get her to develop a taste for it. Although the New York ending has become the standard one, Williams never developed a taste for it any more than Cheryl Crawford did for feta cheese.

Because of its use of Williams's original last act, one London critic described the production as "one third of a world premiere." In the *Illustrated London News*, J.C. Trewin wrote, "I am happier with the third act we have at the Comedy than with that played in New York when Big Daddy . . . reappeared to tell the [ribald] 'elephant story.'" And

Kenneth Tynan, writing in the *Observer*, said, "I still prefer the author's third act to the modified version approved by Mr. Kazan." This sentiment was not universal, though: W.A. Darlington of the *Daily Telegraph* voted for the Broadway version. "When [Big Daddy] is on stage, roaring and bullying . . . the play seems vastly worthwhile," he wrote. "Without him, the last act . . . has little significance."

Reviews for the play were mixed. The *News-Chronicle* called it "Tennessee Williams' most enthralling play." The *Daily Mail* said "it struck London last night like a whiplash across the face," and the *Manchester Guardian* called it "an evening of many powerful moments." But the primal passions of the play put off some critics. The *Sunday Times* complained, "In *Cat on a Hot Tin Roof*, there is no sanity. No important character in it is wholly sane." The *Times of London* said the play was not moving because the characters behaved with such animal ferocity that they ceased to resemble human beings. Another reviewer called it "a[n] hysterical erotic hotpot of bedroom life in a human zoo" and "the latest example of the American passion for abnormality among the inarticulate."

Kim's notices were largely enthusiastic, though. In the *Daily Telegraph*, W.A. Darlington said she gave an impression of stretched nerves and was refreshingly American (writing for the *New York Times*, though, he said she was "pretty good, but does nothing to modify, let alone efface, one's memory of Barbara Bel Geddes"). Other critics called her performance "[one] of great authority and some pathos" and "extremely intelligent," with one saying, "Only Kim Stanley is exactly right." She had her detractors, though: In the *Tatler*, Anthony Cookman said, "Miss Kim Stanley, the gifted Broadway actress, may possibly be a little to blame for the slowness of the first act . . . She has the proper anxious air of a hurt wife but hardly the shameless sinuous tenacity of the Cat." In an allusion to the infamous Method pauses, he adds, "Her interpretation possibly is one that requires some of the long pauses that Mr. Hall arranges for it." And Derek Monsey in the *Sunday Express* called Kim's Maggie "an artificial, tricksy performance."

That wasn't how the play's writer or director felt: In a letter to Maria St. Just, Tennessee Williams wrote, "I feel I ought to be on hand to supervise this production as I am not happy over the reports I've heard, excepting Kim Stanley." And Sir Peter Hall says Kim took a back seat to no one. "Barbara Bel Geddes was excellent," he says. "However, Kim was sexier, more vulnerable, and funnier." And he feels she was funnier than Elizabeth Taylor in the film version. Taylor, in London at the time with then-husband Michael Todd, came backstage to see Kim. "She was charming," Kim later recalled. "She said, 'When I do [the film version], I'm going to steal some things.' I said, 'Go ahead. Be my guest. We all do.'"

Kim did not feel so collegial toward her co-star Paul Massie. A year later, Kim's agent Lucy Kroll spoke with Helen Hayes about a conversation Hayes had had with Hugh Beaumont, producer of the London *Cat*. "Most horrendous time," Kroll's notes indicate. "[Kim] would not take it to Paul Massie . . . crush on him . . . played a few weeks . . . Kim stopped speaking to him . . . tried to get Binkie to fire him . . . Binkie said he would not fight with her . . . Massie crying . . . in dread of going on stage."

Shortly before Kim opened in *Cat,* Lucy Kroll had good news for her: She had just won the Sylvania Award, on a prestige par with an Emmy, for her performance in the *Studio One* version of *The Traveling Lady.* At the awards presentation, master of ceremonies Don Ameche said, "It was difficult for the panel of judges to give the award to this actress as she had very strong competition: Her runner-ups were Kim Stanley in *The Glass Wall* and Kim Stanley in *Clash by Night.*" He then announced Kim as the winner.

Well aware of Kim's femme fatale nature, Kroll, who was her friend as well as agent, wrote after a transatlantic phone call between them, "I have passed on your love to Nathan [Kroll's husband] but not your kiss." She also kidded Kim about her headstrong older daughter: "I suspect she'll be presented to the Queen very soon if I know my Lisa." In that letter, she marks the first known appearance in Kim's personal life of New York corporate attorney Joseph Siegel, whom Kim would eventually marry. "I was at the opening of Beckett's *Endgame* and sat right next to that nice Joe Siegel," Kroll wrote. "He made me jealous by saying that you had been writing to him."

Cat ran for 132 performances, closing on May 25, 1958. After it finished in the West End, it had a two-week run in Liverpool. The audience lacked the polish of Broadway or the West End, but Kim took to them. "They talk to you as a character," she later said. "'Maggie, don't do that!' Or, if you're doing something they approve of, 'That's right!'"

O N APRIL 16, her debut film was released and Kim sent Lucy Kroll an anxious telegram on April 25 asking how *The Goddess* was doing. The news wasn't good. In February, while Kim was still in London doing *Cat*, Harry Cohn had died. Kim did not mourn the vulgar autocrat of Columbia who had been so rude to her while she was trying to land the part of Alma in *From Here to Eternity*. But his death, coupled with that of his brother Jack the year before, left Columbia adrift. Blockbusters like *Bridge on the River Kwai* did well, while a film like *The Goddess,* which needed help finding its audience, did not.

Unhappy with *The Goddess*, which it thought sounded like a classical drama, the marketing department at Columbia thought about substituting a comical range of new titles for it, including "Love Me a Little," "Love Me a Lot," "The Beautiful Nothing," "Shoot for the Stars," "One Sin," "Her Sin," and "My Sin." Although the film opened nationally on April 16, 1958, it didn't open in New York until June 25, and not in a large Broadway or downtown theater, but at the Fifty-fifth Street Playhouse, a 253-seat theater normally reserved for art films. (Ironically, it was Chayefsky who had insisted on identifying *The Goddess* as an art film.)

One thing that made *The Goddess* difficult to market was its humorless, claustrophobic, and didactic nature. Although Paddy Chayefsky was a genius, all of his worst traits as a writer are showcased in this film: portentousness, pseudo-psychiatric blather, and preachy dialogue. Young Emily Ann Faulkner whines at one point, "I don't expect you can understand the shame and degradation a girl feels when she's not invited to a Sweet Sixteen Party." Similarly, Steven Hill as John Tower, Rita Shawn's first husband, tells her, "You don't know what loneliness is—you don't know the great ultimate ache of desolation." There's also an unintentional howler when a film studio executive introduces Rita Shawn to another exec: "Rita, I don't have to tell you who this is. This is R.W. Luray, one of our vice presidents."

But whatever the film's shortcomings, Kim's performance is extraordinary. Michael Morrison, who studied acting with Kim and later became an acting teacher himself, always shows his classes the scene where Kim, as a high school girl, goes for a ride with rich boy Burt Brinckerhoff. "Very few times does the camera cut away from her or take the scene from different angles," he says. "Her character has to go through a rainbow of emotional revelations with little help from her co-star. We see her anger, desperation, vulnerability, obsession, self-loathing, eagerness, and shame, all within a few lines of dialogue. It's a moment that reveals the entire life of the character within her."

After Rita Shawn has her nervous breakdown in Hollywood, her mother, who has temporarily come out to help her, tells her she's leaving, something the troubled star does not want to hear. As Kim anxiously listens to the bad news, she moves her fingers toward her lips in a typical gesture of concentration. But then she opens her mouth and her face starts to contort into a barely concealed mask of rage. She sticks a few fingers in her mouth as if she were going to start chewing on them, her whole body trembles and a fleeting look of sadness and resignation comes across her face. It's a short reaction shot, no more than three or four seconds, but you feel wrung out by the end of it.

Shortly afterwards, Kim's rage as her character's mother (Betty Lou Holland) leaves the house and gets into the cab is like an exploding volcano. "NOTHING I do pleases you, does it? Nothin' I ever did pleases you!" (It's easy to imagine Kim thinking about J.T. as she spit those lines out.) At the start of one scene, Kim asked Marie Kenny, the film's continuity supervisor, where her hands were supposed to be. Kenny, dazzled by Kim's acting, momentarily didn't know what Kim was talking about.

Some critics liked the film, notably Bosley Crowther of the *New York Times*, who wrote, "Get set for heartbreak at this one . . . Evidently, Mr. Chayefsky has studied this subject thoughtfully, for the meshing of human contacts and emotional relations is clear and sound. Furthermore, he has conveyed them in finely written scenes and dialogue." But Wanda Hale, in the *New York Daily News*, called it "a morbid drama unrelieved by one iota of lightness or humor." And the *New Yorker*'s John McCarter said, "She [Rita Shawn] seldom shuts her mouth and the things she has to say are of no particular moment." Although *The Goddess* was promoted as a lacerating portrayal of Hollywood, one critic was unkind enough to note that, given the lack of filmmaking and sense of Hollywood as a place in the film, it could have been about a "harassed heroine" in just about any field of endeavor. Once again, though, Kim received superlatives for her performance. But because of her publicity recalcitrance, there was no Oscar nomination.

The Goddess did receive a few honors. Most notably, the Motion Picture Export Association chose it, along with *The Old Man and the Sea,* to be shown at an international film festival in Brussels, where it won a special jury prize for exceptional qualities. But it won no honors at the box office. About sixty-five American films released in 1958 grossed $1 million or more; *The Goddess* was not one of them.

Kim's attitude toward her first film role, initially enthusiastic, soured quickly. As filming began, she had said that in places, the character delineation was like Eugene O'Neill. When *The Goddess* came out, though, she expressed disappointment that the lighter moments had been cut. And interviewed three years after it was released, she said, "It was a great script, but it didn't turn out well . . . When I saw the picture, I thought, 'If that girl cries once more, I'll shoot her.'"

No interviewer seems to have asked her, nor does she appear to have reflected, on the similarities between herself and Rita Shawn. In her review of *The Goddess,* Wanda Hale of the *New York Daily News* writes:

> Kim Stanley . . . gives a frenzied portrayal of a little Southern tramp who becomes a Hollywood glamor queen and remains a tramp. The mixed-up girl is ever bedeviled by loneliness and insecurity, drowning her phobias in alcohol, living with a self-destruction compulsion, trying marriage twice . . .

Kim sustained close ties to most of her husbands, even after divorce, but many of these unflattering characteristics apply to her as well as Rita Shawn. *The Goddess* is a film about Kim's childhood as she imagined it and her adulthood as she lived it. Even choosing it as her debut film speaks to self-sabotage, as she turned down better vehicles like *Marty, The Rainmaker,* and *Summer and Smoke.*

N LATE JULY, Kim returned briefly to England to do a third version of Horton Foote's *The Traveling Lady* for ABC-TV, a regional affiliate of Britain's ITV Network. Denholm Elliott played her husband in the broadcast, which aired on July 27.

Interviewed by a British reporter as part of the show's publicity build-up, Kim chain-smoked nervously. She called Foote one of the few Southern writers with a tender quality, adding, "Every time I play Georgette, I discover something new in her. She's so full of real basic goodness." (Kim's insights into her character and the play had an effect on co-star Denholm Elliott. "At first, my part in *Traveling Lady* did not appear to have any special significance," he said in an interview, "but since rehearsing it with Kim Stanley, it has grown on me. The theme is so slight that the profoundness of the play dawns only gradually upon one.")

As was her habit, Kim indulged in some embroidering of her past, telling the interviewer she had earned a degree in psychology with the intent of becoming a social worker, but never worked as one because she became too emotionally involved in the cases. Discussing her early struggles to establish herself as an actress in New York, Kim also showed an ability to adapt to local slang. "I thought it was going to be all skittles," she said, referring to a British pub game similar to bowling, "but I didn't work for two and a half years." No kinescope of this show remains, which is unfortunate, as Kim later told Foote she thought it was the best version of it.

While Kim was still in London doing *Cat,* she was visited by Harold Clurman, who brought a script of the next Broadway play he was going to direct, Eugene O'Neill's *A Touch of the Poet.* Kim read it and was intrigued by the role of Sara Melody, the headstrong daughter of Cornelius "Con" Melody, a disgraced former Irish military officer who runs a down-at-the-heels tavern outside Boston in the 1820s.

As Kim and Clurman were in a taxi going through Piccadilly Circus, she asked him who was going to play Sara.

"Are you interested?" Clurman asked.

"Yes."

"You are."

A Touch of the Poet would reunite Kim with Clurman and Robert Whitehead, the team that had staged *Bus Stop.* They had hoped to get production rights for *Long Day's Journey into Night,* but Carlotta Monterey, O'Neill's widow, infuriated Whitehead by granting production rights to Jose Quintero, even though Whitehead had been the first to ask and had already done a successful revival of *Desire Under the Elms.* As a consolation prize, she granted Whitehead rights to the American premiere of *A Touch of the Poet.*

Mrs. O'Neill would prove a difficult collaborator: When the play went into rehearsal, she warned Whitehead and Clurman not to cut a line, or even a word. And she would know: The play had a part written for her, and she had typed it four times. Clurman promptly cut half an hour from it. When Monterey called Robert Whitehead to complain about cuts, the canny producer asked her what was missing. She gave several examples, but in each case Whitehead assured her the material was still there. As Clurman later recalled, O'Neill had repeated everything ten times, so even with five or six repetitions removed, everything was "still there."

The British actor Eric Portman was chosen to play Cornelius Melody, Sara Melody's father. Pretending to be an ex-nobleman, he spends more time carousing with so-called friends and hangers-on (including Kim's ex-husband Curt Conway as Jamie Cregan) than running his tavern on the outskirts of early nineteenth-century Boston. Helen Hayes was cast as Nora Melody, Sara's mother, browbeaten by the arrogant and disdainful Con Melody, but still in love with him. Betty Field played Deborah, the aristocratic mother of Kim's unseen love interest (a Henry David Thoreau–like figure named Simon), who shows up at the tavern one day to learn more about her prospective daughter-in-law and her family. Following a brawl with Deborah's husband, Con Melody finds a measure of peace of mind by abandoning his claims to nobility and accepting the egalitarian nature of his new country.

In a letter to Kim, in London working on *Cat,* Lucy Kroll waxed enthusiastic about *A Touch of the Poet.* "Bob [Whitehead] was really jubilant. I can't tell you how Helen sits by the hour just dreaming of the privilege of working with you. And Bob has communicated Portman's great excitement and delirious joy [at the prospect of] working with you." Even allowing for a certain amount of ego-fluffing blarney here, both Hayes and Portman did make financial concessions to get Kim into the play, giving up 2 ½ percent of their 10-percent stakes in the show to make Kim's 5-percent stake possible.

Before she started rehearsals for *A Touch of the Poet,* though, Kim had important personal business to attend to. She had gone to London to do *Cat* without Alfred Ryder because of problems between them. But now, those problems were smoothed out, and on August 2, 1958, she married him in a Jewish ceremony at Riverdale Temple in the Bronx. Alfred Corn (aka Alfred Ryder) and Patricia Beth Reid (aka Kim Stanley) were joined in marriage by Rabbi Charles E. Schulman.

In preparation for her marriage, Kim apparently converted to Judaism, but her daughter Rachel, herself a reconstructionist Jew, does not remember her mother as the most devout of Jews. "I don't recall ever being inside a synagogue with my mother," she laughs. "She talked about it a lot. For some reason, she decided that Judaism is the only organized religion that was worthwhile. However, that did not translate into practice. She noted holidays like Hanukah and Passover, but I don't recall that Rosh Hashanah or Yom Kippur were ever observed in our household."

After the wedding, a reception for the newlyweds was held at Janice Rule's Manhattan apartment. Lee Strasberg, Harold Clurman, and other leading lights of the New York theater world were there, as was Eva Klein, Kim's psychiatrist. "She came up to me and said, 'How could you be so mean to Kim (in *The Goddess*)?'" Betty Lou Holland recalls. "I hope she was joking, but it really didn't seem so."

Four days later, rehearsals for *A Touch of the Poet* began in New York's Bijou Theatre. Old-school Helen Hayes was put off by the eloquent Method director Clurman, whom she came to regard as an erudite blabbermouth. "He talked too much," she later wrote. "After listening for several days to his explanations of why O'Neill had written this or that, or what was suggested in some character's subtext, I grew impatient. His analyses may have been brilliant, but he was conducting a college seminar, not a rehearsal." Eric Portman, who shared her concerns, frequently refused to accept direction from Clurman, putting him in the humiliating position of having to "direct" Portman by passing notes to him through Whitehead, the stage manager, or others.

As for Kim, Hayes wrote, she "drove herself mercilessly to discover 'the dramatic truth' of whatever character she portrayed," adding sardonically, "if she couldn't find the truth, the fault had to be the playwright's, not hers." On one occasion, Kim had trouble because a line had the word "cute" in it. She had never used that word in her life, Kim said. Plus it wasn't used back then. Rehearsal was suspended so a dictionary could be found. It turned out that "cute" was common back then (and in Irish slang as well), but Clurman allowed Kim to drop the word, which offended Hayes, who believed the text should be respected, especially when written by someone like O'Neill.

A Touch of the Poet opened in New Haven on September 6 and in Boston ten days later. In a sign of looming trouble, Kim complained to Robert Whitehead that Eric Portman was striking her too hard in one scene where, angry at his daughter's defiance, Con Melody slaps Sara. "Bob Whitehead . . . promised me out of town that Eric Portman would be replaced," Kim later said, "because Eric was beating me up onstage. It's not in the script." It's unlikely that Whitehead made such a promise, and it *is* in the script: In O'Neill's stage instruction, Con Melody gives Sara more of a playful push than a slap, but it knocks her off-balance.

Boston critics were enthusiastic, with the *Boston American* noting, "A brilliant cast was recalled again and again by a wildly enthusiastic audience," while the *Boston Traveler* called it "a production long to be remembered." One critic complained that Portman was not enunciating his lines clearly, but there were no such complaints about Kim. Elliot Norton, the dean of Boston critics, singled out her performance.

"Whatever happens in New York to *A Touch of the Poet,* it will bring new prestige to Kim Stanley," he wrote in the *Boston Daily Record.* "Playing with Helen Hayes, Eric Portman and Betty Field in an all-star production, she is working with the best. From now on, she must be ranked with the best. She can do anything any of the older stars can do, and much that is beyond their reach," adding with unintentional prescience, "Nothing but misfortune can keep her from whatever glory a stage career can bring."

Although not always eager to immerse herself in the publicity process, Kim provided one interviewer with a quote that was somewhat racy by the standards of 1950s family newspapers. "When we first opened out of town, I didn't even know what Simon looked like," she said of her unseen fiancé. "Now I see him vividly. I know how he talks and just where he touches me."

When *A Touch of the Poet* opened on Broadway October 2, 1958, it was the first time Helen Hayes had appeared in the theater which had just been named after her. Reviews followed the largely enthusiastic vein of Boston. "The effect . . . is electric," Brooks Atkinson wrote in the *New York Times*. "O'Neill used to feel that his dramas seldom or never had the force on the stage that he had imagined when he wrote them. If he could have seen the stunning performance that Harold Clurman has directed, it is possible that for once he might have been satisfied." Robert Coleman of the *Daily Mirror* called it "magnificent," "a masterpiece," and one of O'Neill's best plays, saying it had a heart that many of them lacked.

Critics were tougher on O'Neill than the performers. John Chapman of the *Daily News* said the play was not great O'Neill like *The Iceman Cometh* (although he felt it still made much contemporary theater look pallid), Richard Watts of the *New York Post* said that with a running time of just under three hours, it was one of O'Neill's mastodonic dramas (and this was after Clurman's cuts), while John McClain of the *Journal-American* didn't care for the characters, calling Con Melody an impossible fake and a bore, his wife just plain stupid, and his daughter humorless and nagging.

While Eric Portman got his share of good reviews (Herbert Whittaker of the *Herald-Tribune* called his performance "the core of the production"), he drew more critical fire than any of the play's principals, mainly for his failure to speak clearly. Kim and Hayes, on the other hand, took home the lion's share of the laurels. Brooks Atkinson wrote:

> *A Touch of the Poet* brings us the two finest actresses of their respective generations . . . Miss Hayes' genius . . . has been happily familiar for years . . . Nor does Miss Stanley's vividness of communication come as a surprise. She has been a fresh and creative actress for a number of seasons. But the fullness of her characterization, the tempestuousness of her emotions, the inte-

rior life of the character as well as its external expression represent Miss Stanley well on into an extraordinary career.

Atkinson was especially taken with one scene between Kim and Hayes late in the play. Sara Melody has just had her first sexual experience with her unseen fiancé, but her mother, preoccupied by her husband's having gone into town to get into a brawl with the fiancé's father, barely notices what her daughter is telling her. "Miss Hayes and Miss Stanley have made [the scene] a classic," Atkinson wrote. "Mother and daughter alone in the night in the dining room of the inn, drawn together, absorbed by each other, yet thinking different thoughts—it is a scene that is alive, profound and unforgettable." Kim also received high praise from a son of the auld sod. Writing in the *Irish Echo,* Edward L. Brennan said, "Although not of Irish parentage, Kim Stanley gives what I consider this season's outstanding performance."

A Touch of the Poet brought Kim the first of her two Tony nominations and an ANTA Award. In newspaper photos of her with co-ANTA-award winner Jason Robards, she throws her head back and laughs so heartily you can practically see her dental work. That creative satisfaction was fleeting, though: Asked after the play closed if she thought she had done well in any of her roles, the perfectionist Kim told a reporter, "I gave three performances in *A Touch of the Poet* that were quite good." The article noted she had given 180 performances in the role.

Another person who wasn't impressed was Kim's older daughter Lisa. Seeing that her mother's part was much bigger than her father's and unaware that she had probably helped him get it, the seven-year-old detected parental hypocrisy. "You tell Jamie and me to share," she said unhappily, "but you don't share!" Kim, delighted with her daughter's misguided precocity, explained that it was the playwright's decision, not hers.

KIM WOULD SOON FIND HERSELF embroiled in a bigger and more public controversy regarding her younger daughter. On December 29, she filed papers with the State Supreme Court of New York in Manhattan to have Laurie Rachel Conway renamed Laurie Rachel Ryder to reflect that Alfred Ryder was her father. Ordinarily, paternity cases are not a matter of public record, but word somehow leaked out and a tabloid scandal ensued. Page one of the *Daily News* for December 30, 1958, consisted of a blaring, three-deck headline, "Kim Stanley Files to Name Daughter's Dad," along with a picture of Kim and Alfred Ryder at their wedding. An article in the *Daily Mirror* began, "Kim Stanley, whose high-voltage emoting in Eugene O'Neill's *A Touch of the Poet* won her critical kudos . . . starred yesterday in [a] surprise four-character legal drama." There was also coverage in the *New York Post* and other New York City tabloids.

In her filing, Kim asked the court to approve the issuance of a new birth certificate changing her daughter's name from "Laurie Rachel Conway" to "Laurie Rachel Ryder" and identifying Alfred Ryder as her father. Ryder acknowledged paternity in an affidavit that accompanied Kim's petition.

At the time, Kim refused public comment on the matter. But several months later, in an interview with Robert Wahls of the *Daily News,* she said, "It was the only honest thing to do under the circumstances. I love my children more than anything else in the world. And I had no thought of hurting any one of them. Not to establish paternity would have been unfair to the child." This is a noble sentiment, but in light of the fact that Kim wouldn't tell Jamie who his father was until he was almost fifteen, it's also quite audacious.

As happened on *Bus Stop,* Kim would develop an allergy to the long-running *A Touch of the Poet.* Almost from the start of the show, she started calling in sick. On November 25, Lucy Kroll wrote to Robert Whitehead, telling him that because of a bad cold, Kim had played the last five weeks with a hacking cough and a viral infection that were difficult to cure because of the intense nature of her role and drafty conditions backstage and in her dressing room.

While Kim customarily realized that she was ill before show time, on one occasion she felt the onset of her virus just before her big scene with Helen Hayes. This resulted in Hayes being left alone onstage, with Kim's understudy, Nancy Malone, having to scurry out and pick up the role on the spot. By March of 1959, Kim had been out of the show thirty-one times. Early in the show's run, whenever Kim was absent, Eric Portman would ask her upon her return, "Feeling better?" We don't know if his tone of voice was solicitous or sardonic, but this is when Kim stopped speaking to him.

Her anger at Portman, who played her father, was another source of her unhappiness. Robert Whitehead later recalled that Portman was not an easy man to get along with. "Eric Portman was very difficult to work with, very temperamental," he said. "He could go into spasms of criticism, which would be brutal and true. He was quite deadly in the way he could take apart some situation onstage and make whoever was involved feel like shooting themselves.

"He wasn't a darling companion. But he was a very talented actor," Whitehead continued. "His qualities for the part were better than anybody who ever played it. He had the Black Irish anger in him. He also had a truthfulness that was devastating onstage."

Alcohol fueled the feud between Kim and Portman: "He accused her of drinking and she accused him of drinking," Whitehead added, taking a plague-on-both-their-houses stance, "and they were both right." (This is confirmed by Patricia Frye, the second wife of Kim's brother Justin. While abidingly fond of her sister-in-law, she remembers Kim keeping a pint-size silver flask of vodka in her purse while working on the play.)

On March 4, Whitehead arranged a backstage meeting between Kim and Portman. When it failed to reconcile them, Kim decided to leave the play. (Oddly, she also told Lucy Kroll that she wanted to declare bankruptcy, although it's unclear why: Her income, while erratic, had been considerable: $54,900 in 1955, $23,400 in 1956, and $64,800 in 1957. That was real money in the 1950s.) Ordinarily, Kim's desire to bolt the show would have been a serious problem, as her contract ran until June of 1959. But Whitehead, ever the gentleman producer, graciously allowed her to leave, despite the financial hit he would take as a result. Everything seemed prepared for Kim's smooth exit: On March 12, Whitehead told Lucy Kroll he would accept Kim's resignation from the show on the grounds of health problems. Furthermore, he would not press charges against her with Actors Equity.

But later that day, Kim decided that she would not accept illness as a cause for leaving the show. Instead, she was going to call the newspapers and Actors Equity to air her complaints about Portman. At 11:30 A.M. the next day, Friday the 13th, a disturbed Whitehead called Kroll, saying Kim had told him she was feeling fine and not ill in the least. It would be difficult to protect Kim if she wouldn't protect herself, he said. Later in the day, Whitehead spoke with Kroll again, saying he was sympathetic to Kim, although he noted her pattern of leaving shows, which he called "a goddamn shame." He said that Portman had her feeling down, calling him ruthless, intelligent, and subhuman.

True to her word, Kim gave a statement to entertainment reporter Louis Calta of the *New York Times* a week later, just as she was about to exit the show. Calta felt Kim's remarks were so libelous they could not be printed as is. While checking with the city desk to see what he could use, he was scooped by the *New York Post,* which provided the overture to a media circus that ran for several weeks. "Kim Stanley's Exit: A Touch of Mystery" ran in the *Post* on Saturday, March 21. In it, Kim blasted the play's tense backstage atmosphere, but, tantalizingly, didn't identify whom she felt was the source of the trouble.

All weekend there was a buzz of speculation along Broadway as to who Kim had in mind: Portman or Helen Hayes. As the tabloid scandal unfolded, each of the three great actors cast themselves in what they felt was their strongest role: Portman, whose spirit was as dark and malevolent as any "Black" Irishman, would play the perfect and slightly puzzled English gentleman; Hayes, formidable to the point of ferocity, would portray herself as a gray-tinged Mary Pickford; and Kim, who would sooner be eaten alive by a pack of wild dogs than serve out her contract in a long-running play, said she was leaving because the play wasn't up to her artistic standards.

On Monday, March 23, the *New York Times* reported, "Shubert Alley's most puzzling mystery of the season was solved last night when Kim Stanley named Eric Portman as the main reason for her quitting." In the *Journal-American,* Kim said, "Mr. Portman's behavior had annoyed me to the point of distraction. And the general artistic atmosphere of the play . . . Well, I have just had enough."

The main charge Kim lodged against Portman was that he routinely slapped her too hard. "There's one scene where he slaps me," she told the *Daily Mirror.* "Now any senior in a dramatic class knows how to hit another actor without hurting him. Mr. Portman is too good an actor not to know that. But he would slap me so hard tears would come to my eyes, and I often found it difficult to finish the scene . . . I had two wisdom teeth aggravated by the constant slapping and irritation." *Mirror* reporter Sidney Fields told her that under the circumstances, the thing to do would have been to file charges against Portman with Actors Equity. Kim replied that neither producer Whitehead nor director Clurman would do that. But it's something Kim could have done herself.

This is not to deny that Portman may have struck her too hard. Asked to assess the probability years later, Whitehead said, "He possibly did. He did spontaneous things that drove everybody crazy." Portman's response to Kim's charges consisted of elaborately polite denials. "I am very sorry for Miss Stanley," he told the *Journal-American.* "She must have a slightly remorseful feeling about all this. She must have been very tired to make such a statement [saying he was the reason she was leaving the play]." Asked specifically about whether he had slapped Kim too hard, he angrily protested, "I don't go bashing people in the face. It's outrageous to suggest that I did." *Time* magazine called it "Broadway's most spectacular feline feud in years."

Although Kim directed the brunt of her wrath at Portman, Helen Hayes was also drawn into the media maelstrom. When the first *New York Post* article hit the newsstands with Kim attacking an unnamed co-star, speculation swirled about Hayes as well as Portman. On Sunday, March 22, as she left for her vacation home in Cuernavaca, Mexico, Hayes issued a denial that she was the target of Kim's barbs.

"There have never been any differences between us," she told the *New York Times,* not realizing Kim was going to clear up the mystery later in the day. "We have worked together with the greatest understanding and sympathy. I am an innocent bystander in this thing and I am distressed at these reports." She added that Kim had some kind of emotional upset, but that it had nothing to do with her. Kim then denied that she had had any emotional upset, adding that Hayes had said what she did in an effort to protect everyone in the cast.

Once Hayes was drawn into the mess, her friends jumped in as well.

"Portman was just a red herring," a friend of hers told *Time* magazine. "The trouble was between Kim and Helen." In one case, Kim supposedly told Hayes that she didn't want to be touched during their intimate mother-daughter scene. Other times, Kim was supposedly too tactile, with Hayes telling a friend, "I've got two elbows down my throat from the girl." On one occasion, Kim didn't respond to Hayes, going so far as to keep her eyes closed. When Hayes complained, according to the backstage grapevine, Kim said she couldn't stand opening her eyes as she couldn't endure seeing Miss Hayes. If Kim did say that, Hayes probably gave as good as she got: It was her name on the theater, and she had more box-office draw than either Kim or Portman. "Probably there were a few evenings when Helen expressed herself," Robert Whitehead said later, "because Helen was very clear-minded."

On March 21, Hayes called Lucy Kroll at home in the fashionable Apthorp Apartments on Manhattan's Upper West Side and had no trouble expressing herself, as Kroll's notes indicate: "Cover-up for Kim . . . vicious woman . . . killed all my laughs . . . only once . . . did Helen show irritation at her behavior . . . she [Kim] is self-centered and inhuman person."

Kroll's husband, Nathan, was so furious with family friend Hayes that he promptly sat down and wrote her a scathing letter. "Frankly I am in a rage," he said. "Not being omnipotent, Lucy cannot control willful personalities any more than she can control inept press agents. I don't know what you said to Lucy at noon today or what she said to you, [but] her hurt as she left the house after your call was more than I could watch." Robert Whitehead also felt the lash of Hayes's tongue. "She blamed me for not keeping order backstage," he later recalled. "I'd done three plays with Helen and we had a very deep affection for one another. [But] she said, 'You're a rotten producer' and really went after me."

Although she couldn't stand Kim, Hayes did express admiration for her in an April 22 letter to the editor of *Variety*. "Nothing will wipe out the memory of those early months of our run and the all-too-rare thrill of working with a perfect actress," Hayes wrote. "I had some of the happiest and most glowing moments of a long career playing with Kim."

She added, however, that it hadn't all been a bed of roses. "[T]here were times, late in the run, when Kim would have tried the patience of a saint with her striving for opening [an] opening-night level of perform-ance—even on rainy Thursdays." Later informed of Hayes's comments, Kim shot back, "I would never want to go back and repeat it as on open-ing night. I'd expect it to be better."

More than one writer called Kim's exit from the play Brando-esque. "Is Kim deliberately trying to be a female Marlon Brando?" asked Robert Wahls of the *Daily News*. "Does she lack the emotional maturi-ty to handle the responsibilities of stardom?" And one writer used Medusa-like imagery to describe her, saying, "Miss Stanley stomped out of *A Touch of the Poet*, sultry lightning in her eyes, her blonde locks writhing like snakes."

With Kim out of the play, the question turned to her replacement, but even here *A Touch of the Poet* was snakebit. Understudy Nancy Malone had gone on for Kim more than thirty times and knew the role cold. Whitehead offered to triple her salary, from $150 a week to $450 a week. But Malone refused, holding out for $500.

Considering her age (twenty-four) and the fact that she did not have much Broadway experience (two plays), Whitehead told a reporter, "I think the offer is eminently fair." But Malone wasn't having any. "Actors have been mistreated for a long time," she said. "I've decided not to lose any more dignity." Lucy Kroll came down on Whitehead's side, scribbling after a conversation with him, "Nancy not a genius."

Cloris Leachman was hired to replace Kim as Sara Melody. Although old Broadway hands speculated the controversy would be good for busi-ness, the opposite proved true: Everyone was exhausted by the mess, and the show, which probably would have run longer otherwise, closed on June 13, 1959.

FOLLOWING THE STURM UND DRANG of *A Touch of the Poet*, Kim decided to take a year off from acting. Her resolve evaporated, though, while vacationing in the summer of 1959 at a lake near Lovell, Maine, with husband Alfred Ryder and the children. Robert Lewis sent her the script of a play he was to direct that fall, *Cheri*, based on two novellas by Colette, and Kim found it irresistible.

The play, adapted by Anita Loos, follows the romance of Lea de

Lonval, an aging Parisian courtesan, and Cheri (Horst Buchholz), a handsome but spoiled and emotionally underdeveloped young man who falls in love with her. The action takes place over a twenty-year period around World War I. To the extent that the play has a theme, it's that she's a high-class hooker and he's a spineless invertebrate, but they're redeemed (and made miserable) by love.

There were several reasons why Kim did the play: For one, she liked Actors Studio co-founder Lewis. As Eli Wallach notes, Lewis had a sure touch for light and fantasy material that had made him a standout amid the proletarian seriousness of the Group Theatre. Also, Lea de Lonval gave Kim the chance to play an older woman (one critic would memorably say that in the last act she looked like Benjamin Franklin), as opposed to the girls, ingenues, and young women that had been a staple of her career. Kim also jumped at *Cheri* because Lewis agreed she could have only a three-month contract, figuring that once the play was up and running he would get someone like Simone Signoret to step in for Kim.

It was a good time for Kim to start picking non-ingenue roles, because she was beginning to display non-ingenue weight. One reporter who interviewed her at this time described her proportions as "opulent," adding "no toothpick, she." Her uncle Herbert Miller and his wife, Flo, were then living in a Maryland suburb of Washington, DC, where *Cheri* had its out-of-town tryout. "After the show, we went back and talked to her," Flo Miller later recalled. "She looked fat in *Cheri*, compared to when we had known her as a young girl. She told us that she had had to gain all that weight for the part."

Kim's preparation for the role was extraordinarily thorough. In rehearsals, she would wear clothing from the role, including tight-fitting corsets and high heels, to give her a sensory feeling for the part. In Washington, she went to the Phillips Gallery, where she studied Renoir's painting *The Luncheon of the Boating Party*. "I actually got feelings from it that I could use in my part," she said. "The way those women lean on their hands, the physicalization of it, that lovely roundness they have." Kim also made a study of cocottes, the French courtesans of the late nineteenth and early twentieth centuries.

The *New York Times* noted that while Lea de Lonval aged from forty-three to sixty and her weight increased from 140 to 290 pounds, Kim believed in using only the barest minimum of makeup to create the illusions of youth and age: "I think it should come from within the character itself," she said. While the weight gain would be accomplished with padding, the *Times* noted Kim's face would undergo its changes without layers of greasepaint.

Kim's thoroughness worked: "Every day, another Lea peeled off her [in rehearsal]," Robert Lewis said. And Tad Mosel, who saw the play in New York, says Kim's performance was a triumph of mind over matter. "Colette, in her book, described Lea as the most beautiful woman in Paris," he says. "Well, Kim wasn't the most beautiful woman on West Forty-fifth Street. She had a heavy jaw, rather small eyes and her nose was a little too large. Everything was wrong. But she walked on the stage and you said, 'There is the most beautiful woman in Paris.' And nobody can tell me how she did that. Nobody."

Lewis chose Horst Buchholz to play Cheri after seeing him in the film version of Thomas Mann's *The Confessions of Felix Krull,* in which Buchholz played the seductive Krull. Target audiences for the play were women ("In the folklore of Shubert Alley, the hand that rocks the cradle picks the shows to see," *Variety* noted) and gays. Expressing himself with late-'50s obliqueness in a telegram to Sam Zolotow of the *New York Times,* Richard Coe of the *Washington Post* said, "Think Bwy. will like, especially females of all genders."

Cheri opened at the National Theater in Washington, DC, on September 21, 1959. Giving it a qualified endorsement, *Variety* said "With *Lady Chatterley's Lover* outselling epsom salts in most drugstores, *Cheri* might make a go of it." A similar mixed review came in the telegram from Coe to Zolotow. "*Cheri* bitter tea for many, but a rare and striking blend," he said. *Variety* praised Kim's performances, but had reservations about Buchholz. "His Washington audience seemed to think he was overacting and laughed in the wrong places," it noted. "[His] near-striptease . . . may be somewhat shocking to sensitive playgoers."

Presumably, anyone who could handle *Lady Chatterley's Lover* could handle *Cheri,* but *Variety* made a good point about the quasi-Victorian sexual ethos of the late 1950s. In a profile of Kim for *Cheri,* a reporter recounted the tale of how Kim had bound her breasts with daughter Lisa's diaper to get the part of Millie in *Picnic.* But the reporter did not use the word *breasts,* referring instead to "that upper area where a woman's interesting measurements begin."

Backstage, *Cheri* was the opposite of *A Touch of the Poet* and its court-of-the-Borgias mood. "The atmosphere surrounding this play has been quite unusual," Kim told a reporter. "There have been no crises, no chaos and no personality clashes." Unfortunately, there was also no box office. The day before *Cheri* opened, Kim told a reporter from the *Herald-Tribune,* "There's a quality in [Lea]—the French thing, the Colette quality—that doesn't come natural to me." She added that she hoped to get it if the play had a long enough run. "People who had already booked for the early performances must have been somewhat daunted by this information," Kenneth Tynan observed in the *New Yorker.* But only people who booked for early performances got to see the show: When it opened at the Morosco Theatre on October 12, 1959, New York critics slammed it.

Richard Watts Jr. of the *New York Post* called it "[a] startlingly dull, prosaic and . . . foolish piece of theatrical claptrap." John Chapman of the *Daily News* gibed that after its Broadway run, it could be made into a French musical movie with Kim having the hit number "Thank Heaven for Little Boys." And Robert Coleman of the *Daily Mirror,* noting that the play was based on Colette's novellas *Cheri* and *The Last of Cheri,* said "as far as we're concerned, this can definitely be the last of Cheri."

Again, Kim outshone the play she had chosen. "Colette would have thought of you as her own child," Maurice Goudeket, Colette's widower, told Kim. Not all the critics agreed (*Time* said she was "as French as corn flakes"), but many praised her highly.

"Miss Stanley mops up in the dream role of the older woman," *Variety* said. "The part offers just about everything in the way of mood, from light banter to torrid love scenes and hysterical emotion and an age range of 18 years . . . Although Miss Stanley has given highly praised performances before, this is her most impressive thus far." Frank Aston of the *World-Telegram & Sun* added, "Kim Stanley is magnificent as she rises above this mire with a beauty that is both personal and artistic."

A dissenting note came from Richard Watts Jr. in the *New York Post*. "Everyone knows by now that Kim Stanley is an excellent actress," he wrote. "But her portrait of the distraught mistress . . . rarely seems to get deeply or movingly into the characterization." Walter Kerr of the *Herald-Tribune* also had his reservations.

"The evening requires that Miss Stanley suffer for love of this prancing colt, that she find the strength in herself to send him packing, and that she mature—or decay—into a level-eyed, solidly built realist who looks rather like Benjamin Franklin," he wrote. In accord with Sidney Lumet's characterization of Kim as a "little girl lost," Kerr affectionately noted, "She wears, as her birthright, the expression of a child who has been awakened out of a sound sleep on Christmas morning to be told that there is no Santa Claus." But he felt her performance was missing a key ingredient.

"Miss Stanley would seem to be an actress of a certain kind: one whose resources are entirely interior," he wrote. "She would seem to do little by discipline, almost nothing through conscious style. It is perhaps here that the spine of the sophisticate eludes her." (Sometime after *A Clearing in the Woods*, Kim thought about doing summer stock and asked Arthur Laurents for his recommendations. "I said *Private Lives*," he recalls. "She said, 'That piece of shit? Why should I do it?' I said, 'Because you'll learn to play style, how to wear clothes, hold a cigarette and hold a martini.' But she wouldn't do it.")

A larger criticism about how *Cheri* fits into the arc of Kim's career is made by actress Anne Jackson, who questions both Kim's intensity and her play selection. "Unless she went into a frenzy of emotion, she didn't think she was giving it her all. I did feel she went over the top with some of her work. And," adds Jackson, who admired Kim's work as a comedienne, "sometimes in plays that weren't worthy of her talent."

The play's elaborate sets by Oliver Smith and costumes by Miles White were praised by the critics, but you can't sustain a long run on settings and costumes. Attendance was poor: After a second-week box office take of $31,500, receipts plummeted to $20,800, a swan dive they never recovered from. Kim agreed to a 20-percent pay cut, which would be redirected to the show's advertising budget (Buchholz, Lewis, and Loos made similar agreements), but these steps were futile.

On other occasions the show might have scraped by, but it had fierce competition: *My Fair Lady* was halfway through its six-year run, and *The Sound of Music* opened twelve days before *Cheri* closed. When theater-club women could envision themselves learning the social graces from Rex Harrison or escaping the Nazis by hiking over the Alps, yodeling show tunes as they went, the prospect of watching Kim Stanley turn incrementally into Benjamin Franklin wasn't so appealing. Also, a new show was booked for the Morosco, so the producers of *Cheri* would incur the costs of moving the money-losing show to a new house. Rather than do that, they closed it on November 28, after a run of six weeks.

There was also bad news in Kim's family. During the play's run, Alfred Ryder filed a petition for bankruptcy following a car accident in which a fourteen-year-old girl was injured. If Ryder was driving without liability insurance, filing for bankruptcy would have made sense. After he paid about $8,000 to the girl's guardian, his bankruptcy was discharged.

While it may not have weighed as heavily on Kim, her oldest brother underwent a mid-life crisis at this time. Living in Amarillo, Texas, with his wife, Lucile, and their two sons, everything seemed to be going well for psychiatrist Howard Reid: His marriage appeared solid, the kids were healthy, and his career was prospering. Along with several partners, he had just established the High Plains Neurological Center, the only facility within several hundred miles that brought together practitioners of psychiatry, psychology, neurology, and neuropsychiatry. They were building a new building on West Seventh Avenue in downtown Amarillo. It should have been a moment of triumph for Howard Reid, but instead he hurriedly left the state under circumstances that remain ambiguous, abandoning his wife, sons, and colleagues.

While saying that her first husband had the kind of winning personality that could sell ice to Eskimos, Lucile Reid Brock adds, "Howard had a serious mental illness. He committed professional, social, and familial suicide." Kim would tell her children that he had lost his Texas medical license for performing lobotomies upon Indians after that practice had been banned. The lobotomy charge is baseless—Howard Reid was a psychiatrist, not a neuropsychiatrist—but it does reflect Kim's visceral aversion to her oldest brother.

As she had also done after *A Touch of the Poet*, Kim announced to the media that she would abandon acting for a year. The *New York Times* reported that she declined to explain why, but suggested it was because she was taking her family to California. A *New York Post* article said that except for one television appearance, she didn't intend to stir from her Riverside Drive apartment until the next fall, planning to do "hundreds of personal citizen type things" in the meantime. "Now, nothing will entice me back," she said. "I've been sent at least fifty scripts and have turned down a beautiful part in Lillian Hellman's new play." (The play was the long-running *Toys in the Attic;* the part was Carrie Berniers, the female lead opposite Jason Robards, which then went to Maureen Stapleton.)

Kim's next TV appearance was a milestone: her last live television drama. But it almost didn't happen for her.

P*LAYHOUSE 90*, the last outpost of quality live TV drama, aired *Tomorrow*, a William Faulkner short story adapted by Horton Foote, on March 7, 1960. It's the story of a man who hangs a jury that otherwise would have acquitted a farmer of shooting a young thug to death. The thug turns out to have been the son of a poor pregnant country girl, played by Kim in a flashback sequence, which occupies much of the show. Abandoned by her husband, she turned up at an isolated rural mill where the renegade juror (Richard Boone) worked as a watchman. He married her and, when she died shortly after childbirth, raised the boy as his own. He developed an affectionate relationship with the boy, but the woman's ignorant, small-minded brothers forcibly took him away from Boone and the boy became a juvenile delinquent.

The first obstacle for Kim was that producer Herbert Brodkin didn't want her, hoping to get Julie Harris, Piper Laurie, Eva Marie Saint, or Lee Remick. But Horton Foote fought for Kim and prevailed. Then there were Lucy Kroll's hardball negotiating tactics: Kim had only second-star billing (her part was smaller than Boone's), but Kroll still demanded a $10,000 fee for her. Negotiations with CBS nearly collapsed, but the network relented, and Kim was on.

Her role, Sarah Eubanks, was a difficult one, as she is always lying down—first on the ground outside the mill where Boone discovers her, her low moans blending with Christmas Eve winds that swirl around the watchman's shack. The rest of the time, she's in bed, preparing for, then attempting to recover from childbirth. She couldn't use her body or make any clothing changes. She had to convey character only through her face and voice, and rose to the challenge. "She was in a very good mood," Foote recalls. "She loved doing that show, I think."

In one notable scene, Boone goes out to chop kindling wood to keep the fire going. Kim's character, mistakenly believing he's abandoning her to die alone, lets out an animalistic shriek that brings Boone back in a hurry. But the live TV camera later catches her in a rare lapse: After she dies, she's covered with a blanket up to her shoulders. Although she's supposedly dead, the blanket clearly rises and falls with Kim's breathing.

Less than two months later, *Playhouse 90* aired its last original show. After another year and a half of reruns, it went off the air after the show of September 19, 1961. The live, intimate, New York–based anthology dramas were replaced by filmed and taped action-oriented series based in Hollywood. While some of those series are class acts, those who have never seen live TV drama—just about anyone under sixty-five—have no idea what they missed.

"Car chases are the polyester suits of television. But that's what they think of as action," JP Miller has said. "There's no such thing as internal action . . . You create a magnificent human drama and push the camera right up close to Kim Stanley and she doesn't do anything but respond inside and maybe there's a slight twitch of her eyelid or something. And it breaks your heart. That's all gone. You have to be hit over the head with a brick now."

Married life appeared to be agreeing with Kim. When a reporter arrived at her Riverside Drive apartment for an interview, he found that Kim, along with Lisa and Laurie Rachel ("two delightful, well-trained youngsters") had just recaptured a pair of parakeets that had flown the coop. During the run of *A Touch of the Poet*, Kim could often be seen dining with her children at Childs restaurant on Broadway, or romping with them in the park along Riverside Drive. "There was always something strange and new happening in the apartment," Jamie recalls. "I had all of Riverside Park to enjoy. There were always people coming and going."

Professionally, Alfred Ryder was as busy as Kim. In the spring of 1956, he replaced Franchot Tone as Astroff in an off-Broadway production of *Uncle Vanya*. In 1958, he was the standby for Sir Laurence Olivier as Archie Rice in *The Entertainer*. He then portrayed D.H. Lawrence in *I Rise in Flames, Cried the Phoenix,* winning an Obie, and replaced Jason Robards as Claggart in a televised version of Melville's *Billy Budd*.

Kim felt strongly about the importance of being a good mother, telling the *Daily News,* "Every actress must choose, on occasion, between her children and the theatre. I would never choose in favor of the theatre. It would make me feel too guilty." But her actions may not have kept pace with her good intentions. "I don't think that she functioned too effectively as a mother," Robert Whitehead later said, "although she gave a hell of a lot of time trying to feel that she did."

An example of this dissonance comes in an interview she gave the *Herald-Tribune*. Asked what she would have done if she had stayed away from the theater for a year after *A Touch of the Poet,* she said, "I have three children. I want to make a home for them before I get much older." Where would she make it? She implied to the reporter that she and Ryder had had a home together on Long Island (it had been her and Conway, of course), but that commuting to New York meant that she saw very little of her children. If she had taken a year off, she added, she would have moved her family back to the country, so she could be an attentive mother. But commuting would mean that after her hiatus year, she would see less of the children again.

While she tried to be a good wife and mother, Kim's heart continued its errant ways. "She sat at the front table of the Russian Tea Room with Robert Herridge of *Camera Three* every night and got drunk," says writer Roger O. Hirson. "They sat there and admired each other. I think they had a love affair." Harold Clurman, who had known Isadora Duncan, described her as "wild and magnetic" and believed her prolific love life was sustained by a special kind of spirituality; perhaps the same was true of Kim. While her serial infidelities were shielded from the public, they were well-known in the theater community, and could have been no secret to her husbands, who may have felt it was simply part of the price they paid for being married to Kim.

Three weeks after "Tomorrow," she was due in Palm Beach, Florida, to star opposite Kevin McCarthy in *Two for the Seesaw* at the Royal Poinciana Playhouse. This wasn't the first time she had been considered for the play. In November of 1956, two months before he offered the career-making role in the Broadway production to Anne Bancroft, producer Fred Coe sent the script to Kim. Author William Gibson went to see her in *A Clearing in the Woods*, but was dubious ("She was so much a shikse that I didn't see how she could play the part [of the Jewish Gittel Mosca]," he said). So was Kim, who turned it down.

The Palm Beach version of *Two for the Seesaw* would represent a first for Mr. and Mrs. Alfred Ryder: He would direct the show, she would star in it. But Ryder bowed out when he landed the role of Sewell, the first mate, in the Broadway production of *One More River*, and was replaced by Alan Schneider. The show's principals have differing memories as to why Kim followed suit, leaving the show shortly before it opened.

Schneider, who had the impression Kim was doing the play because she needed some money in a hurry, later said Kim walked out three days before it opened, saying she wasn't right for the part. "I wanted to kill her," he writes in his memoirs, "but underneath I couldn't bring myself entirely to blame her." Kevin McCarthy, who later crossed swords with Kim in the Actors Studio version of *The Three Sisters*, has this dour recollection: "After one rehearsal, or maybe two, they 'say' she went into the hospital. Or something. She decided she wasn't right for it. Or something." It's the memory of Kim's understudy, Mary Tahmin, who successfully took over for her, that Kim, in the early stages of pregnancy, had a miscarriage. Newspaper reports from the period support Tahmin's version.

In light of her already-demonstrated penchant for prematurely leaving shows in as dramatic a manner as she performed in them, Kim worried everyone would say she just didn't want to do the show, but she was still out. When *Seesaw* didn't come together as a collaboration for the Ryders, they decided to try again, this time with a Broadway play.

Kim, at about fourteen years old, blooming and anxious.
(Courtesy of Raymond and Camille Hankamer)

Kim's father, J.T. (Jesse Taylor) Reid, at right, along with her brothers Justin (left) and Kenneth (center). A stern and imperious autocrat, J.T. would cast a long shadow over his daughter's life.
(Courtesy of Erik Ireland)

Kim's mother, Rubyann (Miller) Reid. The only family member to encourage Kim in her acting, Rubyann was high-spirited, good-natured, and emotionally erratic.
(Courtesy of Raymond and Camille Hankamer)

A beaming Kim as an undergraduate at the University of New Mexico in the early 1940s. The leading lady of the school's drama department, a friend also recalls her as the queen of the campus. (Courtesy of Jinx Witherspoon Rodger)

Pasadena **PLAYHOUSE NEWS**

December 12   **"NIGHT MUST FALL"**   1945

Kim's first husband, actor Bruce Hall, whom she met at the Pasadena Playhouse, where she studied acting in 1945. Their marriage was short-lived. (Walt Mancini photo/Courtesy of the Pasadena Playhouse)

Kim shortly after her arrival in New York in 1946. (Billy Rose Theatre Collection, the New York Public Library for the Performing Arts, Astor, Lenox and Tilden Foundations)

One of the jobs Kim held while struggling to establish herself as an actress was as a cocktail waitress at the Sheraton. She appears on the left in this spring 1947 ad from Cue magazine. (*The Fales Library & Special Collections, New York University*)

We're at the
Sheraton Lounge!
Where are you?

ENTERTAINMENT FROM 5 P.M.
HOTEL SHERATON
LEXINGTON AVE. AT 37th ST., N. Y.

Kim's early off-Broadway shows included an offbeat 1949 play called Too Many Thumbs. *Kim played the girlfriend of an ape who evolves into a man and then a saint. Gene Saks (center) was a professor of religion and Dick Robbins the starchy anthopologist Kim leaves for the ape-man.* (*Billy Rose Theatre Collection, the New York Public Library for the Performing Arts, Astor, Lenox and Tilden Foundations*)

Curt Conway, Kim's second husband, whom she met when he was called in at the last minute to direct Too Many Thumbs. *Her marriage to the popular actor and director was vital but contentious, as were her other three marriages. (Players Guide)*

Kim with her first child, daughter Lisa Conway. Kim tried to be a good mother, but as one colleague said, "She wasn't cut out for motherhood." (Corbis)

Kim (standing) as Adela, the headstrong youngest daughter, in the 1951 ANTA production of The House of Bernarda Alba. *(Billy Rose Theatre Collection, the New York Public Library for the Performing Arts, Astor, Lenox and Tilden Foundations)*

Kim as Anna Reeves and Lonny Chapman as Knub McDermont in Horton Foote's 1952 play The Chase, *which began a long friendship and artistic collaboration between Kim and Foote in theater, live television drama, and film. (Daniel Blum's Theatre World/Courtesy of Helene Mochedlover)*

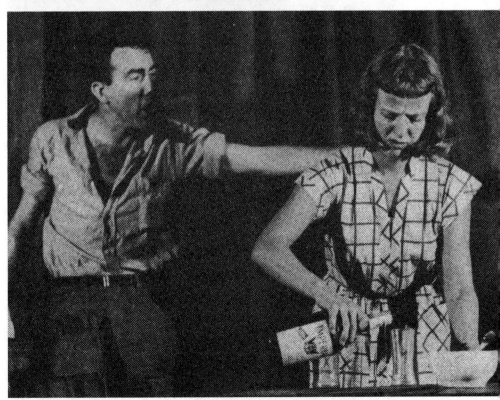

Kim at about the time she appeared in The Chase. *(Guy Gillette photo)*

During the summer of 1952, Kim appeared as Blanche DuBois in A Streetcar Named Desire *in Houston, which she may have done to impress local family members with whom she and her mother had lived as poor relatives a decade earlier. This photo is from rehearsals. (Courtesy of Robert Traweek)*

Kim's breakthrough role was Millie Owens, the angst-ridden, intellectual tomboy in William Inge's 1953 play Picnic. *Here Hal Carter (Ralph Meeker) laughs at Millie's difficulties learning to dance. (Zinn Arthur photo/Billy Rose Theatre Collection, the New York Public Library for the Performing Arts, Astor, Lenox and Tilden Foundations)*

Having arrived as a Broadway star, Kim paints her name above the title of The Traveling Lady *in this 1954 publicity photo. It was the first time in the history of the Playwrights Company that it had voted to elevate a performer to above-the-title status after a play had opened.* (Leo Friedman photo/Courtesy of the Library of Congress)

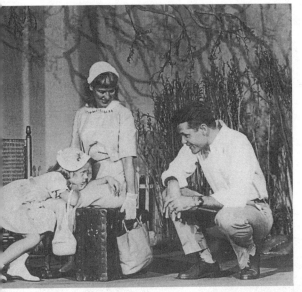

Kim rose to stardom in Horton Foote's 1954 play The Traveling Lady *as Georgette Thomas, the beleaguered but plucky wife of a convict and mother of young Margaret Rose (Brook Seawell). Here they encounter helpful law-man Slim Murray, played by Jack Lord, whom Kim disdained as an actor. (Fred Fehl photo/Courtesy of Gabriel Pinski/www.FredFehl.com and the Billy Rose Theatre Collection, the New York Public Library for the Performing Arts, Astor, Lenox and Tilden Foundations)*

Kim with playwright William Inge (left) and Jerome Courtland, the original choice to play Bo Decker, in a publicity photo for Inge's 1955 smash hit Bus Stop. *(Louis Melancon photo/Billy Rose Theatre Collection, the New York Public Library for the Performing Arts, Astor, Lenox and Tilden Foundations)*

Kim as Cheri, the nightclub singer from the wrong side of the tracks, squaring off with Albert Salmi, who replaced Courtland as rambunctious cowboy Bo Decker in Bus Stop. *(Zinn Arthur photo/Billy Rose Theatre Collection, the New York Public Library for the Performing Arts, Astor, Lenox and Tilden Foundations)*

Kim was the leading lady of live television drama, which flourished in New York in the 1950s. Here she appears with Joanne Woodward (at left) in Horton Foote's A Young Lady of Property, *which aired April 5, 1953, on the Philco-Goodyear Television Playhouse. (Wisconsin Center for Film and Theater Research)*

Opposite: *As Cheri in* Bus Stop, *Kim did a memorable, show-stopping rendition of "That Old Black Magic" on a tabletop, accompanied by Crahan Denton as Virgil. On the play's opening night, Robert Whitehead's wife, Virginia, shortened Kim's costume without telling her, and the upset Kim had to go on in it. (Zinn Arthur photo/Billy Rose Theatre Collection, the New York Public Library for the Performing Arts, Astor, Lenox and Tilden Foundations)*

Another of Kim's live TV drama appearances was a reprise of her role as Georgette Thomas in Horton Foote's The Traveling Lady, *which aired April 22, 1957, on* Studio One. *Robert Loggia (center) played her troubled convict husband and Steven Hill was Slim Murray, the lawman with whom she falls in love. (Wisconsin Center for Film and Theater Research)*

Kim rehearsing for A Clearing in the Woods *with Onslow Stevens, who played her father, and Barbara Myers, who played one of her three younger selves. Kim took an intense dislike to Stevens and worked with several other actresses in the show to make his life backstage miserable. (Billy Rose Theatre Collection, the New York Public Library for the Performing Arts, Astor, Lenox and Tilden Foundations)*

Kim, ethereally beautiful in a Lucinda Ballard gown as Virginia, the troubled heroine of Arthur Laurents's 1957 Freudian drama A Clearing in the Woods. *(Wisconsin Center for Film and Theater Research)*

*Kim talking to Harold
Clurman at the reception
following her third marriage,
to actor and director Alfred
Ryder, on August 2, 1958.
The intensity Kim shows here
was often displayed in her
onstage performances.*
(Courtesy of Ellen Adler)

*Kim, Eric Portman, and Helen
Hayes in the 1958 world premiere of Eugene O'Neill's*
A Touch of the Poet. *Brooks
Atkinson wrote that "[the play]
brings us the two finest
actresses of their respective
generations," but backstage
fireworks among the three
principals caused Kim to
make an early exit from the
long-running show. (Alfredo
Valente photo/Billy Rose Theatre
Collection, the New York Public
Library for the Performing Arts, Astor,
Lenox and Tilden Foundations)*

When Kim, as Rita Shawn, is being deserted by her mother in The Goddess, *she goes to the door of her Hollywood Hills mansion and unleashes a tirade that is blood-curdling in its primordial ferocity. (*The Goddess © 1957, renewed 1985 Columbia Pictures Industries, Inc. All rights reserved. Courtesy of Columbia Pictures and the Academy of Motion Picture Arts and Sciences)

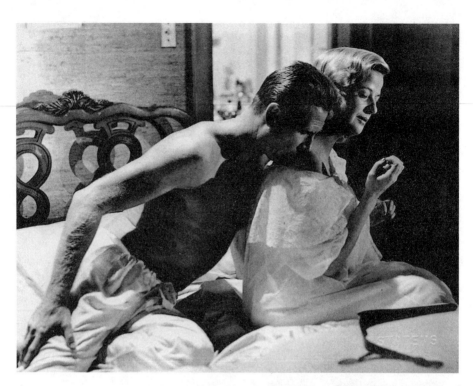

Kim as movie star Rita Shawn with her second husband, boxer Dutch Seymour (Lloyd Bridges), in her film debut, Paddy Chayefsky's The Goddess *(1958).* (The Goddess © 1957, renewed 1985 Columbia Pictures Industries, Inc. All rights reserved. Courtesy of Columbia Pictures and the Academy of Motion Picture Arts and Sciences)

A publicity photo of Kim for The Goddess. (The Goddess © 1957, renewed 1985 Columbia Pictures Industries, Inc. All rights reserved. Courtesy of Columbia Pictures and the Billy Rose Theatre Collection, the New York Public Library for the Performing Arts, Astor, Lenox and Tilden Foundations)

DAILY NEWS 5¢

NEW YORK'S PICTURE NEWSPAPER ®

WEATHER: Cloudy, cold.

Vol. 40. No. 161 — Copr. 1968 News Syndicate Co. Inc. — New York 17, N.Y., Tuesday, December 30, 1968★

KIM STANLEY FILES TO NAME DAUGHTER'S DAD

Kim Would Add Ryder Clause. Actress Kim Stanley and Alfred Ryder smile at their wedding in the Bronx last August. Yesterday, Kim asked Manhattan Supreme Court to list Ryder as the father of her daughter, Laurie, 2, on the child's birth certificate. Kim was Mrs. Curt Conway until a few months before the child was born. The child's certificate lists no father at all now. —Story on page 3

Shortly after Kim's controversial exit from A Touch of the Poet, *she found herself again embroiled in public scandal when it was revealed that her younger daughter, Laurie Rachel, was the child of her third husband, Alfred Ryder, rather than her second, Curt Conway, as she had previously claimed.* (New York Daily News)

Kim as Lea de Lonval, an aging Parisian cocotte, or kept woman, parries an attempt by young Horst Buchholz to relieve her of her necklace in the 1959 play Cheri. *The show was a bomb and closed after fifty-six performances. This is one of three drawings of Kim throughout her career by Al Hirschfeld.*
(© Al Hirschfeld/Margo Feiden Galleries Ltd., New York. www.alhirschfeld.com)

In May of 1960, Kim sailed to England on the Queen Mary *to do an English TV drama,* The Cake Baker. *Seeing her off in her stateroom are, clockwise from left, daughter Lisa, son Jamie, daughter Laurie Rachel, and a friend of theirs. (The Queens Borough Public Library, Long Island Division, New York Herald Tribune Photo Morgue)*

Kim's third husband Alfred Ryder (left) directed A Far Country *(1961), the first Broadway play about Sigmund Freud. With him at a reading are Kim, playwright Henry Denker, and Salome Jens, who played Freud's wife. (Billy Rose Theatre Collection, the New York Public Library for the Performing Arts, Astor, Lenox and Tilden Foundations)*

In a pre-Broadway publicity photo for A Far Country *are, from left, Sam Wanamaker as Dr. Joseph Breuer, Steven Hill as Sigmund Freud, George Gaynes (later replaced by Patrick O'Neal) as Frederick Wohlmuth, and Kim as Elizabeth von Ritter, one of Freud's earliest patients. (Billy Rose Theatre Collection, the New York Public Library for the Performing Arts, Astor, Lenox and Tilden Foundations)*

Kim as drug-addicted lawyer Faith Parsons, with Vince Edwards in a two-part 1963 episode of Ben Casey *that won her the first of her two Emmy Awards. Although brief, the scene in which she goes through withdrawal was praised for its harrowing realism. (Wisconsin Center for Film and Theatre Research)*

Donnie Barker (Gregory Rozakis) is tied a little too closely to his mother's apron strings in William Inge's 1963 Oedipal drama Natural Affection. *Kim played Sue Barker, a middle-aged Midwestern working mother forced to choose between her son and lover Harry Guardino. (Martha Holmes photo/Billy Rose Theatre Collection, the New York Public Library for the Performing Arts, Astor, Lenox and Tilden Foundations)*

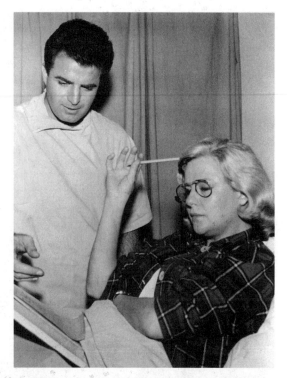

Kim as unbalanced medium Myra Savage in Seance on a Wet Afternoon, *talking her husband Billy (Richard Attenborough, who also produced the film) into kidnapping a young girl so she can "find" her. (Courtesy of Bryan Forbes and the Library of Congress)*

Keyhole shot from Seance on a Wet Afternoon *of Kim, as Myra Savage, impersonating a nurse in order to try and convince kidnap victim Amanda Clayton (Judith Donner) that she's actually in a hospital. (Courtesy of Bryan Forbes and the Academy of Motion Picture Arts and Sciences)*

Throughout her career, adjectives such as "brilliant," "illuminating" and "incandescent" were applied to Kim's acting. This haunting publicity still from Seance on a Wet Afternoon *displays her at her luminous best.* (Courtesy of Bryan Forbes and the Library of Congress)

Kim and her fourth husband, attorney Joseph Siegel, at a reception in Mount Vernon, New York, after their marriage on July 19, 1964. Siegel was the only one of Kim's husbands from outside show business. Their brief marriage was unsuccessful and coincided with the end of Kim's stage career. (Courtesy of Sally Siegel Radin)

Geraldine Page as Olga, Kim as Masha, and Shirley Knight as Irina in the Actors Studio production of Chekhov's The Three Sisters. *The 1964 production in New York was well-received, but its 1965 London production was one of the most spectacular failures in the modern English-speaking theater and the last time Kim would ever go on stage. (Billy Rose Theatre Collection, the New York Public Library for the Performing Arts, Astor, Lenox and Tilden Foundations)*

Videotaping The Three Sisters *in the fall of 1964. Kim as Masha and Kevin McCarthy as Vershinin are seated; Tamara Daykarhanova, Luther Adler, and others are in the background. The taping was contentious. (Peter Basch photo/Billy Rose Theatre Collection, the New York Public Library for the Performing Arts, Astor, Lenox and Tilden Foundations)*

In the early 1980s, Kim went to Hollywood, where she made a brief comeback. Her supporting role as Lillian Farmer in Frances *(with star Jessica Lange) earned her an Oscar nomination; she also appeared in* The Right Stuff *and did several TV shows. (© 1982 CANAL + IMAGE UK—Tous Droits Reserves/Courtesy of the Academy of Motion Picture Arts and Sciences)*

Kim in the early 1980s, with friend Elizabeth Wojcik at right, outside the large Craftsman-style bungalow on Hillcrest Avenue in Hollywood where she lived. (Rietta Netter Oppenheim photo)

Kim at home in Hollywood in the early '90s, with lifelong friend Rietta Netter Oppenheim at right. Years of drinking, binge eating, and isolation had taken their toll on Kim. (Courtesy of Rietta Netter Oppenheim)

CHAPTER 7

LAST TANGO ON BROADWAY

(1960–1965)

IN MAY OF 1960, Kim signed a contract to appear in *Taffy,* a Broadway play about a young woman in contemporary Louisiana with a dark secret. The next month, she, Alfred, and the children left New York City and moved to Suffern, a hamlet with many actors and artists in Rockland County, just up the Hudson River from New York.

In 1960, the Cold War still simmered between the United States and the Soviet Union. The Soviets shot down an American U-2 spy plane over Russia in May, a proxy conflict was brewing in the Belgian Congo, and Americans nervously built fallout shelters. There was also conflict at home, with the early stirrings of the civil rights movement in the South. Among the distractions Americans chose from the news were dancing the twist, jumping on trampolines, and listening to "Theme from *A Summer Place*" by the Percy Faith Orchestra.

Although civil rights was not the theme of Kim's new play, *Taffy* did have a multi-racial cast. Kim was to play Taffy, an unhappily married thirty-two-year-old woman. Now living in New York, she returns home to Lousiana for the first time since she was sent away sixteen years earlier, when, as a tennager, she bore a son to her lover, Ewing (Michael Tolan).

To prevent a scandal, Taffy's still-young mother raised the child as her own, but neither Ewing nor the son knew who the boy's true father was. In the course of Taffy's return visit, the facts of her son's paternity come out. Angry with Taffy for not having told them the truth, Ewing and her son reject her; she then commits suicide.

Jack Ragotzy was to have directed the play, written by Anna Marie Barlow, but when Kim insisted on Alfred Ryder, he was in and Ragotzy was out. Among the cast members were veteran character actor Edward Andrews and Crahan Denton, who had played Virgil in *Bus Stop*. There were also three talented black newcomers: Lou Gossett Jr., James Earl Jones, and Cicely Tyson.

Kim and Alfred worked together well. In one case, Kim had a problem with Taffy's suicide scene at the end of the play. Anna Marie Barlow remembers what happened in rehearsals. "When we would get to the part where she had to kill herself, she would begin wiping her forehead, stopping and calling, 'Alfred! Alfred!'" Barlow says. "And Alfred would say, 'Okay, everybody, take a little break.'

"One day, she said, 'I know what's wrong. I look like a weak person, like I'm begging for sympathy if I do this after they [Ewing and Taffy's son] leave. But leave them on the stage, their backs turned to me. I'll get a knife off the kitchen table and kill myself with them standing there. That says anger. I don't want to be weak, I want to be angry.' The minute she said it, I thought, 'My God, she's right.'" Barlow changed the script to accommodate Kim's insight.

Kim made it work on the stage. "Both Lucy Kroll and Audrey Wood, my agent, were at [a] rehearsal," Barlow says, "and as they saw Kim begin to crawl toward the knife, both of them were pushing back in their seats, saying, 'Oh, no . . . Oh God, no . . . oh no . . .' It was very powerful."

One of the challenges of playing Taffy was that Kim started out age thirty-two, went back to sixteen, then returned to thirty-two. Lou Gossett marveled at how she made the first of those transitions. "It was rehearsal. There was just tape on the floor," he says. "There were no costumes, no wardrobe. And she did it by just maybe letting her hair down. She walks to another circle and she's sixteen. Without lights and stuff. She was so remarkable."

Sylvia Davis, another cast member, remembers watching with fascination the rehearsals of a sexually charged bedroom scene between Kim and Michael Tolan that ended with Kim lighting and smoking a cigarette, then exhaling with the relief of pent-up passion. Tolan, who beat out many male actors for the chance to work opposite Kim, was also impressed.

"When we started run-throughs, I was working the way I usually worked, trying to really nail down what we'd been doing and found that Kim wasn't through," he says. "Like the very few brilliant actors we have, not just the very good or the excellent ones, there was a sense of danger. Kim had the tremendous skill of not only repeating what we'd been doing in rehearsal, but leaving [herself] about 15 or 20 percent open to whatever new impulse might happen. I said, 'Holy Christ, you have to be dead not to respond to that.' And then when you respond, she responds to that! Ever since then, I've said to myself, 'Michael, you're not finished after dress rehearsals. Keep your eyes and ears open and throw something at somebody.' I learned more from Kim than I did anywhere else."

For James Earl Jones, Kim was like one of the greatest male actors of the day. "I considered her to be, for women actors, what Marlon Brando was for male actors," he says. "She carried that great depth of exploration and dealt with a well of passion and feelings that the character had, just like Marlon did." And yet, "there was always something 'girl' about her—something fragile, feminine, and delicate," Jones says. "That very vulnerable person she gave us in *The Goddess*. Not woman, girl. There was something very girl about her."

Gossett remembers Kim encouraging him as an actor, and adds she was attuned to the issue of civil rights long before it became fashionable. "She would be more sensitive to civil rights than I was," he says. "I came from a neighborhood that was kind of ideal [the Coney Island section of Brooklyn]." Kim decried racists as "ugly Americans." "'Just like the Nazis,' she would say. She'd almost go to tears. She couldn't figure out what that disease was, what made people think that way."

Rehearsals of *Taffy* went well, and the play was scheduled to open on Broadway in November of 1960. But producers George Hamlin and Malcolm Wells made a fatal mistake: $50,000 of the play's $125,000 capitalization was to come from an estate. When that estate became tied up in a court battle, they weren't able to find an alternate funding source. On the verge of leaving town for tryouts in New Haven and Boston, the play never even made it to the New York Thruway. "It was something that was quite common on Broadway," James Earl Jones says philosophically. "It didn't work, the backers pulled out, and there you were, left with the old scripts."

A PRE–REVOLUTIONARY WAR DUTCH STONE COTTAGE on 63 acres in Suffern was now home to Kim, Alfred, and the children: Lisa, Kim's nine-year-old daughter by Curt Conway; Jamie, her seven-year-old son by Brooks Clift (although, in a *Taffy*-like deception, he was still told Conway was his father); and Laurie Rachel, their four-year-old daughter. Although Alfred had a sharp edge, he and Kim were indulgent of the children.

"My father was very intense, very intellectual, and very impatient with those who were not intense or intellectual," says his daughter, who as an adult would simply go by Rachel. "He could be incredibly engaging or charming, but also very insulting if he thought you were stupid. But never to us children," she notes, adding with gentle amusement, "He adored us and we could do nothing wrong and were never in error at any time." Her mother, she says, had a similar attitude.

"They both raised us to believe that we were very special. I don't think that was always so wonderful," says Rachel Zahn, now a successful pediatrician. "All children should be raised to feel that they're special, but we were raised to feel we were more special than others and didn't have to deal with mundane real-world problems because we were destined to greater things."

Kim's cooking was not one of those greater things. Lillian Ross, who profiled Kim for the *New Yorker* during this period, remembers Kim preparing a delicious dinner of roast chicken. But this was a minority view. "Kim was not a good cook," Rachel says. "She would cook huge pots of chili. It was so hot I couldn't quite taste it." Playwright Henry Denker visited Kim around this time. "She wanted to be a housewife and cook dinner for me," he says. Asked how the dinner was, he pauses and says, "Well—she was a hell of an actress."

Kim's next play was Denker's *A Far Country*, the story of one of Sigmund Freud's earliest breakthrough cases. Elizabeth von Ritter, the scion of an upper-middle-class Viennese family, had lost her ability to walk owing to repressed guilt over having longed for her brother-in-law while nursing her dying sister. Plays with psychoanalytical themes had appeared on Broadway since *The Fatted Calf* (1912), which dealt with the use of psychotherapy to treat paranoid symptoms. But *A Far Country* was the first Broadway play in which Freud was a character. Real-estate mogul Roger Stevens was an unlikely man to produce it: He was dubious of the benefits of psychoanalysis and said he was probably the only person connected with the New York stage who had never been psychoanalyzed.

Because Freud was the leading role, rather than Elizabeth (who is off-stage half the time and doesn't appear until almost a third of the way through the play), Denker did not expect Kim to take the role. "Lynn Austin was the production supervisor for Roger Stevens," Denker recalls. "She said, 'What about Kim Stanley?' And everybody said, 'Naw—it's not really the leading role.' And at that time, she shouldn't have taken anything less than the leading role. But she took it and made it the leading role."

In their third try, Kim and Alfred finally got a play to the stage as star and director. He was highly receptive to her needs, telling one reporter, "She is an extremely sensitive instrument. She is so delicately attuned to direction that if it is wrongly phrased, she can be thrown into confusion for three or four days. If it is phrased rightly, she takes fire from it."

But even with Alfred as the director, there was always an extent to which Kim called the shots. On one occasion, he told a reporter, "I find as a director it's a great advantage to be married to the actress." Kim then spoke up. "Dear," she asked Ryder, "Do you have my bobby pins?" "Yes, dear," he replied, fishing them out of his pockets. In later years, Denker mused, "What transpired between the star and her husband at night after rehearsals I know not, but I always had the feeling that Kim really directed that production."

Elizabeth von Ritter was a difficult role: First, Kim had to spend much of her time, like any early psychoanalytical patient, lying on a couch. Although the couch was raised so that the audience could see

Kim's face, she still bridled. "I hated that couch during rehearsals," she said. "Take away an actress's legs and you might as well take away her voice. I felt confined and threatened."

She also didn't like the crutches she needed to hobble across the stage. "During my hatred for playing a paralytic, I actually hurled my crutches across the stage, narrowly missing the director, who happens to be my husband," Kim told *Daily News* reporter Robert Wahls. Alfred helpfully added, "When she threw the crutches at me, she didn't aim at me."

To prepare for the part, Kim spent days in the New York Public Library reading Freud's writings about Elizabeth and looking at late-nineteenth-century Viennese prints that showed the physical constriction of women of the time. She studied the social context of the part and, even though she found it burdensome, rehearsed on crutches.

Kim came to regard Elizabeth, who learned from Freud to face her problems and lead a productive life, as "a many-faceted, hard jewel that cracks open." A key moment in that process comes at the end of the second act, where repressed memories crowd in on Elizabeth and, fighting to repel them, she emits a blood-curdling scream. Reviewers described Kim's scream as "burst[ing] through the surface as a submarine explosion suddenly tosses the sea violently into the air" or "like a pistol shot in a silent tomb."

To achieve that effect, Kim's used the Method's sense-memory technique. "In order to do the scream I used my brother's own death at first," she later said, "and when the necessary emotion to arouse me in the scream wasn't there anymore, I had to substitute things. I can remember that I used an obscene sexual image and that at one time I 'fixed hate' for Steven Hill [who was playing Freud]."

Hill, who had not been on Broadway since 1950's *The Country Girl*, was the source of much angst on this production. Salome Jens, who played Freud's wife, recalls a lot of tension between Alfred Ryder and Hill. At one point, Kim's agent Lucy Kroll wrote a letter to Horton Foote on Kim's behalf asking Foote to talk to Hill.

"Kim says Steve is completely withdrawn in his work," she wrote. "He is antagonistic at every rehearsal, and any suggestion becomes a personal insult to him . . . She feels that he is acting like a baby, that when he gets a simple suggestion like crossing the stage, he takes half an hour to decide if he ought to do it or not." Hill's performance, Kim felt, was designed less for the live theater than for live television cameras, which could pick up subtle gestures that would elude theater patrons in the balcony.

"He would mumble his way through rehearsals and we couldn't know what he was thinking or feeling," Henry Denker recalls. "We were not getting anything out of him. This held true right into New Haven. [Co-producer] Joel Shenker and I talked to Roger and said, 'Let's get rid of Steve, and put Sam Wanamaker [who played Joseph Breuer, a colleague of Freud's] in that part and find another actor to play Dr. Breuer.' Kim said no, she wouldn't allow that." Hill would get better and prove Kim right.

Playwright Denker got off on the wrong foot with Kim at the play's first reading: He was wearing a shirt and tie, a habit acquired from working in network television. But to Kim, it meant only one thing: He was a financial backer of the play and did not belong. So she glared at him. "Having spent all her time at the Actors Studio, she had never seen a playwright in a shirt and tie," Denker recalled years afterward. "She did apologize to me later."

Even at the first reading, Denker noted that Kim had a way, consciously or not, of silently expressing her concerns about lines or scenes that bothered her. It could be a look, a pause, or wrinkling of the brow. But Denker paid attention to those unspoken notes of Kim's and used them to improve the play. "Kim was a star in the true sense of the word, yet without ever acting 'the star,'" Denker says. "She was most solicitous of her other cast members. She never made star-like demands. She was, for a person of her talent and reputation, actually a very shy person."

Denker would go on to write a novel, *The Actress,* whose heroine, Kit Lawrence, is based on Kim. In it, he would note her extraordinary talent ("Certain of the lines . . . she delivered with the same brilliant pizzicato effect that Heifetz could extract from a violin"), but also her deeply troubled nature. A woman in the novel, whose husband has slept with Kit, bitterly describes her as "lovely, loveable, alcoholic, psychotic, darling Kit."

Although Steven Hill indulged himself to the consternation of his colleagues, Salome Jens, who greatly admired Kim, acknowledges that she did so as well. In an early scene, Freud tries to hypnotize Elizabeth by telling her she is floating. But Kim took too long trying to float herself into hypnosis.

"She would be doing this 'floating' thing, and Steve would be waiting for her and waiting for her and waiting for her. Finally, he cut the line out," Jens says. This was around the time Alan Shepard became America's first man in space as part of the Mercury Program. When Kim asked Hill why he had dropped the line, he replied in his best offstage Freudian manner, "Well, I think it's very bad for the audience, because they've got those astronauts floating around up there."

In another scene, Jens, as Freud's wife, brought Kim on stage. She was supposed to ask Jens about her pregnancy. "At one of those performances, she started taking off her gloves and watching me and no dialogue was coming," Jens remembers. "I entered the room and tried to do whatever I could to stay onstage, because she was supposed to ask me about the baby I was going to have, and she doesn't. She just took longer and longer and longer, and finally I left the stage because I had run out of things to do. I couldn't, you know, just stare at her. She would indulge herself that way."

The first road town for *A Far Country* was New Haven. There, Kim got to meet her second cousin Robert Ball. A grandson of Lena Hankamer, Rubyann's sister in Houston, he was a freshman at Yale. "Even though officially they pretended to disapprove of her, my mother and grandmother were very proud that she was a famous actress," Ball says. He called Kim up and she provided him with tickets to the show. Afterwards, they met in the bar of the Taft Hotel although Ball, the scion of a family of good Texas Baptists, had never had a drink in his life.

"She had a big table—there must have been ten people," he recalls. "She had me sit right next to her and I swiftly found out she was interested in pumping me for information about my grandmother and my mother. Whatever falling-out they had had, she still had quite a lively resentment of it and couldn't help being curious as to what was going on with that part of the family.

"She talked fast and loud and was used to being the center of attention," he says. "But she was very gracious to me." The next time he met his mother and grandmother, they were equally curious. "They were dying to hear all about her," he says. "How did she look? Was she currently divorced or married? Did she have on too much makeup? I remember that question."

After a second stop in Boston, *A Far Country* arrived on Broadway April 4, 1961, at the Music Box, the scene of Kim's triumphs in *Picnic* and *Bus Stop*. As she did whenever she could, Kim brought her children to the theater, sometimes with adverse consequences. During one show, Laurie Rachel was in the dressing room of Lili Darvas, who played Freud's mother. The four-year-old picked up a makeup pencil and began drawing faces on the cloth wigstands, inadvertently ruining them. Rather than scolding her, Kim thought it was delightful.

Critics responded to the show with mostly rave reviews. In the *New York Mirror,* Robert Coleman called *A Far Country* a "tautly written play about Dr. Sigmund Freud . . . We've been getting too many plays about petty people, too many small slices of life. Here's a tense drama about a big man. A valiant man." Howard Taubman of the *New York Times* wrote, "Mr. Denker has captured the dramatic core of an unforgettable experience in human revelation," while Frank Ashton of the *World-Telegram & Sun* wrote, "Henry Denker's *A Far Country* is a psychiatric detective story with drama, suspense and a spellbinding finish. Its conflicts are believable, its emotions are elemental and its intellectual range is gratifying." The only cautionary note came from Walter Kerr of the *Herald-Tribune,* who wrote, "It has some difficulties . . . the potential drama is diminished by a second-act feeling that we are simply not getting on with things."

Kerr had no such reservations about Kim's performance. His insightful criticism of her portrayal of Elizabeth is almost eerie in the way it sounds like an appraisal of the actress as well as the performance:

What Miss Stanley does that is most stunning is to display the eternal tease in the confirmed neurotic. Her face is quite naturally a face peculiarly susceptible to shadows. The least trace of a cloud that crosses it leaves a delicate, almost imperceptible, yet permanently wounding mark. In time she becomes a recording corridor of veils, gauze upon gauze masking a knot of anger and self-accusation that must exist somewhere . . . but cannot be seen . . . The coy defiance of the self-made sick tinkles about the stage like glass in the wind.

In the *Journal-American,* John McClain led off his review by writing, "Kim Stanley is as gifted as anybody acting today, and . . . she is happily back in business in a compelling and incisive play which gives full range to her very distinct talents." And *Newsweek* noted, "Miss Stanley plays to perfection the beautiful self-deceiver who has so little to hide and so much to gain. Although immobilized throughout the play . . . the actress nevertheless dominates the scene as the focal point of the drama."

Kim electrified the audience as well as the critics. Future acting coach Larry Moss, then fifteen, attended a performance of *A Far Country,* and still recalls the end of act two. Just before the curtain, Freud suggests to Elizabeth von Ritter that the paralysis in her legs is the subconscious result of her having refused to walk upstairs one night and give medicine to the sick father she had long been nursing, because she secretly wished he would die.

Sitting in the front row of the theater, I watched Kim Stanley's cheeks turn bright red; then suddenly tears shot out of her eyes so fast and in such torrents that I clutched the edge of my chair. At that moment, the curtain started coming down as Ms. Stanley screamed with everything in her, "No, it's a lie!" And when the curtain hit the stage floor, she continued screaming in the darkness.

Thirty seconds later they brought the houselights up, and the theater went mad. People started talking to each other, grabbing at each other, for they had just witnessed a great actress give a performance that didn't seem to be a performance at all but a trauma in a real person's life that we shouldn't be allowed to watch.

Praise for Kim reached such a fever pitch that critic Whitney Bolton, a fan of hers, felt obliged to put things in perspective. "My colleagues . . . seem to believe that if Miss Stanley did nothing more demanding than peel an orange, it would be the greatest and most overwhelming feat of orange peeling since man stopped walking on all fours," he wrote in the *Morning Telegraph*. And he spoke critically of her tendency to keep working on her performance throughout a play's run.

"After a play has run some weeks, Miss Stanley, like others in the Method dedication, begins personally and, I think, willfully, to trifle with and distort her performance," he said, adding, "Her performance in *A Far Country* is extraordinary, high in its level of resource and brilliance. I cannot vow that it will remain so."

While not a criticism of Kim's performance, several critics noted she was starting to put on weight, saying that she "has a figure out of Titian or Rubens," or that she "illuminates the stage with her buxom fragility." A reporter granted an interview wrote, "Kim paced her dressing room in what looked like a maternity dress."

The critics had plaudits as well for Alfred Ryder's direction, Steven Hill's Freud, and for Sam Wanamaker, who, as Dr. Joseph Breuer, was making his first American stage appearance in more than a decade after having gone to England when he was blacklisted. Salome Jens as Freud's wife, Lili Darvas as his mother, Ellen Weston as his sister, Eda Reiss Merin as his bossy housekeeper, and Patrick O'Neal as Elizabeth's brother-in-law also won praise.

On April 12, 1961, little more than a week after the show opened, Kim and Alfred acted together for the only time in their careers. The day before, Steven Hill suffered an attack of kidney stones. The show's management, feeling his understudy was insufficiently rehearsed, cancelled the performance at the last minute, sending home a disappointed audience that included Joseph Kennedy (President Kennedy's father), Jack Benny, and composer Richard Rodgers.

The next day, Alfred Ryder was sent out in costume with a copy of the play's script in his hand to substitute for Hill in both matinee and evening performances. The *Herald-Tribune* noted he rarely looked at the script and finished the matinee to solid applause.

In addition to her critical approval, Kim received several in-person compliments from playgoers. Some would drop by her Music Box dressing room after the show to complain their legs hurt. "They talk as if they are a little bit angry, but really it is a kind of compliment," Kim told the *Newark Evening News.* Then there was the woman who came to her dressing room and told her, "I hate you. You were cured in two and a half hours. I've been in analysis for thirteen years and I'm still at it."

Her dressing-room visitor would not have envied her finances, however. Early in the show's run, she found herself short $200. Lucy Kroll loaned her the money and deducted it from her salary. A year and a half later, when Kim moved from Suffern, she would be short $4,000 on the closing costs for her new house. These were not rare occurrences: Kim was often short of money.

A Far Country would run for eight months. As often happened with Kim in a long-running show, she began to leave the play before it left her. "She missed thirty-eight performances in New York," says Henry Denker. "It was a psychological thing. Some nights she would show up with a collar on, a neck brace, and couldn't go on. Things like that, for which there was no physical basis." This created a lot of work for Kim's understudy, Nancy Marchand.

Because Denker lived in New York, he would go to the theater once a week. One night, as he walked up to the box office as the show was beginning, a woman was leaving the theater in tears. "I didn't know if they gave her the wrong tickets or what," Denker recalls. "I stopped her and said, 'Madam, what's wrong?' She said, 'This is the third time I've come to see the show, and she has not appeared yet.'"

Years later, Denker remains flummoxed about Kim's difficulties going onstage. "There was no insecurity once she got onstage," he says. "Before she got to the stage was where the problem was. I've thought about it a lot, but frankly, I just can't figure it out." He's more certain about the essence of Kim's greatness as an actress. "If I had to say it was one thing, I would say it was her own self-torment. If she weren't as tormented a person as she was, I don't think she could have had all those emotional responses. She was able to bring emotions to the surface that other actresses couldn't quite do. I don't know what would have happened to her if she didn't have the stage."

Kim received her second Tony nomination as best dramatic actress for her role as Elizabeth in *A Far Country,* although the award went to Margaret Leighton for *The Night of the Iguana.* And the magazine *Show Business Illustrated* named Kim "Theater Actress of the Year," as she learned in a telegram from its publisher, Hugh Hefner.

When *A Far Country* ended its New York run on November 25, 1961, Kim was one of the few cast members who appeared in its brief West Coast tour. This is the only time after she became a full-fledged star that she toured, something she may have done because Alfred Ryder was just finishing up a West Coast tour of Eugene Ionesco's *Rhinoceros* and it gave them a chance to spend time together.

Replacing Steven Hill as Freud for two weeks in Los Angeles and two more in San Francisco was Michael Tolan from *Taffy.* He was glad to work with Kim, but ambivalent about the role. "It was an impossible part to play," he remembers. "It was on every single page of the script. It started at a high emotional pitch, it kept going on and on, characters coming in and out, and old Freud had to hang in there. I remember going to Kim and saying, 'This fucking part is impossible. Please let Steve Hill finish it out.' She said, 'No, no, Michael, you've got to do it. I want you.'

"As I was having extreme pain trying to [learn] this part, I said, 'Let me see what Steve Hill is doing' and I went to a performance. He was doing it as though he were doing *Dragnet.*" Assuming a clinical monotone, Tolan continues, "Yes. How are you? I see. You can't walk? Hmmmn . . . Did you hate your father? I see. That's too bad . . ."

Tolan switches back to his own voice. "Having been working on the script, I said to myself, 'Son of a bitch, that's the only way you can get through it.' If you tried to play it emotionally from the very beginning, it was impossible. However, I couldn't do it the way Steve Hill did and wound up playing the hell out of it and having a horrible time. On the very last day in San Francisco, we had a little party in Kim's hotel room, and I remember Kim saying, 'Michael, I couldn't tell you before, but the part has no orgasm.'"

The West Coast tour opened at the Huntington Hartford Theater in Hollywood on November 29, 1961. Kim's hometown newspaper, the

Albuquerque Tribune, said it would be the Los Angeles stage debut for "the noted Albuquerque actress," a description that would have appalled Kim, who believed she was as Texan as four-alarm chili. Opening night was dramatic, and not just because of Kim's performance.

A baggage car carrying the show's set was delayed twenty-four hours between New York and Los Angeles. At 8 P.M. curtain time, the set wasn't ready, and an audience featuring the cream of Hollywood had to wait more than an hour. "The curtain did not rise," Henry Denker later recalled. "All the audience could hear were backstage noises of hammering, sawing, sets being moved and hung, and angry whispers of the crew saying, 'Damn it, we're working as fast as we can.'"

Once the curtain rose sometime between 9:15 and 9:30, the audience was spellbound. "The evening concluded after midnight with a deserved tumult of bravos," the *Hollywood Reporter* noted. "Did [Kim] shine that night," Denker recalled forty years later. "People who were there still talk about that performance."

In an "only in Hollywood" review, one critic compared the show to a cowboys-and-Indians shoot-'em-up, saying, "We see Freud driving to a new frontier, harried by the Indian arrows of his reactionary colleagues, tormented by the awareness that his figurative covered wagon may be wrecked in failure." Kim's reviews were mercifully free of this analogy. Alluding to the delayed curtain, Harrison Carroll of the *Herald-Express* said, "Miss Stanley is worth waiting any length of time to see." And Dick Williams wrote in the *Mirror,* "Just to watch the delicate nuances of changing expressions on her mobile face is a bewitching experience. The expressionless little movie starlets who fancy themselves actresses and would-be stars should be at the Huntington Hartford getting first-hand instruction on how it is really done." Kim's notices were similarly good in San Francisco, where the show was the last ever seen at the Alcazar Theater: After the set of *A Far Country* was struck, they razed the Alcazar and put up a parking lot.

During the show's run, the *New Yorker* published a profile of Kim by Lillian Ross, conducted over a three-day period at Kim's home in Suffern. "She was a very attractive, warm, smart, perceptive and alert person with deep convictions," Ross recalls. When she published *The Player,* a series of more than fifty interviews with leading actors (including Melvyn Douglas, Zero Mostel, Katharine Cornell, Sidney Poitier, and Angela Lansbury), Ross put Kim's interview first, because of her quote keynoting the book's theme: "Unlike other artists, the actor has only his own body and his own self to work with. To exhibit oneself on the stage is quite a brave and wonderful thing to do."

Consistent with Stanislavski's observation that every artist wants to create within himself a more interesting life than the one that surrounds him, Kim embroidered her life for Ross's benefit. She said she had received a B.A. in psychology from the University of Texas in 1945 (Kim never graduated from college, studied psychology, or attended UT). She said Jamie was the son of Curt Conway, rather than Brooks Clift. Her father was a professor of philosophy and part Indian, her mother an interior decorator (she had been one for a few months when they lived briefly in Texas; otherwise, she was a disaffected hairdresser and artist manqué). Kim's improvements upon the truth burnished her academic credentials and made her life more conventional to please her father, while consoling her mother for the disappointments she had endured.

Her resentment of her father seeped out, though. "My father always thought acting was very silly, and I wanted his approval," she said. "To him, acting was not a serious occupation. I think he still regards fishing as more important." On the last point, she was almost certainly right.

Kim had glowing words for her father figure, Lee Strasberg, though. "He's an artist in his own right. He made it possible for the world to open up for me," she said. "Through his teaching, Strasberg gives you tools that make it possible for you to accomplish what you want to do . . . Each person Strasberg works with comes out a much broader, fuller, deeper person, because Strasberg is not interested in exploiting talent but in nurturing it and making it grow."

Kim said she wanted to convey the playwright's meaning on stage, and expressed a sense of mystery about the rehearsal process. "When you begin to rehearse with other people, things begin to happen," she said. "What it is exactly, I don't know and I don't want to know. I'm all for mystery there. Most of what happens as you develop your part is unconscious, most of it is underwater."

Despite her reputation as the female Brando, Kim would never act opposite him, although not for lack of trying. As early as 1958, she talked about playing Ophelia to his Hamlet. A year later, she held out the possibility of playing Gertrude. By the time of her interview with Ross, she was back to Ophelia. But Brando was gone to Hollywood and would not be lured back, not even (or perhaps, given his fear of returning to the stage, especially not) to play opposite Kim.

KIM'S NEXT ACTING JOB WASN'T IN THE THEATER, but on television, where she appeared in *That's Where the Town's Going,* a videotaped show airing April 17, 1962. Written by Tad Mosel and directed by Jack Smight, it co-starred Patricia Neal, Jason Robards, and Buddy Ebsen, only months away from becoming Jed Clampett in *The Beverly Hillbillies.*

The story is about two middle-aged sisters who live together in a small Midwestern town with their dying mother. The dreamy and impractical Wilma (Kim) gets in touch with a successful ex-boyfriend (Robards) in the hope of marrying him and escaping loneliness and endless caretaking. But the cunning, practical Ruby (Neal) steals him, and Wilma winds up with the town's aging lecher (Ebsen). Neal recalls Kim giving Ebsen a very hard time. "She was just terrible to Buddy Ebsen," she says. "Oh God! I've never seen anything so bad." (Her hostility was not related to Ebsen's ability or the lack thereof; Tad Mosel says, "He played all his scenes with Kim and kept up with her every step of the way.")

This was the first time Kim and Neal had seen each other since Kim, newly wed to Bruce Hall, had frostily stared at her over tea because Neal was Hall's previous girlfriend. Although working on the show kindled a friendship between them, Tad Mosel says it was not all sweetness and light. After a tape of the show was put together, director Smight invited Kim and Neal to watch it with him. Afterwards, Neal phoned Mosel. "Pat Neal called me from the airport, and I think she'd had a couple of drinks," Mosel recalls. "She said, 'Well, that was just one big fat close-up of Kim.' It was kind of a resentment of her talent, in a way."

One of the most popular TV series of the early 1960s was the medical drama *Ben Casey,* starring Vince Edwards, with Sam Jaffe as his mentor, Dr. Zorba. In late October and early November of 1962, Kim went to Hollywood to do her first filmed TV show, a special two-part *Ben Casey* episode written by Norman Katkov: "A Cardinal Act of Mercy." She apparently did it to get money so she and Alfred could buy a new home in Rockland County.

Once Kim was signed, producer Matthew Rapf and twenty-eight-year-old director Sydney Pollack felt she might be a little overweight for the part of Faith Parsons, a belligerent and domineering attorney addicted to heroin, who's brought to the hospital after collapsing from pain and exhaustion. "The producer and director have asked if you could try to lose about five or six pounds," Lucy Kroll wrote to Kim, "as they feel the character of a dope addict would have a slightly starved look." Kim said no, and Kroll wrote back to the producers: "Kim asked me to [say] that even if she lost a lot of weight, her face would never look emaciated, because she just doesn't have that kind of bone structure."

Because of Faith Parsons's volcanic temper, Kim got to play her in full Vesuvius mode. After she goes through surgery, anesthesiologist Maggie Graham (Bettye Ackerman) tells Casey, "She'll be able to talk in an hour. Yelling, in two hours." When Casey prescribes large doses of morphine virtually on demand, Parsons becomes more cooperative. Dr. Zorba orders Casey to cut off her morphine. Parsons then dupes the son (Timmy Everett) of another patient (Glenda Farrell) into getting drugs for her. Casey finally forces her to go cold turkey. The show's upbeat ending is tempered by Casey and Zorba acknowledging that only one percent of addicts are ever truly cured.

Producer Matthew Rapf later recalled that Vince Edwards was nervous about working with Kim. "Vince behaved like the perfect angel with Kim Stanley. I went to him before the show and said, 'I've got Kim Stanley to play a two-parter . . . She's never done filmed television; she may be a little nervous.' And Vince said, 'She may be nervous? How do you think I feel?' They got along beautifully. She loved him."

Kim *was* especially nervous about doing filmed television. Sydney Pollack remembers getting a phone call at home from Kim, who was staying at the Chateau Marmont on the Sunset Strip. "She called me 'Mr. Pollack,' which made me feel silly. I was a young kid," the director recalls. "She said, 'Mr. Pollack, I have some bad news.'" What bad news, he grimly wanted to know. Kim explained that she had never done filmed TV before. She was so obviously beside herself that Pollack went over to Chateau Marmont.

"I knew right away what the problem was," he says. "In film, you're forced to repeat things from many different angles, to repeat what you did physically. That's not what Kim was accustomed to. She was used to a certain kind of freedom to follow new impulses, which is why she was such a great actress. So I did a very unusual thing for *Ben Casey*. I shot three cameras, sometimes four, at the same time, so I could combine the close-up, medium shot, master shot, over-the-shoulder shot, whatever, so she wouldn't have to match anything. She was grateful, and was great to work with."

In Pollack's experience, most actors relaxed when they had lines while off-camera. But not Kim. "Even when the camera was on someone else, she was acting up a storm," he later said. And producer Rapf noted, "She worked so hard that she got laryngitis and had to be put to bed for two days. Then she wanted to come back to work too early, she didn't want to hold up our production."

Although in awe of Kim, Pollack was surprised to learn how vulnerable she was when he gently offered her constructive criticism on the withdrawal scene. "It was the only time I really 'fiddled with the performance,'" Pollack says. "After we had done one take, I went to Kim and said, 'It's wonderful. It's full of little pearls that are beautiful in themselves, but it needs an overall bit of connection, something to string the pearls together.' We went back and did another take, and in a few minutes I saw her crying. I asked what the matter was, and she said, 'I'm just upset that you didn't like what I was doing.' It was a startling insight into how delicate she was, in spite of the fact that a lot of directors were petrified of her." Kim's star turn in the show's brief but harrowing withdrawal scene was effectively showcased by Pollack's direction, the dark, noirish visuals from director of photography Ted Voigtlander, and a downbeat, foreboding score by Richard Markowitz.

Like J.T. Reid, the father of Faith Parsons was a relentless, driving perfectionist. However much she accomplished, it was never good enough for him. In a quiet scene between Faith and Ben Casey, she tells him that when her friends played "Three Musketeers" as children, she was always D'Artagnan. "Why not M'Lady?" Casey asks. Faith ducks the question, but one possible answer is that if she had been a boy, her father would have loved her as a son, the same situation Kim had faced as a girl in Albuquerque.

Kim received her usual rave reviews for the show, which aired on January 14 and January 21, 1963. "Kim Stanley [was] outstanding as a brilliant femme lawyer on the hypo," the *Hollywood Reporter* said. "Hers was the task of exposing the viciousness and selfishness that warps human decency when morphine is the master and the individual is the slave. Her withdrawal scene was explosive, but not to be negated is the subtly shaded personality she projected almost as frighteningly in the first part." *Variety*'s review, written in classic Varietese, was equally enthusiastic. "Miss Stanley . . . pull[ed] out all the emotional stops and let go with as devastating a display of educated scenery-chewing as has crossed the little screen in some time," it said. "To say she sank her teeth into the plum role would be an understatement. Miss Stanley chewed it, devoured it, digested it and spit out the seeds. Give the lady two ears, one tail and an entry in the Medical Journal under the heading of 'Hysteria for Fun and Profit.' Emmies are optional." Heeding *Variety*'s advice, the Academy of Television Arts and Sciences awarded Kim her first Emmy as best actress in a drama. Kim would not attend the Emmy ceremonies, and Robert Preston accepted for her.

While in Hollywood to do *Ben Casey*, Kim racked up one of her rare film credits. "Credit" isn't exactly the right word, as Kim insisted on being uncredited for her role as the narrator of *To Kill a Mockingbird.* Harper Lee's classic tale of a young girl growing up in the pre–civil rights South was adapted by Horton Foote for an Alan Pakula production directed by Robert Mulligan. Gregory Peck starred as Atticus Finch, a top-flight lawyer and courageous, unprejudiced man. He's also a father who loves his daughter as much as his son, as shown by the film's final image, in which Peck affectionately and protectively holds his young daughter Scout (Mary Badham).

Horton Foote says it was Alan Pakula's idea to have a narrator. Although Kim has only six passages, her voice is pivotal to *Mockingbird:*

It's the first one you hear in the film (save that of a girl humming over the opening credits) and the last. Because Kim did not want a credit, some viewers of the film have thought the narrator was Harper Lee herself. Kim opens the film by saying, "Macon was a tahr'd old town. Even in 1932, when I first knew it . . ." Her voice is rich, evocative, and Southern; it's her *Young Lady of Property* voice, slightly aged.

"She was not very commercial," Horton Foote recalls of Kim. "She loved the film, loved the people doing it, and wanted to make a contribution. And you know, she didn't accept a nickel for it." She did accept a few nickels, but not too many: Pakula-Mulligan Productions paid her $500, and there was apparently a token payment from Universal-International Pictures as well. This is evidence of Kim's artistic integrity, but also of her willful perversity: She was buying a house at the time and needed the money.

Kim's new home was an old farmhouse in the Rockland County town of Congers known as the DeBaun House, which dated back to the Revolutionary War. She would live there for ten years, as long as she had ever lived anywhere. In Suffern, Kim and Alfred had rented; in Congers, they would own the house they moved into in December of 1962. It came with 15 to 20 acres of tree-studded land, so in Congers, Kim would live in a clearing in the woods. Years later, Jamie remembered wandering through wild strawberry fields and finding a buried French flintlock pistol with a cracked octagonal barrel that, for all he knew, had been there since the American Revolution. But there were drawbacks.

"It was a suburban area that had only recently become suburbanized," Rachel says. "That became a major source of horror for Kim. We were this little island in a suburban wasteland—at least that was her point of view. She often despaired of what an unenlightened community it was. She had impulsively bought the house when she fell in love with it, but failed to notice there wasn't an artist or intellectual within 10 miles." There was one welcome neighbor, though: Kim's brother Justin and his first wife, Jeanne, lived in nearby Nyack at this time.

In interviews from this period, Kim gives the impression of being a super-mom who stayed with her children as late in the afternoon as possible before heading to New York for her show, and who drove back to Rockland County afterwards to be with them for breakfast. One interviewer suggested she might be "the world's greatest mother." Her children speak well of her, but acknowledge her flaws.

"She was funny and cheerful, with a great sense of humor," Rachel says. "Most of the time, she was very soft and mild-mannered. I don't remember her losing her temper often at all. My friends adored her." But, she adds, "She was the most intuitive person I have ever known. She could always peg a situation or a person. Which sometimes was not fun if you were the one being pegged."

Jamie says Kim was a hard person to deal with in many ways. "She was somewhat opinionated and definitely flawed," he says. "I saw her sometimes in a very bad light, and yet I loved her." That affection was strained, though. Patricia Neal says, "I was told her son really loathed her," while, years later, Kim's brother Justin put it more diplomatically: "Jamie has felt separate from his mother for a long time."

Kim also strove in her interviews to create a portrait of suburban domesticity. "The children go to the local public school," one profile read. "Kim is in the PTA. Alfred Ryder, between assignments, works around the house . . . [T]he Rockland County fruit trees put out blossoms . . . the air is soft, the grass fresh green and the sharpest noise the cries of the kids climbing over rockpiles in the yard . . ."

No matter how she tried, though, Kim was not your standard Suburban Madonna: She would read Don Marquis's *archy and mehitabel* to the children of Clifford Odets and their friends when they visited. "Kim would read all the parts—the cockroach and the cat and maybe there was someone else," Walt Odets recalls. "For a seventeen-year-old, it was totally riveting." But those entertaining skills came at a cost to Kim. "She had that remarkable kind of intensity that you saw in her acting," he says. "She was like that all the time. She was kind of like, never turned off, unless she just passed out. Kim was possessed. Kim was a possessed person. I don't know how else to put it."

Her strongly held principles led Kim into some improbable adventures. A dedicated pacifist, one night she led Alfred and several friends on an expedition to dig up a cannon on display in downtown Congers as part of a patriotic memorial. For several hours, they tried to dislodge it, failing to reckon with how tightly it was bolted down. Finally, they were picked up by local police who took them home rather than arrest them.

The house was decorated in a style Rachel describes as "eclectic Kim." "She would find something in an antique store, fall in love with it, and buy it. The styles didn't necessarily go together. When we still lived in New York, it was a sort of French antique style. Later, she got more into Country American and things she rescued from thrift stores." Kim's taste in music ran to Mozart and that period of classical music, although Rachel remembers Kim's fondness for Roger Miller and her piping "King of the Road" through the house on the intercom.

An important, if intermittent member, of the household was Kim's mother, Rubyann. She sometimes lived with them in Congers, and played an important role in helping Kim raise her children. Other times, Rubyann stayed at her apartment on West Fourth Street in Greenwich Village, which Kim paid for. Rachel recalls her grandmother as slight but not fragile, with long white hair in a bun on the top of her head and a pronounced Texas accent. "As was Kim's," Rachel says, "when she chose to reveal it."

Jamie remembers Rubyann as "a really strong person who did a lot for us, who had a lot of love. She was one of the strongest people you can imagine. We called her Mamaw." Rachel calls her "a little Texas firecracker," saying she was very energetic, always doing something, never sitting still. And, Rachel adds, she "took crap from no one." Rubyann was also more versed in the domestic arts than her famous daughter.

"My grandmother was an incredible Southern cook," Rachel says. "I've never had anything like the fried chicken she'd make." And Jamie remembers her gardening skills. "We had a small tomato garden in Congers with some corn. But it was Mamaw who tended it," he says. "Kim always seemed to have a love of growing flowers and tried to grow vegetables, but didn't seem to have the greenest thumb." The abiding fondness her grandchildren feel for Rubyann is manifest in Jamie's minutely observed description of her eyes: "blue with flecks of green and orange." There was also a series of housekeepers to keep an eye on the children when Kim was working and Mamaw was in Greenwich Village.

Jamie says their household never suffered for a lack of visitors. "We really had one hell of a childhood," he says. "Too many people came and went, but it was the best of both worlds." The two worlds were Rockland County and the Greenwich Village apartment Kim's children sometimes got to use as they grew up. "In some ways, I had three fathers [Brooks Clift, Curt Conway, and Alfred Ryder]," Jamie adds. "And many people that were somewhat nurturing."

It was a Bohemian household. "All these people were very unconventional," Jamie says. "Although they were still under convention in the public sense, the relationships were far more dynamic than whether or not they were staying together for twenty years or having your everyday middle-class life." Rachel agrees with Jamie's "three-father" observation.

"All these people were really, in their fashion, very attentive parents, very doting," she says. "We have incredible memories of things they would create for us. This was not a 'Mommie Dearest' childhood by any means. There was a lot of love in our house from our biological parents and our non-biological parents."

In Boston during the pre-Broadway tour of *A Far Country*, Rachel remembers Kim and Alfred having a suite in the Ritz-Carlton in Boston that was bigger than the house she lives in now (and she lives in a good-size house). "Something like one hundred people gave us presents," she recalls. "It was excessive. But it's wonderful when you're five years old. I felt like Eloise at the Plaza." In times to come, Kim could not pay the phone bill and the service would be cut off. "There was not a lot of consistency," Rachel says with a degree of understatement.

During the days of wine and roses, though, there was never a dull moment. Kim's household was wide open. Among the slew of visitors every weekend was Alfred's sister, actress Olive Deering, who would irritate the fastidious Kim by leaving teacups with teabags in them all over the house. And because both parents were of the theater, there was the expected household drama.

"I do remember some screaming fights," Rachel says. "But at that age, I thought that's what married couples did. In the theater world, people scream at each other a lot. Screaming arguments in my home were not an unusual thing, and they didn't always involve my parents." Kim and Alfred were clearly in love, she says, adding, "in a very intense way. Everything they did was very intense. Nothing was boring or mundane or routine," she says with a good-natured laugh.

I N THE FALL OF 1962, Kim signed to do her third William Inge play, *Natural Affection*. Inge was no longer the vital playwright of *Picnic* and *Bus Stop*, though, and Kim was ambivalent after reading the script. It took a personal pilgrimage to Congers by director Tony Richardson to convince her.

In *Natural Affection*, Kim would star as Sue Barker, a clothing buyer for a Chicago department store forced to choose between the unsuccessful car salesman she lives with and her son, just home from reform school, who has an un-natural affection for her. Harry Guardino played her live-in lover Bernie Slovenk, Gregory Rozakis was her son, and Tom Bosley her married, drunk, and closeted gay neighbor. After Sue decides to send her son back to reform school, he becomes enraged when another woman attempts to seduce him by saying, "Come to mama." In an act of displaced aggression, he stabs her to death, puts a twist record on the record player, drinks a glass of milk, and walks out.

Robert Whitehead had originally been scheduled to co-produce the play with Roger Stevens, but bowed out after the show's Phoenix tryout, starring Shelley Winters, because Inge would not make script revisions Whitehead wanted. Stevens, Tony Richardson later said, was not so keen on the play but produced it because he was keen on Kim, with whom it was rumored he had had an affair.

The director was utterly taken with his star. In his autobiography, *The Long-Distance Runner*, Richardson notes that he worked with Vanessa Redgrave, Peggy Ashcroft, Edith Evans, and Jeanne Moreau. "[But] never, before or since, have I worked with someone of such variety and impact [as Kim]," he wrote. "Directing Kim was as if you'd been given a piano and suddenly found you could play as well as Glenn Gould. She was like Larry [Sir Laurence Olivier], only more so." Richardson was so fascinated by Kim that he and his wife, Vanessa Redgrave, named their second daughter, Joely Kim, in part after her.

Mitch Erickson, the assistant stage manager on the play, was also impressed. "Kim would make me cry," he says. "And on different nights, it would be at different places in the script. The stage manager would kid me and say that I needed a new script, because I was shedding so many tears on the one I had."

Well into the rehearsal process, though, Kim had not memorized her part. "She drove Audrey Wood, Inge's agent, up the wall because she didn't learn the lines," Erickson says. "She held onto her script through tech. rehearsals in Washington. But she was listening to what was coming at her from the other actors. I did spend some hours cuing her in her suite at the Willard, but I never felt we were in an emergency situation."

Certainly Inge didn't act as if there were any emergency: Richardson found him inert and passive, his main activity eating a lot of desserts, especially pink custard and Jell-O. The only thing Inge showed any interest in was the Gregory Rozakis problem.

Richardson describes Rozakis as "a slightly catatonic young actor whose presence was effective, but whose impulses were so nonreactive that Kim would sometimes clap her hands in his face to get even a blink. It was the only thing she failed in." Knowing Richardson was unhappy with Rozakis, Inge brought a steady stream of his handsome young male friends to audition as a replacement, but none were much good and Rozakis kept his job.

Bonnie Bartlett, who played the young woman Rozakis stabs to death at the end, shares her director's opinion of Kim. A few rare actors, she says, "go out there willing to fail, to fall down—it's kind of a connection with the gods. You don't know what they're going to do."

Kim was supportive and loving and made you feel anything you did was okay, Bartlett adds. But she had to impose limits in her dealings with Kim. Bartlett was then in the process of adopting a baby. It was a direct adoption, and she and her husband were taking care of the young woman who was pregnant. "We had to place her with a family and Kim wanted to take her," Bartlett recalls. "I said, 'Well, I think you're a little bit too famous.' We arranged for another home for the girl until she gave birth. Even though I loved Kim, her drinking was very difficult for me to deal with."

Kim's transgressive nature made her scary in other ways. "I drove with her a couple of times, and she didn't pay any attention to the signs," she says. When Bartlett suggested she do so, Kim said, in effect, it didn't matter. "She did what she wanted, and that's very dangerous," Bartlett says. "You can't live in a society and not obey some of the rules."

Although Kim got along well with most cast members on *Natural Affection,* Tom Bosley was an exception. In the third act, Kim, Harry Guardino, and several others return from a night out at the Playboy Club. Guardino goes to wake up Bosley, who didn't accompany them because he had fallen asleep in a drunken stupor. "I start to philosophize for about twelve minutes," Bosley recalls. "In the process of staging it, Tony had the other people frozen in the living room. She resented greatly that she had to sit there while I did my schtick in the next room. The pressure she brought upon Tony hit me pretty good, too."

During the out-of-town tryout in Washington "there was one unfortunate evening at the Variety Club in Washington," Bosley recalls. "Kim had a couple of drinks and started to lash out at me verbally. My late first wife was with me. She was a very quiet, soft-spoken gal who, when she had something to say, really said it and kind of put Kim down." Still, Bosley couldn't help but admire Kim's acting and, when not onstage, stood in the wings and watched her work.

Originally, Roger Stevens planned to open *Natural Affection* on Broadway without an out-of-town tryout. But when a newspaper strike hit New York, he decided to open it at Washington's National Theater on January 16, 1963. (Playing elsewhere in D.C. that evening was the "First Family" troupe of comedian Vaughn Meader, which affectionately parodied President Kennedy.) *Natural Affection* got a good review from Richard Coe of the *Washington Post,* who called it Inge's best play yet. Other than that, the reviews augured poorly for Broadway. "This . . . is a family that could startle the most experience-hardened social worker," Jay Carmody wrote in the *Washington Star,* "one whose behavior suggests that Inge has set out at last to parody Inge." And Tom Donnelly of the *Washington Daily News* added, "These people just haven't got the stuff. They are slobs and they face the doom of slobs."

Although largely devoid of merit, the play is not wholly so: Inge has a few good lines, as when Sue (Kim's character) marvels at the ability of her drunken neighbor Vince to keep his job, saying, "He must be using someone else's liver." Kim was so calm backstage on this show, one could almost believe she was using someone else's nerves: She was as relaxed as she had been in *Cheri*, another short-lived and unsuccessful play. Publicity photos from *Natural Affection* show she had also put on weight since *A Far Country*, although Inge described her character as "drifting toward fat and forty," so perhaps she was just getting into character.

New York newspapers were publishing by the time the show opened January 31 at the Booth Theatre on Broadway, although given the hostile reviews, Roger Stevens may have regretted that. "This could have been a strikingly good and perhaps a great play," Norman Nadel wrote in the *World-Telegram & Sun*. "But two major errors have prevented this . . . bad taste and bad judgment. *Natural Affection* could become known as "Natural Function," that being the nature of its emphasis." In the *Wall Street Journal*, Richard Cooke called the play "a baneful bouquet of human unhappiness and derangement," while *Time* said "*Natural Affection* has the roiling, quivering hysteria of a child's uncontrollable tantrum . . . Like a tantrum, *Natural Affection* moves in a circular frenzy of grievance; neither the play's characters nor the play itself can be reasoned with, or placated, or ignored, or resolved."

Even the show's cast members were critics. During a dress rehearsal before the play went to Washington, Tony Richardson invited Tom Bosley to sit with him and watch the staging of the final scene. "At the climax, [a] neighbor wanders in," Bosley recalls. "The boy is drunk. He strangles her [stabs her, actually] behind the couch and performs sex upon her. Now he gets up, goes to the refrigerator, takes a drink, and walks out.

"I couldn't believe what I was seeing," he continues. "And Tony is sitting there just enjoying every minute of it. I turned to him and said, 'Would you like to have a little comic relief at the end?' He said 'What do you have in mind?' I said, 'While the boy is having sex with the dead girl, why don't you have the moving company come in and repossess the furniture?' Then I got up and walked out."

As usually happened with her bombs, Kim's reviews were vastly better than those of the play. Her biographical note in the *Playbill* for *Natural Affection* reads in part, "Her gifts defy category, and the ease with which she projects herself into each role regardless of its age, background, mood or period, is unique in the contemporary theatre." The critics agreed.

"The only way to account for *Natural Affection* is as a vehicle for Kim Stanley," wrote Michael Smith in the *Village Voice.* "Despite the fact that it's not a very good one, she is enchanting as always." *Newsweek* said, "Kim Stanley is an actress whose face can say in three seconds what three pages of script couldn't render as well." In *Show Magazine,* Anthony West said, "In this appallingly difficult part, Kim Stanley proved herself to be the best actress on the American stage today . . . When she is onstage, it does not occur to one that there is an alternative to her reading of the part." And in a joint plaudit for Kim and co-star Harry Guardino, West added, "Every scene they play together . . . is a pure joy to watch, a display without a single fault of the American naturalistic style at its most precise."

There was also praise for director Richardson and other cast members, but the show met the doom of slobs, closing on March 2, 1963, after only thirty-six performances. Its failure continued a distinctive pattern in Kim's Broadway career that began with her breakout success in *Bus Stop:* the regular alternation of hits with flops. Given Kim's keen intelligence, which extended to play selection (she predicted that *Toys in the Attic,* which she passed on, would succeed) and her sometimes physical aversion to going to the theater, it's easy to suspect she chose plays that would fail in alternation with hits so she wouldn't have to go to the theater more than necessary.

Several months after *Natural Affection* closed, another profile of Kim, titled "Kim's Light and Heat," appeared in *Show Magazine,* written by Mary Lukas. It acknowledged that in her personal life, Kim was as protean and varied as her *Playbill* write-up said she was on stage:

> For a woman who has shown so little interest in publicity, Kim Stanley has amassed over the years a large and bafflingly contradictory collection of public images. She has been alternately cited as the female Marlon Brando and the "World's Greatest Mother," excoriated as a voracious femme fatale and praised as

the very model of the quaint suburban housewife. She has been described by some friends as the pampered product of an accomplished, intellectual family, by others as a Little Nell who sewed on upholstery buttons at night to help her mother meet the rent. Acquaintances from different eras in her life have accepted her as, among other things, a Southern belle, a Texas oil heiress and the descendant of a Cherokee Indian.

Gently poking fun at herself and her youthful ambitions, Kim added another image: When she was a student at the Pasadena Playhouse, she said, "what I really wanted was to be Queen of the May."

Kim's ability to generate so many images, Lukas said, was a tribute to her acting skills. "Kim Stanley is probably the greatest young actress of her time," she wrote, noting that to William Inge she was the actress who generated the deepest aura of mystery. While noting the fondness many people had for her, Lukas added some words of caution.

"To those who love her—and they are many—she has always been 'a being deeply involved in life,' warm and full of sudden generosities, intensely preoccupied with her children, staunchly loyal to her friends. To more critical acquaintances she is certainly all these things, but beneath the softness, they sense a terrifying tension, 'something,' one has explained, 'like a high C held too long.'"

And remarkably, given that Kim was on top of the theater world, she talked to Lukas about "ditching the stage" and retiring to the country "just to be a mother." Among the people who knew Kim, Lukas said, the suggestion that she would retire was received with skepticism. "It's on the stage Kim really lives," they noted. "It's there she takes on shape and life and color."

By the spring of 1963, Kim and Alfred had been married for five years and together for seven. Unfortunately for Alfred, that was about as long as Kim could sustain a relationship. Mary Lukas wrote that "the last two years have been on the surface relatively quiet . . . rumors about difficulties in her private life have faded as quickly as they have come." But that simply wasn't so.

Just as *Natural Affection* ended, Alfred was directing and starring in an off-Broadway play, Oliver Hailey's *Hey You, Light-Man.* Joanna Frank played the ingenue lead and daughter of Ashley Knight, Alfred's character. "Alfred was drunk all the time," she says. "Kim would come running down the aisles during rehearsals and they would have the most extraordinary screaming battles right there in public. Nothing was hidden.

"I was very young and totally traumatized by this experience," she continues. "There was a moment in the play where I was supposed to sit in his lap. And he would drop me. His legs would give way—he was just so drunk. It was humiliating and scary. My eyes blew up and I had to go to all these dermatologists to find out what was wrong with my eyes. Finally, it turned out I was allergic to Alfred."

Speculating on why Kim's marriages failed, Roger O. Hirson says, "She had a bad father problem. Her men problem may have been a function of her father problem." Anne Jackson says, "I just don't think she was very stable." And Bonnie Bartlett says, "I don't think Kim could live with any man. She was just too strong and too neurotic." Some of Kim's friends speak disparagingly of her poor choice of husbands, but to be fair to them, being married to Kim must have been like living on the rim of a volcano, constantly having to peer down into the caldera for signs an eruption is imminent. Kim loved babies, marriages in the first flush of romance, and shows that had just opened. But sustaining her attention to them was always a problem.

U NTIL NOW, Kim had only appeared in one movie, *The Goddess,* and it had not been a happy experience: She didn't like filmmaking in general or Hollywood in particular. "No matter what you do in a film, it is, after all, bits and pieces for the director, and that's marvelous for the director, but it doesn't allow the actor to learn to mold a part," she told Lillian Ross. "In films, it is the director who's the artist," she said, adding, "It's in the very nature of the medium—waiting for lights and technicalities, starting and stopping your part for a minute or two at a take—that your sustained feeling gets cut off."

British director Bryan Forbes nonetheless wanted Kim for his upcoming film *Seance on a Wet Afternoon.* It was about Myra Savage, a disaffected lower-middle-class British housewife and self-styled medium who bullies her husband into kidnapping the daughter of a wealthy industrialist so she can "prove" her psychic powers by finding the girl.

"We offered it to a number of people—Simone Signoret, Deborah Kerr, et cetera—all of whom turned it down, I think, because of the subject matter," Forbes says. "Lucy Kroll was very dubious about it. She said, 'Well, you must go out into the country. Perhaps Kim will see you, and if you can talk her into it, fine.' So I went up and found her surrounded by children. She gave me tea and apparently liked me. I got her to see two films of mine, *The L-Shaped Room* and *Whistle Down the Wind*. She seemed to like the way I worked, she liked the script and said 'Yes.'"

Although Kim was not Forbes's first choice, producer and co-star Richard Attenborough says she was his. "The complexity of dramatic impression vital to the credibility of Myra was hard to find," he says. "Also an intellectual ability to follow and understand the character. I didn't believe Simone could convey, as Kim did, the otherworldliness which this woman inhabited in her private fantasies."

In late June of 1963, Kim sailed to England on the *S.S. United States* in a first-class outside cabin with a private bath. A photo of a smiling Kim being greeted by an equally smiling Forbes and Attenborough appeared in newspapers across Great Britain. Attenborough was especially happy with the press coverage, he told Lucy Kroll, in light of the Profumo scandal, which was "taking up 99 percent of every paper." (The Monica Lewinsky scandal of its day, the Profumo affair exploded in the British press when it was revealed that beautiful young English call girl Christine Keeler had been romantically involved with both British secretary of war John Profumo and Evgeni Ivanov, an official at the Soviet Embassy in London.)

Rather than settling right in, Kim moved several times, staying first at a flat in St. Peter's Square in London, then at the Bell Hotel in Maidenhead/Berks, and finally at the Oakley Court Bungalows along the Thames River near Windsor, with swans swimming up to shore.

While Kim was working on the film, Rubyann came over to visit with Lisa and Laurie Rachel. Jamie remained Stateside, staying with Curt Conway in Southern California and playing baseball. "I'm out of my head to see the children, and so sorry Jamie isn't coming now, but I can see his point," Kim said in a letter to Lucy Kroll. "And thank God he wants to be king of the baseball players!"

In the course of her visit, six-year-old Laurie Rachel became jealous of Judith Donner, the British child actress who played the kidnapped girl in the film. "Who was this impostor, who not only had the attention of my mother, but got a lot of great lines as well?" Rachel said years later. "Why couldn't I have played that part? Wasn't I as deserving as she? Just as adorable? Kim's real daughter? When I told my mother this, she was amused and horrified. As far as she was concerned, child actors were being cruelly exploited by both the studios and their parents. Not her child!"

Alfred Ryder did not visit Kim while she was working on *Seance,* but a man who was becoming an increasing part of her life did: attorney Joe Siegel. His sister Sally Radin remembers he went to England several times to visit Kim during filming to provide her with moral support.

One of the things that would make *Seance* a happy experience for Kim is that, unlike most films, it was shot in sequence as much as possible. "I can't tell anything about the film—as so much of it has to do with spooky lighting, shots, etc.," Kim said in a letter to Lucy Kroll, "but the atmosphere is quite genial and thank the dear god and Bryan—we're shooting in sequence so my amateur status in the medium doesn't show up quite so blatantly!"

The focal point of the film, the home of Myra (Kim) and Billy Savage (Attenborough), was a large, half-timbered house with a turret at 41 Marryat Road in Wimbledon that manages to look spooky even on a bright spring morning. The woman who owned the house agreed to let Forbes use it, but asked why he chose it. For the turret, Forbes said. "That figures," the woman said, "the last owner committed suicide in that room." The house's spooky qualities apparently carried back to Pinewood Studios, where much of the film was shot. "When we built a replica of the seance room at Pinewood Studios, it was never warm," Forbes says. "It was always cold. It was strange."

Despite Kim's worries, filmmakers Forbes and Attenborough found her to be a remarkable film actress. "She always went beyond the evidence," Forbes later wrote, "never taking the easy route and constantly surpris[ing] me and Richard Attenborough with the purity of her invention." Attenborough adds, "She was an extraordinary actress. She was driven by a passionate intuition which overtook any research and logic and thinking about the thing. When it came to playing on the floor, she just took off.

"She so occupied the psyche of this extraordinary woman, it impelled her to take certain moves and make certain decisions which just a good actress, a really very good actress, simply wouldn't get anywhere near," he continues. "She transferred her viewers into the world which she occupied."

In the course of doing so, though, Kim gave her colleagues heartburn. "It was quite complicated when I put my actor's hat on," says Attenborough, who also produced the film. "Because you never quite knew what she was going to do, not merely in terms of the delivery of her lines. It used to drive the camera operator to his wits' end—you didn't know which side of the set she was going to be on.

"[In 1963], the constraints on lenses and microphones and so on were considerable," he continues. "Now, if somebody's two or three feet off their marks, it couldn't matter less. You're capable of holding, with a good focus puller, whatever you want. In those days, you couldn't be a foot off your mark, unless the dolly pusher was absolutely superb. But the end result was bewitching."

Bryan Forbes also remembers how Kim's free spirit made for difficult moments during filming. "There was one notable occasion when I was panning her through the kitchen (of the Savages' home) with the child out to the back yard. And she suddenly stopped, but the camera operator went on, and I had to say 'Cut!' I said, 'What's the problem, Kim?' She said, 'I was relating to the oranges.' There was a bowl of oranges on the table. So I said, 'What a brilliant idea. I wish I'd thought of it. Unfortunately, Kim, it's a waste shot. Why don't you relate to them on the move, instead of stopping and relating?' She was a tortured soul in many ways. She was really too good an actress to suffocate herself with all that Method shit."

Kim would also drive the continuity supervisor batty by saying she didn't want to smoke in a scene where she had already been smoking.

("Here's how we get 'round it," Forbes would tell her, "as soon as I say 'Action,' stub it out.") Or she would change her hairstyle when they had filmed only part of a scene. But, Forbes adds, "I can't recall, apart from the problems she gave herself, that she was unhappy. She got on with everybody and was a delight to work with."

Although she claimed otherwise, Kim drank while working on *Seance*. Forbes and Attenborough have different memories of it. "She would leave the set," Attenborough says. "Bryan and I knew she was going to have a little snifter . . . She never appeared to be inebriated at all. But she needed that courage, whatever it was for."

Forbes adds, "On one occasion I asked the wardrobe mistress, 'Where is she getting it?' It was classic—the "Lost Weekend" syndrome. She had a bottle of vodka inside the toilet tank, suspended on a string. I said to her, 'Kim, dear, we don't have Prohibition here. If you want to drink, I'll have a drink with you.' She looked me straight in the eye and said, 'How dare you? I never drink when I'm working.' So I had to say 'Fine.'"

A few days before she was scheduled to finish shooting her scenes on August 16, an anguished Kim threatened to walk off the film. "I was sitting at home one night," Bryan Forbes recalls. "She rang and said, 'I can't come in in the morning. He's dying and I have to go to him.' I said, 'Who's dying, Kim?' and she said Clifford Odets. I said, 'We can't possibly restrain you. But if you go, Dickie [the future Lord Attenborough] and I are broke.'" They tried to juggle the schedule to shoot around her while she was gone, but the matter was resolved when Odets died before Kim could get on a plane.

Kim was calmer when interviewed by the *New York Times* during filming. She spoke about the myths surrounding Method acting while mixing a gin and tonic. The reporter added, "Another myth that Miss Stanley is quick to destroy is that there is any 'mystery' about her. 'I'm not in the least mysterious,' she said. 'I don't know why anybody should think I am.' To look at her was to share her sense of the absurdity of the charge. Frank, steady blue eyes [they were hazel, but perhaps they were acting blue]; rumpled fair hair, ash-tinted; no make-up; a simple, loose pink-check gingham dress. No hint of mystery or intensity anywhere." It was another successful performance by Kim.

When Kim finished filming, she planned to take a brief vacation in southern France. "Lying in the sun all day long doing absolutely nothing is my idea of heaven," she told the reporter. The image of Kim as happily indolent, lazing away endless hours in the sun, is not one that crops up frequently in her career, but she chose to project it here. Less publicly, she shared her impressions of English men in a letter to Lucy Kroll, implying that their well-bred manner was suggestive of homosexuality, and that only the acid test of sex could answer the question: Were they or weren't they? "The men never cease to amaze me," Kim wrote. "Even the most masculine seem effete—and how's one to know without the 'act of darkness'—*quelle dommage* [what a pity]!"

Although *Seance,* with its child abduction and somewhat unsympathetic leading characters, could be seen as uncommercial, it would have been more so if Bryan Forbes hadn't altered several plot points of the Mark McShane novel. In the book, Kim's character slaps the kidnapped girl. And during a seance attended by the girl's mother (played in the film by Nanette Newman, Forbes's wife), the Richard Attenborough character accidentally suffocates the girl when she cries out from the next room.

While tension-ridden, *Seance* moves, for the most part, with agreeable slowness. The one notable exception is the rapid-fire Leicester Square sequence, when Attenborough goes to pick up ransom money from the little girl's father (Mark Eden), while, at the same time, a detective comes to the Savages' house to snoop around for possible evidence of the girl. The naturalism of the scene in Leicester Square was heightened by Forbes's shooting with hidden cameras. He did such a good job of concealing them that part of the scene had to be reshot: Unaware that a movie was being made, several prominent Londoners such as Sir John Gielgud were captured on film wandering about the square running their daily errands.

Impressive in its technical achievements, *Seance* is also a moving film. Early on, the henpecking Myra scolds Billy over his lack of mediumistic powers. "You know what I sometimes wish?" she asks. "I sometimes wish I were ordinary like you . . . Dead ordinary. Ordinary and dead like all the others." By the end, when Attenborough stands up to Kim, it's a testimony to the resilience of the human spirit and gives the film, despite its gloom and shadows, a profoundly humanistic core.

The humanism of *Seance* also appears in its well-placed literary allusions. Late in the film, Kim says to Attenborough, "It's so bright after a seance. Brightness just falls from the air." As *Newsweek* astutely noted, this was a reference by screenwriter Bryan Forbes to *In Time of Pestilence*, by sixteenth-century English poet Thomas Nashe, who wrote, "Brightness falls from the air/Queens have died young and fair/Dust hath closed Helen's eye/I am sick, I must die." The allusion is apt here, as the kidnapped girl is in mortal peril: Myra has decided that instead of releasing her, they should kill her, so she can become a playmate in the afterworld for their stillborn son, Arthur. (Instead of killing her in the film, Billy leaves her where she can be found and restored to her parents.)

While putting the film together, Forbes was impressed with Kim's performance, although he knew she would not be as laudatory. "I am trying to finalize a cut of the film," he wrote to Lucy Kroll in October. "Everybody is eulogistic about Kim's performance. I cannot promise you that it will satisfy her! But I think lesser perfectionists will find nothing to complain of."

Among those lesser perfectionists were the bulk of the English film critics. When *Seance* was released in England in June of 1964, the *London Express* called *Seance* "a superbly atmospheric film." And in the *Sunday Telegraph,* Philip Oakes called it "an original, intensely exciting film which runs the worthwhile risk of alienating its audience . . . compassionate, intelligent and absorbing." Kim did just as well by the critics. "With her ravaged beauty and tortured quasi-ethereal voice, the American actress Kim Stanley is superb" as "this suburban Lady Macbeth," said the *Evening News and Star.* The *Sunday Telegraph* said, "[The] lady medium [is] lambently played by the American actress Kim Stanley," using an arcane term for "flickering lightly" or "shining gently." Ernest Betts in *The People* said, "Kim Stanley's performance as the half-mad wife is a masterpiece." In the *Observer,* Penelope Gilliatt added a cautionary note, however. "Kim Stanley does it horribly well," she wrote. "It's a pity she couldn't manage the English accent better."

Oddly, the Berlin Film Festival refused to accept *Seance* as an entry, saying they didn't understand it. A more serious setback came in the form of the English weather in the summer of 1964: It was beautiful, and no one wanted to be inside when they could enjoy the glorious sun of York. "Attendance figures everywhere have been considerably reduced," Bryan Forbes wrote to Lucy Kroll. "The expectancy for the gross in the U.K. has now been cut by 50 percent . . . The sunny weather was literally of a freak nature and could not have been anticipated. We normally have a pretty putrid July and might well have come out with marvellous figures. This was not to be and we have lost the gamble."

Kim's finances were in an even greater state of disarray. An account she had at the Trade Bank and Trust Company of New York was overdrawn by $2,000. She had ignored several bills from the legal firm of Weissberger and Frosch, which did her accounting. And another account she had in a Congers bank was also overdrawn. "Now, darling, as to your Congers bank account. Please don't write any more checks on it because, my darling girl, there ain't no money in that account anymore," Lucy Kroll wrote to Kim while she was filming *Seance,* adding, "I'm just asking you to learn to live on $500 a week." (In 2005 money, that would be more than $2,700 a week.)

Fortunately, *Seance* was a commercial success when it opened in the United States in November. Distributed by former bandleader Artie Shaw's Artixo Productions, it was a critical success as well. In the *New York Herald-Tribune,* Judith Crist called it "the perfect psychological suspense thriller and a flawless film to boot," while Bosley Crowther of the *New York Times* wrote, "It isn't often you see a melodrama that sends you forth with a lump in your throat, as well as a set of muscles weary from being tensed for nigh two hours. But that's the condition you may expect to be in after watching *Seance on a Wet Afternoon.*"

Kim's performance won similar praise. "Miss Stanley gives a horrifying, pitiful, utterly compelling performance," the *Hollywood Reporter* said. "She has a final scene in which she pulls together the character she is playing that is one of the most shattering in all screen acting." (In that scene, the film's concluding seance, Myra suffers a nervous breakdown while performing a seance for the police investigator who correctly suspects her of masterminding the girl's kidnapping.) And in *Life*, Roald Dahl wrote, "With a seraphic smile, she forces [Attenborough] to do the most terrible things, and I think that many a husband in the audience, after watching Stanley's performance, will look rather carefully at his own wife the next time she gives him her sweetest, most angelic smile."

As in the British reviews, Forbes and Attenborough also came in for their share of well-deserved plaudits. Several theaters, such as the Plaza in New York, refused to seat people once the movie had begun so as not to distract viewers with latecomers shuffling around during suspenseful sequences.

Kim would get an Oscar nomination as best actress for the film. (She did not attend the Academy Awards, though: Bryan Forbes was there to accept on her behalf if she had won.) She also received a nomination from the British Academy of Film and Television Arts as best foreign actress, and several other nominations and awards, including the award for best actress from the New York Film Critics. "In all but the best actress category, the 13 critics had difficulty agreeing on a winner," the *New York Times* noted. "[But] Kim Stanley easily captured the acting prize." In doing so, she beat out Julie Andrews in *Mary Poppins*, Sophia Loren in *Marriage, Italian Style*, and Audrey Hepburn in *My Fair Lady*.

After a sneak preview at New York's Cinema East in January of 1965, *Seance* opened in Kim's hometown of Albuquerque on February 19 at Don Pancho's Art Theater. On March 2, there was a special tribute to her that featured Albuquerque Mayor Archie Westfall (who had owned the UNM bookstore when Kim worked there as a student) and J.T., Kim's father. Kim was absent, although if she didn't show up for the Oscars and Emmys, she could hardly be expected to appear in Albuquerque, a city whose legitimate claim to her she would vigorously deny to her last breath.

J.T. was proud to accept the accolade on behalf of his daughter, but as Kim wisely told Lillian Ross, it wasn't as important to him as fishing. At about this time, he was teaching a course on fishing at UNM Extension. One day, the class went out on Lake Conchas in northeastern New Mexico. Marilyn Murphy, a friend of Carol White, Kim's half sister, was in the class, and J.T. invited her to go out in a motorboat with him. Far out on the lake, strong winds came up and the boat was in danger of capsizing. Murphy thought they would not make it back, but J.T. calmly took the helm and steered her safely back to shore, something he would never be able to do for Kim.

WHILE KIM WAS SAILING BACK FROM EUROPE after making *Seance,* Lucy Kroll cabled her aboard the *Leonardo da Vinci* to see if she was interested in the role of Marilyn Birchfield, Rod Steiger's romantic interest in Sidney Lumet's *The Pawnbroker.* It didn't happen, and the role went to Geraldine Fitzgerald. At this time, the possibility of working with another Sidney arose: Kim was interested in doing a stage version of *Othello* with Sidney Poitier. But nothing came of that, either.

Having not done a comedy since *Bus Stop,* Kim decided to do *The Owl and the Pussycat,* a two-character play by TV sitcom writer William Manhoff about the romance that blooms between an ill-matched pair of neighbors: Felix, a nebbishy pseudo-intellectual writer, and Doris, an actress-model working as a call girl. On May 16, 1963, before sailing to England to do *Seance,* she had signed a contract to appear in it on Broadway.

Alexander Cohen was going to produce the show and Stanley Prager would direct, but it didn't happen, either, at least not for Kim. Philip Rose, who produced it on Broadway in 1964, believes they had problems coming up with the right leading man. But securing a director was an even bigger problem.

On July 2, 1963, Stanley Prager bowed out of the project because, Lucy Kroll felt, Prager was afraid of working with Kim. A host of directors was considered, and it looked for a while like Josh Logan, Kim's director on *Picnic,* would rescue the project. At first, the manic-depressive Logan was manic ("Josh Logan loves *The Owl and the Pussycat,*" Lucy Kroll wrote to Kim on July 11. "He has been waiting for a long time . . . to work with you again"). Then, two days later, he turned depressive ("Logan said play has such severe problems," Alexander Cohen told Lucy Kroll on July 13) and withdrew. Eventually directed by Arthur Storch and starring Alan Alda and Diana Sands, *The Owl and the Pussycat* made Broadway history as the first black-white romance not specifically written into the script.

Kim's next project was a two-part episode of TV's psychiatrically themed series *The Eleventh Hour,* which aired on March 25 and April 1, 1964. The somewhat soap-operatic plot featured Kim as Carol Fields, an anxious social climber married to an engineer husband (Philip Abbott) who is frequently out of town. Their daughter, Gina (Kim Darby), develops personal problems and is sent to the school counseling program headed by Dr. Starke (Ralph Bellamy). Carol makes a pass at Dr. Starke's associate, Dr. Graham (Jack Ging), who is treating Gina. When he rebuffs her, she tries to sabotage the school counseling program by accusing Dr. Graham of offering sex education. She also hopes this will score her points with town social arbiter Maggie Britt (Joan Tompkins).

In one scene, Kim lightheartedly and flirtatiously tells Drs. Starke and Graham they know too much about her through their treatment of her daughter. She then accidentally drops her purse, spilling its contents, and her high-strung character viscerally screams "Damnation!" with no transition from the social banter preceding it. Although the show is no great shakes, this is Kim at her best.

Philip Abbott also does a good job as Kim's husband. Angered at her lying about Dr. Graham and at her refusal to buy furniture for their almost-vacant house until she can afford more expensive pieces, he lashes out, "Carol, there's got to be a point where illusion ends and reality takes over. Will you please leave that fantasy land of yours where you're always the Queen of May and grow up!"

As the emotionally troubled but sensitive and precocious adolescent daughter, Kim Darby comes close to stealing the show from Kim. In one scene, Darby unleashes a Kim Stanley–quality screaming burst right in Kim's face. The script doesn't call for Kim's character to return fire, which is unfortunate, as Darby gives the impression of being one of the few actresses she ever worked with who was able to go toe-to-toe with Kim.

A scene toward the end of the show's second part allows Kim to showcase her quieter side. Kim's character throws a party at her house to collect signatures calling for the resignation of Dr. Graham. The party is broken up when Drs. Starke and Graham bring home Gina, who has run away. Everyone leaves and Kim wanders through her now-empty house. Even before she picks up a petition and throws it in an ashtray,

Kim somehow lets you know she's going to heed her husband's advice, abandon her flighty fantasies, and start working to restore their marriage. She holds you rapt as she moves from room to room in the empty house, with no dialogue or other characters to interact with, something only the best actresses can do.

In real life, though, Kim's marriage to Alfred Ryder was beyond repair. Around the spring of 1964, he went to Mexico to obtain a divorce. Adding to his woes was the misfortune that befell him playing Hamlet in New York's Central Park on June 10, with Julie Harris as Ophelia. The play would be televised nationally the next night, and Alfred was primed for a triumph.

But it was an unusually chilly evening for early June and, as the show went on, Alfred developed laryngitis. "The arch villain in last night's presentation of *Hamlet* . . . turned out to be not so much Claudius as laryngitis," the *New York Times* said. "Through a long and chilly evening, it seemed that [Ryder] was in a race to see whether or not he could complete the performance before his voice gave out completely." While saying "a Hamlet deprived of his vocal equipment is like a fiddler without a bow," the *Times* praised Alfred for his courage and show-must-go-on spirit. It was a doubly cruel blow to the man who had aspired to be the definitive Hamlet of his generation.

O N JULY 19, Kim married for the fourth time, to attorney Joseph Siegel. The wedding was held in the living room of Siegel's mother in Mount Vernon, New York; Kim was thirty-nine, her groom thirty-five. Joe Siegel worked in real estate and corporate and securities law. He also had an affinity for artists and show business and would co-produce several off-Broadway plays.

Joe's sister Sally Radin remembers him as brilliant and generous. "He entertained beautifully, too," she adds. "If he came to the house, he didn't bring two bottles of wine, he brought eight. He would come in like Santa Claus." But one Army buddy describes him as tense, and Justin, Kim's brother, didn't care for him. "[He was] a highly dependent-type person who took a ride with Kim," he says. "I don't mean to say that he didn't have some positive aspects, but he was easily dominated and ready to say people were taking advantage of him."

Other acquaintances say he was good-natured and easygoing. Mel Juffe was with Siegel in the Army when both were stationed in Germany during the Korean War. He remembers the "half and half" story Siegel liked to tell on himself.

"When we were in Germany, he took relief and went to London," Juffe says. "He had fantasized about going into a British pub and saying, 'Bartender, I'd like an "arf 'n arf."' That was a classic thing to have at a British bar—you would see it in the movies. He found the picture-perfect pub, walked up to the bar, and said, 'I'll have an "arf 'n arf."' And the bartender said, 'Arf of what and 'arf of what?' And Joe said, 'The trouble was, I didn't know the answer.'"

Siegel and Juffe had been in the 301st Radio Broadcast and Leaflet Group, a psychological warfare unit. Siegel was handsome, charming, and stylish, as well as a successful attorney who moved easily in entertainment circles. But an expertise in psychological warfare has to be one of the last things one hopes to see on the résumé of a prospective spouse.

Kim's daughter Rachel felt he used that training during his three-year marriage to Kim. "He almost immediately began playing us [Kim's children] against each other, and against Kim," she says. If he had a fight with Kim, he would take the children out for ice cream to curry favor with them. Rachel felt her new stepfather was manipulative; Kim's mother Rubyann didn't like him at all. "She hated him," Rachel says. "I think for most of that marriage she was at her apartment in New York." Writer Roger O. Hirson expresses an attitude toward the marriage shared by many of Kim's show-business acquaintances. "I thought the marriage was bizarre," he says, "because he was so straight [not of the theater]."

During their marriage, Kim took a new fashion cue from Siegel, often walking around the house in a top and a pair of his boxer shorts. Her drinking continued unabated, though. "He would tell me about the extraordinary ingenuity of the alcoholic in her," says Robert Lasky, Siegel's law partner at the time. "He would search, search, search—the 'Lost Weekend' thing. The bottles hidden in several levels of the lingerie drawer. You'd find one and if you didn't look further—that was just to mislead you."

Robert Matson, who later joined Siegel and Lasky in their practice, heard stories as well. "I remember his telling me once that they put her in Doctors Hospital, over on East End Avenue near Gracie Mansion," he says. "The hospital was kind of fancy, and you could order food in your room. And he said, 'You know what? They have beer on the menu. She's supposed to be drying out, and she was ordering beer in the hospital.'"

Lasky recalls Siegel's utter frustration with Kim. On one occasion he came into their office bloodied because he'd rammed his fist into a glass door panel. But he still defended her. "Joe was very much a believer that you have to forgive people who make a contribution—who have special attributes," he says. "I frankly disagreed with the notion that just because somebody had a unique ability or even genius that they were entitled to run roughshod over people who were perhaps normal types."

For years, the Actors Studio had considered setting up a production unit, which would allow the Studio's many talented actors to do edgier, more interesting work than standard Broadway fare. Finally, during the 1963–64 theater season, the Actors Studio Theater was created. It staged five plays, including *Strange Interlude*, *Blues for Mister Charlie*, *Marathon '33*, and, oddly, the sitcom-like *Baby Want a Kiss*, starring Paul Newman and Joanne Woodward. The last play of the AST season was *The Three Sisters*, Chekhov's classic about three sisters in provincial Russia whose inability to get to Moscow symbolizes the difficulties we have in fulfilling our dreams, and how we make peace with ourselves when we fail to attain them.

Kim played Masha, Geraldine Page was Olga, and Shirley Knight, Irina. The ensemble cast of Studio players featured Gerald Hiken as their brother, Andrei, and Barbara Baxley as his shrewish wife, Natalya, with Luther Adler as the defeated old Doctor Chebutykin, Albert Paulsen as Kim's ineffectual husband, and Kevin McCarthy as Vershinin, Kim's lover. Robert Loggia was the hotheaded Solioni; James Olson, the idealistic Baron Tuzenbach; Tamara Daykarhanova, the aging nurse; and Salem Ludwig played Ferrapont, the comic relief. Actors Studio artistic director Lee Strasberg would direct the production.

The Three Sisters had not been done on Broadway since the

1942–43 season, when Katharine Cornell played Masha, Judith Anderson was Olga, and Ruth Gordon, Natalya. (The orderly in that production was played by Kirk Douglas.) Strasberg was eager to revive the show because he had seen the Moscow Art Theater do it in 1924, and felt it failed to capture onstage the full emotional richness Chekhov had envisioned.

The drama of casting *The Three Sisters* would equal the drama onstage. Anne Bancroft wanted to play Masha. When offered the role of Natalya by Strasberg, Bancroft responded angrily, "No, no, darling. I play Masha or nothing." It was nothing. Strasberg wanted his daughter Susan to play Irina, but Kim was dead set against it. In the early spring of 1964, an article in *Variety* reported Kim had withdrawn from the show. Then, on April 8, she reversed course. "Kim Stanley, who withdrew several weeks ago from the forthcoming Actors Studio revival of *The Three Sisters,* has changed her mind and agreed to appear in the play," *Variety* noted. "Perhaps by coincidence, Susan Strasberg . . . has withdrawn." As *Variety* wryly suggested, it was no coincidence. The previous October, one of Lucy Kroll's assistants wrote her a note. "Kim feels that Susan Strasberg is wrong for part of youngest sister (also didn't like several other of Strasberg's casting decisions)," it said. "Kim holding contracts until the casting shapes up."

Shirley Knight replaced Susan Strasberg. Knight has good, if bittersweet, memories of Kim. "She was a very loving woman," Knight says. "My daughter Kaitlin was a baby, only six months old. I would bring her to the theater and Kim would just snatch her up and kiss her feet. My daughter would giggle. She just loved that."

Knight recalls how, one night on stage, Kim used a handkerchief to deal with a medical emergency, much as she had done on *The Traveling Lady.* "I have a scar on my right hand because of something that happened onstage," she says. "During a scene, Robert Loggia knocked over a wine glass. It broke, and a piece of it was on the floor. I picked it up, because I knew Kim would be kneeling there, and had it in my hand.

"She had never done this before," Knight continues, "but for some reason that night, Kim grabbed my hand and squeezed it. I had an expression on my face of incredible pain. She looked at me and opened my hand, which was bleeding, took out the piece of glass, and wrapped her handkerchief around my hand. It was such an indication of her humanity and professionalism that she didn't scream and ask if there was a doctor in the house. She simply dealt with it in the moment."

But, Knight adds, "her alcoholism frightened me. I had grown up with uncles and a grandfather who were alcoholic. They were always very frightening people because they were out of control." She feels the combination of Kim's drinking and the depth of her acting took a toll on her. "Most actors don't enter into zones where they're tampering with their psyche, because they're doing what I call pretend acting," she says. "When you enter into very deep emotional work that is tampering with your psyche, you have to be very healthy. And I think acting became too difficult for Kim, for her emotional stability, and the alcohol did not help."

That Kim was on edge was shown by an incident during the play's run. When the curtain goes up at the start, Kim, as Masha, is discovered sitting on a chaise longue at stage center. "There was a pillow on that chaise," Robert Loggia recalls. "Someone inadvertently fussed with the pillow—moved it or touched it, and she went ballistic. It was like 'Keep your fucking hands off the chaise and that pillow!' It was a very private thing. She was getting something from that object."

Another piece of casting Kim was unhappy with was Masha's lover, Vershinin. According to *Three Sisters* stage manager Martin Fried, Marlon Brando was offered the role, but turned it down at the last minute. Kevin McCarthy read for Lee Strasberg one day at the Actors Studio, only to notice someone sitting with him as he auditioned: Kim.

"It was as though she wanted to pass on who was going to play opposite her," McCarthy says. "It was an unattractive action, I thought. But you play your power, and she was playing her power." Kim's power had its limits, though: Strasberg told her one day at lunch he had chosen McCarthy against her wishes. She stormed out of the restaurant where they were eating.

Kim and McCarthy did not get along. When they began rehearsing Act Three, the fire scene, Kim played it in a sad, weeping manner, while McCarthy was laughing and jovial. After several rehearsals, Kim asked McCarthy, "Why are you laughing?" Referring to Chekhov's stage instruction calling for Vershinin to laugh, McCarthy curtly responded, "Because Tony says so."

Coming back to rehearsal one day from lunch, McCarthy picked up his script and discovered that someone had taken it, scratched out the word "Vershinin" wherever it appeared and, in its place, substituted "Father." "I thought, 'What the hell's going on here?'" McCarthy recalls. "Then I realized I'd picked up Kim's script by mistake. She had chosen, evidently, to identify Vershinin as a substitute for her father."

Kim's drinking posed a particular problem for McCarthy. Speaking of the dramatic farewell between Masha and Vershinin in the final act, he says, "At the last moment, she appears and rushes across the stage to Vershinin, throws her arms around him, and gives me this BIG KISS! And this kiss is where I earned my salary. You wondered if she'd been sick to her stomach. You had the feeling that somebody may have been drinking too much!"

Although *The Three Sisters* is an ensemble piece, Kim made the play her own. But to his frustration, director Lee Strasberg did not have much to do with molding her performance. As David Garfield reports in *A Player's Place,* at one rehearsal, the Studio's Michael Wager watched Kim's third-act entrance with her hair streaming down her back. "What's this?" he asked Strasberg. "She looks like she's playing the mad scene from *Lucia di Lammermoor!*" Strasberg, unable to coax Kim away from this interpretation, spluttered, "She's playing it that way because she thinks Masha goes crazy in the third act!"

Another time, Kim was chatting with Gerald Hiken, whose dressing room was next to hers. "Kim said, 'You know, Lee might have been right when he said the way I'm playing Masha, she would have walked to Moscow,'" Hiken recalls. "Which I think is a reference to how fiercely independent she played the character, without regard to the social conventions of the period, which would have made her a little more circumspect."

Although Kim had said her goal in acting was to convey the playwright's meaning, she interpreted that mandate broadly on *The Three Sisters.* Poet Randall Jarrell, whose translation was used for the production, estimated that fully one quarter of the lines Kim spoke were of her own devising. After one performance, Kim reportedly said to him, "I love your translation," to which he responded, "I love yours."

Kim was heedless of the director and translator, at odds with her romantic lead, and working on a different level from her fellow cast members. In *A Player's Place,* David Garfield writes, "There were those who pointed out that the sheer brilliance of her portrayal tended to disturb the balance of the play and to make of the drama a one-woman show." Chekhov would probably no more have recognized a Masha who goes off the deep end than Randall Jarrell recognized his translation as improved by Kim. In taking these liberties, and by not functioning on the same plane as her fellow actors, Kim was crashing through all the collaborative barriers ordinarily inherent in an ensemble piece; Icarus-like, she was flying too close to the sun (in one performance, Geraldine Page said, "I thought Kim had really broken loose and gone into the stratosphere"). Although Kim's career-ending nervous breakdown would not come until after the May 1965 failure of *The Three Sisters* in London, her inability to work with her collaborators in New York suggests she was already beginning to spiral out of control.

The play got mixed but largely positive reviews when it opened at the Morosco Theatre on June 22, 1964. "It is gallant of the Actors Studio to bring in *The Three Sisters* at this time of year," Howard Taubman wrote in the *New York Times.* "The town is richer for residents and visitors with Chekhov's tender, rueful masterpiece." (Not so sure was *Variety,* which said it was hardly the sort of entertainment to attract tourists in New York for the World's Fair.) Emory Lewis, in *Cue* magazine, added "It was a rare and enchanted evening, but I was confused. I kept thinking I was off-Broadway . . . Broadway, as everyone knows, is for musicals and ephemeral sex comedies." And Jerry Tallmer, in the *New York Post,* wrote, "The Actors Studio talks a good deal about truth. Last night at the Morosco Theater it nailed for a lifetime the right to do so . . . It is difficult to believe that there has ever been a more organic and total production of *The Three Sisters* anywhere at any time, whether in Russia or the United States."

More critical was Judith Crist of the *Herald-Tribune,* who wrote, "[T]here is a diffusion of character, a variety of acting styles and a diversity of mood that vitiates the cumulative impact of the play." And, in a sardonic comment on the Method pauses punctuating the play, John Simon wrote, "In the gaping interstices of this production, a whole other one could be staged."

Kim's work was praised by critics and colleagues alike. Robert Loggia and several other cast members, when not on stage, would go down to the wings and watch Kim work, much as Tom Bosley had done on *Natural Affection*. And Ben Gazzara was enthralled with her performance.

"She had a moment that tore my heart out, that was brilliant," he recalls. "She says a simple line: 'I love that man.' She started it low. It was just going to come out 'I love that man.' But from the 'I love' to the 'that man,' there was an eruption, a flood of tears that was just . . ." Gazzara sighs and pauses, ". . . overpowering. It surprised you—you didn't see it coming. That's always the best kind of acting."

Judith Crist said, "Miss Stanley's Masha is a magnificent figure . . . Caught up suddenly in a romantic encounter . . . She seethe[s] with a furious and womanly passion that sweeps the stage and makes it hers . . . relegating Shirley Knight's girlishly hysterical Irina and Geraldine Page's headachy and wispy Olga to the periphery." Similarly, Michael Smith in the *Village Voice* wrote, "Kim Stanley's portrayal of Masha is astonishing. Not only does she achieve a complete and stunning character, with a rare combination of emotional and physical acting, but she also, sometimes single-handedly, establishes the rhythm for whole scenes and focuses them around her." In *Cue*, Emory Lewis called Kim "one of our national art treasures."

A more critical note was struck by Nathan Cohen of the *Toronto Daily Star*, who wrote, "In Mr. Strasberg's production, the sisters are merely discontented small-town women . . . Kim Stanley's characteristically mannered, sighing and crying Masha is particularly objectionable." And Richard Attenborough, an admirer of Kim's, was disappointed. "She was totally ill-disciplined," he says. "The performance varied by half an hour a night. It was extraordinary." Kim's weight was also a factor in some reviews: Judith Crist described her as "a solid, ample figure in black," while Norman Nadel of the *World-Telegram & Sun* said she had the look of a vegetating hausfrau.

Geraldine Page as Olga and Shirley Knight as Irina got good reviews, with consistent enthusiasm for Barbara Baxley's performance as Natalya. While there was praise for Kevin McCarthy's Vershinin, he drew some of the sharpest critical comments, affirming Kim's casting instincts.

Critics were split on Lee Strasberg's direction: Howard Taubman said, "Under Lee Strasberg's direction, the Actors Studio Theater is doing the best work of its youthful career," and Jerry Tallmer wrote, "Lee Strasberg proved . . . that he could direct a play . . . with all the creative truth and strength a human being can command." But Judith Crist spoke of "the strangely disjointed minuet through which Lee Strasberg, rather than Chekhov, seems to have guided [the actors]," while Jack Thompson in the *Journal-American* said "his direction is halting and he seems to allow his actors to be eternally fondling things like canes or glasses or just rubbing their heads."

Kim's new husband, who had always been drawn to the theater, used his connection to Kim to act out his "star for a day" fantasy. "When Kim was at the theater, he would go out in the back and sign autographs," says Joe Siegel's sister Sally Radin. "Not his name—he'd just scribble something on people's *Playbills*."

The night the play opened, Kim went to Sardi's with her new family, for whom it was a once-in-a-lifetime experience. "When you walk into Sardi's with the star, everybody gets up and applauds," Radin says. She remembers sitting at the middle table, with several actor colleagues of Kim coming over, quizzically wondering who the nonactors were. Kim proudly introduced the Siegels. "She was generous and charming, as always," Radin says.

But Kim's marriage to Joe Siegel was in trouble from the start. Lucile Reid Brock, the first wife of Kim's brother Howard, recalls the dinner at Sardi's as well. "Patty [Kim] and her husband had a party after the play, at Sardi's," she recalls. "Then they wanted me to go up with them to Congers. He was friendly at Sardi's, but when we went to their house the next day, he was closeted in the bedroom and never came out."

Although the play ran until October 3, Kim left the show after its Friday, August 21, performance. This was just after Lee Strasberg had returned to watch the show and give notes to the actors. His comments to Kevin McCarthy: "Terrific. Just fine. You're coming right along." As McCarthy recalls, "Kim quit the next day. I think she was hoping he would scold me for my performance or something."

On August 21, 1964, a battalion-size force of pro-U.S. South Vietnamese soldiers walked into a Vietcong ambush. Congress adjourned in advance of the Democratic convention in Atlantic City, New Jersey, that would nominate Lyndon Johnson to run against Barry Goldwater. The film *Kisses for My President,* starring Fred MacMurray and Polly Bergen, opened in New York. And Kim Stanley appeared on an American stage for the last time.

Rather than saying she had left the show, Kim kept calling in sick. Audiences, unaware that a Broadway milestone was already in their rearview mirror, kept calling the box office to find out if she was going to be in that night's show. "The box office response to queries about whether she's to appear at any specified show has been that she's expected to do so," *Variety* said. "Audiences, gambling on this info, have been buying and/or holding tickets, only to find out just before the curtain ringup of [her] absence." *Variety* added laconically, "Miss Stanley's failure to show up for performances of *Sisters* follows a pattern for which she's become known in the trade." Kim's understudy, Joan Potter, had gone on for her while she was still in the cast; once Kim left the play, the parts of the sisters were recast, with Geraldine Page playing Masha and Peggy Feury moving into the role of Olga that Page had vacated.

A VIDEOTAPED VERSION of the New York stage production was made in late October of 1964 as a fundraiser for the Actors Studio; it was later transferred to film and released in 1977. Except for Sandy Dennis substituting for Shirley Knight as Irina and Shelley Winters in for Barbara Baxley as Natalya, it was the original cast. Paul Bogart directed. Even though it was taped after Kim had left the cast, she was apparently convinced to come back for it, since it was a Studio fundraiser.

"The men were wonderful," Bogart recalls with ironic good humor. "Luther, Jim Olson, Kevin McCarthy, Bob Loggia. All of them came to me in turn to say that they knew their parts weren't the biggest ones in the show, but that the play was about them."

Kim would make an enduring impression on Bogart. "She was a very intense woman," he says. "It was that very intensity she brought to the part that was so electrifying. She did things so wonderful, she made the hair on the back of my neck stand up and crawl, and I don't know how she did it. At her most critical peak of passion, she would grab Geraldine Page and whisper in her ear, 'I think I'm going out of my mind.' And it was the very quietness of it that was so frightening."

Some of Kim's behavior just left Bogart scratching his head, though. "She did some weird things that I never did understand," he says. "She would mock her lines sometimes. Deliberately—she knew what she was doing. It didn't make much sense to me."

While entranced with Kim the actress, Bogart was less taken with Kim the person. "She was very exciting to watch," he says, "but she was a pain in the ass." Kim wouldn't come to rehearsals much of the time, and when she did, would glare at her fellow actors or insult them, particularly Kevin McCarthy.

"She was rehearsing a scene with him," Bogart says. "She was sitting in the foreground and Kevin was walking around in back of her. She looked at me and mouthed the words, 'I hate him.' Unmistakably. My face must have fallen, because Kevin said, 'What's the matter?' And I had to say 'Nothing.'"

Then there was Kim's weight. "She was overweight," Bogart recalls. "And that would have been fine, because the ladies then were. They had corsets and were wasp-waisted and big-bosomed. But she agonized over her weight. She wore the corset, but her body sort of—hung out over the top of it. So I sent somebody out to put a little shawl on her. She understood why I'd done it, and was just frantic. I never saw her laugh or enjoy herself," he adds. "It was all a dark experience, it was all painful to her."

While not as troubled as Kim, Shelley Winters was also a handful. "Shelley has many, uh, intonations of New York, although I don't think she was born and raised there," he says. For Winters's Natalya, "Olga" became "Ahlga." "Bobik," the affectionate term for her baby, became "Bubik," like the Yiddish "bubbele." The three-pronged utensil Natalya finds lying on the ground in act four is a "fahrk." And Winters was very sensitive to status distinctions.

Although he did not allow actors in the control room, Bogart let Kim in one day to watch some of her performance for reassurance. Geraldine Page came in as well. "Shelley found out they had been invited," Bogart remembers. "I could hear her in the studio through the soundproof walls saying, 'I am a star! Why am I not allowed in?'

"Everybody was at the end of their rope by the time we were finishing," Bogart concludes. "After a while, I couldn't wait to get it over with. If you ever watch it, you can see that act one is very carefully made, act two is a little less so, act three even less so, and act four is 'Hurry up, let's get out of here.'"

O N JANUARY 31, 1965, the *New York Times* ran a profile of Kim, "Kim Stanley on a Snowy Afternoon." It began by assessing Kim's professional status, flavored with her penchant for self-mythologizing. "Great actresses are rare," Eugene Archer's article began. "Great American actresses are rarer. Kim Stanley, Texas-born and not yet forty, is one." In it, Kim raised the prospect of not returning to the stage:

> "I don't want to say I don't want to act again," she murmured in her country home the other day, pleasurably stretching out her womanly arms before the fire. "That sounds so awful." It did not sound awful at all. It was also completely untrue.

One moment later, Kim was full of plans. "Pierce the surface tension of this gifted delineator of modern feminine psychoses and it is easy to detect the soul of a buoyant comedienne," Archer noted, adding, "At the notion of reviving *Private Lives* with Rex Harrison, she was bubbling over with delight. 'We're going to do it,' she said positively. 'I just won't think about the problems—we're going to do it!'" Although the production never came off, it was not idle talk: Saint Subber was interested in producing it, and Mike Nichols in directing.

In the article, Kim said she had wanted to do the film version and London stage premiere of Edward Albee's *Who's Afraid of Virginia Woolf,* but Albee didn't want her. "He thought I was too soft and womanly," Kim said, "but I don't think that woman should be dikey, do you?"

If she had gotten the part, Kim added, she would have had a few suggestions for Albee. "I'd have played that role differently," she said. "To me, if that couple had lived with their imaginary child for 20 years, it would have been part of their lives—and important all through the play, not a sudden revelation at the end."

At about the time of Kim's "Snowy Afternoon" profile, Actors Studio cofounder Cheryl Crawford received a letter from Peter Daubeny, who was organizing the 1965 World Theatre Festival at the Aldwych Theatre in London. Leading companies from around the world came to play two weeks of repertory there. Daubeny invited the Actors Studio, and they accepted.

To go, the Studio had to raise $50,000. But the State Department spurned a request for funding. Paul Newman got Pan Am to grant Studio members free airfare, raised much of the money from the movie studios, and kicked in the balance himself. It was a noble act, but in an evil augury, Crawford later noted that the money came through belatedly, hampering preparations and not leaving much rehearsal time.

Kim did not want to participate: She didn't get along with Kevin McCarthy, and, according to Robert Lewis, was unhappy with Lee Strasberg because he had tried to get her to approximate the performance of Masha he had seen in the 1924 Moscow Art Theater version. "To get her to say 'yes' to the London appearance, the Studio heads put pressure on Kim, telling her they'd have to call it all off if she wouldn't go, since hers was the most important performance," Lewis later recalled. "Without *The Three Sisters*, America would have no representation at the World Theatre Festival and, finally, her refusal would deal a mortal blow to the Studio."

This full-court guilt-giving apparently worked, and Kim signed on. But in another omen, Lucy Kroll wrote to Joe Siegel on March 11, reporting her conversation with John Roberts, general manager of the Royal Shakespeare Theatre. "He tells me that unless a visiting company is bringing the cream of its artists in their presentations, it would be subject to great critical disfavor," she said. "If the Studio does *Three Sisters* with Shelley Winters [as Natalya] and Nan Martin [as Olga], Kim [will be] . . . surrounded by a second company, and the burden will be enormous on her."

In an interview with the *Herald-Tribune* during one of the last rehearsals before the company left for London, Lee Strasberg said, "I am very pleased, flattered and, I must say, a little scared at the interest in London." His fears may have led him to bully the actors during rehearsals. As Foster Hirsch reports in *A Method to Their Madness,* Strasberg yelled at Sandy Dennis in front of the company after she completed a speech with her trademark hesitations and pauses. "My God, what are you doing up there?" he asked. "Are you trying to ruin my play?" After a brief pause, Dennis responded, "You can't speak to me this way. I'm a human being." Strasberg did not take this approach with Robert Loggia. "He browbeat some people if he felt he could get away with it," Loggia says. "He was kind of scared of me, and for good reason: I'd knock him on his ass."

Neither Kim nor Kevin McCarthy wanted to work together again. Author David Garfield reports that Kim's first choice for Vershinin in London was Montgomery Clift, with whom she rehearsed their scenes. But Strasberg, concerned about Clift's physical and mental condition following his 1957 Hollywood car crash, rejected the idea.

George C. Scott then stepped into the breach. Kim later said he did it as a favor to her, because she needed all the help she could get. But Robert Loggia says Scott had an ulterior motive: He was pursuing Ava Gardner and thought he could get her to attend opening night.

In discussing what went wrong with the London version of *The Three Sisters*—and there was little that didn't go wrong—it's useful to begin with Elia Kazan's speculation as to why Lee Strasberg was so dead set on going to London despite numerous warning signs. In 1961, Kazan was invited, along with Robert Whitehead, to run the theater company of the new Lincoln Center. But the Studio was not invited to become the resident theatrical company, nor was Strasberg or anyone else from the Studio invited to participate. Strasberg took it as a personal insult, and it was Kazan's theory that Strasberg envisioned the London expedition as a way to revenge himself upon the Lincoln Center board by showing them they had made the wrong choice.

The Actors Studio Theater brought two shows to the World Theatre Festival: James Baldwin's *Blues for Mister Charlie,* which ran from

May 3–12, 1965, and *The Three Sisters,* whose May 13–22 run would ring down the curtain on the festival. *Blues for Mister Charlie,* starring Al Freeman Jr. and directed by Burgess Meredith, did not get good reviews. Strasberg held a press conference after the reviews came in and ungraciously attacked the playwright. "It's partly Baldwin's own fault that the play does not sufficiently convey the human conflict," he said. In addition to offending members of his own troupe, Robert Lewis later recalled, Strasberg's harsh criticism offended the British audience, with its deeply ingrained sense of fair play.

Although neither show had had sufficient time to rehearse, *The Three Sisters* labored under an additional handicap: Kim refused to fly with company members to London, sailing with Joe Siegel instead. This further cut the amount of time the company could rehearse together. Salem Ludwig, who played Ferrapont in *The Three Sisters,* was also the company's Equity representative and said the Aldwych Theatre management was not very helpful.

"We had no rehearsal space," he noted. "They gave us tennis courts and armories, never a theater. Then when we finally got access to the Aldwych, we found that it was a raked stage with an eighteen-foot apron—we didn't have time to adjust to this. The costume fittings were all wrong. Lighting was not strong enough, and it wasn't the same lighting plot as in New York."

Robert Loggia remembers the steep pitch of the raked stage. "It was like a ski run," he says. "Furniture had to be nailed down, and we had [only] one dress rehearsal. All of us were lurching around like drunken bums on a trawler." During one rehearsal, Tamara Daykarhanova fell and broke her arm. The gaping apron stands out in the memory of Gerald Hiken. "It was as big as the set we were playing on," he says. "The distance between us and the first row was enormous."

According to playwright Meade Roberts, George C. Scott had trouble learning his lines because he was busy over at the Savoy Hotel beating up Ava Gardner. And because his uniform wasn't ready in time, Scott had to rehearse with Kim under embarrassing conditions. Cheryl Crawford writes in her memoirs:

On the afternoon of the opening, I went to watch Kim and George rehearse, to find him playing a poigniant scene in long johns that had a sagging back flap (his uniform was being pressed). The British stagehands peered out from the wings, their faces incredulous. It was almost an omen.

Another omen was the attitude of the British audience as to what constituted good Chekhov. "The audience was quite used to daughters of generals being on the aristocratic side," Gerald Hiken says. "Their idea of Chekhov characters are upper-class English people who live in the countryside." One London reviewer would say that the men in the production talked as if they had come straight from the Fulton Fish Market.

Hiken remembers the cast's getting through the first half of their lighting cues the day of the show, then being sent to their dressing rooms because it was time to let the audience in. "Nobody called us to places," he says. "When we finally went upstairs the audience was stamping [its feet] because the curtain was late." Once it went up, the show would drag on for four hours, rather than the scheduled three hours and ten minutes.

It was one of the legendary disasters of the modern theater. The audience booed the actors, calling out, "Yankees, go home!" When Sandy Dennis as Irina said, "It's been a terrible evening," someone in the audience called out, to general hilarity, "It sure has!" Robert Loggia recalls, "At the curtain call, we were hooted and hollered at and things were thrown."

At this moment of utter rout, Kim would recall, the stage manager gave the company eight curtain calls. "The stage manager, to whom the Studio was God . . . kept raising the curtain. Again and again," she remembered almost twenty years later. "My God! We were being crucified and he kept raising the curtain. Finally, the eighth time, I stepped downward, turned to face the cast and bowed to them, and we left." Gerald Hiken also remembers Kim behaving heroically under fire. "Kim was wonderful at the curtain call," he says. "We were booed by someone in the audience and Kim applauded him. It was like, 'Thank God someone knows what's going on.'"

One person not in the audience, much to the chagrin of George C. Scott, was Ava Gardner. "After opening night, when Ava Gardner didn't attend, George C. Scott chug-a-lugged a quart of gin," recalls Robert Loggia. "I mean chug-a-lugged it, which could kill you. He didn't make the performance the next night." Author Peter Hay notes that Laurence Olivier came backstage to comfort the actors "and helped cushion the blow . . . by sweeping the company off to a party . . . for them at which they proceeded to drink heartily."

This saved them from having to read the reviews. "This is not only the last production of the season, but the worst," Bernard Levin wrote in the *Daily Mail.* Another critic said, "After the fire of *Blues for Mister Charlie* comes the still small voice of Chekhov—and it comes no stiller or smaller than this." The *Illustrated London News* called it "an occasion to have raised Stanislavsky's ghost." "Lee Strasberg's production seemed to be one long pause occasionally interrupted," it said. "The cast had various players of resource, but what in the world did they think they were doing?" Perhaps the most ferocious blast came from Penelope Gilliatt in the *Observer.* "The admirable World Theatre's dismal task has been to mount the suicide of the Actors Studio," she wrote. "The whole endeavor is absurd and agonizing, like playing the harpsichord in boxing gloves, like filling the Spanish riding school with hippopotami."

There were a few touches of compassion among the reviews. While saying that *The Three Sisters* moved at a paralytic pace, Milton Shulman of the *Evening Standard* added, "This production did not . . . deserve the disgraceful and rude reception it received from the gallery. As guests laboring under technical difficulties which may have accounted for some of the ponderous effects, they merited courtesy rather than hyena laughter and boos."

Kim was not spared from the critical shellacking. The *Sunday Times* said, "Masha and Irina are ludicrous and painful." In the *Manchester Guardian,* Philip Hope-Wallace said, "Kim Stanley flashed a whole battery of naturalistic details at us, patting her hair, laughing under her breath, watching her hands." And Milton Shulman added, "Outside of a school for stammerers, I have never heard such long and unintelligible pauses. Kim Stanley, as Masha, was particularly guilty." Such criticisms were not confined to the English. Cheryl Crawford later wrote, "They gave an unbelievable, self-indulgent performance. Kim was lethargic and allowed herself a performance one of the actors said 'you could drive a truck through.'"

Kim did get a few good reviews, though. The best came from a critic who said, "Kim Stanley's Masha was a marvelously timed performance, hinting at the passion for life she could never consummate." In the "faint praise" category was the *Times* of London, which said "Kim Stanley's Masha is at present an unformed and exploratory reading which might develop into something interesting; but the other performances seem all too well formed."

Of the three sisters, Nan Martin got the best reviews. George C. Scott got consistently good notices, while Sandy Dennis took a pasting, with Bernard Levin of the *Daily Mail* sharing Strasberg's aversion to her pauses, writing, "Irina (Miss Sandy Dennis) has one trick: Saying 'I—er—I—ah' for the first person singular pronoun."

After the reviews came out, Lee Strasberg called a meeting of the company and said the critics were right. It was a repeat of his post–*Mister Charlie* performance and George C. Scott had had enough. "Scott, who always referred to Strasberg as Lee pardon-the-expression Strasberg, stood up in a rage and advanced on Lee, threatening him with bodily harm," Robert Lewis wrote in his memoir *Slings and Arrows.* Studio historian David Garfield quotes Scott as saying, "Mr. Strasberg, you called us together to tell us the papers were right? That we're lousy actors?" With Scott closing in on him, Strasberg turned around and walked out. Robert Loggia attributes Scott's anger to Ava Gardner's decision not to attend. "George was fueled with anger because Ava Gardner didn't show up," he says. "She went back to Madrid, to the bullfighter. And that ended that."

During the show's run, Kim and five other members of the company (Luther Adler, George C. Scott, Sandy Dennis, Nan Martin, and Gerald Hiken) were interviewed on the BBC by host Ian Dallas on a soundstage with huge portraits of Stanislavski, Chekhov, and Lee Strasberg looming over them. Unlike the air of almost matronly serenity Kim had projected in her televised interview with CBS's Martin Agronsky eight years earlier, here she displays a dark, restless, and edgy vitality, with anxious looks occasionally seeping out of the corner of her eyes. It's emblematic of how beleaguered the Studio actors felt that, years later, Gerald Hiken would recall Dallas as hostile and condescending, although a viewing of the show's videotape reveals that the BBC interviewer was utterly intimidated by these bristling and high-powered stars of the American theater who had just endured one of the greatest critical drubbings of their lives.

There were some positive reviews later in the show's two-week run, notably one by Francis Wyndham, who said, "the mercurial Russian temperament—the sudden switches from enthusiasm to despair, from excitement to indifference—made sense in this production as it never has on the English stage." And, he added, "Kim Stanley's Masha was among the finest performances ever seen on the London stage . . . [It] was not a star performance, it was a great one. Overwhelming as it was, it would have been even more effective if all the other actors had been her equals."

But the damage had been done. May 22, 1965, the last day *The Three Sisters* ran in London, was the last time Kim performed on stage. The Aldwych Massacre also marked the end of Lee Strasberg's career as a director and the death of the Actors Studio Theater.

Robert Lewis later speculated that Kim's leaving the stage stemmed from her guilt feelings over having pressured Strasberg to do *The Three Sisters* in the first place, given the botch he made of it in London. Studio historian David Garfield also believes she felt betrayed by Strasberg for not having "been there," for not having stood behind her. (Years later, he would add insult to injury by saying, "She waddled on the stage . . . I don't know what she did.") A distant, harsh, and judgmental father figure exhorts his daughter to achieve but fails to support her in time of need: Strasberg the father figure now resembled J.T. the father. Kim had tried to conceal her Albuquerque roots and traveled far from them, but now it was as if she had never left.

Joe Siegel accompanied Kim on this ill-fated trip, and after the show's run, they traveled briefly in Europe. Remarkably, only three months later, Kim was sailing to London again, to appear in the Daniel Petrie film *The Idol.* It would star Kim as a middle-aged Englishwoman who has an affair with her son's friend, played by Michael Parks.

Daniel Petrie had risked his participation in the project by telling producer Joseph Levine he would only do it if Kim starred. Levine approved Kim if Petrie could get her, so in June, he went to Congers.

"When I saw her, I almost blurted out that she was pregnant," Petrie recalls. "She was really big and heavy, fat and flabby. I didn't say anything, except to hint that the mother of this kid was very with-it, that she played tennis and was very active." He told Kim that shooting would start in eight weeks. She got the hint, saying that would be enough time to lose her excess weight, adding, "After all, I have to be tennis trim."

As it turns out, Petrie may not have been wrong about Kim being pregnant: On June 28, Edward R. Morse from the Paramount casting department wrote a deal memo to Lucy Kroll confirming Kim's participation in *The Idol*. The next day, Kroll spoke with Joe Siegel. Notes she made from the conversation indicate that Kim was pregnant, that it was illegal for her to withhold that information from the film's producers, and that Joe Siegel would discuss that with Kim. As to what may have become of this pregnancy, Kim's brother-in-law Lynn White has said, "She had three or four abortions."

On August 11, Kim sailed to England on the *Queen Elizabeth,* arriving August 17. Paramount apparently asked Kim to get a physical before sailing, because on August 13, Lucy Kroll wrote to Daniel Petrie and his wife Dorothea, who had worked with Kroll, saying, "Kim is on the boat, and the insurance doctor gave her 100 percent good health affidavit." The doctor did so prematurely. There was an acquaintance of Dorothea Petrie's in a stateroom near Kim's. "All he saw was the vodka going in and out," says Petrie. "He never saw her."

When Kim arrived in Southampton, she exemplified the old Polish saying, "vodka in excess, brain in recess." Daniel Petrie took one look at Kim and saw she was not tennis trim—and that she was emotionally unstable. On August 23, when rehearsals were supposed to begin, Petrie called Lucy Kroll, whose notes include:

Dan Petrie called from London . . . Kim not doing picture . . . very ill . . . staggered off boat . . . want[ed] to take next boat back . . . why hadn't she said this before . . . thought it all the time . . . Dottie [Dorothea Petrie] spent four hours with her . . . [Kim] wanted to talk to Horton [Foote] . . . very ill . . . trying to get a plane at three o'clock . . . to go home with her . . . must have a nurse to accompany her . . . voice all garbled . . . speech slurred . . . terrible mess . . . very unfortunate.

Why did Kim go if she had no intention of appearing in *The Idol?* Petrie hazards a guess in his unpublished short story, *Directed by Jack Phelan,* based on his dealings with Kim on *The Idol*: that she wanted an all-expenses-paid opportunity to drink her way across the Atlantic. In that story, Petrie describes Julia Lambert, the heroine based on Kim, as wearing "the bottle scars of four marriages, 11 psychiatrists and 10,000 puce-colored hangovers."

Dorothea Petrie went to the Savoy Hotel, where Kim was staying, because they feared she was suicidal. "You really had the feeling that she might go out a window if you weren't there," Dorothea says, adding that Kim was a tangle of free-floating fears. "She was very concerned that she had cancer, and that it was in her hip," Dorothea recalls. "I called the hotel doctor. He came up, and of course, it was not apparent. These were her fears, and she had so many. She was such a gifted actress with so many demons that one suffered both for and with her . . . It was an emotional breakdown." After seeing how much time and effort Lucy Kroll put into helping Kim keep herself together, Dorothea Petrie realized the agenting field was not for her.

Joe Siegel came over to get Kim, and on August 24, Kim flew back to New York on Pan Am Flight 103, probably heavily sedated. Jennifer Jones replaced her in *The Idol.*

During 1964 and '65, Kim considered several other films: *Reflections in a Golden Eye,* in which she would have acted opposite Marlon Brando; *The Loved One,* in which she would have played Aimee Thanatagenos, the astronaut's wife; and *This Property Is Condemned,* in which she would have played Natalie Wood's mother. But she appeared in none of them. Nor did she appear in the stage version of *The Lion in Winter,* for which she was apparently considered for the role of Eleanor of Acquitaine.

When Daniel Petrie returned to New York after filming *The Idol,* he ran into Albert Paulsen, who had played Kim's husband in *The Three Sisters*. Paulsen told him that several friends of Kim's from the Actors Studio had just gone up to Congers to visit her, bringing a box of chocolates. When they arrived, Lisa took the chocolates and devoured them. After a long wait, Kim appeared at the top of the stairs, theatrically greeted her companions, then tumbled down the stairs, landing in a heap at the bottom. They put her to bed and left. As an actress, Kim had taken the worst of spills as well. It would be seventeen years before she made another film. Her stage career was over.

PART THREE

THE LOST YEARS

CHAPTER 8

THIS HOUSE OF WOMEN

(1965–1972)

I N 1965, KIM TURNED FORTY. She had achieved her dream of theatrical stardom but was unstable and burned out, her newly minted fourth marriage already in trouble. Dr. Ross, the psychiatrist in Henry Denker's novel *The Actress,* speaks of Kit Lawrence, the heroine based on Kim, as having "a devilishly adroit mind . . . the ingenuity of a borderline psychotic . . . [and] the charm and technique of a great actress." During this period, Kim would display all of those characteristics and become well-acquainted with members of Dr. Ross's profession.

When she was returned to New York from London following her crack-up on *The Idol,* Kim apparently underwent a brief hospitalization in New York, possibly at Doctors Hospital in upper Manhattan. During the summer of 1966, she visited Janice Rule and Ben Gazzara, then living in the exclusive Westwood section of Los Angeles. "She was drinking, drinking, drinking, drinking—and then it got really bad," Gazzara recalls. "We were forced to commit her to a psychiatric ward at UCLA with the help of Ralph Greenson, who was Marilyn Monroe's psychoanalyst."

When Rule and Gazzara went to visit Kim in the psychiatric ward, she wasn't angry at them for having institutionalized her. She joked that the other women on her ward were fans of Gazzara's, then starring in the TV series *Run for Your Life,* and asked him to sign autographs. "She always had a sardonic sense of humor," Gazzara says.

It's not clear where Kim went when she was discharged after several days in the UCLA psychiatric ward. "They let her out and she went her merry way back to New York and continued drinking," says Gazzara. "What are you going to do?" But Patricia Frye, then married to Kim's brother Justin, has a different memory. "Roddy McDowall took her to a recovery place in Maryland," she says. "I think they just kidnapped her at the behest of Justin and Janice Rule and Ben Gazzara."

It reflects the mystery of Kim's whereabouts during this period that no one can agree where in Maryland she was taken: Arthur Laurents says it was Johns Hopkins, but *Miracle Worker* author William Gibson, whose wife Margaret is a psychiatrist who consulted with Kim at this time, says it was Chestnut Lodge. Patricia Frye says Chestnut Hill, Kim's daughter Rachel says Silver Hill, and the facility where Kit Lawrence goes in Henry Denker's *The Actress* is called Silvermine.

Horton Foote was then living in New Boston, a small town in New Hampshire. "Kim became so difficult that they threatened to commit her because of her alcoholism, I suppose," he recalls. "She said if they wouldn't do that, she would voluntarily talk to William Gibson's wife, who was a psychiatrist, and follow her advice.

"Mrs. Gibson suggested a place for her to go. They raised a considerable amount of money and asked me if I would be in charge of it and I agreed. People were very generous." (Among the many contributors: Geraldine Page, Steven Hill, Paul Newman, Bryan Forbes, and Arthur Laurents.)

"She seemed to be doing very well," Foote continues. "Then Mrs. Gibson called me and said, 'She's asked to go home for Thanksgiving.' I thought to myself, 'I hope this isn't too soon.' The next thing I knew, I got a call from, I believe, Mrs. Gibson, saying Kim was locked up in her mother's apartment in Greenwich Village. She wouldn't go back to the sanitarium and was drinking very heavily.

"Kim's mother had said I was the one person who could get to her. They asked if I would go into New York and I said, 'No, I won't do that.

She's never let me see her drunk, and I don't want to unless she asks for me. The person who can [do this] is Vivian Nathan.'"

But Foote relented and flew down to New York from Manchester. Vivian Nathan, who may have had a key to the apartment, went in first; if Kim agreed to see Foote, he would talk to her. "By the time Vivian got there, Kim was quite sober, so when I was called in, we kind of made light of the whole thing," Foote recalls. "But she never went back for treatment. And from then on, it was a kind of spiraling downward, I think."

How did Kim get out of the sanitarium? Arthur Laurents says, "She was such a consummate actress. Thanksgiving was coming, and she said, 'I'm much better—I know I'm not all better—but just let me go home to cook Thanksgiving dinner for my children and I will come back.' They let her go and she never came back."

Ironically, during the 1966–67 school year, Kim's children weren't on the East Coast: They had been sent to Southern California, where Lisa went to boarding school in Ojai, while Jamie and Laurie Rachel lived with Alfred Ryder in the San Fernando Valley and went to public school. It was another bravura performance by Kim, but one that worked to her detriment.

Kim's brother Howard, now living in Bemidji, Minnesota, offered to help her as well, according to Sally Radin, the sister of Joseph Siegel. "Her brother the psychiatrist wanted her to come out where he was," she says. "And she just didn't want to go." Given the history of ill will between Kim and Howard, her refusal isn't much of a surprise, though.

Back in New York, Kim attended the play *Luv,* starring fellow Actors Studio members Eli Wallach and Anne Jackson. "People would laugh so hard they would fall in the aisles," Wallach says. "Kim came backstage and said, 'This is one of the saddest plays I've ever seen.' What I loved is that she didn't join the bandwagon. Each character in the play tries to outdo the others in the misery of their lives. Kim identified with that."

On May 1, 1966, Kim paid her respects to a seminal figure of the Actors Studio, Lee Strasberg's wife, Paula, by attending her memorial service at the Riverside Memorial Chapel in Manhattan. Kim was among 700 mourners, including Anne Bancroft, Estelle Parsons, Harold Clurman, William Gibson, and Senator Jacob Javits. Her presence showed the high regard she had for Paula, if not for Strasberg himself in the wake of the *Three Sisters* debacle in London: Kim had a morbid fear of funerals and memorial services and rarely attended them.

Kim was not just unhappy with Strasberg; she was unhappy with the Method and its sense-memory exercises, telling playwright Paul Zindel she blamed her problems on them. "To arrive at true realism, Kim had to tap into her personal sense memory of pain and recreate it totally," Zindel later said. "It was a matter of using your trauma and joys and re-creating them exactly as they were, re-experiencing them in front of an audience. This was her undoing. By courting her demons, she was walking a fine line of madness. She would sacrifice her sanity for the sake of achieving realism.

"She told me this was why she hated the Actors Studio and Lee Strasberg and was turning her back on Stanislavski and the Studio," Zindel added. "She found out there are other ways to arrive at realism that wouldn't mean having to do all that stuff."

Kim was saying sense-memory is a good technique in moderation, but taken too literally and ridden too hard, can fry your spirit. Experts in the Method, of whom this author is not one, may legitimately question Kim's interpretation of sense-memory and the extent it played in her unraveling, but it's what she told Zindel.

With Kim in psychological disarray, it was only a matter of time before her odd-couple marriage to lawyer Joseph Siegel became another casualty. In addition to Siegel's fascination with the theater, he was also active in politics and a member of the Village Independent Democrats. In 1966, he went to work for Robert Kennedy's successful run for the U.S. Senate from New York.

Kim and Siegel split their marriage between her home in Congers and his ground-floor apartment at 12 East Eleventh Street in Greenwich Village. Her first three marriages had not hampered Kim's libertine tendencies, so it's ironic that her marriage to Siegel foundered when she mistakenly suspected him of infidelity with Jackie Kennedy.

One day, Siegel and Robert Kennedy were in a car with another political operative when a question came up. Kennedy said his sister-in-law Jackie would have the answer. He gave her unlisted number to Siegel, who wrote it down and called her.

"That night, when Joe came home to their apartment in the Village, he emptied his pockets and put everything on the dresser, including the piece of paper with Jackie Kennedy's phone number," a friend of Siegel's recalls.

"Kim came down from Congers quite late that night and in her cups, you might say. She let herself into the apartment with her key. Joe was fast asleep. She was a very suspicious person, and started going through his effects on the dresser. When she came across the piece of paper with Jackie Kennedy's name and number, she picked up one of Joe's shoes and started beating him on the head and saying, 'You son of a bitch, you're cheating on me with Jackie Kennedy!' She turned around and left, and shortly after that, they were divorced."

In getting the divorce, Siegel may have followed the advice of Robert Lasky, then his law partner. Robert Matson, who later joined their practice, says, "Apparently Lasky kind of leaned on him and said, 'You know, I'm your best friend, and no matter how enamored you are of this woman, you've got to leave her, because it's ruining you.'"

With her fourth and last marriage over, Kim's behavior became increasingly self-destructive. Alice Hirson, then appearing in a play with Vivian Nathan, remembers her getting a call one evening: Kim had been drinking and was hemorrhaging. And Nathan's goddaughter, Elissa Myers, only nine years old at the time, recalls another evening when Nathan had to ride to Kim's rescue. Now a successful casting director (which she attributes in part to what she learned from Kim), Myers remembers with sadness what she witnessed one evening at Kim's home in Congers.

"Vivian made a frantic call to my mother that we had to go to Kim Stanley's house because Kim was on a binge and Vivian was very concerned," Myers says. "We drove to her house in the country—I don't remember where my mother was in all this. I followed Vivian into the house for which she had the key. As we entered the kitchen, Kim was on the floor and there was vomit all over the place.

"I remember Vivian giving me her dirty clothes and putting them in the sink and washing them up. Vivian put everything together. I remember her dressing Kim in a nightgown and sitting in the living room and giving her tea. It was so scary and yet it was so precious. Vivian was the greatest person in the world." Somewhat ruefully, Myers adds, "Kim did this to herself. No one did it to her."

THE SPRING OF 1967 marked two years since the *Three Sisters* debacle in London. Kim had not acted again, and Arthur Penn, who had done several live TV dramas with her, was determined to get Kim back to work. He was producing and directing a drama called *Flesh and Blood* for NBC, and campaigned to get her. "He wants you desperately," Lucy Kroll wrote to Kim on March 30. "Those are his words." When Kim's lapsed membership in AFTRA became a potential stumbling block to her participation, Penn advanced her the money to renew her membership.

Flesh and Blood was written by William Hanley, who had had some success with several one-acts and the full-length Broadway play *Slow Dance on the Killing Ground*. But the plot of *Flesh and Blood* is like a country-and-western song on steroids: A family lives in a condemned apartment building. The construction worker father (Edmond O'Brien) wants to step off a girder and kill himself. His wife, Della (Kim), had one of their three children (Kim Darby) by his brother, the moody, alcoholic, diabetic defrocked priest (E.G. Marshall), but has never revealed the truth of her paternity. Their older daughter (Suzanne Pleshette) has marital problems because she doesn't like her husband's wife-swapping idea or his suggestion that she get silicone breast implants. Their son (Robert Duvall) is in a vegetative state from war injuries that also resulted in the loss of his hands. Other than that, they're your basic all-American family.

Originally destined for Broadway, *Flesh and Blood* was rerouted to TV when NBC bought it for $112,500 (in 1967 money). Although she took the role of Della, Kim was not enthusiastic about it, with Lucy Kroll noting during a telephone conversation with her, "The lady is a bitch . . . No way to play her except as a phony or no life at all . . . [Kim] understand[s] why [Penn] wants her to supply what is not there." Rehearsals for the show were held the first three weeks of July in the ballroom of the Riverside Plaza Terrace hotel on West Seventy-third Street, so Kim would not have to travel all the way downtown from Congers. In-studio rehearsals and taping would take place the last week of July at NBC's Brooklyn Two Studio in the Midwood section of Brooklyn.

The making of *Flesh and Blood* was difficult for Kim: She was beginning to have memory problems, and the show would have to be taped virtually line by line as a result. Laurie Rachel, then eleven, would help cue her mother on lines, the first time she had ever done this. Kim's problems would make the show's production an arduous one and, to make matters worse, both Edmond O'Brien and E.G. Marshall were having personal problems as well.

Toward the end of rehearsals at the Riverside Plaza, Kim disappeared for several days. There were fears Kim had killed herself, and one technician who worked on the show says it was the only time he ever saw Arthur Penn cry. Kim had gone on another multi-day drinking binge. Several psychiatrists, including Margaret Gibson, were consulted. Penn got Colleen Dewhurst to stand by, in case Kim couldn't complete the show, and the decision was made to replace her. In a note on July 22, Lucy Kroll wrote, "Arthur is to tell her the bad news . . . She will be distraught . . . She won't accept medical [help]." Later that day, Penn broke the news to Kim, who somehow managed to talk him out of it. But he had a condition.

"Arthur Penn said, 'I don't want her to go back to her house and start to drink. We'll never get her back here,'" says Phil Hymes, the show's lighting director. "So he said, 'I've got a great idea. We'll get a hotel for her in Brooklyn.' So he rented a room and thought, 'Well, she could still go out and get a bottle of booze.' So he had the assistant director stay at the same hotel with her. Unfortunately, he was a heavy drinker, too. So the next day was pretty hectic, but gradually Arthur got a performance out of her." The hotel that Kim and the assistant director stayed at, the Half Moon, was best known for a 1941 incident in which mobster Abe "Kid Twist" Reles, scheduled to testify against mob boss Alberto Anastasia, fell to his death from his sixth-floor hotel room while in police custody.

Author William Hanley praises Kim, saying, "Her performance was brilliant. With all of her personal difficulties, she showed up every day, did her work, and gave a beautiful performance." But the show's technicians do not remember her so fondly.

"Sometimes she would step out of her key lights and it would have to be lit all over again," says set designer Warren Clymer. Might a nervous Kim have been unaware of what she was doing? "Oh no, no, no," he says. "She was too sharp. She was very sharp. She knew exactly what she was doing." And Phil Hymes, a veteran of live television, adds, "The problem with tape is that a person who had a weakness could express it, because they knew you could do it again. Kim Stanley wasn't a dope. She knew, 'I blew the line—let's do it again.' That's what drove Arthur crazy. I remember Duvall being really pissed off, because he just couldn't take working like that."

The show aired on January 26, 1968, and ran into a buzz saw of criticism. In the *New York Post,* Harriet Van Horne wrote, "Rarely have so many screaming crises—not one of them credible—been visited upon one ordinary, dreary family." *Variety* called it "a dreary two hours of prime-time TV with lots of spinoff potential for a daytime soaper." And in the *New York Times,* Jack Gould referred to William Hanley's big payday: "His tax accountant must be overjoyed, and Broadway can be grateful to NBC for what it was spared."

There was some praise, though: While calling it "two hours of unrelieved melodramatics," the *Hollywood Reporter* added, "Producer-director Penn, after an eight-year absence from TV, returned in high fashion and with a veteran's touch to make the show an evening of exceptional entertainment." And Rex Reed loved the show, saying, "Here at last is a play that sweeps away the absurdly conventional gauze surrounding the myth of the American family and probes the reasons why people do agonizing and unforgivable things to each other in the name of love." And he spoke highly of Kim's performance:

If for no other reason, see *Flesh and Blood* for Kim Stanley's devastating work as the mother. Touching her daughter's earring with love in the middle of a speech, placing her hands over the vegetable's [Robert Duvall's] ears when her husband raises his voice to curse, rubbing an eye when somebody utters a truth she doesn't want to hear and listening, always listening, she is an actress for whom adjectives become about as forceful as water dropping on gasoline.

Reed acknowledged, though, that Kim had seen better days:

No longer the darling Cheri of *Bus Stop,* her face is now a roadmap of human suffering—bags under the eyes, red streaks in the eyeballs, lines in the chin. Where have you been, Miss Stanley? The world has lamented the absence of your genius.

As usual, Kim was no genius about her finances: A letter to her from her accountant the day *Flesh and Blood* aired informed her she had not made her last two house payments nor paid an insurance premium. And he told Lucy Kroll several weeks later he was being "hounded by the tax man."

Kim needed money, and there was easy money in store from CBS, then airing *CBS Playhouse,* an occasional series of quality dramatic specials. One was *Secrets,* written by Tad Mosel and directed by Paul Bogart. All Kim had to do was appear in one scene as an aging actress and get $10,000.

Bogart knew Kim was having trouble and, despite the difficult time he had had with her on the videotaping of *The Three Sisters,* wanted to help. "It had a wonderful scene in the middle for a remarkable character, an actress," he recalls. "I could put her in exotic makeup, dress her so she would look slender. She sat at a table, so she wouldn't have to get up and move around.

"I asked her to play it and she accepted. Then I got a call from wardrobe saying she had not turned up for any fittings. So I called her again, and she said, 'Oh yeah, okay, okay.'

"Then they called me back again and said, 'She has not turned up.' So I called her back again and said, 'What's going on?' She said, 'Who gives a damn about the show? It's crap. Television is crap. It's all crap. I'm not interested—give it to somebody else.' So I replaced her with Eileen Heckart, who did a marvelous job. But it wasn't the same as Kim. It would have been like the cherry on the ice cream [sundae]."

One of the sticking points for Kim had been her transportation to Hollywood, where *Secrets* was produced. She wouldn't fly, which meant the train. But she wanted a drawing room, not just a first-class compartment, and there were no drawing rooms on trains anymore. CBS put out a statement saying Kim would not appear because her part had been cut down to one scene (all it had ever been) in rewriting.

That February, a new neighbor of Kim's knocked at her door, bringing home-baked cookies and the offer of professional companionship. Joan Turetzky was participating in a production at the Elmwood Theater, a community theater in nearby Nyack, and invited Kim to join.

"She said, 'A community theater? That's the last thing I need,'" Turetzky recalls. "I assured her that most of the members were former professionals, and the play was *The Iceman Cometh,* a very brave undertaking. Besides, I thought, but didn't say, 'You could get out of the house and make some social contacts.' A short time later there was a notice in the local paper that she was in the hospital. It seems she fell asleep with a cigarette." Kim's face was burned in the incident and required plastic surgery.

Lucy Kroll heroically continued seeking work for Kim. In the spring of 1968, the Long Island Theatre Society in Mineola was going to stage Robert Lowell's *Phaedre,* directed by Andre Gregory. Kroll thought it would be good for Kim. "I am trying to do what I can to supplement [your] income," she wrote to her. But it fell through.

During this period, Kim began shedding friends as well as acting jobs. Shirley Knight, one of her co-stars from the Broadway version of *The Three Sisters,* had just had another baby. "She would call me at two in the morning and talk to me for a couple of hours," Knight remembers. "Our relationship really ended because of that. I had children and couldn't be talking on the phone in the middle of the night. One night I said, 'Kim, please call me during the day. Don't call me at night. It's so hard.' Then she stopped calling."

Dorothy Land, Kim's sorority sister and fellow drama major from the University of New Mexico, had married and moved to Suffield, Connecticut. "I talked to her on the phone and invited her to lunch," she recalls. "She was going to come up. My mother was visiting, and we were so excited. A day before, I thought, 'I'd better call her and just make sure she knows the way,' but I couldn't talk to her. One of her daughters said she was ill. And I never heard from her again."

The next to go was Lucy Kroll herself, Kim's friend, confidante, mother hen, and agent all the way back to *Picnic.* In July of 1968, a terse listing in the "Artists & Agents" column in the *Hollywood Reporter* announced, "Peter Witt Associates Inc. has signed Kim Stanley for representation in all fields." There was no elaboration, and the relationship that had outlasted all of Kim's marriages and sustained her through the bulk of her Broadway career was no more.

During the 1968–69 school year, when Laurie Rachel was in sixth grade at Rockland County Day School, her best friend was Betsy Norton. Norton fondly remembers Kim's energetic mother, and, like Kim's children, calls her "Mamaw." "She was full of fun, full of life, and could fix anything," Norton later recalled. "She took care of the house, the groceries, the dog—everything.

"Mamaw was so strong. You would never know that anything bad had happened to this woman. If Rachel and I were upstairs, she would just walk in, sit down on the bed and start talking to us. She was so cute. And she was the family protector, the bodyguard. With that little body."

Norton remembers that Kim always wore a hat and didn't go out much (one exception: Laurie Rachel's graduation from RCDS). But Kim still had her signature laugh. "I can hear her laugh right now," Norton says. "I don't want to call it an infectious laugh, [but] it was a laugh that came from deep down within."

Jamie remembers his mother being a perfectionist about colors. "She did seem to take an inordinate interest in colors," he says. "When shopping for her, we could never seem to get it right—whether it was green, blue, whatever—clothing, flowers, shelf paper." She was also fussy about table settings, with no packets of sugar or ketchup bottles allowed.

"We were not allowed to have any paper or plastic cartons or containers of any kind on the table," Rachel says. "When milk was served, it had to be transferred from the carton to a pitcher first. Butter always had to be in a butter dish." And only fine china on the table? "In a sense," she says. "[But] it never matched. It was beautiful, but Limoges and Wedgwood at the same meal."

Betsy Norton remembers Lisa as beautiful, with many boyfriends, and rarely at home. Jamie was "an artist, a cool guy, gorgeous." He was also rarely home. Laurie Rachel was usually at home, but Kim's erratic behavior made it difficult for her twelve-year-old daughter. Her father, Alfred Ryder, lived on the West Coast, and faithfully called her every night. When he could tell things were going badly, Ryder would call Betsy, who would tell her parents, who would call Kim and "invite" Rachel over, then come and get her. "She was a straight-A student without working," Norton says of her friend, "so she had something there that was okay."

But things were increasingly not okay in Kim's household. In a development straight out of *Flesh and Blood*, Kim had a surprise for her own flesh and blood in 1969. The exact timing is unclear, but sometime that year, Kim had a talk with Jamie. Curt Conway, the man you've always thought is your father, is not, she said. Brooks Clift, who you've always thought of as a friend of the family, is your true father.

While he was shocked, Jamie maintains he took the news in stride. "I think it [the secrecy] was just carried on too long," he says. "But it was not traumatic to me in any way. You know, I'm not sure I can figure it out." But the revelation had a dramatic impact on his life: Shortly afterwards he left home, never to return. He was not yet sixteen.

"I kind of knew school wasn't for me. Kim supported me in that," he says, referring to Kim by her name, rather than as his mother, a custom his sister Rachel would develop as well. "I knew I wanted to paint, so I left. And there were personal reasons, but not really anything I can talk about, because I just had a unique situation. I think I grew up a little too early." Why did Kim wait so long to tell him? How did she get Curt Conway and Brooks Clift to participate in the cover-up, and how did they feel about having to do so? These are some of the mysteries which linger in the wake of this episode.

The playwright Paul Zindel met Kim around this time. "Jamie was running around on communes down there [in New Mexico]," he says. "She said, 'Jamie? He knew enough to get out of this house of women.' The kid was like only fifteen, but he had the good sense to flee. That's how she interpreted it." With Joseph Siegel long gone, Kim presided over a household as matriarchal as the one she grew up in had been patriarchal. Like the house of Bernarda Alba, Kim's had several daughters and was dominated by a powerful woman whose mother had a history of erratic behavior. But rather than being stern and repressive, Kim was tolerant and permissive, with the possible exception of table settings.

AFTER THE FAILURE OF *THE THREE SISTERS* IN LONDON, Kim vowed never to return to the theater. Actors Studio co-founder Robert Lewis later recalled, "Kim said to me on her return to America: 'When I was making a film and something went wrong, I could always say,

"Oh, come on, Kim. It's only a movie." When I did a TV show and was unhappy I'd say, "Oh, come on, Kim, you're only doing it to make money." But when I entered the Cathedral and found that to be corrupt, well, there was nowhere else to go. Bobby, I'm never going to act on the stage again.'" But she did make one more effort.

In its pre-musical, pre-Sondheim incarnation, *Company* was a series of seven seriocomic one-act plays by George Furth about a husband, his wife, and a friend of theirs. It was going to be produced by Porter Van Zandt and Philip Mandelker, and directed by George Morrison. Kim would play all seven wives, John McMartin the husbands, and Ron Leibman the best friends. As Morrison recalls, Kim had just come out of an institution of some sort. It isn't clear if this was the facility in Maryland or somewhere else.

At least one reading of the script was held in the living room of co-producer Porter Van Zandt on the fourteenth floor of 118 West Seventy-ninth Street in December of 1968. "We did a reading with Ron Leibman and John McMartin," Morrison recalls. "I remember her arriving. She had just gotten off a plane and was in disarray of some sort when she came in. She seemed a little odd.

"She settled down, and they started to read. It was a scene in which the three characters smoke marijuana and get high. She started out and was literally taking one-minute pauses between her lines. I remember sitting there thinking, 'Boy, this is the ultimate Method actress.' [But] Kim was an extremely powerful presence. Nobody dared say anything to her.

"So we're just waiting through these one-minute pauses. She picked up a cigarette from a coffee table. She didn't even light it. But she started to drag on it as though it were a joint, and she passed it around among the three of them. They joined in this pantomime of drawing in the smoke and holding it in their lungs.

"She picked up the pace, very gradually. And within five minutes or so, all three of them seemed like they were absolutely stoned. As the scene developed, it was so funny that tears were running down my cheeks, I was laughing so hard. And I actually—everyone talks about this metaphorically—fell out of my chair. I think it was the most brilliant piece of acting I've ever seen in my life.

"And the scene didn't have any gags or jokes," Morrison says. "It was what she brought to it, and how she pulled these two guys in, pulled them in psychologically."

While in awe of Kim's acting ability, Morrison was aware of her dark side. "There was an enormous hostility inside her," he says. "She lay in wait all the time, and could lay anybody out in two seconds." At the same time, he adds, Kim was unmistakably poignant, a figure of pathos.

"She had a great sweetness," he says. "She said one thing that's stayed with me all these years. Once, when we were alone, she said, 'I ask just one thing of you, George.' I said, 'What, Kim? Anything.' And she said, 'Don't treat me as though I'm crazy.'

"I knew exactly what she meant, because we were all treating her like she was crazy. We were tiptoeing around her, and she didn't want that. She was acutely aware that people were making allowances all the time.

"Now the fact is, if it had been somebody else, I would have said, 'What's the matter with you?' or something, but I didn't," he adds. "I don't think I succeeded in obeying her plea, but I knew what she meant and was touched by it." The producers were unsuccessful in their efforts to bankroll the play, and Morrison feels part of the responsibility lay with Kim, who was well known for alcoholism and not showing up when a play became a hit.

As a musical, *Company* would be a gigantic hit. "When the production didn't materialize, George asked me what to do with the plays and I suggested sending them to Hal Prince," Stephen Sondheim recalls. "Hal suggested making them into a musical and the rest is, as they say, history." *Company* opened on Broadway April 26, 1970, and ran for almost two years. When the nonmusical version of *Company* was abandoned, George Furth wrote Kim a note saying, "I owe you a play." For two or three years afterwards, she called him in various stages of inebriation, leaving messages on his answering machine that ranged from seductive to a furious "You owe me a play, George!"

O<small>N</small> A<small>PRIL</small> 17, 1969, Kim made one of her now-rare television appearances in the telefilm *U.M.C.*, a pilot for the series *Medical Center.* The show's illustrious cast included Edward G. Robinson,

Maurice Evans, Kim's ex-husband Alfred Ryder, and Kevin McCarthy, her nemesis from *The Three Sisters*. It made a poor prognosticator out of *Variety*'s reviewer, who wrote, "Although it shapes up as no big winner, *U.M.C.* does seem to have some texture against [Marcus] *Welby*, which is sort of a *Peyton Place* on a gurney and strictly DOA."

Four months later, a brief item ran in a "question-and-answer" style column in the *Albuquerque Tribune* asking for information about Kim. It was the first of several such questions that would appear in celebrity q-and-a columns through the years, all of them essentially asking Rex Reed's question: "Where have you been, Miss Stanley? The world has lamented the absence of your genius."

In 1970, Kim took the role of Mrs. Nell Buckman in the western *The Wild Rovers*, starring William Holden, Ryan O'Neal, and Karl Malden. She was on location with cast and crew near the Mexican border, but couldn't pull it off. Diana Douglas Darrid recalls in her memoirs, "Kim Stanley was having emotional problems, whether fueled by alcohol or not was a moot point, but she was unable to work, and they needed a replacement in a hurry." Darrid replaced her, but ended up leaving the film and was replaced by Leora Dana.

Kim's next prospect of work came when a rising young playwright tried to sign her for his sophomore production. Paul Zindel, who won the Pulitzer Prize for *The Effect of Gamma Rays on Man-in-the-Moon Marigolds,* desperately wanted Kim for the role of Catherine Reardon, the title character in *And Miss Reardon Drinks a Little.* The play about three sisters in the Queens borough of New York and their tangled family relationships would co-star Julie Harris as flighty Anna Reardon and Nancy Marchand as Ceil Adams, their haughty, married sister. Owing to Zindel's success and the marquee value of Harris and Marchand, the production would not have to depend on Kim's name for financing.

"It just seemed to me that Kim was an extraordinary instrument for the stage," Zindel later recalled. "And because she hadn't been on the stage in a long time, I felt that whoever brought her back was going to cause a furor. It would be fabulous." Kim expressed interest in the script, so Zindel went up to Congers. There he formed a strong impression of Rubyann, then living with Kim and the children.

"Her mother was a tremendous character, a bit like Mammy Yoakum, a straight shooter. It seemed there was always a tension between them," he said. "Kim and I began to talk about the play. Very shortly, she said she needed to get out of there, how about if we go out and have a drink? Not knowing very much about her, I said sure. We got into my car and drove away. I said, 'What bar would you like to go to?' She said, 'Just head south.' Little did I know that she was going to come down and move into my apartment on Staten Island." Kim was wearing an overcoat, with perhaps only a nightgown underneath.

"I knew I was in an adventure, but I didn't know the size of it," Zindel said. "I was rolling with the punches and said, 'Yeah, sure,' like there was nothing unusual happening. So within a matter of hours, I now have Kim Stanley living in my apartment on very ordinary Staten Island.

"I had a rather large liquor supply, not because I drink—I'm kind of allergic to alcohol—but in case I'd get lucky enough for any lady to come that drank," said Zindel. "Kim behaved in a very proper manner until I went out to get something," he says. "When I came back, I had to break down the door, because she was drunk."

Kim had passed out in Zindel's bed. Before she came to, he took his entire remaining liquor supply and deposited it with the building's superintendent. Once Kim woke up and learned the spigot had been turned off, she insisted Zindel drive her back to Congers, and he cheerfully obliged.

Despite this episode, Zindel maintained his professional pursuit of Kim. When he learned Julie Harris had agreed to play Anna Reardon, he called Kim, hoping this would secure her participation.

"Julie Harris wants to play Anna. I thought that would seal the thing," Zindel said later. "But Kim said, 'Julie Harris? You can count me out!' I said, 'Why?' She said, 'Because when Julie Harris shows up for the first rehearsal, she has the play all memorized and worked out, so there's no room for visceral growth.' I was shocked, and didn't even know what it meant at the time." The role of Catherine went to Estelle Parsons.

Like many who knew her, Zindel was struck by Kim's dual nature. "She would speak two different ways to me: from the point of view of the purity of developing a play with great truth, bringing it to the highest realism through the Stanislavski-Strasberg process. Then there was this other person who would drink all my alcohol and pass out on the bed. I had both the idealist and this reckless woman filled with demons, and I was never sure exactly who I was talking to."

On another occasion, Zindel and Kim were going to dinner at the Russian Tea Room. The young playwright got to see Kim's theatrical power at the expense of a hostile Manhattan cabbie. "The taxi cab driver was driving a little bit swift and a little bit rudely. She said, 'Would you slow down?' in a very demanding tone. He said, 'This is the way I drive!' Then he did a couple of more maneuvers, even faster and rougher. She said, 'I told you to slow down!' He still didn't, and then she screamed at him, 'If it's too hot in the kitchen, GET OUT!' At which point, he brought the cab to a screeching halt and told her to get out. I was quite willing to exit with her. That's when I glimpsed the stage power in real life."

Zindel would transmute his experience of Kim into the play *Ladies at the Alamo,* about a power struggle for control of a community theater in mythical Texas City, Texas. Shirley Fuller, one of the main characters is brilliant, fragile, erratic, and modeled on Kim. Zindel's stage instruction when Shirley Fuller enters is:

Her hair is dramatic, in fact everything about her is dramatic, twitching, in motion. She's always "on." She smiles broadly, smokes grandly, and it is obvious her primary philosophy is that "a thing in motion would sooner catch the eye" . . . She is well-spoken, her voice resonant, but a fair judge of character would sense there is much tension underneath.

When Shirley Fuller comes on stage early in the first act, she's dressed in a coat which seems slightly out of place, but she keeps wrapping it around herself as if she's got a slight chill. Late in the second of the play's two acts, another character pulls the coat off to reveal she's wearing nothing underneath. It was an evocation of the time Kim had briefly moved in with Zindel.

NOTHER EFFORT TO GET KIM ON STAGE was made in December of 1970. Ashley Feinstein was going to produce *Ten Cents a Dance,* a play by Claire Burch about a mother and her daughter, who's in a mental hospital. The play would be directed off-Broadway by Jose Quintero. Feinstein wanted Kim for the mother; the daughter would be an unknown young actress named Louise Lasser.

Again, Kim expressed interest, and again a hopeful acolyte of the theater made the pilgrimage to Congers. Feinstein had a 4 P.M. appointment with Kim at her house; he was so nervous that he got there an hour early on a freezing-cold snowy winter day. Feinstein went to get lunch and returned to knock on Kim's door at exactly four.

"The house looked sort of dark, but there were lights on, very ghostlike," he says. "I knocked and knocked and knocked—and nothing. I must have waited an hour. I kept knocking and no answer, and figured maybe she'll come up late. Then all of a sudden, I could see movement through the windows of the house. And I went again and knocked, and there she was. She said nothing about why she was late."

Kim was much heavier than the last time Feinstein had seen her, in *Seance on a Wet Afternoon* six years earlier. He gave her the play. She liked the idea of working with Quintero, but kept asking Feinstein why he was doing it off-Broadway. Because it's less expensive, he told her. Kim kept pressing for Broadway. Even when he gained admittance to the house, though, Feinstein still found Kim's behavior mysterious.

"When I came in, she said, 'You must be freezing. I'll give you something to drink if I have it. I don't drink.' She made that very clear," Feinstein says. "She said in a Southern accent, 'Ah have either Scotch or blackberry liqueur.' I said, 'I'll have Scotch. Plain. On the rocks.' She went in and brought back the Scotch. She kept leaving the room a lot, and at one point, I followed her stealthily and saw her go into the kitchen, open the cabinet, and take out the blackberry brandy. She poured it into a glass, drank the whole thing, then came out again."

Kim decided to pass on the play, much to Feinstein's disappointment. "It could have been brilliant for her, and it's too bad it wasn't done, especially with Jose Quintero," he says. "But I'll always remember looking through the window and seeing her shape moving through the house. She was dressed all in black, a long black dress, and was like a mixture of all her characters. She was not the least bit disappointing. She was just magnetic."

In 1970, Kim did another TV show. Except for *Flesh and Blood* and *U.M.C.*, it was the first assignment she had completed since her nervous breakdown. *I Can't Imagine Tomorrow* was one of two one-acts by Tennessee Williams airing under the title *Dragon Country* on January 9, 1971. It appeared on WNET in New York, one of the stations that eventually formed the Public Broadcasting Service. The show was directed by Glenn Jordan.

Kim played a spirited but ill woman visited by a timid, ineffectual suitor (William Redfield), who's lost his teaching job because of psychiatric problems. It was the first time Kim had acted with Redfield since he played the title role in *Montserrat,* her Broadway debut. One exchange between them is strikingly evocative of Ashley Feinstein's visit to Kim:

> *REDFIELD:* Well, as I came up the drive, I saw you at the window. Then you closed the curtains.
> *KIM* (coquettishly, with a slight Southern accent): What's wrong with that?
> *REDFIELD:* I had to knock and knock before you opened the door.
> *KIM* (laughing graciously): You nearly knocked that old door down!

As on *Flesh and Blood,* Kim was unable to memorize the script. Instead of shooting it in one take, like a play, they had to tape it in short individual takes. Even so, several of Kim's flubs are preserved on tape. "They had to bring in extra coaches to try to get her to learn her lines," said Paul Zindel, an acquaintance of director Jordan. "They wrote lines on every piece of furniture they could find." The play is not top-drawer Tennessee Williams, and Kim was not at her best. But even so, she hadn't lost her ability to dazzle the critics. "Miss Stanley's performing was the program's saving grace," *Variety* said, "her face and inflections imparting greater depth to her role than the mere words provided."

By recent standards, 1971 was a busy year for Kim. Later in January, she did an episode of *Medical Center.* And in February, she was in an episode of *The Name of the Game* called "The Happy Ghost of Will Cheyenne," playing the wife of a missing movie stuntman who is interviewed by reporter Robert Wagner. Then in October, Kim appeared in an episode of *Rod Serling's Night Gallery.*

On "A Fear of Spiders," Kim plays Elizabeth, the lonely, like-to-get-to-know-you-better upstairs neighbor of Justus (Patrick O'Neal), who always rejects her advances. One night, after he's harshly spurned her, a large spider appears in his bedroom and keeps growing (no matter what size it is, unfortunately, it always looks like something from the plush-toys department at FAO Schwarz).

Ten years earlier, O'Neal had carried Kim onstage as her brother-in-law in *A Far County.* Now she had gained so much weight she looked as if she could snap him in half without breaking a sweat. The show isn't much and Kim is a shadow of her former self, but she still has flashes of brilliance.

In one scene, she mocks O'Neal's fearful obsession with the growing spider, which he alone can see. "You're cruel," he tells her. "No, I am not cruel," she replies. "I am refreshingly blunt." When Kim says, "I am refreshingly . . .", she rolls her eyes in disdain and sets her mouth in anger, which then spreads through the rest of her face and hardens like quick-drying cement on "blunt." It's the visual equivalent of a knockout punch.

By now, Elissa Myers, Vivian Nathan's goddaughter, had entered adolescence. One day, she sat in Nathan's living room on Christopher Street in Greenwich Village, talking with Kim. "Kim asked me, 'So Elissa, what do you want to be?'" Myers recalls. "And I said, 'Oh, I want to be an actress in the theater!' She picked up a pewter jug with a bone handle she had just given to Vivian and threw it at my head. Her feeling was that I was loved, and a loved one should not enter the theater." Kim had turned her back on Broadway, off-Broadway, and the community theater. New York held nothing more for her, and it was time to go back home.

CHAPTER 9

"GOD HAD HIS HAND ON MY SHOULDER"

(1972–1981)

In the spring of 1972, Kim sold the house on Kings Highway in Congers. Jamie had left home several years earlier, and Lisa was away at college; Laurie Rachel, still a student at Rockland County Day School, boarded with a teacher until the end of the school year. That summer, Jamie drove Kim back to New Mexico. He recalls that after a brief stay in a Taos motel, she lived in Questa.

At the base of majestic, snow-capped Flag Mountain, Questa is a small Hispano (the New Mexico term for "Hispanic") village 20 miles north of Taos across sagebrush plains and a forest of spruce and pine; it's so insular that a restaurant waitress can tell you're from out of town if you don't know that cherry is the pie of the day. Kim's whereabouts here are unclear, perhaps because she stayed for only a few months. Some think she may have actually lived in nearby El Rito, then a commune which ran heavily to artsy Anglos.

The picture becomes more clear when Kim moved down to Taos in the early fall. She rented an apartment in a large house on Ranchitos Road, not far from the Harwood Foundation, where she had lived with her father thirty years earlier. The house was owned by Frances Minerva Nunnery, also known as Frances Martin, a rancher, real estate saleswoman, and one-time nightclub singer living with Janice Mars, who had played several small roles in the Actors Studio version of *The Three Sisters.*

It's evidence of Kim's low profile that several ex–New Yorkers who had known her and now lived in Taos had no idea she was there. One person who did know Kim in Taos was Native American artist R.C. Gorman: Kim came to his house several times for lunch. "She had the most beautiful hands," he said. "She was quiet and friendly. She didn't seem to be depressed." Virginia Dooley, who manages Gorman's gallery, says, "I always thought she was rather exuberant. Intelligent, of course. She wasn't the greatest social butterfly, but you would see her at things (such as new shows opening at local galleries)."

But evidence that Kim was not doing well came from her abortive connection with the film version of Edward Albee's *A Delicate Balance.* Tony Richardson, who had directed her on Broadway in *Natural Affection,* was eager to help Kim restart her career. He visited her in Taos and found her overweight, but in good spirits. She agreed to play Claire, the alcoholic younger sister of Agnes (Katharine Hepburn), and Richardson accepted the directing job on the condition that Kim would play Claire. Producer Ely Landau reluctantly agreed.

Paul Scofield was to play Tobias, Agnes's husband. Joseph Cotten and Betsy Blair played Harry and Edna, the frightened couple who want to move in with Tobias and Agnes, and Lee Remick played their daughter, Julia, whose fourth marriage is falling apart. During pre-production, there were complaints from the Landau Organization of erratic phone calls from Kim and pressure to recast her, but Richardson brushed them off as lies and gossip from a production company that hadn't been eager to hire her.

Kim arrived in England several days early and stayed with Richardson and his wife, Vanessa Redgrave. Kim hadn't lost her excess weight as promised, but otherwise appeared fine, refusing drinks when offered. The cast gathered at Richardson's home for a first reading, and he told them to read in a casual manner, not to act. That's how it worked for the first act, but then came Kim's scenes in the second act. This description is from Richardson's autobiography, *The Long-Distance Runner:*

Gradually she started to act, not read. She began to improvise on Edward's text, she crawled on the floor, she sputtered, she cried. Looked on one way it was a parody of the stereotypical view of Method acting. In a London first-floor drawing room, expressing her emotions, her flesh, her bulk, it was almost obscene. "How could you have let that happen to us?" Paul . . . hissed violently at me when we finally broke up. But it was magnificent—its reality so compelling, so violently and truthfully exposed, that there was more knowledge of the depths of human experience and of alcoholism than I've seen in any other performance. It transcended anything I'd ever imagined could be in the play, and I knew instantly how to direct it. It had the ugliness, the truth, the understanding of great art. But it was clear that Kim's truth was at the expense of everything else— the other performers, the text of the play, and the exigencies of the production. If we had had a year to shoot I could have gotten something so disturbing on film it might have been unwatchable. [But] we had two weeks' rehearsal and then four weeks to shoot.

After Kim's display, Hepburn announced she was withdrawing from the production. Kim tried to meet with her, but Hepburn refused. Richardson called in his doctor to examine Kim. He diagnosed her as a severe alcoholic and uncovered several quarts of vodka she had stashed around the Richardsons' house. Under pressure, Richardson reluctantly fired her. Producer Landau generously agreed to pay Kim's salary in full, then hired Kate Reid to replace her.

"Hepburn worked from the top. Kim started at the bottom and worked up. I'm not knocking it, it's just a different way of working," says actress Bonnie Bartlett. "And it must have made Hepburn very nervous to be around an alcoholic, because she lived with one [Spencer Tracy]." Kim's departure from the cast was noted by the *Hollywood Reporter.* "How sad that Kim Stanley still doesn't seem to be emotionally stable enough to resume her career, hard as she has tried," it said. "Even with Tony Richardson keeping a protective eye on her during her houseguest-ing with him and her own conviction that she could make it, when it came time for her to leave for the studio, she just couldn't manage it. Now back in New York, Kim, lunching with Harold Clurman at the Russian Tea Room, looked so great, you wouldn't think she had a problem in the world. And here's hoping this brilliant actress can eventually prove she hasn't."

It was seven years since Kim had been on Broadway, and her fans missed her. In the syndicated column of Robin Adams Sloan of December 19, 1972, J.S. of Rochester, New York, asked what had become of Kim, adding, "Wasn't she supposed to surpass the late Laurette Taylor?" Sloan responded that Kim's life had been "somewhat disturbed," adding that she was living in Taos, teaching retarded children. (Tony Richardson had heard she was teaching autistic children, although it isn't clear what Kim would have had to teach them.) And in Sloan's column of October 9, 1973, H.J. of New York asked, "Is it true Kim Stanley will never act again? I saw her in the film *The Goddess* and in several Broadway plays and thought she was the greatest." Sloan again compared Kim to Laurette Taylor. "She wants very much to return to Broadway," Sloan wrote, "and she will if somebody finds her the right play."

While Kim was living in Taos, daughters Lisa and Laurie Rachel came to visit her, along with Laurie Rachel's friend Betsy Norton. They flew into Albuquerque, where Kim picked them up at the airport and drove them back to Taos. The ride unnerved Norton: Kim drove extraordinarily slow on the high-speed interstate ("It was scary—she drove about 12 miles per hour the whole way"), as if the drive were one long Method pause.

On April 17, 1974, Curt Conway died suddenly in Los Angeles of a heart attack, one month short of his sixty-first birthday. Kim's immediate reaction is unknown, but years later, she said, "I've been married four times . . . and all of them except the last one [Joseph Siegel] are still my friends. Even the one that's dead is still my friend."

I N THE FALL OF 1974, Kim moved down to Santa Fe, drawn by its endless powder-blue sky, the earth tones of the adobe-style buildings, and the cool sage-scented Rocky Mountain air after a springtime storm. She also had family nearby: Her son, Jamie, lived in the area, and her brother Justin and his third wife, Paula, spent much of the '70s in nearby Chimayo. "When I came out of the spin [which began with her 1965 nervous breakdown], I really had a lot of assessment to do on my own self and needed a quieter arena to do it in," Kim later told an interviewer. "Which is why I went to Santa Fe. The combination of the mountains and that gorgeous sky and the horizon which goes on forever . . . [is] very comforting to me . . . That's when I found out quite fortuitously—God had his hand on my shoulder in some way—that I'm extraordinarily good at teaching."

Shortly after arriving in Santa Fe, Kim approached the performing arts department at the College of Santa Fe, which is affiliated with the Catholic church, and sought work as an acting teacher. In a letter to Edward Purrington, the outgoing department chairman, Kim told him (although he doesn't appear to have asked) why she wasn't looking for work at the University of New Mexico. She said that would seem logical, since her father had taught at UNM. But, she added emphatically, she did not want to live in the ugly city of Albuquerque. (Take that, Dad!)

In a handwritten résumé prepared for incoming performing arts chairman John Weckesser, Kim listed her many career accomplishments and made up a few as well. In addition to having appeared on Broadway in Garcia Lorca's *The House of Bernarda Alba,* she said she had also done *Yerma.* Supposedly, she had also appeared off-Broadway in Cocteau's *The Eagle Has Two Heads,* studied acting at the Actors Studio for twenty years, and served as an assistant acting teacher to Lee Strasberg. Even with this embellished résumé, Kim would not ordinarily have been hired. "She didn't come in with the teaching credentials that we would expect if I were doing a search for an acting teacher," says John Weckesser, the department chairman to this day. "But she came in with this halo, and that was a substitute."

As the newly minted department chairman, Weckesser was thrilled that a Broadway star of Kim's stature was joining his small department. "I was ecstatic, because this was one of the renowned actresses of the day. We met in my office at the college," he says. "She came across as the genuine article, completely honest and committed to the idea of working with aspiring actors. We hit it off just fine. The first year was a terrific experience." Soon after Kim started teaching at the College of Santa Fe, Gregory Peck visited and spoke with the students. Weckesser was talking with him in the lobby of the college's Greer Garson Theater one day during a reception, and complimented Peck on his acting. "I'm no actor," Peck said, looking across the lobby at Kim, "there's THE actor."

Kim started teaching at CSF in January of 1975. It was the middle of the school year, but she was eager to start, and a place was made for her. She would serve as a catalyst in the department's effort to establish a Bachelor of Fine Arts in acting degree. She also wanted to establish an ensemble group or repertory company of acting students within the department. The department approved, although it would later have second thoughts.

Student reactions to Kim ran the gamut. Meredith Alexander is now a director and master teacher in acting at the University of Iowa. "My initial impressions were of somebody with the most extraordinary charisma, spirit, and presence that I had ever met," she says. "Her desire to know in the deepest places, and to let you know you were being known, was seductive in every respect. She could draw you into her world, into her reality." But, she adds, that came with a downside. "Kim's sobriety was always an issue," she says. "She was nipping out in her car or in her office or something. The students sometimes were in extraordinary psychological pain from things she'd said."

One of them was Sue Ann Carpenter, who would play Cherie, Kim's signature role on Broadway, in a version of *Bus Stop* that Kim directed at the College of Santa Fe. "She was unpredictable in her moods, so sometimes she wasn't very kind. And that was hard," she says. "She hurt me, but I loved her anyway, because she gave me so much."

Katharine Lee was in awe of Kim's powers of concentration. "She listened unbelievably," Lee says. "She had a way of paying attention and listening that was quite extraordinary. I would often look over at her and wonder what it was that she was seeing."

For Stephen Reynolds, what stood out was a deeply ingrained sense of sorrow. "One of the things I got from her as a teacher was a great sadness. She was obese and terribly unhappy—you could sense that," he says. "And yet, when she would get up onto the stage, for just a glimmer, all of that just dropped off and she was once more a great beauty."

Kim's classes, Reynolds recalls, were essentially the Method as taught by Lee Strasberg at the Actors Studio during the 1950s, including affective memory (in which an actor conjures up a memory or experience from his past to help simulate an emotion on stage) and private moments (in which an actor shows how a character would act when alone). "I wanted to move into scene work," says Reynolds, who was then in his mid-twenties and already had some acting experience. "That was my particular frustration with her, that we kept doing these exercises."

But Wayne Sabato, who was studying acting for the first time, was enthralled. Now artistic director of the Santa Fe Performing Arts Company, he says, "Her work was intense, and not everyone took to it. There were students who were frightened by it, who were intimidated by it. And then there were those of us who were drawn to it. This craft is never-ending. It forces you to face your demons if you're truly pursuing the character within yourself. And Kim was rather relentless in pushing her students to the depths of their work."

Kim's first year at the College of Santa Fe was a good one and, had she so chosen, she could have settled down in Santa Fe to a long run as a distinguished and revered teacher of acting. But long runs weren't in Kim's blood, and at the start of her second year, things began to happen.

"I can almost pinpoint when I thought I was getting in trouble," says John Weckesser. "There were some problems—she missed a few classes. I didn't pay any attention to it. But she was getting sick a lot. Friends who were somewhat savvy about the professional theater alerted me that she had had problems when she was working in New York. I refused to believe that. I was probably in denial, to use the contemporary lingo." At one point, Broadway producer Arthur Cantor was in Santa Fe, to visit Greer Garson. He stopped in at the department and chatted with Weckesser. "I said to him, 'Arthur, I've been told that Kim had some problems with drinking when she was in New York,'" Weckesser recalls. "He just rolled his eyes and said, 'Mon-u-mental!'"

Although he had no way of knowing it, Weckesser had another problem: He was a male educator in a position of authority over Kim, which meant appearing to her as a father figure. As such, he might as well have had a bull's-eye painted on his back. Then there was Weckesser's desire to have her direct a version of *Bus Stop* at the college. "I always wanted to do that play," he says. "She was reluctant at first. One time we were talking about it and she began to weep silently. She said, 'I'll do it for Bill' [William Inge]."

The Kim Stanley–directed version of *Bus Stop* was staged at the college from February 12–15, 1976, but would prove to be a bumpy ride, due in part to a severe kidney problem Kim developed during its production. Before she was taken to Albuquerque for an operation, she was in St. Vincent's Hospital in Santa Fe. While she was there, rehearsals of *Bus Stop* were videotaped so Kim could provide director's notes from her hospital bed.

"She was born with a duplicate kidney. It never functioned—it was just sort of there," says her daughter Rachel. "I guess about that time it either became infected or caused some kind of problem and they removed it." But doing so was not easy.

"She was deathly ill," John Weckesser recalls. "I thought we were going to lose her. They wouldn't deal with it in Santa Fe—they had to rush her down to Albuquerque. I followed the ambulance down and stayed overnight in a motel across from the hospital, expecting a call." Kim's operation was at Presbyterian Hospital in Albuquerque, on Central Avenue at Interstate 25, not far from where she had grown up. Her hospital bill in Santa Fe was paid for by the indigent fund at St. Vincent's Hospital, and may have been in Albuquerque as well. (You can be young without money, Maggie the Cat says in *Cat on a Hot Tin Roof*, but you can't be old without it.) Kim was out much of the term, and Vivian Nathan came from New York to teach her classes.

Before she went into the hospital, though, Kim toyed with Sue Ann Carpenter, who wound up playing Cherie, Kim's role, in *Bus Stop*. One night Carpenter was at Kim's place, the guest quarters of an isolated house on a hilltop north of Santa Fe. She was eager for the role. Kim told her that if she could pick out which of the pillows on her sofa was a gift from Rubyann, she could have the part. Then, after an uncomfortable pause, Kim assured her the role was hers. "It was like she haunted me," Carpenter says. "She'd call me at night and say, 'My dog is sick—I need help,' and hang up. I would worry all night, because I didn't have her phone number and couldn't get up to find her and it would be snowing."

After Kim told Weckesser several times she wasn't interested in a full-time teaching job for the 1976–77 school year, he hired someone else. She then decided she wanted it after all, but it was too late. In a letter Weckesser wrote to her on June 15, 1976, he suggested other ways Kim could maintain her affiliation with the department: directing a production of *Waiting for Godot* they had discussed, getting involved in acting classes taught by other professors, and using the college's facilities to offer private acting lessons.

Kim apparently acted on all three suggestions, directing *Waiting for Godot* at the college November 18–21, 1976. A dark meditation about the human condition, it's an oddly surrealistic play, like a Magritte painting come to life. And, as Kim was fond of pointing out, it's a funny play as well.

Kim scored a coup by getting her friend Maureen Stapleton to come down from New York to play Estragon. (Bill Jones played Vladimir, the other person waiting for Godot. Other than he and young Herman Varos, who played The Boy, it was an all-female cast.) Kim and Stapleton enjoyed bantering with each other in the press. "This is an unusual play, but Kim says she understands it, so she can explain it to me," Stapleton told the *Santa Fe New Mexican*. "It's not what I'm used to doing, and I figure I'll learn something from it. Or maybe I won't." And Kim told the *Denver Post*, "I called Maureen and said, 'How'd you like to do *Waiting for Godot*?' and she said, 'Sure, what's it about?' No, really her first question was, 'Can I wear chiffon?' I said, 'No, no chiffon.'"

The drama editor of the *Denver Post* said Kim was looking radiant, an observation confirmed by Sue Goodson, one of the actors in *Godot*. She noted how Kim enjoyed a good laugh, the clarity of her eyes, and her flowing hair. Wearing a gauze-textured frock with a patterned scarf over her shoulders to add a splash of color, she strode purposefully about in leather moccasins.

Oddly, Kim told the *Denver Post* she had lived in Taos for six years, when it had only been two. And she took a cheap shot at Lee Strasberg, her former mentor. Kim told the *Post* she picked Herman Varos to play The Boy in *Godot* because he didn't want to be an actor, adding, "He's not an actor, he's a child, but he knows more than Lee Strasberg."

As had happened on *Bus Stop, Waiting for Godot* would be a difficult production, but not because of Kim's physical health. "The opening night of *Godot,* Kim was plastered," says John Weckesser. "Even that didn't bother me. But there was a strangeness that I found embarrassing, a kind of groping and making borderline inappropriate remarks. I kept her out of the theater for the first act. She was talking very loud, and her behavior could have stopped the show. We stayed in the lobby. She did go in for the second act and it was fine."

Also making a late entrance was Marlon Brando. "He sat right behind me," says Sue Ann Carpenter, who was seated toward the front of the house. "Then the next thing I knew, he was gone. I heard that a helicopter was waiting for him outside the theater, but more than likely it was a car." Actually, it was a Winnebago. Frances Martin and a group that included Brando had come down from Taos in a recreational vehicle. "After the play, Marlon wanted to take over the driving and do a little sight-seeing, though it was very late," Martin later wrote. "He drove over every curb on Santa Fe plaza on our way home. He was the worst driver I ever saw in my life."

About this time, Kim had another visitor who remembers that she wasn't looking well. Edward Balcomb had been a boyfriend of Kim's more than thirty years earlier at the University of New Mexico. Now an engineer overseeing the construction of a law office in Santa Fe, he learned Kim was living there and dropped in on her. "She was quite heavy," he says. "The weight she'd put on was—watery, I guess. And she drank a lot of wine. I didn't like her condition, but it was nice to see her."

Things weren't so pleasant for John Weckesser. Kim started calling him in his office and late at night at home, her calls sometimes coming in swarms. "She was exceedingly mean and abusive," he recalls. "She would call me names and accuse me of not knowing what I was doing. What business did I have running a department? It went on long enough that it began to get to me. I remember coming home one evening and telling my wife, 'I just don't know if I can take this anymore.' She said 'She's an alcoholic, John. You can't pay any attention to it.' Finally, I had to accept that."

Kim was causing academic problems as well. She had a favored group of students, known as "The Group," who were the only ones allowed to take Kim's upper-division classes. "That produced a great deal of resentment from people who weren't selected," Weckesser says. "In a small undergraduate program, you really can't afford to have that kind of thing. You expect it in big university programs, but not here."

Dissatisfaction with Kim reached the point that a meeting with drama majors was held on December 6, 1976. In a letter written to Kim a month later, Weckesser summed up the anger at Kim many of them felt, along with concerns from the performing arts faculty. "They [the students] felt that frequently you had been drinking prior to classroom or private sessions," Weckesser wrote. "I cannot and will not tolerate your coming to class after you have been drinking."

Weckesser added that Kim's erratic and capricious behavior during the production of *Godot* had created widespread ill will in the department, although he noted that Kim had produced an excellent show. But, he added, her treatment of the department's two scene designers was inexcusable. "You treated your fellow artists in an incredibly unprofessional, cavalier way throughout," he wrote. "They deserve the same respect as yourself. If after all your years in the professional theater, you are not able to read a 'ground plan' or identify major technical or design problems when the initial concepts are presented to you, you have problems, they don't." Weckesser also noted Kim's drunkenness on opening night, and told her meetings of The Group were no longer to be held on campus.

One night, Weckesser was at a faculty party. Kim had not shown up at her classes for about a week. He got a call that something was badly wrong with Kim and someone needed to get over to the small apartment she now had on Booth Street in downtown Santa Fe. He left the party and went to Booth Street. Another faculty member had beaten him there and gotten in. Kim was being taken away in an ambulance. She had passed out drunk on a heating grate in the floor and burned her leg raw. When the paramedics entered, there was a smell of roasted flesh in the apartment. Kim had third-degree burns on her leg. She had long since reached the point identified by Charles Jackson in *The Lost Weekend* where one drink was too many and a hundred not enough.

On February 25, 1977, the academic dean at the College of Santa Fe wrote to Kim, telling her she would not be offered a full-time teaching position for the upcoming school year. She appears to have left the college soon afterwards. There were still good times for Kim, though: In 1977, Harold Clurman and his old friend Aaron Copland came to Santa Fe and visited Kim. "We took a trip to the country and saw the historic Puye ruins and the beautiful purple colors on the tall mountains," Kim later recalled, gently poking fun at the man who had directed her in *Bus Stop* and *A Touch of the Poet*. "Aaron and I were just thrilled by what we saw, but Harold kept talking about music, theater and the arts."

Kim's forlorn fans continued to write to columnist Robin Adams Sloan. E.O. in Cody, Wyoming, said, "I just adored actress Kim Stanley. She seems to have disappeared. What can you tell me?" Sloan inaccurately reported that Kim was now teaching theater courses at the University of New Mexico, adding "Most of her show biz pals have deserted her, except for a few loyal friends, including Maureen Stapleton." This makes Kim sound like a victim of show business callousness, when in reality she did everything short of turning a blowtorch on some of her old friends to drive them away.

Kim was not the only one of her siblings in dire straits during this period. To her growing distress, Kim's half sister, Carol White, developed a growing awareness of her own bisexuality. Although married with children, she started dating other men—and women. Her weight ballooned, just as Kim's had. Carol left her job as a popular and well-regarded junior high school teacher and became a medical receptionist. When she and her husband, Lynn White, were divorced in 1978, he was granted custody of their children.

About the time Kim left the College of Santa Fe, a leading gossip columnist had hopeful news for her fans. "Kim Stanley . . . ran away from Broadway to direct and teach acting in Santa Fe," Liz Smith wrote. "Now they say she is so thrilled over a play a student wrote about Virginia Woolf she's reconsidering trodding the boards." Kim was also considered for a Woody Allen movie—his dark and brooding *Interiors*. "Woody was a great admirer of hers, so he thought it was a really good idea," says Juliet Taylor, Allen's casting director. "[But] by then she was teaching out in New Mexico. She was sort of semi-retired, and we just decided not to get involved because of that. Then we focused on Geraldine Page."

However, in early 1978, Kim did decide to move back to New York City, where she would remain for three years. A January 20 item in the *New York Times* noted, "Kim Stanley, who has been living in New Mexico, is returning to New York. The distinguished actress is not coming back for a play, however; she will return to teach two four-hour sessions a week at the Lee Strasberg Theater Institute." Despite the harsh words she'd had for Strasberg, he offered her the position, probably having heard his former star protégée was adrift.

Kim came back East in the spring, attending her younger daughter's college graduation in Washington, DC, with ex-husband Alfred Ryder. With some prompting from Kim, Laurie Rachel Ryder was now Rachel Ryder. "Laurie is a name that I had always disliked," she says. "I felt it was a diminutive name, and since I was a diminutive person (5 feet 2 inches), I really didn't think I needed a diminutive name. I was complaining to Kim: Why did she give me the first name of Laurie when Rachel was such a better name? She said, 'Well, why don't you just drop it?'"

Although Alfred Ryder was presentable at his daughter's graduation, he had, like his ex-wife, fallen on hard times. He was now living with his sister Olive Deering at the Whitby Apartments in midtown Manhattan. Alfred and Olive would go into Times Square restaurants, run up tabs, and leave without paying. "They were kicked out of Joe Allen's," says publicist Bill Schelble. "They used to come in and get very drunk. Joe told them never to come back."

Kim was teaching at the Lee Strasberg Institute by the summer of 1978. Larry Gold, now an acting teacher, studied with her. "A lot of our teachers were really big name-droppers, you know, Bobby and Dusty and

Al," he says, referring to DeNiro, Hoffman, and Pacino. "You never, ever got that from Kim." One thing he did get from her, though, was a sense of the importance of props.

"She was big on working with props and treating them like characters," he says. "That's what I do in my class: The playwright said to pick up a coffee cup. Is it just a coffee cup, or is it something more? The way you hold that cigarette—what is it saying about you? Think of everything you work with on stage as being a part of your character. A lot of that I got from Kim."

Despite her insightful teaching, Kim was still prey to her demons. Gold and another student from the Strasberg Institute ran into Kim near the railroad flat she had at 24 King Street in Soho at a time when she had missed several classes. She was carrying some bags of groceries. "We ran over to help her. And I just have to think she was tanked up or something," Gold says. "She didn't recognize us and just turned around and said something like, 'You—I kill. And I don't kill many.' And she kept on walking."

Kim's teaching at the Lee Strasberg Institute only lasted several months: By the fall, she was on her way out. In an interview with the *Los Angeles Times* several years later, Kim again blasted Strasberg, saying, "George Scott (who never studied the Method) knew more about Stanislavsky's theories than Lee Strasberg ever will . . . Lee wants to be a millionaire, and he is, and so the Studio as we knew it doesn't exist any more. If you get greedy you lose whatever it was you had." In a letter to the *Los Angeles Times* Strasberg's publicist John Springer responded, "Miss Stanley is one of the most extraordinary talents the theater has known, but she should not forget that, at a time when her fortunes were at a low ebb, she was invited and welcomed to the faculty of the Lee Strasberg Institute. Her own personal problems ended that association."

In New York, Kim often played poker with Maureen Stapleton. "Mo will call up and say, 'You lonesome?' I'll say, 'Okay, let's try it,'" Kim later recalled. "Maureen deals a good hand of cards. But she cares about winning—I don't," a statement contradicted by Patricia Frye's story about Kim's chili recipe.

Given her imagination, Kim didn't even need cards to play cards. One night in the autumn of 1978, student Matthew Armstrong was at Kim's apartment. "We decided to pretend we were on a train," he recalls. "Every so often, one of us would lurch as if the train were careening around a bend.

"Then Kim said, 'Let's play poker,' at which point she grabbed an imaginary deck and dealt out five imaginary cards and set the deck in the center of the table. We played for a long time, maintaining our poker faces, shuffling, cutting the deck, arranging our cards, raising our bets, staring at our hands and watching the other's face as the train rolled on into the night. We were going clear across Texas, I think. It was strange and wonderful and hilarious. And, as I remember, she won."

After leaving the Strasberg Institute, Kim taught private classes at various places in Greenwich Village and midtown Manhattan, including the Harold Clurman Theater on Forty-second Street and the Shelter West Theater (now the Soho Playhouse) on Vandam Street. One student even remembers a class at the Metropolitan Opera. Classes were three nights a week when they met, which could be inconsistent.

"She would teach for six weeks or so, then she'd go off and the drinking would start," recalls Jackson McGarry, one of her students. "She would disappear for a couple of weeks. She'd come back and say, 'Well, I had a nervous breakdown.' She was always having 'nervous breakdowns.'" John Tyrrell, another student of Kim's, recalls the distinctive method of paying for her classes. "She passed a paper bag around the class," he says. "You paid by the class. It was sort of like she didn't have responsibility when she went off on a toot—we hadn't paid her, so when she didn't show up, she didn't owe us any money."

Kim accepted Jackson McGarry into her class on the basis of a telephone interview, and he looked forward to his first class with nervous anticipation. "We kind of just sat on the floor. I didn't see her yet. She came out of a side room. She was very huge. And she had this really weird hat on, a black fedora. She looked like a clown from the circus," he says.

"I watched this woman work and it was un-be-lievable," he continues. "It was like being around white light. When she wanted something done, she would go up there and do it. And when you watched her work, you were just mesmerized. For years after that, I couldn't go to the theater because, I thought, what was the point? I had already seen the greatest performance in the world."

Kim's classes consisted of four parts: an animal-improvisation warmup activity, sense-memory or affective memory work, need exercises, and scene work. Robert Ellerman, who studied with Kim in New York, remembers that she put her own distinctive stamp on these exercises. "Instead of the classic animal improvisation, where it was an individual exercise, Kim would say, 'You're in a jungle. You're in a barnyard.' And she would have fifteen people up there," he says. "This would last about forty-five minutes. When they were over—and I'll never forget the first time I saw her do this—she would start at the beginning of the improvisation with each actor and go through almost the whole thing. Everything they did. And she didn't take notes. I don't know of anyone who has that level of concentration."

Katharine Lee, who had studied with Kim at the College of Santa Fe, remembers a class at the Clurman Theater where Kim gave a memorable display of the sense-memory technique. She was talking about the importance of evoking a physical environment and began to describe a tree standing behind her, scooping her hand through an imaginary stream at her feet. Twenty years later, Lee could still see in her mind's eye a large white oak rustling behind Kim, with drops of water falling off her fingers back into the stream. But she could also see the unfinished brick wall behind Kim and dirty floorboards beneath her as if in a double exposure, Kim's vivid imagination transcending her mundane environment.

"What I learned from Kim was specificity," says Jackson McGarry. "She would say, 'Okay. You're standing in a field. What time of day is it? Where is the sun hitting you?' She went down to the month, the time of day, the nettles on the ground. Was it a dry heat or a humid heat? And if you couldn't get it, she'd do it. This woman would create an environment. A living, pulsating environment in her eyes."

Then came need exercises. Ellerman says "need" was Kim's word for "objective" in the Stanislavski system. Two students would get up before the class. One would need something from the other student, who in turn would need something from the first. Behavior was essentially physical, silent, nonverbal.

"Kim did not like Lee Strasberg at this point in her life," says McGarry. "I guess she was more in tune with Stella Adler, who was big on imagination. But this is where it got a little bit nuts. She would say to us, 'There are only four needs in the world: the need to destroy, the need to seduce, the need to seduce in order to destroy, and the need to celebrate.'" (Another need Kim could have mentioned was the need to transgress, a powerful need in her own life.)

Scene work then followed. Doing all this with a group of fifteen or so students took time. "Class would start around 7 P.M. and would end whenever she felt she was through," McGarry says. "On [some] occasions, we walked out of class and the morning sun was coming up over the Manhattan skyline." Robert Ellerman remembers class routinely ending at 2 or 3 A.M. "These modern acting classes where it's an hour or two hours are a waste of time," he says. "Because you don't get to what Kim Stanley does that quickly. It takes a long time, a lot of work, to find that place of reality and imagination and truth, so you can begin to pull that stuff up."

Kim strongly communicated to her students an aversion to mediocrity. In one class, she set up a few props and told the students they were in a funeral home. They were to imagine paying their last respects to someone who had been close to them. "One by one, the actors came in and all indicated their asses off," says former student Carl Palusci, using an acting term that means telling rather than showing. "Kim was totally disturbed by what she saw.

"She began to talk about what it meant to walk into a funeral home and face someone you had loved dearly. And she began to relive it. She started talking about her brother and how close she had been to him, how he would never see the sun shine again, or the blue sky. The things they had shared," he continues. "I'd never thought of death that way. She became the person reliving that experience."

Kim had seamlessly moved from a description of the mood to the mood itself. That made her a remarkable actress, Palusci says, but caused confusion in her life. "As far as I'm concerned, Kim could not distinguish life from acting," he says. "There was no distinction between the two. If you were on stage, you became that character. You were that character."

She didn't usually talk about emotion in class, but one day a student asked about the role of emotion in acting. "You want to know about emotion?" Kim asked. She sat in a chair and took off her shoe. She was dry-eyed, but projected such a forlorn quality that the students began crying without knowing why. Kim just put her shoe back on and said, "That's emotion."

As she had done at the College of Santa Fe, Kim began calling her students at all hours. Victor Slezak got a call at 2:30 or 3 one morning. He picked up the phone, and Kim said in a light, breathy voice, "I've got some very, very bad news for you." "What?" he asked. "You're not the Messiah," she answered and hung up.

Kim began to haunt her students' dreams. In one, Slezak was doing a jigsaw puzzle, and as he was putting it together, he realized it was Kim's face. When he put the last piece of the puzzle in, it came to life. Kim looked at him and said, "Oh, you've gotten this far." The next thing he knew, she was on a cherry picker looking down at him. "How did you do that?" he asked her. "How did you *do* that?" Kim just shook her head and smiled.

Whether her students were novices or celebrities, Kim showed them equal respect—or disrespect. Author and playwright Martin Duberman took acting lessons from Kim. "He was doing a scene from a play called *P.S. Your Cat Is Dead*," says Arthur Laurents. "She stopped him and said, 'You have to know what you want in this scene. You want to suck his cock. Say it!' And he said okay and she said, 'No, say it! Say, "I want to suck his cock!"' And she made him say it."

Another of Kim's students was actress and model Lauren Hutton. Carl Palusci recalls Hutton having a difficult time at the beginning, with Kim screaming at her. One time Kim threw a shoe at the Revlon girl. "Fortunately, it missed her," he says. "It went right past her head."

"There was something extremely authentic about Kim in a way that most people are not," says John Tyrrell. "There was something awe-inspiring, but also a little bit frightening, because they're not going to pull any punches with you."

Horton Foote attended several of Kim's classes and found her an inspiring and dedicated teacher. But if her classes looked good, her living conditions were appalling. Carl Palusci served as her assistant and remembers Kim asking him and Jackson McGarry up to her apartment to help move some things.

"The place was very, very dirty," he says. "The smell was unbearable. There was vomit in the bathroom and a sour stench that made me heave. The kitchen was filthy and full of roaches." Kim had a mattress on the floor, with a clock next to it, and a little TV on a wooden crate. The place was sparsely decorated. "When I saw it, I was kind of aghast," Palusci continues. "I said, 'Kim, if you don't mind, I think we could give you a hand cleaning this.' I didn't know how to put it—you had to be very delicate. Finally, she relented and said yes." Rather than inviting people up to her place, Kim would meet them at the restaurant Café des Artistes.

On May 6, 1979, a gala celebration organized by a group that included Aaron Copland, Bess Myerson, and Brendan Gill staged a "backstage bash" in honor of Harold Clurman as the Broadway theater at 412 West Forty-second Street was renamed for him. Among the many leading lights of Broadway in attendance were Julie Harris, Maureen Stapleton, Elia Kazan, Arthur Miller, Cheryl Crawford, Robert Lewis, and Robert Whitehead. "But," Rex Reed wrote in the *Daily News*, "the real attraction is a rare appearance by America's greatest and most reclusive actress . . . Kim Stanley, who will recreate her role as Cherie in *Bus Stop* to act as hostess in the 'Bus Stop Bar.'"

The event was held in a yellow and white tent behind the theater, decorated with vines, flowering trees, and *Playbills* from the more than forty plays Clurman had directed. Kim wore a red Mexican fiesta dress as she greeted guests in the Bus Stop Bar. She told a reporter from *Women's Wear Daily* that she had been keeping a low profile while teaching in New York, spoke of her hopes for creating an ensemble theater, and added, somewhat cryptically, "I've been working quietly—from within."

Asked if she planned to return to the stage to act, she said, "Of course I will." But Robert Whitehead knew better. "I loved her," he later said, "and when I saw her, it was with a great feeling of nostalgia and a feeling that what a shame she's not going to come back and act, because I knew she wasn't." In June, along with her daughter Lisa, Kim made another public appearance, attending the opening of the revival of Arthur Miller's *The Price* at the Forty-eighth Street Theater.

One event Kim didn't attend was her father J.T.'s ninetieth birthday party, held in Albuquerque at the Kirtland Air Force Base Officers Club on August 19, 1979. It was attended by about fifty people, although there were three significant no-shows at the celebration for the man fondly known in Albuquerque as "Pop" Reid: his three surviving children by Rubyann. Kim was teaching acting in New York. Justin was in Big Sur. Although a highly successful lawyer, he was so distraught by the breakup of his third marriage that he stood at the edge of a cliff overlooking the Pacific Ocean and contemplated jumping, finally deciding to attend sessions at the Esalen Institute instead. Howard was now living in the small town of Bemidji in the north woods of Minnesota. He practiced psychiatry and had lived there with his second wife, Merrillee, since taking it on the lam from the Texas Panhandle twenty years earlier.

The only one of J.T.'s children who attended was Carol White, Kim's half sister, who read a letter of tribute to J.T. from Kim. The letter, though brief, was effusive to the point of gushing and recalls Henry James biographer Leon Edel's injunction to examine "the excessive endearment that conceals a certain animus." The occasion was festive, despite the voluntary absence of most of Pop's kids, with many speeches of tribute. J.T., who was still active in fishing and real estate, gave a brief talk in which he managed to sound as hard and flinty as a man only half his age.

A MONTH LATER, the *New York Times* published a profile of Kim. "She was in a Greenwich Village restaurant, and she was looking splendid," reporter John Corry wrote. "In her years of isolation, she had exorcised painful old ghosts, and she had lost unwanted weight . . . Once again, she was beautiful." The latter observation, while gallant, is not borne out by photos that accompany the article, but Kim may have acted beautiful for the interview. In it, she talked again about her desire to create an ensemble acting company.

"It's what I want to do with the rest of my life—establish an ensemble group," she told Corry. "I've been working on an ensemble group in my head for twenty-five years . . . we have some actors from Santa Fe, where I was teaching, and we have a place to work [the Shelter West Theater on Vandam Street, now the Soho Playhouse], and I have Harold Clurman as a mentor.

"I want to be involved with the great plays," she added. "There are so many actors who can play all the big roles—Ben Gazzara, Nehemiah Persoff, Martin Balsam—so many actors who want a place to do the great parts of literature. I want a place for them." Another goal was a film about Virginia Woolf. "I have no interest in exploiting the suicide; that's a very small part of it," she said. "But the relationship with Leonard—fascinating."

Kim continued to tantalize her fans with the prospect of a comeback. "I miss acting," she said. "I will act again, and there are things I want to do: Electra, Medea, but not Lady Macbeth. Shakespeare didn't write for women." And, acknowledging how difficult she found acting, she added, "You can't be good in the theater unless you've immersed yourself in the marvelous detective story of the human spirit. But it's difficult, terribly difficult. None of my children, thank God, went into the theater."

Kim now had the chance to make a comeback in an uncommonly good film. In 1979, John Guare and Louis Malle were putting *Atlantic City* together. There was a part in it for an old gangster's moll, and when Guare learned Kim was in New York, he enthusiastically told Malle about her. "We have to have her," Malle said. Guare got Kim's phone number and called her. She picked up the phone, speaking in a sleepy voice. Guare told her they wanted her for the role of Grace. Kim laughed and said, "You can send the script, but I don't think I'm available." Guare sent the script and never heard back from Kim. Just as the producers of *A Delicate Balance* had done, Guare and Malle turned to Kate Reid instead.

In 1980, it looked like Kim's dream of an ensemble theater might become a reality. Although it isn't clear who her backer was, several students say Kim received financial support from an affluent figure with an interest in theater so she could create her long-cherished ensemble company. "Kim was attempting to carry on Harold Clurman's dream of a permanent acting company," says Robert Ellerman. "It's no accident that two of Kim's husbands [Curt Conway and Alfred Ryder] were associated with the Group Theatre. Kim wanted a real theater to work in, based on an acting company in the Group Theatre tradition."

Kim had a theater, a group of actors, and several plays in mind—including, remarkably, *Cheri*, one of her less successful shows. But she didn't have the organizational knack to turn her dream into a reality. "I think Kim, because of her alcoholism, was incapable of bringing any plans she had to fruition," says Carl Palusci. "I never really got the sense that she knew how to let the plays materialize. There was never any planning. She talked about it, but she was a dreamer. Kim was haunted by demons. She was the most tormented human being I've ever met." Palusci says it was appropriate that Kim loved the work of Edvard Munch and the Expressionists. "Expressionism is all about human anxieties, nightmares, fears, traumas, and terror," he says. "It seemed to me that Kim was a character right out of Munch."

However tormented Kim was, there was still time for romance: Several students recall the fifty-five-year-old Kim getting involved with a student at most in his early thirties. If love was no problem for Kim, though, money was: She charged only forty dollars a month for classes, not enough to meet her expenses. Carl Palusci recalls Kim telling him that Gregory Peck was sending her money; Jackson McGarry says Paul Newman and Lauren Hutton helped to pay her rent. Unlike Blanche DuBois, Kim did not depend on the kindness of strangers, but she did depend on the kindness of friends and colleagues.

That March, Kim got to see Tennessee Williams again at the premiere of his short-lived Broadway play, *Clothes for a Summer Hotel*, starring Geraldine Page and Kenneth Haigh as Zelda and F. Scott Fitzgerald. Kim invited Palusci to attend with her. When they disembarked from the cab at the Cort Theatre, several older people ran up to Kim and took her picture. Kim was flattered to be recognized, but the scene had an odd feeling to Palusci, as if Kim's aging fans were plants who had been sent by a well-wisher (Page?) to boost her spirits.

The show was not a success, which did nothing to enliven Kim's first meeting with Williams since *Dragon Country* ten years earlier. "He was livid, pacing back and forth, because the show's closing notice had already gone up," Palusci says. "He was not warm to her. It was just 'Hello.'"

After the show, Kim, Geraldine Page, and Palusci were invited to dinner at the home of two costume designers in Greenwich Village, going down by taxi. "Geraldine Page was trying to get Kim to go back on the stage," remembers Palusci, who sat between them in the cab. "Kim kept saying, 'No, I can't do it. I just can't do it.' I think this was the basis of the problem with Kim—it was a painful experience for her to become the character, whatever character it was. Geraldine Page said, 'You have to start enjoying it. I have so much fun on the stage. I enjoy every moment!'"

In the fall of 1981, Kim turned her back on New York again without having tried to go on stage. Robert Whitehead had been right: She had not come back to New York to act. She had Jamie drive her to Bemidji, Minnesota, where Rubyann now lived in a nursing home near Kim's brother Howard and his second wife, Merrillee. Rubyann had remained in the West Fourth Street apartment in Greenwich Village for several years after Kim left New York in 1972. But when she could no longer live alone, Rubyann went to Bemidji to live in a nursing home near Howard.

The plan appears to have been for Kim and Jamie to visit Rubyann and take her for a ride. They did, but instead of returning her to the nursing home, they kept heading west. Unbeknownst to Kim's brother Howard, Kim had just kidnapped their mother.

"I'm quite sure Kim viewed the 'heist' as a noble act," Kim's daughter Rachel says. "I would guess Mamaw was unhappy and missed Kim—their bond was very strong. Kim probably thought, or imagined, Mamaw was being mistreated or cruelly ignored by Howard. Since Kim didn't consider kindness to be one of Howard's attributes, she would have felt it was an awful way for Mamaw to spend her last days."

With Kim's father in decline, she decided to return to Albuquerque and try to make peace with him. While she was there, Hollywood came calling.

CHAPTER 10

EXIT, PURSUED BY DEMONS

(1981–2001)

IN THE SPRING OF 1981, Kim was living in her childhood hometown, or, as she had recently called it, "the ugly city of Albuquerque." One day that summer, there was a family gathering at the home Kim's father had shared for decades with his second wife, Florence, on North Dartmouth Street in University Heights.

As everyone sat in the backyard, Kim repeatedly tried to engage J.T. in conversation, but, to her growing frustration, he kept bobbing and weaving away from her. Because he had begun to suffer from senile dementia, it's hard to say how much of this was passive-aggressiveness and how much the downward course of his illness. But it was the capstone of a lifetime of frustration and anger Kim felt with J.T. She was a legend, had awards and the awe of her theater colleagues, but she didn't have a sense of reconciliation with her father, nor would she ever.

While Kim was trying to connect with her father, Jonathan Sanger and Graeme Clifford, the producer and director of a projected film about 1930s movie star and stage actress Frances Farmer, were in New York interviewing actresses for the role of Farmer's mother Lillian. "We had met with the usual suspects," Sanger says, a group of four or five actresses including Kim Hunter and Celeste Holm. "But no one knocked us out. I knew who Kim Stanley was and just wondered about her."

Sanger found Kim in Albuquerque and sent her a copy of the script. She expressed interest when they talked on the phone, so he arranged a layover of several hours in Albuquerque on a flight from New York to Los Angeles. Kim met Sanger at a coffee shop in the airport, where they talked for several hours. "When I got to L.A," Sanger recalls, "I called Graeme and said, 'You have to meet Kim Stanley.'"

Shortly afterwards, Clifford went to Albuquerque, where he would find Kim equally impressive—and colorful. "It was typically eccentric in a very Kim way," Clifford recalls. "She met me in a diner somewhere near the airport, no better than a truck stop. She had big sunglasses on and a big hat pulled down over her face. She looked very much from her era: the movie star incognito.

"Not many people in Albuquerque would recognize Kim Stanley, especially in a diner at the airport," Clifford continues. "But the impression I got was not that she was doing it for effect so much as just not wanting to take any chance she would be recognized." Kim liked Clifford and decided to play Lillian Farmer in 1982's *Frances*, the biographical film about the brilliant, free-spirited film and stage star of the 1930s who was lobotomized after a long-running series of troubles with her family (especially her overbearing stage mother), personal life, and the Hollywood studio system.

It would be Kim's first film in eighteen years. Unless one counts some location shooting from *The Goddess,* it was also her first Hollywood film. *Frances* was shot at the Zoetrope Studios in Hollywood, with location shooting in Southern California and Seattle. Like Frances Farmer, Kim had always had a deep-seated aversion to Hollywood: the place, the filmmaking process, and the now-faded studio system. But during the filming of *Frances,* she still chose to live in Hollywood, moving into the Magic Hotel on Franklin Avenue.

A slew of Hollywood stars was reportedly interested in the part of Frances that eventually went to Jessica Lange, among them Tuesday Weld, Diane Keaton, Cathy Lee Crosby, Goldie Hawn, Kim's former student Lauren Hutton, Natalie Wood, Jane Fonda, Sissy Spacek, and

Valerie Perrine. But if actresses were lining up to play the part, producer Sanger worried that the film's downbeat subject matter might keep moviegoers from lining up at the box office, telling journalists the film was not depressing or negative at all. The *Los Angeles Herald-Examiner* was unconvinced, though, headlining a brief interview with him, "Frankly, We'll Wait for the Musical."

Beyond their aversion to Hollywood, the parallels between Kim and Frances Farmer are striking: In his book *Shadowland,* William Arnold called the Farmers "a family tinged with brilliance and . . . a certain madness." Like Kim, Frances Farmer was talented and willful, with a strong independent streak. According to Arnold, Frances was "incapable of dissembling" and "could not abide dishonesty." She was also a devotee of the theories of Stanislavski, involved with the Group Theatre, had an affair with Clifford Odets, and played the role of Melanie in Robert Ardrey's *Thunder Rock,* as Kim had done as a student at the University of New Mexico.

According to Kim's daughter Rachel, her mother was at first dubious about working with Jessica Lange, whom she knew mainly as the star of the remake of *King Kong.* "I remember Kim telling me that when Jessica Lange was going to play Frances, her first thought was, 'Oh my God, not that girl in the monkey movie,'" Rachel recalls. (Kim had another connection with the "monkey movie": Its screenwriter was Lorenzo Semple Jr., with whom Kim had had an affair in New York in the late '40s.) But Kim and Jessica Lange would forge a close personal and professional relationship.

Graeme Clifford says that Kim helped his directorial debut beyond the quality of her performance. "It was very inspiring," he says, "because working with an actress who has such a reputation and who is so creative and demanding—demanding of herself, mostly—sort of brings everyone's game up a notch." Jessica Lange benefited, Clifford says, but she wasn't the only one.

"It helped Jessica an awful lot to have Kim to play against as her mother," he says. "And she inspired most others in the cast, whether or not they were in scenes with her. She was just a consummate professional." Jonathan Sanger notes that Jessica Lange had done only a few films at this point, and this was the first one she carried as the star. "Having someone as solid and experienced as Kim to rely on was really important to her being able to achieve the performance that she did," he says.

Sanger adds that Kim helped Jessica Lange in another way: keeping her in line when she acted on the set as the younger Kim might have done. "If I had a problem, ever, it was Jessica," he says. "We needed her on the set, but she'd go back to her trailer. Kim had a conversation with her, which I overheard, where she was saying, 'Look. You don't have to act out in order to do this.'"

The mother-daughter conflict in *Frances* comes to a boil in a scene when Frances returns to her parents' home in Seattle after her first psychiatric hospitalization in Hollywood. Frances announces to Lillian Farmer, the ultimate stage mother, that she has no intention of returning to Hollywood. She then tries to leave the house for a walk, but Lillian blocks her path. "They just went at each other physically," Clifford says. "That's the way we'd rehearsed it, but when you're doing a scene like that, you don't really rehearse until you start shooting. You can't give that level of emotional performance in a rehearsal and repeat it too many times." As played by Kim and Jessica Lange, the scene is one of visceral intensity.

Like many who worked with Kim, Clifford compares her acting to Brando's. "Kim was probably the most perceptive actor I've ever worked with," he says. "She could get to the bottom [of a character] by digging. I would hazard a guess that she worked in a similar way to Marlon Brando. It would have been great to see them in a movie together." Clifford was also struck by the intensity of Kim's Method. "She wasn't one of those actors that can just turn it off and turn it on like a tap," he says. "She got into the character and stayed there. So you had to talk to her as if she was Mrs. Farmer and not Kim Stanley. This was the first time I had encountered an actor who inhabited a character to such an extent."

Among Kim's fellow cast members on *Frances* was Bonnie Bartlett, who had appeared with her on Broadway in *Natural Affection* almost twenty years earlier, and who plays the snippy hairdresser Frances Farmer slugs after showing up late on a film set. Despite Clifford's accolades, Bartlett felt Kim was no longer the actress she once had been. "Whether it was her age or what, she had lost her muse," she says. "She still did very interesting work, but it wasn't the same."

Dorothy Land, Kim's friend and sorority sister at the University of New Mexico, was surprised by her appearance when she went to see *Frances*. "She didn't look like herself at all," she says. "I think she grew tired of things." Even Rex Reed, one of Kim's greatest admirers, described her fading looks with a block-that-metaphor intensity, saying, "Now sixty-one [she was fifty-six when *Frances* was shot] and many kilos overweight, her face [is] ravaged and lined like a map of Argentina . . ."

Graeme Clifford believes that one reason Kim never liked working in films is that even when she was a youthful beauty, she didn't like to look at herself. "I think she was so critical of herself and her work that being able to see it was something she didn't like," he says. "Whereas on stage, of course, you never saw what you were doing.

"She never looked at the dailies," he adds. "I'm not sure that she ever saw the finished movie. She may never have, as far as I know." It's probably no coincidence that in the two mediums in which Kim shone most brightly—theater and live television drama—you can't see your performance. When your work is done, it vanishes into the air.

Much of the film's dialogue is surprisingly resonant with Kim's life. When the grown Frances leaves the Farmers' house one day, Lillian yells after her, "Frances, remember that the surest way to lose an appetite is to drink. I don't want you drinking, Frances!" And when Frances decides not to return to Hollywood, Lillian says, "You'd throw it all away? Just throw it away, huh? You had it all—beauty, a brilliant career, a wonderful husband . . ." In the *New Republic*, Stanley Kauffman observed, "Kim Stanley, who was a theater figure of importance twenty or twenty-five years ago, plays Lange's mother with competence and truth. Stanley's career was hampered by illnesses; and for those who know a few of the facts, some of the lines she speaks about her daughter have an extra edge."

As do some of the lines she speaks about her own character. When Lillian Farmer spitefully condemns her daughter to the psychiatric commitment that will result in her being lobotomized, she says at the court hearing, "Doctor, you see, all my life I have been trying to live up to my parents' sense of excellence." The same was true of Kim and her siblings, with sometimes-devastating results.

Unfortunately, it was not just Frances who suffered the unkindest cut of all, but the film itself. Kim told one interviewer that Clifford had to cut forty-five to fifty minutes out of *Frances* involving scenes that showed why Frances and her mother were so inextricably bound to each other. Clifford acknowledges the cuts, but says Kim exaggerated their extent.

"Universal wanted Jonathan and me to cut twenty minutes out of the early part of the movie, because, like most studios, they wanted to get to the action quicker," he says. "To be honest with you, it was probably more like ten minutes. Jonathan and I resisted, but to no avail. There were some early scenes between Frances and her mother that were extremely important to the movie. Because otherwise you would not understand why she kept going back home. But the studio didn't care. They just wanted to make it shorter."

Unfortunately, Clifford, adds, if you're waiting for a director's cut of the film, don't hold your breath. After making the film, he left it in storage with a production company that held onto it for a few years, then disposed of it without telling him. "Unfortunately, all of the trims and the negative, the stuff we had in storage, got thrown away," he says. "So those things don't exist anymore."

In addition to a Golden Globe nomination, Kim received her second Academy Award nomination for her supporting role as Lillian Farmer. Had she chosen to attend the Oscar ceremonies a year later, she could have reunited with Lou Gossett Jr., her fellow cast member from the ill-fated Broadway play *Taffy*, who was named best supporting actor for his role as Sergeant Emil Foley in *An Officer and a Gentleman*. Kim had also worked with three of that year's nominees for best director: Richard Attenborough, who won for *Gandhi*, Sydney Pollack *(Tootsie)*, and Sidney Lumet *(The Verdict)*. But, as was her custom, Kim did not attend the awards ceremonies.

IN JANUARY OF 1982, just after finishing work on *Frances*, Kim gave an interview to Paul Rosenfeld of the *Los Angeles Times*. Its unintentionally ironic headline, "Kim Stanley Plays with a Full Deck," was a reference to Kim's stated fondness for playing cards with friends when she had recently lived in New York. She was in good spirits, laughing as she told Rosenfeld that she had recently been contacted about a retrospective of her films. "Retrospective?" she guffawed. "I've only done two." For all her humor, though, Rosenfeld noted that interviewing Kim was a challenge, comparing it to going headfirst into a pencil sharpener. "[She] is both contradictory and compelling," he wrote.

Rosenfeld noted Kim was growing philodendron and planning new projects. "Immediately," she said, "I'm going to Broadway. I want to do Noel Coward's *Tonight at 8:30*. There's a lot of stuff I want to do before I'm too long in the tooth. But producers say to me, 'Kim, we're not buying that stuff this season.'" Kim's assertions of setting out for Broadway are a frequent refrain of her later years, and bear an eerie resemblance to Chekhov's three sisters' assertions of an imminent departure for Moscow.

Kim reasserted her fictional Texas roots ("Stanley, daughter of a psychology professor from San Antonio, went on to the University of Texas, graduating and briefly considering pre-med," Rosenfeld wrote). While insisting she was ready for Broadway, she added that she didn't miss the stage at all. "Life," she said, lighting yet another cigarette, "is much more fun than anything that ever happened on the stage. To be in love, to have children, to watch them grow up . . . There is not a moment on the stage that can equal that."

On February 9, 1982, Kim's father, J.T., died in Albuquerque of pneumonia at age ninety-two. His ashes were scattered over Elephant Butte Reservoir, where he had fished for fifty years, in a desolate area of southern New Mexico known by seventeenth-century Spaniards as Jornada Del Muerto, the journey of the dead. In an interview publicizing *Frances* for her hometown *Albuquerque Tribune,* Kim played the role of the loyal native daughter. "We had a nice visit last summer and I'm happy about that," she said. "His death decimated me . . . [This interview] is for Pop and the old home town."

Scarcely a week later, Kim's father figure died: Lee Strasberg, the embodiment of the Actors Studio, was dead of a heart attack in New York at age eighty. Although he had guided Kim to stardom and given her a job at the Lee Strasberg Institute in the late '70s, Kim never forgot or forgave his failed captaincy of the London version of *The Three Sisters.*

That April, Kim was again the houseguest of Paul Zindel, as she had been ten years earlier on Staten Island, when he was trying to entice her to appear in *And Miss Reardon Drinks a Little.* Zindel, now married, was living with his wife, Bonnie, a psychologist and author, and their two young children in Beverly Hills. "She moved in on my wife and me," Zindel later recalled. "She came in again and hit the liquor supply. I started hiding all the liquor again." But Bonnie Zindel, who was meeting her for the first time, was enchanted by Kim.

One night after they finished dinner, everyone was sitting around the table. The Zindels' daughter Lizabeth had changed into a pale pink satin nightgown. "She was sleepy, so she curled up in my lap, and I started rocking her," Bonnie Zindel recalls. "I remember watching Kim's face— no, her being more than her face. She was taking all this in. She was suddenly the actress or the artist. I could see her memorizing in the cells of her body what it was like to hold a little girl in your arms, someone you love, and rock them to sleep."

But she adds that Kim's impulsiveness got her into trouble. "At that time, we had a big Great Dane and a sheepdog," she says. "I cooked some stuff for the dogs and figured we'd give it to them the next day. But then Kim came down in the middle of the night and started eating it. Afterwards, she said, 'That chicken was terrible. I got sick all night from it.' But who knew she was going to eat it? It was for the dogs."

Although Zindel wasn't Jewish, his wife was, and this seemed to awaken the Jewishness Kim had casually embraced when she married Alfred Ryder. As Passover approached, she asked the Zindels to hold a Passover seder, which led to a night memorably different from all other nights. Before the seder, Kim said, "Oh my God, you don't have flowers on the table," Bonnie Zindel recalls. "I said, 'Flowers are not something you'd think of putting on the table. You think of matzoh or bitter herbs.' So she said, 'Don't worry, I'll take care of it.' She went up and came down with the most magical thing! She found the kids' Tinkertoys and made a flower arrangement from them. It was the most fabulous centerpiece I have ever seen. I saved it for the longest time—it had such a sense of whimsy and imagination."

For all his fascination with Kim, Paul did not share his wife's enthusiasm. "This was one of those occasions when her Jewish side would pop up," Paul Zindel later recalled. "She wanted the seder to be done properly. So my wife went out and bought all the books on how to run it."

"When Kim came down, she took control. We had these haggadahs. Someone started doing something, and she said, 'Paul, you have to do it. You're the man of the house. You have to run it.' Incidentally, she arrived at the seder wearing her dead father's fedora. After all the years and battles and drunks—suddenly, it fell into place when she was wearing the father's fedora.

"There she was, ordering me about in front of my wife and kids, making me into an absolute fool and idiot. She was doing the thing that most triggers me to go bananas, which is to have a dominating female lacerating me," he laughed.

"So I stopped my participation in the seder and told her that's not the way it's going to be run. I had a big blowup with her, a major explosive screaming match. I was mortified at being an inept seder performer. I was the failed father, and she was wearing the father's hat.

"She went up to her room sometime that night, got ahold of more liquor from the bar, and set her bed on fire with a cigarette. We smelled the smoke and broke down her door. My son was about seven years old and in the next room. Now she's endangering my children. That's when I said, 'Okay, you're out of here. There are limits to what I can tolerate.'" The seder from hell was over.

By night, Kim raged at her father and father figures. But by day, she could give a thoughtful and incisive analysis of the stresses buffeting men in our society, telling an interviewer, "I'm really for Men's Lib; little boys are taught from a very early age the way to behave because they're going to have to decide very soon what chute they're going to go down, they're going to be a doctor, a lawyer. And so a lot of intuitive stuff is almost cut off . . . 'Don't cry—that's not manly' . . . it dries up all the real stuff. It's very unfair, I think. Men have it much harder than women . . . We have it much easier to get at our real selves. Women have so many more options."

Kim's oft-stated desire to create an ensemble theater company looked like it might happen in the spring of 1982, with the creation of the redundantly named Hollywood Opera and Theatre Ensemble Theatre. Based in the Hollywood Masonic Temple on Highland Avenue, it was to feature a three-theater complex and an ensemble including John Cassavetes, Janice Rule, Jean Stapleton, and Martin Balsam. Kim would serve as the group's artistic director. But it never got off the ground for reasons that are unclear.

In the wake of *Frances,* Kim continued expressing interest in returning to Broadway. "To prove Kim is really back on track, she just signed with agent Robbie Lantz and says she'll return to the Broadway stage!" columnist Liz Smith reported enthusiastically in May. "There's talk of a revival of *The Glass Menagerie.* But I opt for the life story of late actress Laurette Taylor, which Judy Holliday tried to bring to the Main Stem. *Laurette* closed out of town. But I'll bet now with Kim Stanley back, it could make it." Both projects, evocative of Laurette Taylor, would have been good vehicles for Kim, but neither happened.

On July 10, 1982, Kim's fourth husband Joseph Siegel, a young and apparently healthy fifty-three, died of a heart attack while playing tennis in Southampton, New York. Kim, who had severed all connections with him, was probably unaware of it.

Happy news came later in the year from Kim's younger daughter, Rachel, who married attorney Peter Zahn in New Jersey the first week of September. Although Kim did not attend the wedding, she paid for it. "Kim begg[ed] off due to a sudden dental abscess," Rachel says. "I always thought it was a combination of her fear of flying and discomfort with that sort of social situation with non-showfolk." Rachel would begin medical school in the fall of 1985, getting her M.D. at Rutgers in 1991, then moving to Southern California, where she would have a successful career as a pediatrician in San Diego.

But later in the fall of 1982, there was more bad news: On October 31, Kim's mother, Rubyann, died of a heart attack in an old-age home on Fairfax Avenue in Los Angeles. The newly married Rachel flew out to Los Angeles to be with her mother and grandmother, but Rubyann died while she was en route. Rubyann was buried in Forest Lawn Hollywood Hills Cemetery. Her plaque, paid for by Kim, read:

ANN REID
LOVED AND WAS LOVED
1896–1982

Rubyann Miller, who had abandoned her youthful dreams of stardom only to see them realized in her daughter, was laid to rest in Hollywood among movie stars.

"Kim was very moved by her mother's death, and had many guilt feelings there, how she treated Annie and ordered her around and asked more of her than she should have in terms of getting to help with the children and things like that," Kim's brother Justin says. Tellingly, when asked about Kim's reaction to J.T.'s death, he simply says, "I don't really have much for you there." Similarly, Rachel didn't even learn from Kim that J.T. had died until several months after the fact. This was a season of death for Kim, as her older brother Howard died during this period as well.

ON THE HEELS OF *FRANCES*, Kim chose to make another film, her last: *The Right Stuff* (1983), Philip Kaufman's saga of the early years of the American space program, based on the book by Tom Wolfe. A large and impressive cast featured Sam Shepard as test pilot Chuck Yeager, Ed Harris as John Glenn, Dennis Quaid as Gordon Cooper, Barbara Hershey as Yeager's wife, and Mickey Crocker, who had studied with Kim at the College of Santa Fe, as the wife of astronaut Deke Slayton.

Kim played Pancho Barnes, the tough-talking owner of Pancho's Fly Inn, the desert bar that becomes a hangout for test pilots at Edwards Air Force Base in the high desert of Southern California. It's a small part, with two minutes and forty seconds of screen time. But Kim makes the most of it: In one scene, a young woman asks Pancho Barnes why a hotshot pilot sitting in the bar doesn't have his picture on the wall along with other pilots. "Whaddya have to do to get your picture up there, anyway?" she asks. "You have to die, sweetie," Kim responds in a superficially polite but curt and conversation-stopping manner that implies it was a dumb rookie question. And when Sam Shepard as Chuck Yeager appears shortly afterward, Kim's line is "Well, Yeager, you old bastard. Don't just stand there in the doorway like some lonesome goddamn, mouse-shit sheepherder. Get your ass over here and have a drink." Kim wisely underplays the line, which is ripe for overplaying.

She looks better in her scenes, both in terms of weight and overall appearance than in *Frances* or in the several TV shows she would subsequently do. Remarkably, if she had played the Hollywood game and worked harder to publicize *The Goddess,* her brief stint in *The Right Stuff* might well have been her only film appearance for which she was not Oscar-nominated.

By the end of 1982, Kim was living at 6175 Glen Oak, a short, dead-end street in Beachwood Canyon, in the shadow of the Hollywood sign. There, she gave her last interview, to entertainment writer John Kobal. Critics such as Rex Reed had heralded Kim's appearance in *Frances* as the start of her comeback. But Kim said, "From where? I hadn't gone anywhere. I'd been working my ass off. I was forming a group theater. But I couldn't get any money to back it."

Although Kim was a strikingly independent woman, she never identified herself with feminists, whom she derided as "libbers." In her interview with Kobal, she knocked then-popular feminist-themed plays such as *I'm Getting My Act Together and Taking It on the Road,* saying, "I can't tell you how many plays I've refused where the final scene is: 'I'm leaving you, Charles, and I'm going out to find myself.' Excuse me!"

She slammed the superficiality of Broadway, saying that in the 1950s, "Tennessee and Bill Inge and Arthur Miller, all from their own viewpoint, were writing about something. Now I find that nobody's writing about what's really going on today. I haven't read even one passable play that has to do with the nuclear problem.

"Everybody's so immobilized that they just want to go see somebody tap dance, and do something that happened in 1930 or 1920 or 1928, or dress up and put the sequins on and please don't let me think about anything," she added. "And that certainly is not the function of a living art, is it? I like *Guys and Dolls* and musicals and *A Chorus Line,* but you can get sick eating too much of that stuff."

Contradicting herself, Kim then praised Doris Lessing for having written a play about the nuclear issue and said she had wanted to do it, but couldn't get funding. And she repeated her desire to do the classics. "I want to do the big shows. I want to do Clytemnestra; I want to do *Ghosts;* I want to do *Medea;* I want do to Noel Coward, with George C. Scott. But it's not anything that's selling on Broadway." One can almost hear the echo of *Sunset Boulevard's* Norma Desmond: "I'm still big. It's Broadway that got small." And that's true, but many of Kim's talented peers still somehow managed to keep their acting careers alive.

During this period, Kim did several TV shows, including an episode of *Quincy, M.E.*, starring Jack Klugman as a feisty medical examiner in the L.A. County Coroner's Office. On February 2, 1983, Kim guest-starred on the episode "Beyond the Open Door," playing Edith Jordan, a psychic who uses her clairvoyant abilities to help Quincy track a serial killer who preys on young women. Unlike Myra Savage in *Seance on a Wet Afternoon,* she's a genuine psychic, although she tends to misinterpret her own visions and usually needs Quincy to make sense of them. Getting her to do the show was no easy matter. "I heard she was in town and I wanted to use her," Klugman recalls. "I had to go to her house and knock on the door. She wouldn't answer. Finally, I got her on the phone and said, 'Come on, Kim. Please.' Finally, she said okay."

The first time Kim and Klugman had acted together, in the 1949 off-Broadway version of Shaw's *Saint Joan,* she had been the star and he the supporting player. Now their roles were reversed. It isn't clear whether Kim had any input into the script, but the troubled family history of Edith Jordan remarkably parallel's Kim's own: "Even my own father hated me because I had the gift [of psychic powers]," she tells Quincy. That was because she had foreseen the death of her brother in a flaming crash, although it was a bus crash, not a plane crash like the one that killed Kim's brother Kenneth.

Klugman's admirable loyalty to Kim extended beyond getting her to do the show. "I sent a limo for her to take her to work, but nobody knew who she was," he says. "It pissed me off, because they gave her a little dressing room. I said, 'I told you to give her a suite.' And they said, 'Well, who is she?' I said, 'She's just one of the best American actresses we've ever had, and don't you ever treat her disrespectfully or I'll have your ass.' So she was treated royally and was wonderful, although she had difficulty remembering her lines." Kim was also slated to appear in an episode of *Trapper John, M.D.*, starring Pernell Roberts, with whom she had appeared on Broadway in *A Clearing in the Woods*. But for reasons that are unclear, she was fired by the producers and replaced.

In mid-1983, Kim moved into the upper floor of a large Craftsman-style bungalow at 1914 Hillcrest Avenue in Hollywood, just west of Highland Avenue and north of Franklin Avenue. That winter, she was one of several illustrious cast members who gathered at the Sunset Boulevard studios of KCET, Los Angeles's PBS station, for the taping of *Cat on a Hot Tin Roof*. Jessica Lange and Tommy Lee Jones starred as Maggie the Cat and her husband, Brick, with Rip Torn as Big Daddy and Kim as Big Mama. The show was directed by Jack Hofsiss, with David Dukes as Brick's brother, Gooper, and Penny Fuller as his wife, Sister Woman. Doing the broadcast was a homecoming of sorts for Kim, who had starred as Maggie in the play's 1958 British premiere in the West End.

The show was a co-production of the fledgling cable network Showtime, which would air it in the spring of 1984, and PBS, which aired it on June 24, 1985. The taping was difficult because of the schedule (eight days, each twelve to fourteen hours long) and Rip Torn's irascibility. Producer Phylis Geller says Kim and Torn weren't crazy about each other, but managed to be polite. Politeness wasn't Torn's signature trait during the taping, though.

"He would get upset from time to time," Geller recalls. "I remember he was smoking a cigar, then stopped the take and started yelling that the prop person didn't have the cigar the right length, and it wasn't going to match the take before. Kim really had very little patience with any lack of professionalism. She had no patience for acting out.

"Kim was kind of an anchor, because Rip and Tommy Lee didn't get along too well, either," she adds. "We would always look to her—we knew that when she came on the set everybody was going to behave. She was really Big Mama on the set as well."

By this point in her life, Kim had consumed enough alcohol to float the Spanish Armada, but her gift had not entirely deserted her. In the third act, upset at the machinations of her son Gooper, Kim's Big Mama yells "Crap!" with an impressive primal ferocity. Just as Big Daddy says Maggie has life in her body, Kim still does, too. At the same time, she looks like hell: She's grossly overweight, her face more like Ben Franklin's than it ever was in *Cheri* and her teeth, owing to her fear of dentists, are in obviously poor shape.

Reviews for the show were mixed, with *TV Guide* calling it "less than compelling." Kim came off somewhat better: John J. O'Connor of the *New York Times* observed, "Miss Stanley . . . retains the practical shrewdness behind Big Mama's flighty hysterics."

When Kim finished her work on *Cat,* there were a few days of taping left with the rest of the cast, Phylis Geller recalls. "I was saying goodbye and thanking her," she says. "She took my hand and sweetly said, 'Well, dear, you have two more days. I'll be praying for you.'" So saying, Kim took her leave of Geller, the KCET studios, and an acting career that had begun forty-five years earlier at Lincoln Junior High School in Albuquerque. She would never act again.

As if to mark this milestone, Kim was inducted into the Theater Hall of Fame on March 4, 1985, a few months before *Cat* appeared on PBS. The ceremony was held at the Gershwin Theater in New York; other inductees included Kim's *Bus Stop* and *Touch of the Poet* producer Robert Whitehead, James Earl Jones, Edward Albee, Richard Burton, Melvyn Douglas, and Robert Preston. Kim, of course, did not attend.

GIVEN'S KIM'S THEATRICAL ALLURE, writers never stopped trying to get her back onstage. Chuck Blasius, a young actor who had studied with Kim in New York, sent her a play he had written with a part he felt was ideal for Kim. A few months later, she called him in New York and said she wanted to workshop it with her students. "I saw myself as the playwright who was going to bring Kim Stanley back to the theater and started rehearsing my Pulitzer acceptance speech," he says with wry humor. "I was only twenty-two, remember."

Over a period of months, he sent her rewrites and tried to follow the work's progress. Not hearing back from Kim, he called her one night at midnight her time. Kim was incoherent and started giving incomprehensible notes. Election day was approaching and Kim asked Blasius if he was going to vote. When he gave a noncommittal answer, she launched into a tirade against the younger generation and hung up. He never heard from her again.

It wasn't only Kim's recent acquaintances with whom she burned her bridges (and, as Tad Mosel has observed, Kim tended to burn her bridges before she crossed them), but old friends as well. Lonny Chapman, who had appeared with Kim on Broadway in *The Chase* and *The Traveling Lady*, was living in Los Angeles with his wife, Erma. "We knew Kim was out here teaching because we would see her ad in the papers," she says. "But we never did see her."

Kim did stay in touch with Brooks Clift, Jamie's father, who lived in Hollywood between 1984 and '86 in an apartment on DeLongpre Avenue with his fifth wife, Joanna. He and Kim often spoke late at night on the phone prior to Brooks's death at age sixty-seven on September 29, 1986, from a cerebral hemorrhage.

A tragically premature death occurred in Kim's family during this period when Dana Reid, the daughter of Kim's brother Justin and his first wife, Jeanne, died of asphyxiation in Albuquerque following the end of an unhappy romantic relationship. Some family members believe it was a suicide—if so, another case of Reid family brilliance overshadowed by self-destructiveness.

Given Kim's burgeoning weight, she took to wearing large and free-flowing garments. "She was very heavy, so she dressed in caftans, the odder the better," Kim's daughter Rachel recalls. "They could be Chinese or Indonesian or Russian, but it was always sort of costume-like." Michael Morrison, an actor who studied with Kim in Hollywood, believes Kim had her teeth pulled during this period, although Rachel thinks it was more like the mid-'90s. "She had pretty decent dentures," Rachel recalls, "but hated them, even though her vanity wouldn't allow her to not wear them."

As she had done in Santa Fe and New York, Kim continued to teach acting in Hollywood. Alan Rachins and his wife Joanna Frank took her class together in 1983. In different ways, they found her extraordinary. "When she spoke to you, she might say, 'It's kind of hot out there,' and all of a sudden, she'd be hot," Rachins says. "She could register these things in a very unusual way. She'd go in and out of sensual emotions like that. I think that was part of her gift."

Similarly, Frank was struck by Kim's remarkable openness. "In every moment of being with her, just looking at her face or into her eyes, she registered the sum total of her life's experiences on an emotional level," she says. "Kim was alive from within herself in a way that was very visible and visceral. Most people are shut down or covered over, so you only get what they choose to show you. But she allowed everything to seep through her pores and that made her a most unusual person to be around."

Kim's class reflected that uniqueness. Rachins remembers one night when they were doing animal improvisations. "We were animals in the forest and I was, I think, a lion, and this other guy was a panther," he says. "We started snarling at one another. And I thought, 'This guy is not backing down. It could escalate into a fight.' And I wasn't going to back off. Luckily, he did. I wondered when Kim would have stopped it, when she would have stepped in."

"She was excited by danger," Frank adds. "That quality ruled her own life. She went further than what was safe or comfortable or accepted."

That going further included Kim's alcoholism. "However long this class was supposed to be, it doubled or tripled in length of time," Rachins says. "Many nights we got the phone call, 'Kim will not be having class tonight.' Some people in the class took on the role of rescuer, and got involved with taking the liquor away or having long talks with her. We didn't do that. We were there strictly to enjoy the benefits of her gift, and if she couldn't have class, *ç'est la vie,* we'll see her next time. There were a lot of people who were the equivalent of groupies. To be near her was a privilege. So they would get sucked into that role."

They would prove no more successful than others who had tried to lead Kim to sobriety. Tom Hatcher, who acted with Kim in *A Clearing in the Woods,* recalls two women trying to get her into AA. Sally Radin, the sister of Kim's fourth husband, Joe Siegel, remembers Kim's brother Howard trying to intervene. Kim did attend one or two meetings of a women's AA group in Hollywood in the mid-'80s, but she appears to have made no concerted efforted to fight her alcoholism. "How can you save someone that doesn't want to be saved?" a character muses in Horton

Foote's play *The Midnight Caller*. "Because he doesn't want to be saved. Nor from drink, not from loneliness, not from death."

In the fall of 1991, eight years after Rachins and Frank, Anna Gunn studied with Kim. As far as she knows, Kim was not drinking at that time. Just as Kim bared her own soul, she says, she expected you to bare yours—and could see through you even if you didn't. "It was like being in the presence of somebody who recognized all of you, who asked you to bring forth everything, to not leave anything behind or hide anything," she says. "You felt Kim knew you by looking at you. She listened and watched so carefully and intently that she got a lot of who you were through things you weren't even aware you were letting out."

Kim's intuitive approach surprised and energized Gunn. At one point, she was working on a scene from *Mourning Becomes Electra* and spoke with Kim on the phone. "Now, darling, for next time, I want you to think about this," Kim said. "Did you ever go into your mother's closet, stand next to her clothes, and try them on?" A surprised Gunn, who had, but who had never told Kim about it, said yes. "Alright," Kim said, "I'll leave it there. See you next time." Then she hung up. "And I thought, 'What does that mean? What am I supposed to do with that?'" Gunn recalls. "It was meant to unlock something in me. That was the beauty of working with her. She would give you images and fragments. If you were open to them, they would open a door, sometimes into the true nature of the scene or the character."

Kim could also be demanding. "She wanted more than you thought you ever could give," Gunn says. "I would think sometimes, 'I've just exhausted it. I gave it all I had.' My guts were on the floor. And her comment would be, 'There's more there. I want deeper, I want more.'"

For Kim's neighbors, having an acting studio in their midst helped to stave off the boredom and monotony of daily life. One day, a neighbor glanced through Kim's window as he came home, saw her being held at gunpoint, and called the police. But it had just been an acting exercise in which Kim had played her part all too well.

Nor was this the only time the police were called to 1914 Hillcrest. One night a female student, a grown woman, was preparing for a private moment exercise, in which she would act as the character would if completely alone. She left the grounds around Kim's house and went out onto Hillcrest wearing only a short nightgown, holding a teddy bear, with her hair in pigtails. She ran up and down the street crying, pulling at her hair and, occasionally, bursting into song.

She then returned to Kim's place, to be replaced on Hillcrest by a male student wearing army fatigues and brandishing a rifle. He appeared agitated, muttering and grunting as he marched up and down the street. After about fifteen minutes, he returned to Kim's and was beginning his private moment when loud footsteps were heard on the porch, the door was kicked open, and two policemen burst in with guns drawn.

"The students were completely petrified," recalls Anna Gunn. "We all put our hands up in the air. The police were equally bewildered. From the back of the room, Kim rather indignantly said, 'Excuse me, what's going on here?' One of the policemen said, 'Ma'am, we received a phone call reporting a hysterical woman in a nightgown fleeing from this house followed by a guy in fatigues with a gun. Also we've had several complaints from your neighbors reporting that there appear to be screams of torture coming from inside this house.' There was a long pause and then Kim replied, 'Well yes, officer. We're working.'"

Rochelle Tetrault bought the craftsman cottage where Kim lived in 1988. Kim's new landlady heard rumors that Roddy McDowall was paying Kim's $1500-plus a month rent, although it was always Kim's name on the check. Tetrault was struck by Kim's little-girl quality. "Her voice was almost like a whisper, like Marilyn Monroe," she says. "I often wondered if Marilyn Monroe got it from her. Both had the same hair and the same voice," she adds. "I always thought, 'God, what magnificent hair.' It was just naturally very silky." Later learning Kim's birth name, Tetrault felt the name Kim didn't match Kim's girlish quality; Patty Beth did.

For ten years, from 1983 to 1993, Kim's downstairs neighbors were Craig Strong and Randy Bennett, both active theater professionals, which may have made them ideal neighbors for Kim. They found Kim pleasant if not chatty, but Bennett was able to bribe her into conviviality.

"I found out that her favorite thing in the world was Southern salmon croquettes," he says. "We cooked all the time and our kitchen was right below hers. One time she called and said, 'I would just give anything if I could taste your salmon croquettes.' I would bring her food, and in exchange, I would get to sit with her and have tea and hear stories about her early days on Broadway."

Among the regular visitors to Kim that Strong and Bennett observed were Jessica Lange, who studied with Kim, Roddy McDowall, Shelley Winters (during whose visits loud peals of laughter could be heard), and Kim's children Jamie and Rachel. But when Kim was alone, she reverted to old habits. "Her bedroom was directly above ours, and it was hardwood floors," Bennett recalls. "Sometimes we would hear bottles just hit the floor on other bottles and then hear her fall. It was devastating."

On one occasion, after Kim had been on a five- or six-day drinking binge, she called Strong and asked him to get her some milk. He bought a gallon, and knocked on Kim's door. "She opened the door and returned to bed. I've never seen anyone like that," he says. "She was kind of purple and green all over, and just wrung out. She looked a little like Jabba the Hut from *Star Wars*. She took the milk and drank almost the entire gallon right out of the carton. It was really frightening. Then she asked to be let alone. About three days later, she called and thanked me for having taken care of her." Strong says Kim's drinking problems clustered in her early years on Hillcrest; as far as he's aware, she didn't drink after 1988 or '89.

Increasingly, Kim turned into a recluse. Strong says she hardly ever went out in her early years at Hillcrest, and that was extroverted by her later standards. After 1988, "she never left the house," says Rochelle Tetrault. "A hundred percent never left the house. She only left the house when she went back to New Mexico [in 1995]." Kim had turned into the lady of mystery evoked by her character Wilma Thompson in *A Young Lady of Property,* locking herself in her home and letting the vines grow all around.

Several times Kim called the paramedics, then wouldn't let them in, so they would break down her door. On none of those occasions did Kim need hospitalization. Rochelle Tetrault had to replace the locks several times. She believes Kim wouldn't let the paramedics in out of willful perversity, while Bennett and Strong think Kim's impaired mobility made it hard for her to get to the door.

While Kim remained secluded, life went on around her. Her daughter Lisa was married in Oakland in 1988 or '89 to attorney David Ostrander; Kim, not feeling well, did not attend. This good news from Lisa was offset by dreadful news from Rachel and Peter Zahn: On July 8, 1988, they lost their first-born child, son Justin, to neuroblastoma, a childhood cancer. He was only four years old. Kim did not go back East to comfort her daughter, who generously explains Kim's absence. "She was terrified of death," Rachel says. "Of her own, of the death of those around her. As far as I know, she never went to a funeral. So I think that when Justin died, she had no clue how to comfort me. Because to her, it was so unimaginable to lose a child."

Even when Kim sealed herself off from life, though, life came to her. On April 29, 1992, following the acquittal of several Los Angeles police officers who had been videotaped beating black motorist Rodney King, Los Angeles erupted in riots and flames. Several blocks south of Kim's apartment, the famous lingerie store Fredericks of Hollywood burned. Even closer, a convenience store at Franklin and Highland, barely two blocks away, went up in flames. Some of Kim's neighbors on Hillcrest turned cars over to barricade their block against looters and arsonists, and manned the barricades with guns. "And [they were] drinking!" Randy Bennett recalls. "We were more scared of them than of the rioters!" Kim was terrified by the Brueghelian panoply unfolding around her.

"We talked several times and would go up and bring her things," Craig Strong says. "This was when she was not walking well. There was a concern as to how we would get her out of there if we needed to evacuate. We talked with some of the neighbors because [in light of Kim's size] we were afraid we would need their help."

Strong went up on the roof of Kim's apartment and hosed it down, as embers from nearby fires were landing all around. "She was crying," Randy Bennett says. "She was so afraid that we would leave her. If we left, she wanted us to take her with us." But Strong and Bennett were in a bind: They were about to produce a play called *One of Those Days* at a local theater, and their car was packed full of lights and props for it. Fortunately, the block was not overrun and Kim didn't have to be evacuated.

Despite living in the Mediterranean climate of Southern California,

Kim was cold much of the time. "Those apartments were not particularly warm," Strong says. "That building was built into a hillside. It could be very damp. And it had high ceilings, so that frequently the warmth went up. She was frequently cold. She had circulation problems."

Compounding her misery, Kim took a bad fall sometime in the early 1990s. Badly bruised, she was taken to the hospital and would not teach again in Hollywood. And the death she so feared stalked her life again: Alfred Ryder died April 16, 1995, in the Actors Fund Nursing Home in Englewood, New Jersey, of liver cancer. He was seventy-nine and the third of Kim's husbands to die.

THAT MONTH, Kim returned to Santa Fe for good. If you're cold much of the time, a move from Los Angeles to Santa Fe might not seem sensible, but it was a second home to her and her son, Jamie, lived there. For all the emotional estrangement he felt from Kim, he would help during her last days. He was married by now, and his wife, Jolene, would prove as attentive to Kim as if she had been her daughter.

In Santa Fe, Kim lived in Villa Teresa at 1501 Montano Street, a dead-end street parallel to nearby Cerrillos Road, the commercial strip entering Santa Fe from the south. Villa Teresa is an HUD project for older people with disabilities, and, as the awkwardly handpainted and misspelled sign out front says, it provides "Equal Housing Opportunitunity." It's a simple, well-maintained place, but a long way down from the Ritz-Carlton.

Various people still in Kim's life—her brother Justin; Tom Hatcher, from *A Clearing in the Woods;* and Wayne Sabato, who studied with her at the College of Santa Fe—believe Kim was no longer drinking, although there is anecdotal evidence to the contrary. She retained her sense of humor, telling Rachel's friend Betsy Norton that in November she was planning to start an acting workshop. If no students showed up, Kim said, she would teach the prairie dogs to act.

Kim's return to Santa Fe allowed her niece Solea, the daughter of Justin and his third wife, Paula, to become better-acquainted with her aunt. "I almost felt like she was acting, even when I was talking with her," Solea says. "Not in a bad or inauthentic way—she was just very theatrical in her everyday being." In a sense, Kim was still performing, just for smaller audiences. "You could tell there was an underlying bitterness that she was where she was," Solea adds. "She maintained this behavior and way of talking that was disbelieving of it." As if she were still the queen of Broadway? "Exactly."

In September of 1997, Kim's younger half sister, Carol White, died in Albuquerque. She had been a popular middle-school teacher before leaving to manage a doctor's office. The later part of her life was characterized by emotional instability, the possible result of her inability to reconcile her strict Baptist upbringing with a growing awareness of her own bisexuality. The former student body president of Albuquerque's Highland High School died alone, her body so decomposed by the time it was found that coroners were unable to perform a proper autopsy.

Upon Kim's return to Santa Fe, she reconnected with Wayne Sabato, her former College of Santa Fe student, now artistic director of the Santa Fe Performing Arts Company. She served as a final reader for plays the group was considering, and planned to teach there as well. "We were beginning to put together a group of people to work with her, about four of us," Sabato says. "Her health was not great, though, and this is an old, drafty theater." Kim worked with the group for only a year or so.

Her expertise was still in demand, as working film actors called from New York and Los Angeles to ask for her advice. About 1998 or '99, Edward Albee did some workshops with the Santa Fe Performing Arts Company, and the idea of them doing his *Three Tall Women* was discussed. "I mentioned it to Kim," Sabato says. "She was not interested in getting onstage. I also talked to her about the possibility of directing it, and she said, 'My dear boy, I would rather not go there right now.'"

Nearly forty years after the *New Yorker* had published a profile of her, Kim flirted with the possibility of another one, this time with *New Yorker* staff writer Hilton Als. "We were going to do the piece," he says. "I wanted to come down to Santa Fe to see her. But then one got the sense she really didn't want to be seen. This strange phone relationship started where she would be sober sometimes or out of it. She would sometimes leave messages or hang up on my machine. You could hear her breathing, but she wouldn't leave a message." Als abandoned the profile, but afterwards received Valentine's Day cards from Kim.

During her final years, Kim shed friends and renewed old acquaintances with no discernible pattern. Although pleasant on the phone to Craig Strong and Randy Bennett, her downstairs neighbors from Hollywood who now lived in Santa Fe, she never saw them again. And she rebuffed Rietta Netter, her friend since she had been a sixteen-year-old in Taos. "I talked with Kim about a year before she died," Rietta says. "She didn't want me to call her. I could tell she must have been drinking or was very, very ill. She just wasn't herself and almost pleaded with me not to call her." Rietta never did. But Kim did renew her friendship with Horton Foote at this time. Kim also stayed in touch with Rachel's friend Betsy Norton almost until the end. The last time they talked, she told Betsy she was still teaching at the College of Santa Fe, where she hadn't worked in almost twenty-five years.

In 1999 or 2000, Arthur Laurents made the last effort to get Kim back on stage. He had written *2 Lives,* with a part for a mother. He called Kim, found her charming, and asked if she wanted to come to New York. Only to work, Kim said. "So I told her I had a play and sent it to her," Laurents recalls. "She loved it, but said she was all wrong for the part. I asked why. She said, 'My voice is wrong. That woman has a high, silvery voice and my voice is basso.' She sang 'Happy Birthday,' and it was indeed basso. She was right," he says, impressed that Kim knew his character better than he did. "It was the wrong voice."

In early 2001, Kim began to have severe pains. Her brother Justin and his fourth wife, Patricia Burger, took her to the doctor. "We had to hold her down, because she was in such pain," Burger recalls. "She was absolutely frightened. She kept asking for a tranquilizer, so I asked the nurse or doctor and they said no, they didn't have that in the office. So I said, 'Kim, let's do some deep breathing.' We'd sit, she did it and it calmed her down." In February, tests revealed Kim had uterine cancer.

In Santa Fe, Kim renewed her acquaintanceship with *New Yorker* writer Lillian Ross. On March 18, she wrote to Ross, saying she would be going into St. Vincent's Hospital in Santa Fe for a hysterectomy, adding that she'd much rather go see Duke Ellington's band. Shortly afterwards, Ross called Kim. "She was leaving for the hospital," Ross recalls. "She was so scared and nervous. I tried to give her the standard pep talk, but it was so moving because she was saying she had cancer. It shook me up."

After the operation, Wayne Sabato recalls, Kim said it wasn't as bad as she had feared, and that she was feeling well. "She was sent to a recovery-rehab type of place," he says. "I think she did go back to her apartment for a brief period, and then it turned. Maybe some type of infection or something. It didn't take long."

About this time, Jean Moss, who had studied with Kim at the College of Santa Fe, visited her in the nursing home. Kim was sitting in bed, her face scrubbed clean and shining, her eyes alive, her hair neatly combed behind her ears. Kim spoke about staging Chekhov's *The Seagull* and suggested two actors in Hollywood who might play Nina and Constantine. Moss said the actors were too old for those roles.

"Oh, well," Kim said, waving her hands in the air, dismissing Moss's objection, "that doesn't matter—we aren't that Hollywood trash, darling." Mischievously, Moss said, "Well, I'm not." Kim raised her eyebrows and said, "Oh, I see—you're not, but you have your doubts about me?" and they broke up laughing.

On one visit to Kim during her last days, her brother Justin was accompanied by his ex-wife Paula. She had observed some heated arguments between them through the years—usually one attacked their father and the other defended him; they switched roles. But now she noticed brother and sister steering away from the shoals of old arguments.

Justin visited Kim twice in the summer of 2001. The first time, Kim's eyes were still open. Afterwards, he went to California with his son and grandson for a fishing trip. "When I came back, she couldn't open her eyes," he says. "She was semi-comatose and a few hours from death. I began to talk with her, and I could tell from what happened in her face that she could hear me. We both knew it was the last time we were going to be in each other's presence."

Some time after Kim's hysterectomy, a staph infection had developed. Doctors tried to treat it with antibiotics, but it proved resistant. The second week of August, she experienced acute kidney failure. Her weakened health was further undermined by alcoholic dementia. Kim died in St. Vincent's Hospital on August 20, 2001, age seventy-six. The woman whom director Mark Rydell later described as a legendary brilliant raw wound of an actress was no more. It had been more than fifteen years since she had gone before the public, nearly forty since she had last appeared on the American stage.

In his *New York Times* obituary, Robert Berkvist wrote, "[Kim's] infrequent but luminous stage portraits brought her to the edge of greatness, but [she] ultimately shrank from the pressures of performance and stardom." Noting her youthful wish to be Queen of the May and her brilliant but all-too-short stage career, he added, "She had, in effect, achieved her childhood dream of becoming the May Queen, but chose to leave the parade before its end."

Newsweek recalled her quote "You can't be good in the theater unless you've immersed yourself in the marvelous detective story of the human spirit." But, it added, many of the riddles in her own life went unsolved. Her death was also reported, often with long and detailed obituaries, in the *Los Angeles Times,* the *Washington Post, Time* magazine, the Associated Press, Hollywood trades, and elsewhere.

Kim's death was also news in Great Britain. The *Times* of London ran a long remembrance of her, as did many British newspapers, including the *Independent,* which called her one of Broadway's most admired actresses. It described the 1965 Actors Studio production of *The Three Sisters* that ended her theater career, however, as "one of the legendary fiascos of the London stage." In Manchester, the *Guardian* noted that in *The Goddess,* she had played a movie star who moves from promiscuity, alcoholism, a nervous breakdown, and broken marriages to an eccentric lonely middle age. "Although the film was based tangentially on Marilyn Monroe's life," it noted, "there were similarities with Stanley's own career."

The fictions Kim had spun about herself now arose to bedevil obituary writers on two continents: the fiction that Jamie's father was Curt Conway, the fiction that she had a degree in psychology, the fiction that she had graduated from the University of Texas. "The reporter from the *L.A. Times* called me three times to ask if Kim had graduated from the University of Texas," Kim's daughter Rachel says. "And I have no clue! It was new to me when I read it in the *New York Times.* I never heard it growing up."

On September 9, 2001, a memorial service was held for Kim at the

College of Santa Fe, organized by her students Anna Gunn, Katharine Lee, and Jean Moss. Many of Kim's celebrity colleagues sent reminiscences, and some of her students spoke as well. Kim's daughter Rachel attended and spoke; Lisa did not attend, nor did Jamie, who still lived nearby (Jamie's wife, Jolene, did, though). But Lisa still managed to make her presence felt, giving a living voice to Kim's dark side.

"After the memorial service here, Lisa called me out of the blue," says John Weckesser, then still CSF performing arts chairman. "The switchboard said, 'Somebody is calling for you and is really scary.' I said, 'Well, put them through.' She was a dead ringer for Kim's voice and slurring manner of speech, the accusations. 'What do you know?' she said. 'You fool! I'll preside over your death!'"

Lisa did attend the standing-room-only memorial service for Kim at the Actors Studio in New York on October 12, 2001. Rachel had planned to go, but in the wake of the terrorist attacks of September 11, decided to stay with her two sons and daughter in San Diego. The memorial service featured a clip reel of highlights from Kim's career. Mistress of ceremonies Estelle Parsons called Kim the greatest actress of the century.

In a light moment, Rex Reed drew laughter when he noted the irony of having a critic speak at an actor's memorial, saying, "This is like a Nazi visiting a bar mitzvah." Playwright John Guare recalled watching Kim's moving performance on live TV's *A Young Lady of Property* when he was growing up in Queens. "Something disappointing had happened to [her character], some betrayal," he remembered. "Her look of pain hit me in the gut. It was the first time I ever cried at home over a nondomestic event."

Playwright Henry Denker fondly recalled how Kim had glared at him at the first reading of *A Far Country* because his shirt and tie caused her to mistake him for one of the play's financial backers. Sir Peter Hall, who had directed Kim in the British premiere of *Cat on a Hot Tin Roof,* sent a letter, which read in part: "Acting . . . requires integrity, judgment, and, above all, though it frequently teeters on the borderline of excess, it must have discretion, so that passion is never self-indulgent. Kim Stanley was a very unique actress who lived and worked on this borderline. She made her audience contemplate unbearable pain, but . . . did so by the use of an accomplished technique which was always in control."

And in his letter, Bryan Forbes, writer and director of *Seance on a Wet Afternoon,* noted, "Kim had a passion for the truth, filling the shadows of her performance with a rare substance. Nobody can adequately describe her brilliance, for actors are sculptors who carve in snow. But we must consider ourselves fortunate that, trapped on the emulsion of film, for future generations, her genius will never melt."

Also speaking were Elaine Stritch, Elizabeth Wilson, Vivian Nathan, Michael Tolan, and Kim's student Victor Slezak. Letters from Vanessa Redgrave and Horton Foote were also read. That weekend, the Actors Studio screened a series of Kim's best TV shows.

Only one of Kim's husbands survived her: Bruce Hall, who had run away with her from the Pasadena Playhouse and shared her early struggling years in New York. He died of pulmonary problems from emphysema in Newburgh, New York, on August 8, 2002.

In *The Actress,* Henry Denker's novel based on Kim, Kit Lawrence pulls out of her nosedive and returns to Broadway to bask in the adulation due a star of her magnitude. Laurette Taylor, to whom Kim was often compared, came back triumphantly in 1946 for *The Glass Menagerie.* This book has no such happy ending. Depending on your point of view, Kim's story is either the tragic tale of someone who failed to tame her demons or the exasperating story of someone who indulged them and expected others to pay the freight. But it's not an easy call: Despite all the facts available about her, Kim retains much of her mystery, like the Sphinx or the Mona Lisa. "None of us ever knew what anything meant to her," King Charles says in the epilogue of *Saint Joan.* "She was like nobody else, and she must take care of herself, wherever she is."

Having no resources, Kim left no will. She made arrangements to have her body cremated. Her student Meredith Alexander would later recall Kim saying, "The thing that matters most to me, where I think I achieved the most, is my children. That's what I'm proudest of."

Kim's older daughter, Lisa, would work in the publishing industry. Like Kim, she was an intelligent blonde beauty with a sometimes erratic temperament. Like Kim, Jamie would become a capable and talented artist, but also somewhat reclusive. Unlike Kim, Rachel would overcome personal tragedy to balance a rewarding life as wife and mother with a successful professional career, something Kim aspired to do and claimed she had done, but never attained.

Shortly after Kim died, Rachel watched *Seance on a Wet Afternoon* with her fourteen-year-old son. In one scene, she was surprised to see the nightgown Kim had worn for years, one intricately woven into Rachel's own childhood memories. Did Kim wear her own clothes on stage and in film because they felt more comfortable? "The easy answer is yes," Rachel says, "but I think it's much more complicated. I think it has to do with the melding of her life and career and art. There were no separations, really. So her life clothes were her stage clothes, in a way.

"Clearly, it wasn't because her clothes so specially fit the part that she couldn't find anything as good," she adds. "And I think it goes back to your question of which was her real speaking voice. Well, who knows? Which were the real clothes? Who knows? She was the role. The role was her."

APPENDIX I

THE STAGE PLAYS OF KIM STANLEY

OFF-BROADWAY

him (Premiered July 22, 1948, at the Provincetown Playhouse) ROLE: One of the Three Wierds. THEATER GROUP: The Interplayers. DIRECTOR: Irving Stiber. PLAYWRIGHT: e.e. cummings. WITH: Gene Saks, Harry Guardino, Janet Shannon.

The Dog Beneath the Skin (Winter 1948 at Carnegie Recital Hall) ROLES: Iris Crewe and the Queen. THEATER GROUP: The Interplayers. PLAYWRIGHTS: W.H. Auden and Christopher Isherwood. WITH: Gene Saks, Janet Shannon.

Yes Is for a Very Young Man (Premiered June 6, 1949, at the Cherry Lane Theatre) ROLE: Denise. THEATER GROUP: Off-Broadway Inc. DIRECTOR: Lamont Johnson. PLAYWRIGHT: Gertrude Stein. WITH: Tony Franciosa, Michael Gazzo, Bea Arthur, Gene Saks.

Too Many Thumbs (Premiered July 27, 1949, at the Cherry Lane Theatre) ROLE: Jenny Macklebee. THEATER GROUP: Off-Broadway Inc. DIRECTOR: Curt Conway. PLAYWRIGHT: Robert Hivnor. WITH: Gene Saks, Nehemiah Persoff, Dick Robbins.

Saint Joan (Fall 1949 at Lenox Hill Playhouse) ROLE: Joan of Arc. THEATER GROUP: Equity Library Theatre. DIRECTOR: Philip Robinson. PLAYWRIGHT: George Bernard Shaw. WITH: Jack Klugman, George Roy Hill, Walt Witcover.

REGIONAL

A Streetcar Named Desire (Sept. 3 to Oct. 6, 1952, at the Playhouse Theatre in Houston) ROLE: Blanche DuBois. DIRECTOR: Vincent J. Donehue. PLAYWRIGHT: Tennessee Williams. WITH: James Gavin, Bob Stevenson, Marguerite Lenert.

TOURS

The Trip to Bountiful (April 20 to May 2, 1954, at the Showcase Theatre in Evanston, IL; May 10 to 15, 1954, at the Lydia Mendelssohn Theatre in Ann Arbor, MI) ROLE: Jessie Mae Watts. DIRECTOR: Vincent J. Donehue. PLAYWRIGHT: Horton Foote. WITH: Lillian Gish, Frank Overton, John Conwell.

A Far Country (Opened Nov. 29, 1961, at the Huntington Hartford Theater in Hollywood; opened Dec. 18, 1961, at the Alcazar Theatre in San Francisco) ROLE: Elizabeth von Ritter. DIRECTOR: Alfred Ryder. PLAYWRIGHT: Henry Denker. WITH: Michael Tolan, Ludwig Donath, Lili Darvas, Eda Reiss Merin, Joanna Merlin, Ellen Weston.

BROADWAY

Montserrat (Oct. 29 to Dec. 24, 1949, at the Fulton Theatre) ROLE: Felisa (Kim joined play halfway through, replacing Julie Harris). PRODUCERS: Kermit Bloomgarden and Gilbert Miller. DIRECTOR: Lillian Hellman. PLAYWRIGHT:

Emmanuel Robles; adapted by Lillian Hellman. WITH: Emlyn Williams, Nehemiah Persoff, Vivian Nathan, Kurt Kasznar.

The House of Bernarda Alba (Jan. 7 to 20, 1951, at the ANTA Playhouse) ROLE: Adela. PRODUCERS: Stewart Chaney in association with Boris Tumarin and Lily Turner for the American National Theatre and Academy. DIRECTOR: Boris Tumarin. PLAYWRIGHT: Federico Garcia Lorca; translated by James Graham Lujan and Richard L. O'Connell. WITH: Katina Paxinou, Helen Craig, Ruth Ford.

The Chase (Apr. 15 to May 10, 1952, at the Playhouse Theatre; Kim left cast May 3, 1952). ROLE: Anna Reeves. PRODUCERS: Jose Ferrer in association with Milton Baron. DIRECTOR: Jose Ferrer. PLAYWRIGHT: Horton Foote. WITH: Kim Hunter, John Hodiak, Lonny Chapman, Murray Hamilton.

Picnic (Feb. 19, 1953, to Apr. 10, 1954, at the Music Box Theatre; Kim left cast May 30, 1953) ROLE: Millie Owens. PRODUCERS: The Theatre Guild and Joshua Logan. DIRECTOR: Joshua Logan. PLAYWRIGHT: William Inge. WITH: Ralph Meeker, Janice Rule, Eileen Heckart, Arthur O'Connell, Paul Newman, Joanne Woodward, Elizabeth Wilson, Reta Shaw, Peggy Conklin.

The Traveling Lady (Oct. 27 to Nov. 20, 1954, at the Playhouse Theatre) ROLE: Georgette Thomas. PRODUCER: The Playwrights' Company. DIRECTOR: Vincent J. Donehue (replaced by Harold Clurman). PLAYWRIGHT: Horton Foote. WITH: Jack Lord, Lonny Chapman, Katherine Squire, Kathleen Comegys, Brook Seawell.

Bus Stop (March 2, 1955, to Feb. 13, 1956, at Music Box Theatre; until April 21, 1956, at the Winter Garden; Kim left cast Nov. 4, 1955) ROLE: Cherie. PRODUCERS: Robert Whitehead and Roger L. Stevens. DIRECTOR: Harold Clurman. PLAYWRIGHT: William Inge. WITH: Albert Salmi, Elaine Stritch, Anthony Ross, Phyllis Love, Lou Polan, Patrick McVey, Crahan Denton.

A Clearing in the Woods (Jan. 10 to Feb. 9, 1957, at the Belasco Theatre) ROLE: Virginia. PRODUCERS: Roger L. Stevens and Oliver Smith. DIRECTOR: Joseph Anthony. PLAYWRIGHT: Arthur Laurents. WITH: Onslow Stevens, Robert Culp, Anne Pearson, Barbara Myers, Joan Loring, Sybil White, Tom Hatcher, Lin McCarthy.

A Touch of the Poet (Oct. 2, 1958, to June 13, 1959, at the Helen Hayes Theatre; Kim left cast ca. March 12, 1959) ROLE: Sara Melody. PRODUCER: The Producers Theatre and Robert Whitehead. DIRECTOR: Harold Clurman. PLAYWRIGHT: Eugene O'Neill. WITH: Eric Portman, Helen Hayes, Betty Field, Curt Conway.

Cheri (Oct. 12 to Nov. 28, 1959, at the Morosco Theatre) ROLE: Lea de Lonval. PRODUCER: The Playwrights' Company and Robert Lewis. DIRECTOR: Robert Lewis. PLAYWRIGHT: Anna Loos; adapted from two novels by Colette. WITH: Horst Buchholz, Lili Darvas.

A Far Country (April 4 to Nov. 25, 1961, at the Music Box Theatre) ROLE: Elizabeth von Ritter. PRODUCERS: Roger L. Stevens and Joel W. Schenker. DIRECTOR: Alfred Ryder.

PLAYWRIGHT: Henry Denker. WITH: Stephen Hill, Sam Wanamaker, Lili Darvas, Eda Reiss Merin, Patrick O'Neal, Salome Jens.

Natural Affection (Jan. 31 to March 2, 1963, at the Booth Theatre) ROLE: Sue Barker. PRODUCER: Oliver Smith in association with Manuel Seff. DIRECTOR: Tony Richardson. PLAYWRIGHT: William Inge. WITH: Harry Guardino, Tom Bosley, Gregory Rozakis, Bonnie Bartlett, Monica May.

The Three Sisters (June 22 to Oct. 3, 1964 at the Morosco Theatre; Kim left cast Aug. 21, 1964) ROLE: Masha. PRODUCER: Actors Studio Theater. DIRECTOR: Lee Strasberg. PLAYWRIGHT: Anton Chekhov; translated by Randall Jarrell. WITH: Geraldine Page, Shirley Knight, Luther Adler, Barbara Baxley, Kevin McCarthy, Robert Loggia, Gerald Hiken, Tamara Daykarhanova, Salem Ludwig, Albert Paulsen, James Olson.

LONDON
Cat on a Hot Tin Roof (Jan. 30 to May 2, 1958 at the Comedy Theatre) ROLE: Maggie the Cat. PRODUCER: New Watergate Theatre Club. DIRECTOR: Peter Hall. PLAYWRIGHT: Tennessee Williams. WITH: Paul Massie, Leo McKern, Bee Duffell.

The Three Sisters (Opened May 13, 1965, at the Aldwych Theatre) ROLE: Masha PRODUCER: Actors Studio Theater. DIRECTOR: Lee Strasberg. PLAYWRIGHT: Anton Chekhov. WITH: George C. Scott, Nan Martin, Sandy Dennis, Luther Adler, Robert Loggia, Gerald Hiken.

APPENDIX II

THE TELEVISON WORK OF KIM STANLEY

(+ *Date listed is when show first aired; date of Kim's appearance is unclear.*)

EARLY TELEVISION APPEARANCES
Hollywood Screen Test, April 1948+.
The Bigelow Show, Oct. 1948+.

LIVE TELEVISION DRAMA
AND OTHER LIVE TV
(*Show title followed by the live dramatic anthology it was part of.*)

Starring Boris Karloff, Sept. 1949+. Episode title unknown.
Sentence of Death (The Trap), 5/27/50.
Cavalcade of Stars, 6/3/50. Scene from *Golden Boy* with John Garfield.
The Vanishing Lady (Sure as Fate), 10/17/50.
The Covenant (Escape), 1950.

Father, Dear Father (Magnavox Theatre), 11/10/50.

The Anniversary (Danger), 1/30/51.

The Bus to Nowhere (Out There), 12/30/51.

The System (Danger), 6/10/52.

The Witness (Goodyear Television Playhouse), 8/17/52.

The Darkness Below (Goodyear Television Playhouse), 11/9/52.

The Final Hours of Joan of Arc (You Are There), 3/1/53.

A Young Lady of Property (Philco Television Playhouse), 4/5/53.

Tears of My Sister (First Person Playhouse), 8/14/53.

The Death of Cleopatra (You Are There), 10/18/53.

The Sixth Year (Philco Television Playhouse), 11/29/53.

The Big Story, 1/1/54.

The Brownstone (Goodyear Television Playhouse), 1/31/54.

Paso Doble (Omnibus), 2/14/54.

The Bet (Danger), 3/23/54.

Hands (Inner Sanctum), 4/24/54.

The Scarlet Letter (Kraft Television Theatre), 5/26/54.

Somebody Special (Philco Television Playhouse), 6/6/54.

H Is for Hurricane (Armstrong Circle Theatre), 12/7/54.

The Trial of St. Joan (Omnibus), 1/2/55. (Contemporary Theater, Film
   and Television gives her credit for this; Television Drama Series Programming
   says it's Kim Hunter.)

The Bridge (The Elgin Hour), 1/11/55.

The Tonight Show with Steve Allen, 3/2/55. Scene from *Bus Stop*.

ANTA Album of 1955, 3/28/55. Scene from *Bus Stop*.

The Waiting Place (Playwrights '56), 12/20/55.

Flight (Playwrights '56), 2/28/56.

Conspiracy of Hearts (Goodyear Television Playhouse), 3/11/56.

Joey (Goodyear Television Playhouse), 3/25/56.

Death Is a Spanish Dancer (Kraft Television Theatre), 5/9/56.

In the Days of Our Youth (Goodyear Television Playhouse), 5/20/56.

The Traveling Lady (Studio One), 4/22/57.

The Glass Wall (Kraft Television Theatre), 5/15/57.

Clash by Night (Playhouse 90), 6/13/57.

Look Here, 11/17/57. Kim interviewed by Martin Agronsky.

The Traveling Lady (ABC, a regional affiliate of Britain's ITV), 7/27/58.

Tomorrow (Playhouse 90), 3/7/60 (rebroadcast 7/18/61).

The Cake Baker (ABC, a regional affiliate of Britain's ITV), 6/11/60.

FILMED AND TAPED TELEVISION

That's Where the Town's Going (Westinghouse Presents), 4/17/62.

"A Cardinal Act of Mercy" *(Ben Casey)*, 1/14/63 and 1/21/63.

Does My Mother Have to Know? (Eleventh Hour), 3/25/64 and 4/1/64.

The Three Sisters (filmed version of Actors Studio stage play), 1965.

Flesh and Blood (NBC), 1/26/68.

U.M.C (aka *Operation Heartbeat*), 4/17/69.

I Can't Imagine Tomorrow (one of two one-act plays shown as *Dragon Country* on *N.E.T. Playhouse*), 1/9/71.

"The Man Who Killed a Ghost," aka "The Happy Ghost of Will Cheyenne" *(The Name of the Game)*, 1/29/71.

"Secret Heritage" *(Medical Center)*, 2/3/71.

"A Fear of Spiders" *(Rod Serling's Night Gallery)*, 10/6/71.

"Death Penalty" *(It Takes Two)*, 10/28/82.

"Beyond the Open Door" *(Quincy, M.E.)*, 2/2/83.

Cat on a Hot Tin Roof (PBS), 6/24/85 (aired on Showtime one year earlier).

APPENDIX III

THE FILMS OF KIM STANLEY

The Goddess (1958) ROLE: Emily Ann Faulkner/Rita Shawn. PRODUCTION COMPANY: Columbia. PRODUCER: Milton Perlman. DIRECTOR: John Cromwell. WRITER: Paddy Chayefsky. WITH: Lloyd Bridges, Steven Hill, Betty Lou Holland, Burt Brinckerhoff, Gerald Hiken, Joyce Van Patten, Curt Conway, Patty Duke.

To Kill a Mockingbird (1962) ROLE: Narrator (uncredited). PRODUCTION COMPANY: Universal. PRODUCER: Alan J. Pakula. DIRECTOR: Robert Mulligan. WRITER: Horton Foote; adapted from the novel by Harper Lee. WITH: Gregory Peck, Mary Badham, Philip Alford, Robert Duvall, Frank Overton, Brock Peters.

Seance on a Wet Afternoon (1964) ROLE: Myra Savage (Academy Award nomination for best actress). PRODUCTION COMPANY: Richard Attenborough–Bryan Forbes Productions. PRODUCER: Richard Attenborough. DIRECTOR: Bryan Forbes. WRITER: Bryan Forbes; adapted from the novel by Mark McShane. WITH: Richard Attenborough, Nanette Newman, Gerald Sim, Judith Donner, Mark Eden.

Frances (1982) ROLE: Lillian Farmer (Academy Award nomination for best supporting actress). PRODUCTION COMPANY: Universal. PRODUCER: Jonathan Sanger. DIRECTOR: Graeme Clifford. WRITERS: Eric Bergren, Christopher Devore, and Nicholas Kazan. WITH: Jessica Lange, Sam Shepard, Lane Smith, Bart Burns, Gerald O'Loughlin.

The Right Stuff (1983) ROLE: Pancho Barnes. PRODUCTION COMPANY: Warner Bros. PRODUCERS: Irwin Winkler and Robert Chartoff. DIRECTOR: Philip Kaufman. WRITER: Philip Kaufman; adapted from the book by Tom Wolfe. WITH: Sam Shepard, Scott Glenn, Ed Harris, Dennis Quaid, Barbara Hershey, Veronica Cartwright.

APPENDIX IV

WHERE YOU CAN SEE THE WORK OF KIM STANLEY

Museum of Television and Radio
25 West Fifty-second Street
New York, NY 10019-6104
(212) 621-6600
www.mtr.org
e-mail: sbrotman@mtr.org (President Stuart Brotman)

465 North Beverly Drive
Beverly Hills, CA 90210-4601
(310) 786-1000
e-mail: lareference@mtr.org

Cavalcade of Stars (Kim does scene from *Golden Boy* with John Garfield.)
Tears of My Sister (First Person Playhouse)
Paso Doble (Omnibus)
The Scarlet Letter (Kraft Television Theatre)
Look Here (Kim interviewed by Martin Agronsky.)
The Traveling Lady (Studio One)
Cat on a Hot Tin Roof (PBS)

UCLA Film and Television Archive
46 Powell Library
P.O. Box 951517
Los Angeles, CA 90095-1517
(310) 206-5388
www.cinema.ucla.edu
e-mail: arsc@ucla.edu

Tears of My Sister (First Person Playhouse)
ANTA Album of 1955 (Scene from *Bus Stop*)
Clash by Night (Playhouse 90)
Tomorrow (Playhouse 90)
"A Cardinal Act of Mercy" *(Ben Casey)*
The Three Sisters (filmed version of Actors Studio stage play)
The Goddess
To Kill a Mockingbird
Seance on a Wet Afternoon
Frances
The Right Stuff

Museum of Broadcast Communications
400 North State Street, Suite 240
Chicago, IL 60610-4624
(312) 245-8200
www.museum.tv
e-mail: archives@museum.tv

Death Is a Spanish Dancer (Kraft Television Theatre)

Wisconsin Center for Film and Theater Research
Wisconsin Historical Society
816 State Street
Madison, WI 53706
(608) 264-6466
www.wisconsinhistory.org/wcftr
e-mail: mfducey@facstaff.wisc.edu (Maxine Fleckner Ducey)

The Sixth Year (Philco Television Playhouse)
Flight (Playwrights '56)

Library of Congress
Motion Picture, Broadcasting and Recorded Sound Division
101 Independence Avenue SE
James Madison Building, LM 336
Washington, DC 20540-4690
www.loc.gov/rr/mopic
e-mail: rhane@loc.gov (Rosemary C. Hanes, Film and Television Research Librarian)

Does My Mother Have to Know? (Eleventh Hour)
The Glass Wall (Kraft Television Theatre; audio track only)

AVAILABLE ON VIDEO

The System (Danger; intermittently available for purchase on the Internet)
Dragon Country (with *I Can't Imagine Tomorrow;* available from Broadway Theatre
  Archive)
"A Fear of Spiders" *(Rod Serling's Night Gallery)*
The Goddess
To Kill a Mockingbird
Seance on a Wet Afternoon
Frances
The Right Stuff

BIBLIOGRAPHY

BOOKS

Arnold, William. *Shadowland: The Search for Frances Farmer.* New York: McGraw-Hill, 1978.

Atkinson, Brooks. *Broadway.* New York: Limelight Editions, 1990.

Biebel, Charles D. *Making the Most of It: Public Works in Albuquerque During the Great Depression.* Albuquerque: The Albuquerque Museum, 1986.

Bosworth, Patricia. *Montgomery Clift.* New York: Bantam Books, 1979.

Botto, Louis. *At This Theatre.* New York: Applause/Playbill, 2002.

Bradford, Richard. *Red Sky at Morning.* New York: Pocket Books, 1971.

Brooks, Tim, and Earle Marsh. *The Complete Directory to Prime Time Network TV Shows.* New York: Ballantine Books, 1992.

Castleman, Harry, and Walter J. Podrazik. *Watching TV: Four Decades of American Television.* New York: McGraw-Hill Book Company, 1982.

Cather, Willa. *Death Comes for the Archbishop.* New York: Vintage Books, 1971.

Clurman, Harold. *All People Are Famous.* New York and London: Harcourt Brace Jovanovich, 1974.

Considine, Shaun. *Mad as Hell: The Life and Work of Paddy Chayefsky.* New York: Random House, 1994.

Crawford, Cheryl. *One Naked Individual.* Indianapolis/New York: Bobbs-Merrill Company, Inc., 1977.

Curnan, Cynthia. *The Care and Feeding of Perfectionists.* Georgetown, MA: North Star Publications, 1999.

Dawkins, Cecil, ed. *A Woman of the Century: Frances Minerva Nunnery.* Albuquerque: University of New Mexico Press, 2002.

Denker, Henry. *The Actress.* New York: Simon and Schuster, 1978.

Fergusson, Erna. *Erna Fergusson's Albuquerque.* Albuquerque: Merle Armitage Editions, 1947.

Flynn, Raymond. *Growing Up a Sullen Baptist and Other Lies.* Denton, TX: University of North Texas Press, 2001.

Foote, Horton. *Harrison, Texas: Eight Television Plays.* New York: Harcourt, Brace and Co., 1956.

Garfield, David. *A Player's Place.* New York: MacMillan Publishing Co., Inc., 1980.

Gianakos, Larry James. *Television Drama Series Programming: A Comprehensive Chronicle, 1947–1959.* Metuchen, NJ, and London: The Scarecrow Press, Inc., 1980.

Hay, Peter. *Theatrical Anecdotes.* New York: Oxford University Press, 1987.

Hayes, Helen, and Katherine Hatch. *My Life in Three Acts.* New York: Harcourt Brace Jovanovich, 1990.

Hellman, Lillian. *Pentimento.* Boston: Little, Brown and Co., 1973.

Hillerman, Tony. *New Mexico, Rio Grande and Other Essays.* Photography by David Muench and Robert Reynolds. Portland, OR: Graphic Arts Center Publishing Co., 1992.

Hirsch, Foster. *A Method to Their Madness: The History of the Actors Studio.* New York: W.W. Norton & Company, 1984.

Hivnor, Robert. *Too Many Thumbs: A Three-Act Play.* Minneapolis: Univ. of Minnesota Press, 1949.

Kazan, Elia. *Elia Kazan: A Life.* New York: Da Capo Press, 1997.

Kobal, John. *People Will Talk.* New York: Alfred A. Knopf, 1985.

Krampner, Jon. *The Man in the Shadows: Fred Coe and the Golden Age of Television.* New Brunswick, NJ: Rutgers University Press, 1997.

Laurents, Arthur. *Original Story By.* New York: Alfred A. Knopf, 2000.

Lewis, Robert. *Method—Or Madness?* New York: Samuel French, Inc., 1958.

———. *Slings and Arrows: Theater in My Life.* New York: Stein and Day, 1984.

Lindsley, John Berrien, ed. *The Military Annals of Tennessee—Confederate.* Nashville: J.M. Lindsley & Co., 1886.

Little, Stuart W. *Off-Broadway: The Prophetic Theater.* New York: Coward, McCann & Geoghegan, Inc., 1972.

——— and Arthur Cantor. *The Playmakers.* New York: W.W. Norton and Company, Inc., 1970.

Logan, Joshua. *Movie Stars, Real People and Me.* New York: Delacorte Press, 1978.

Loggia, Marjorie, and Glenn Young. *The Collected Works of Harold Clurman.* New York: Applause Books, 1994.

Moss, Larry. *The Intent to Live: Achieving Your True Potential as an Actor.* New York: Bantam Books, 2005.

Mazursky, Paul. *Show Me the Magic.* New York: Simon and Schuster, 1999.

McDowall, Roddy. *Double Exposure.* New York: Delacorte Press, 1966.

McNeil, Alex. *Total Television.* New York: Penguin Books, 1984.

McShane, Mark. *Seance on a Wet Afternoon.* Greenwich, CT: Fawcett Publications, 1965.

Morella, Joe, Edward Z. Epstein. *Paul and Joanne: A Biography of Paul Newman and Joanne Woodward.* New York: Delacorte Press, 1988.

Morris, Jan. *Manhattan '45.* New York: Oxford University Press, 1987.

Norman, Charles. *E.E. Cummings: The Magic-Maker.* New York: The Bobbs-Merrill Co., Inc., 1972.

O'Connor, Kathryn Kennedy. *Theater in the Cow Country.* South Bend, IN: Creative Service for Publishers, 1966.

Pilkington, John, ed. *Stark Young: A Life in the Arts, Vol. II.* Baton Rouge: Louisiana State Press, 1975.

Reed, Rex. *Big Screen, Little Screen.* New York: The MacMillan Company, 1971.

Reid, J.T. "Big Texas Family." Unpublished; excerpts in possession of the author.

———. *Fishing in New Mexico: A Guide for Anglers in New Mexico.* Albuquerque: University of New Mexico Press, 1956.

———. *It Happened in Taos.* Albuquerque: University of New Mexico Press, 1946.

Rhodes, Eugene Manlove. *Paso Por Aqui.* Norman, OK: Univ. of Oklahoma Press, 1973.

Richardson, Tony. *The Long-Distance Runner.* New York: William Morrow and Company, Inc., 1993.

Rose, Philip. *You Can't Do That on Broadway!* New York: Limelight Editions, 2001.

Sonnichsen, C.L. *Tularosa: Last of the Frontier West.* Albuquerque: University of New Mexico Press, 1980.

Ross, Lillian. *Here but Not Here.* Washington, DC.: Counterpoint, 1998.

——— and Helen Ross. *The Player: Profile of an Art.* New York: Simon and Schuster, 1962.

Schneider, Alan. *Entrances: An American Director's Journey.* New York: Viking, 1986.

Seldes, Marian. *The Bright Lights: A Theatre Life.* Boston: Houghton Mifflin Co., 1978.

Simmons, Marc. *Albuquerque: A Narrative History.* Albuquerque: University of New Mexico Press, 1982.

Simon, John. *Uneasy Stages: A Chronicle of the New York Theater, 1963–1973.* New York: Random House, 1975.

Stanislavski, Constantin. *An Actor Prepares.* New York: Theatre Arts, Inc., 1936.

Strasberg, Susan. *Bittersweet.* New York: G.P. Putnam's Sons, 1980.

Thomas, Bob. *King Cohn.* New York: G.P. Putnam's Son, 1967.

Wager, Walter, ed. *The Playwrights Speak.* New York: Delacorte Press, 1967.

Walker, Stanley. *Home to Texas.* New York: Harper & Bros., 1956.

West, Ray B. Jr., ed. *Rocky Mountain Cities.* New York: W.W. Norton & Co., 1949.

White, E.B. *Here Is New York.* New York: Harper & Brothers Publishers, 1949.

Williams, Tennessee. *Memoirs.* Garden City, N.Y.: Doubleday & Company, Inc., 1975.

_____. *Five O'Clock Angel: Letters of Tennessee Williams to Maria St. Just.* New York: Alfred A. Knopf, 1990.

Winecoff, Charles. *Split Image: The Life of Anthony Perkins.* New York: Plume Books, 1997.

Winters, Shelley. *Shelley: Also Known as Shirley.* New York: William Morrow and Company, Inc., 1980.

ARTICLES AND PROFILES

Archer, Eugene. "Kim Stanley on a Snowy Afternoon." *New York Times,* January 31, 1965.

Corry, John. "Kim Stanley Returns, Directing Ensemble Troupe." *New York Times,* September 20, 1979.

Fields, Sidney. "Only Human." *New York Daily Mirror,* March 14, 1955.

Gelb, Arthur. "Actress Minus Frills." *New York Times,* April 3, 1955.

"The Girl on Your Set." *Newsweek.* June 17, 1957.

Hewes, Henry. "Goon Girl." *Saturday Review,* April 11, 1953.

"Kim Stanley" entry in *Current Biography,* 1955.

Kobal, John. "Dialogue on Film: Kim Stanley." *American Film,* June 1983. (Expanded version appears in Kobal's book *People Will Talk.*)

Kravet, Edith. "Fast-Traveling Lady." *Newark Sunday News,* May 22, 1955.

Lukas, Mary. "Kim's Light and Heat." *Show Magazine,* July 1963: 65.

Minoff, Philip. "The Forthright Kim Stanley." *Cue Magazine,* February 11, 1956: 12.

Rosenfield, Paul. "Kim Stanley Plays with a Full Deck." *Los Angeles Times,* January 10, 1982.

Rosenfield. John. "Kim Stanley of Southwest," *Dallas Morning News,* November 6, 1954.

Ross, Lillian. "Profiles: The Player." *New Yorker,* October 21, 1961.

Rule, Janice. "The Actor's Identity Crises." *International Journal of Psychoanalytic Psychotherapy,* Vol. 2, No. 1, February 1973.

Wahls, Robert. "Kim Stanley's War with Success." *New York Daily News,* April 5, 1959.

Wilson, Earl. "Gets the Laughs." *New York Post Weekend Magazine,* March 13, 1955.

NOTES

Frequently used abbreviations in the chapter notes:

Publications and Organizations

AJ	*Albuquerque Journal*
AMPAS	Academy of Motion Picture Arts and Sciences
AT	*Albuquerque Tribune*
DM	*Daily Mirror* (NY)
HR	*Hollywood Reporter*
JM	*Journal-American*
LAT	*Los Angeles Times*
LK/LOC	Lucy Kroll papers at the Library of Congress
MG	*Manchester Guardian* (UK)
NY	*New Yorker*
NYDN	*New York Daily News*
NYHT	*New York Herald-Tribune*
NYT	*New York Times*
NYP	*New York Post*
NYPL	Billy Rose Theatre Collection at the New York Public Library for the Performing Arts
NYWT	*New York World Telegram*
PB	*Philadelphia Bulletin*
PI	*Philadelphia Inquirer*
SR	*Saturday Review*
TA	*Theatre Arts*

Individuals

BA	Brooks Atkinson
BF	Bryan Forbes
HD	Henry Denker
HF	Horton Foote
JC	Jamie Clift
JK	Jon Krampner
JR	Justin Reid
JW	John Weckesser
JWR	Jinx Witherspoon Rodger
KS	Kim Stanley
LK	Lucy Kroll
PZ	Paul Zindel
RH	Roger O. Hirson
RW	Robert Whitehead
RZ	Rachel Zahn
TM	Tad Mosel

Miscellaneous

int.	interview
conv.	conversation
ltr.	letter
n/p	name of publication not available
n/d	date of publication not available

After first reference, books (and articles that are listed in the bibliography) are cited by only author's name and page number or date.

CHAPTER 1

(p. 2) . . . gets a special pass . . . and checks out Henry Miller . . . : John Kobal, *People Will Talk* (New York: Alfred A. Knopf, 1985), 688.

(p. 3) "Acting was my ticket out of Texas": Ibid., 691.

(p. 3) His family's ranch . . . : J.T. Reid, "Big Texas Family." Unpublished; excerpts in possession of JK. [Later references as Reid 1.]

(p. 4) J.T. Reid had been a captain . . . : John Berrien Lindsley, ed., *The Military Annals of Tennessee—Confederate* (Nashville: J.M. Lindsley & Co., 1886), 564.

(p. 4) "Those damn Yankees!": Int. with Lynn White, 12/18/03.

(p. 4) he lived to be ninety-five: "Old Veteran Passes Away," *Daily Inquirer* (Gonzales, TX), 6/5/25, 1.

(p. 4) In 1904 . . . his family moved . . . to Lampasas County: Reid 1, chapter 1.

(p. 4) "I'm not raising my boys to be soda-jerking sissies . . .": Ibid., chapter 10.

(p. 4) Milton Miller . . . was a former schoolteacher . . . : Stanley Walker, *Home to Texas* (New York: Harper & Bros., 1956), 131.

(p. 4) a mesquite thorn stuck in [his eye] . . . : Int. with Marvin Miller, 12/4/02.

(p. 4) illustrious ancestors included several Earls of Derby: Walker, 120.

(p. 4) Annie Miller wrote humorous letters: Katherine Norris e-mail to JK, 1/29/03.

(p. 5) Annie . . . kissing him affectionately: Int. with Herbert F. Miller, 12/15/02.

(p. 5) "She was a fairly angry human being . . .": Int. with JR, 12/27/02.

(p. 5) "a consecrated Christian": "Death Claims Mrs. M.F. Miller Sunday," *Lampasas Record,* 1/3/35, 1.

(p. 5) dipping snuff: Int. with Marvin Miller, 12/4/02.

(p. 5) may have . . . addicted her to cocaine: Interviews with JR, 10/31/01, 11/29/01, and 12/27/02.

(p. 5) "In this project, I sometimes had the help . . .": Walker, 89.

(p. 5) Stanley Walker noted that on the drive: Ibid., 55.

(p. 5) a cousin of Kim's thinks they met . . . : Int. with Marvin Miller, 12/4/02.

(p. 5) Justin thinks they met in church . . . : Int. with JR, 10/20/01.

(p. 5) Thanksgiving Day of 1915, they were married: *Lampasas Daily Leader,* 11/26/15.

(p. 6) "Everybody listened and did exactly . . .": Int. with Lynn White, 9/7/02.

(p. 6) "Let the big bad Indians come! . . .": Reid 1, chapter 1.

(p. 6) "Our deserts are truly enchanting . . .": J.T. Reid, *Fishing in New Mexico* (Albuquerque: University of New Mexico Press, 1956), 8.

(p. 6) J.T. calmly forced the point of the hook . . . : Ibid., 65.

(p. 6) he pulled his boat over, shot the deer . . . : Int. with Bob Lalicker, 7/3/02.

(p. 6) "He was a well-liked, beloved gentleman . . .": Ibid.

(p. 7) J.T. had a hard time . . . expressing feelings . . . : Int. with JR, 10/20/01.

(p. 7) "J.T. was from that Southern Baptist . . .": Int. with Paula Reid, 10/4/03.

(p. 7) "You have been chosen because you are well-qualified . . . ": Eupha Brock Morris, former Tularosa schoolteacher, speaking at J.T.'s ninetieth birthday celebration at Kirtland Air Force Base, Albuquerque, 8/19/79. Tape in possession of JK.

(p. 7) "He couldn't have understood Kim . . .": Int. with Patricia Frye, 1/30/04.

(p. 7) "My father always thought . . .": Lillian Ross, "Profiles: The Player," *NY,* 10/21/61, 59.

(p. 7) "He was proud of Kim's acting . . .": Int. with JR, 5/16/02.

(p. 7) "Kim felt left out of these things . . .": Int. with JR, 1/16/02.

(p. 7) "Big Red . . . moved along the boardwalk . . .": Reid 1, chapter 1.

(p. 7) "It was awfully nice and cool . . .": J.T. Reid, speaking at his ninetieth birthday celebration, Albuquerque, 8/19/79.

(p. 8) "There'll be no women-folk talk": Int. with Patricia Frye, 1/30/04.

(p. 8) Proudly claim she had been a full-blooded Cherokee: Edith Kravet, "Fast-Traveling Lady," *Newark Sunday News,* 5/22/55, 26.

(p. 8) "Mixed blood" in his family: Reid 1, chapter 1.

(p. 8) "She had a bad father problem . . .": Int. with RH, 8/24/01.

(p. 8) "Each time Françoise began work . . .": Janice Rule, "The Actor's Identity Crises," *International Journal of Psychoanalytic Psychotherapy,* February 1973 (Vol. 2, No. 1), 57–58.

(p. 9) "In order to meet the perfectionist's standards . . .": Cynthia Curnan, *The Care and Feeding of Perfectionists* (Georgetown, MA: North Star Publications, 1999), 16.

(p. 9) "She wanted to please him and yet . . .": Int. with Lynn White, 12/18/03.

(p. 9) "She was small but mighty": Int. with JR, 3/24/04.

(p. 9) "She was a sweet, very intelligent . . .": Int. with JR, 10/20/01.

(p. 10) "Kim used to say . . . 'Patty Beth Reid! . . . '": Int. with Meredith Alexander, 3/26/03.

(p. 10) "Ruby roomed with Lena one year . . .": Katherine Norris e-mail to JK, 1/29/03.

(p. 10) "She was sassy and cute . . .": Int. with Paula Reid, 10/4/03.

(p. 10) "Kim was kind of the black sheep . . . ": Int. with Catherine Hynson, 12/30/02.

(p. 10) "She stood out just a little bit": Int. with Juanita N. Pileckas, 2/6/02.

(p. 10) "She kind of went and did what she wanted . . .": Int. with Herbert F. Miller, 12/15/02.

(p. 11) "She kind of assumed roles that were grand . . .": Int. with JR, 1/16/02.

(p. 11) Several family members say Rubyann was a paranoid schizophrenic: Interviews with Jeanne Miles, 6/27/02, and Dorthy Miller, 12/4/02.

(p. 11) This condition was over-diagnosed: Dr. Bernice B. Elkin e-mail to JK, 12/2/02.

(p. 11) "As she got older, she was much more difficult . . . ": Int. with JR, 12/27/02.

(p. 11) "My mother was the only one who encouraged me . . .": Ross, 10/21/61.

(p. 11) "Ruby aspired to be an actress . . .": Int. with Lucile Reid Brock, 6/11/02.

(p. 11) "Ruby seemed possessive of Patty . . .": Int. with Dorthy Miller, 12/14/02.

(p. 11) "It was a dysfunctional family": Int. with Lucile Reid Brock, 6/14/02.

(p. 11) "If Christianity covers the world . . . ": Raymond Flynn, *Growing Up a Sullen Baptist* (Denton, TX: University of North Texas Press, 2001), 9.

(p. 12) No one had to go to church on Sunday: Int. with JR, 1/16/02.

(p. 12) "Some families are very close": Int. with Rietta Netter Oppenheim, 1/16/03.

(p. 12) "There were houses there and paths . . .": James B. Simpson, *Contemporary Quotations* (New York: Thomas Y. Crowell Co., 1964), 184.

(p. 13) "[Uncle Jim] was known to have taken nips . . .": Walker, 98.

(p. 13) "There was a quirk in all of them . . .": Int. with Dorthy Miller, 12/4/02.

(p. 13) "There are a lot of secrets in that family": Int. with Robert Ball, 6/8/03.

(p. 14) "The Tularosa country is a parched desert . . .": C.L. Sonnichsen, *Tularosa: Last of the Frontier West* (Albuquerque: University of New Mexico Press, 1980), 3.

(p. 14) "If it has no tenderness . . .": Ibid., 5.

(p. 14) "A tot in love with make-believe . . .": William Glover, "Kim Stanley Not Pleased by Time She's 'Wasted,'" *AJ*, 11/14/54.

(p. 15) "It is a matter of pride that the public schools here . . .": "Artesia History-Makers: The Educator," *Artesia Advocate*, 1/19/28, 2.

(p. 15) J.T. Reid . . . elected vice president of the NMEA . . . : "J.T. Reid Elected Vice President of N. Mex. Educational Ass'n.," *Artesia Advocate*, 11/12/25, 1.

(p. 15) "Even in its busiest districts . . .": Erna Fergusson, *Erna Fergusson's Albuquerque* (Albuquerque: Merle Armitage Editions, 1947), 2–4.

(p. 16) "Three cultures . . . have flourished here . . .": Ibid., 9.

(p. 16) "In New Mexico, Anglo . . . connotes citizens . . .": Erna Fergusson, "Albuquerque: A Place to Live In" in *Rocky Mountain Cities*, ed. Ray B. West Jr. (New York: W.W. Norton & Co., 1949), 170.

(p. 16) "a gangling kid with loose blonde hair . . .": Mary Lukas, "Kim's Light and Heat," *Show Magazine*, July 1963, 65.

(p. 16) Kim was quiet: Int. with Anabel Everett Kelly, 7/14/02.

(p. 16) "I thought of her as being unsatisfied . . .": Int. with JR, 11/29/01.

(p. 16) "As a child and teenager, Patty Beth . . . is remembered . . .": Lukas, 65.

(p. 17) "I lived . . . in a state of continual frustration . . .": Ibid.

(p. 17) "My brother snuck me out of the house . . .": Ross, 10/21/61.

(p. 17) "Howard was a strong Leo personality . . .": Int. with JR, 10/20/01.

(p. 17) "Kim really disliked him and made it clear . . .": Int. with RZ, 1/19/02.

(p. 17) "Kenneth was my hero . . .": Int. with JR, 10/20/01.

(p. 17) Anabel Everett . . . recalls him . . . : Int. with Anabel Everett Kelly, 7/14/02.

(p. 17) "He sounds like a real bright spirit . . .": Int. with Paula Reid, 10/4/03.

(p. 17) "Fat, dumb and happy": Int. with JR, 1/15/03.

(p. 17) "She would accuse me of being like Pa . . .": Int. with JR, 1/16/02.

(p. 18) Justin did have the patriarchal streak . . . : Int. with Paula Reid, 10/4/03.

(p. 18) "Pop tended to dominate . . .": Int. with JR, 12/27/02.

(p. 18) "It was all about new-mown hay . . .": Ross, 10/21/61.

(p. 19) "The only reason I was in that play . . . ": Int. with Edwin Johnson, 6/26/03.

(p. 19) Kim also played an intense Calpurnia . . . : Lukas, 65.

(p. 19) "Patty was the most responsive child . . .": "Albuquerque Actress Voted to Stardom on Broadway," *AJ*, 10/29/54.

(p. 19) "I shall never forget Patty": "Kim's First Drama Coach Cheers Her," *AT*, 5/5/58.

(p. 19) "A lovely, warm, kind lady": Ross, 10/21/61.

(p. 19) "I dreaded the feeling of coming home . . . ": Ibid.

(p. 20) "My mother was trying to find a good place . . .": Int. with JR, 10/20/01.

(p. 20) "I was overcome. I was transfixed . . ." Ross, 10/21/61.

(p. 20) "I think my mother . . . found Kim headstrong": Int. with Robert Ball, 6/8/03.

(p. 21) "The secret lies with the father . . .": Int. with PZ, 11/6/02.

CHAPTER 2

(p. 22) The average annual income . . . : J.T. Reid, *It Happened in Taos* (Albuquerque: University of New Mexico Press, 1946), 10.

(p. 22) the highest infant mortality rate of any county . . . : Ibid., 11.

(p. 22) "[F]or my senior year in Taos . . .": Ross, 10/21/61.

(p. 23) "purtier than an oil well": Earl Wilson, "Gets the Laughs," *NYP,* 3/13/55.

(p. 23) there is no evidence she went (to the University of Texas): Records search performed by Ashley in the UT registrar's office, 11/29/01.

(p. 23) Baylor . . . Patty Reid never went there . . . : Records search performed by Janette in Baylor registrar's office, 11/30/01.

(p. 23) "Kim was intent . . .": Sidney Fields, "Only Human," *DM,* 3/14/55.

(p. 24) "After two years at the University of New Mexico, she switched . . .": Gilbert Millstein, "Kim Stanley," *TA,* Nov. 1959, 14.

(p. 24) "She agreed to study pre-medical courses . . .": Jack Ryan, "'That Broadway Actress' on the Oscar List," *Family Weekly,* 3/28/65.

(p. 24) "She said, 'I'm going to get to the top . . .'" Int. with Falba M. Hannett, 2/7/02.

(p. 24) "The next time I saw her, she said . . .": Int. with Patricia Frye, 1/30/04.

(p. 24) "She always dressed better than anyone else . . .": Int. with JWR, 4/22/02.

(p. 24) "[Patty] lived at the sorority house": Int. with Falba Murphy Hannett, 2/7/02.

(p. 24) the sorority's candidate for "Sweetheart of Sigma Chi": "To Choose Sigma Chi Sweetheart," *New Mexico Lobo,* 11/13/42, 3.

(p. 25) "We were laughing so hard . . .": Int. with Dorothy Land Fitzgerald, 6/25/02.

(p. 25) "Somehow, there was a sadness . . .": Int. with JWR, 4/22/02.

(p. 25) "She used to come and spend . . .": Int. with Falba M. Hannett, 2/7/02.

(p. 25) "The first time I ever had gin . . .": Int. with JWR, 4/22/02.

(p. 25) "It was just so apparent . . .": Int. with Kathryn Lou McIntosh Ely, 6/22/02.

(p. 26) "My first real acting experience was in 1942 . . .": Ross, 10/21/61.

(p. 26) "play acting was not a matter of 'playing' . . .": "Albuquerque Actress Voted to Stardom on Broadway," *AJ,* 10/29/54.

(p. 26) Patty had worked hard both as an actress . . . : "Rodey Stage Laid Groundwork for Career of Kim Stanley," *AT,* 2/5/65.

(p. 26) a week before he was scheduled to graduate: "Two Cadets Die in Plane Crash," *Morning Avalanche* (Lubbock, TX), 11/5/42, 6.

(p. 26) Kenneth Reid was piloting a Cessna T-50 . . . : U.S. Army Air Force report on the plane crash that killed Reid and William Philippe; in possession of JK.

(p. 27) Kenneth's body was completely eviscerated: Death certificate for Kenneth Reid; in possession of JK.

(p. 27) "He had so much promise . . .": Int. with Anabel Everett Kelly, 7/14/02.

(p. 27) Patty and . . . Justin made several tearful . . . : Int. with JR, 10/20/01.

(p. 27) "She had a wonderful background in the theater . . .": Int. with JWR, 4/22/02.

(p. 27) "Patricia Reid, who played . . .": Janet Cromer, "On the Stage," *AT,* 2/18/43, 6.

(p. 28) a sorority sister remembers the large diamond ring . . . : Int. with Falba Murphy Hannett, 2/7/02.

(p. 28) He took her to visit his family . . . : Int. with Mary Helen Cox Ewing, 2/7/02.

(p. 28) "a nervously sensitive young girl . . .": Kathryn Kennedy O'Connor, *Theater in the Cow Country* (South Bend, IN: Creative Service for Publishers, 1966), 68.

(p. 28) "This production requires intimate knowledge . . .": Marion Pearsall, "Campus Wash Comes Clean—As Seen by Lobo Reviewer," *New Mexico Lobo,* 4/14/44, 1.

(p. 28) "very funny in spots": "Campus Musical Opens at Rodey," *AJ,* 4/13/44, 2.

(p. 28) "Miss Reid's performance was excellent . . .": "Rodey Play Accepted by Enthusiastic Audience," *AT,* 4/14/44, 4.

(p. 28) Patty directed *Soladeras,* a one-act play . . . : "Rodey Presents One-Act Plays," *New Mexico Lobo,* 5/12/44, 1.

(p. 28) "Patty's youth and beauty carried her . . .": "Informally," *AJ,* 6/9/44.

(p. 28) "Miss Reid's interpretation of several difficult scenes . . .": "Miss Reid Does Outstanding Work in Rodey Theater *Mrs. Moonlight,*" *AT,* 6/8/44.

(p. 29) "She was perfect in that, enchanting . . .": Int. with JWR, 4/22/02.

(p. 29) "If I think of her today, I remember . . .": JWR e-mail to JK, 4/16/03.

(p. 29) "Patty was the queen of the university . . .": Int. with JWR, 4/22/02.

(p. 29) John Kerr . . . was slated to become a director at the Pasadena Playhouse . . . : "*Right You Are* About in Shape," *New Mexico Lobo,* 9/1/44, 1.

(p. 29) She appeared in . . . : "One-Act Plays Next Thursday," *New Mexico Lobo,* 10/6/44, 1.

(p. 29) Patty jumped up, ran across the room . . . : "Kim's First Drama Coach Cheers Her," *AT,* 5/5/58.

(p. 30) "Kim was so positive that she wanted to be an actress . . .": Int. with Flo Miller Shields, 12/13/02.

(p. 30) everyone in her family except her mother opposed . . . : Ross, 10/21/61.

(p. 30) Aunt Lena . . . paid for the bulk of . . . : Katherine Norris e-mail to JK, 2/2/03.

(p. 30) "Pasadena turned out to be like a glorified junior college . . .": Ross, 10/21/61.

(p. 30) "Patty Beth was never too happy . . .": Int. with Dabbs Greer, 3/4/02.

(p. 31) "I was talking to a friend . . .": Int. with Barbara Turner Double, 12/6/02.

(p. 31) "The reason I never connected her . . .": Ibid.

(p. 31) "She had something that was a little different..": Int. with Jack Harris, 3/4/02.

(p. 31) Pat Reid . . . never did (join Actors Equity): Int. with Pat Reid, 3/4/02.

(p. 32) Guests in . . . Albuquerque's Hilton Hotel . . . saw . . . : Marc Simmons, *Albuquerque: A Narrative History* (Albuquerque: UNM Press, 1982), 368.

(p. 32) "J.T. set up the adult ed. classes . . .": Int. with Lynn White, 12/18/03.

(p. 32) "My grandmother turned . . .": Katherine Norris e-mail to JK, 1/28/03.

(p. 32) He was . . . "a lady-killer": Int. with Charles Callaway, 6/4/02.

(p. 32) "Warner Brothers signed her to a movie contract . . .": *"Theatre Arts* Introduces . . ." *TA,* March 1949.

(p. 32) if there . . . was such a contract, no evidence . . . remains: A 4/29/02 search of the Warner Bros. collection at the USC cinema/TV library by curator Randi Hokett turned up no evidence of Kim's having had a contract with Warner Bros.

(p. 32) "[She] flunked a Warner Bros. screen test": Lukas, 65.

(p. 32) "I went in to see Michael Curtiz . . .": Kobal, 692.

(p. 33) Lucy Kroll . . . was a literary analyst at Warner Bros.: John Pilkington, ed., *Stark Young: A Life in the Arts,* Vol. II (Baton Rouge: LSU Press, 1975), 1421.

(p. 33) Lee Strasberg . . . was directing screen tests . . . : David Garfield, *A Player's Place* (New York: MacMillan Publishing Co., Inc., 1980), 78.

(p. 33) Alfred Ryder . . . had a one-year contract with Paramount: Michael Smith, "Most Seductive Trap—Seducing the Audience," *Village Voice,* 5/27/59.

(p. 33) Deek Kelley . . . told Patty they needed . . . : Int. with Bill Corwin, 1/30/03.

(p. 33) Patty appeared . . . in . . . *Boy Meets Girl:* Eve Mark, *"Boy Meets Girl* Gives Audience Run for Money," *Louisville Courier-Journal,* 5/1/46.

(p. 33) "[It] did nothing to establish a dramatic interest . . .": Boyd Martin, *Lady Honey* review, *Louisville Courier-Journal,* 5/8/46.

(p. 33) now she was Kim Stanley . . . : Ibid.

(p. 34) "They were holding the Kentucky Derby": Int. with Edward Balcomb, 12/14/02.

(p. 34) Kim went on to New York with Deek Kelley: Int. with Bill Corwin, 1/30/03.

(p. 34) a Norman Rockwell drawing: *Saturday Evening Post,* 4/6/46.

CHAPTER 3

(p. 36) "It was the town . . .": Jan Morris, *Manhattan '45* (New York: Oxford University Press, 1987), 6.

(p. 36) she always claimed to have come in 1947: Lillian Ross and Helen Ross, *The Player: Profile of an Art* (New York: Simon and Schuster, 1962), 11.

(p. 37) "The first week I was in New York . . .": John Kobal, "Dialogue on Film: Kim Stanley," *American Film,* June 1983, 27.

(p. 37) Chayefsky, Hayes, and Clurman would compare Kim . . . : Richard C. Wald, "New Chayefsky Screenplay Is Filmed Locally," n/p, n/d (Chayefsky). Press release for *Touch of the Poet* headed "Kim Stanley" (Hayes). Both in KS bio file at NYPL. Marjorie Loggia and Glenn Young, *The Collected Works of Harold Clurman* (New York: Applause Books, 1994), 307 (Clurman).

(p. 37) Kim . . . said she didn't know anyone in the city: Ross and Ross, 11.

(p. 37) "I came to New York in 1944 . . .": Int. with JWR, 4/22/02.

(p. 37) Kim also had a list of movers and shakers . . . : Ross and Ross, 11.

(p. 37) she took a room at a cheap . . . : Ibid., 11–12.

(p. 37) Jinx Witherspoon thinks Kim stayed . . . : Int. with JWR, 4/22/02.

(p. 37) "I went up to Kermit Bloomgarden's office . . .": Kobal, 691.

(p. 37) "I sat everybody down . . .": Wilson, 3/13/55.

(p. 38) "Making the rounds is like . . .": Ross and Ross, 12.

(p. 38) it was at Pompton Lakes . . . : "She's Come Far Since Then," *LAT,* 3/8/65.

(p. 38) the assistant producer had a "yen" for her . . . : Fields, 3/14/55.

(p. 38) "It didn't make me feel . . .": Ross and Ross, 12.

(p. 38) "When this girl did not show up . . .": "She's Come Far Since Then," *LAT,* 3/8/65.

(p. 39) it was on either Thirty-second or Thirty-sixth Street: Ross and Ross, 12.

(p. 39) "This was a trashy area . . .": Int. with Bill Corwin, 1/28/03.

(p. 39) "When the train went by . . .": Ibid.

(p. 40) "She wasn't a heavy drinker . . .": Ibid.

(p. 40) his friend Cliff Robertson recalls . . . : Int. with Cliff Robertson, 11/18/01.

(p. 40) "I don't know. I imagine he's still . . . : Int. with Ethel Winant, 2/26/02.

(p. 40) "I was hired as an outdoor-girl . . .": Ross and Ross, 12.

(p. 40) one of her jobs . . . was touring Southern towns . . . : Ibid., 13.

(p. 40) "I thought I'd save more money . . . : Ibid., 12.

(p. 40) "It was the only time I hated people . . .": Fields, 3/14/55.

(p. 40) "I was one . . .": Philip Minoff, "The Forthright Kim Stanley," *Cue,* 2/11/56.

(p. 41) "She and Marlon were the top . . .": Int. with Georgann Johnson, 6/25/02.

(p. 41) "She had taken to drinking . . .": Int. with JWR, 4/22/02.

(p. 41) "It all seemed to work okay . . .": Int. with Nikki Tachias Barr, 8/2/02.

(p. 41) "Her mother was bugging her . . .": Int. with Lorenzo Semple Jr., 10/24/01.

(p. 41) "I think she bothered Kim . . .": Int. with Gene Saks, 5/16/02.

(p. 42) Rubyann had a nervous breakdown: Int. with Dorthy Miller, 12/24/02.

(p. 42) they found . . . a poured concrete cyclorama: Stuart W. Little, *Off-Broadway: The Prophetic Theater* (New York: Coward, McCann & Geoghegan, Inc., 1972), 40.

(p. 42) "always of a frighteningly high-minded sort": Lawrence Kane, "Five Minutes From Broadway," *TA,* Dec. 1949, 43.

(p. 42) Proclaimed its faith in "the democratic principle . . .": Program for Interplayers' production of *him* in *him* file at NYPL.

(p. 42) "We had philosophical discussions . . .": Int. with Merle Debuskey, 7/14/02.

(p. 42) Kim took her turn cleaning . . . : Little, 40.

(p. 42) "Very embarrassing . . .": Fields, 3/14/55.

(p. 42) they rigged up a primitive air-conditioning system . . . : Little, 40.

(p. 43) "We would go to Forty-second Street . . .": Int. with Merle Debuskey, 7/14/02.

(p. 43) "In the trees, the night wind stirs . . .": E.B. White, *Here Is New York* (New York: Harper & Brothers Publishers, 1949), 35–37.

(p. 43) "She was not a classic beauty . . .": Int. with Merle Debuskey, 7/14/02.

(p. 44) "Don't try to despise it . . .": Program for Provincetown Players' production of *him* in *him* file at NYPL.

(p. 44) Actors in the original version . . . could go to cummings: Charles Norman, *E.E. Cummings: The Magic-Maker* (New York: The Bobbs-Merrill Co., Inc., 1972), 217.

(p. 44) he sometimes walked past . . . but never went in: Little, 40.

(p. 44) Kim [played] as one of the Three Wierds: Int. with Gene Saks, 5/16/02.

(p. 44) "She was a very attractive blonde . . .": Ibid.

(p. 44) Reviews of the "A for effort" variety: Richard Watts Jr., "Interplayers Revive Controversial Play," *NYP,* 7/27/48, and George Freedley, "Interplayers Offer Revival of E.E. Cummings' *him*" in *him* file at NYPL.

(p. 44) Kim played Iris . . . and the Queen . . . : This information comes from what appears to be Kim's bio sketch from *St. Joan,* in her bio file at NYPL.

(p. 45) "I know it must sound . . .": "Theatre Arts Introduces," *TA,* March 1949, 51.

(p. 45) "It is virtually impossible . . . : "Five Minutes from Broadway," *TA,* Dec. 1949, 43.

(p. 45) "New York's hottest summer . . .": Ibid., 47.

(p. 46) "It was my first brush . . .": Ross and Ross, 13.

(p. 46) "She was so beautiful . . .": Int. with Bea Arthur, 8/12/02.

(p. 46) "Kim had gotten involved . . .": Int. with Tony Franciosa, 5/1/02.

(p. 46) "Kim and he had been lovers . . .": Int. with Ben Gazzara, 7/19/02.

(p. 46) "Oh my goodness gracious . . .": Int. with Merle Debuskey, 7/14/02.

(p. 46) "Many afternoons, we sat drinking . . .": Int. with Lorenzo Semple Jr., 10/24/01.

(p. 47) "[Denise] is played very well . . .": Julius Bab, "Gertrude Stein im Cherry Lane Theater," *New Yorker Staats-Zeitung,* 7/13/49.

(p. 47) "They were very dynamic . . .": Int. with Lamont Johnson, 6/7/02.

(p. 47) "Kim was really uptight . . .": Int. with Nikki Tachias Barr, 8/2/02.

(p. 48) "Nobody paid much attention . . .": Int. with Merle Debuskey, 7/14/02.

(p. 48) she, Kim, Rubyann, and Jinx . . . : Int. with Nikki Tachias Barr, 8/2/02.

(p. 48) "It makes the little Cherry Lane Theatre . . .": "Yes Is for a Very Young Man," *The Christian Science Monitor,* 6/11/49.

(p. 48) "When Miss Stein writes . . .": Thomas R. Dash, "Yes Is for a Very Young Man," *Women's Wear Daily,* 6/9/49.

(p. 48) "The most interesting member . . .": Richard Watts Jr., "Gertrude Stein Drama Presented Downtown," *NYP,* 6/7/49, 32

(p. 48) Kim was the most successful . . . : William Hawkins, "Stein Play Given Fine Presentation," *NYWT,* 6/7/49, 16.

(p. 48) "In Kim Stanley, as a young French mother . . .": BA, "Gertrude Stein's *Yes . . .* is Put On at Cherry Lane Playhouse," *NYT,* 6/7/49, 27.

(p. 49) "The superb notices lifted Kim Stanley . . ." Little, 41.

(p. 49) receipts from *Yes* plunged: "Five Minutes from Broadway," *TA,* Dec. 1949, 47.

(p. 49) "In our naïvete . . .": Int. with Merle Debuskey, 7/14/02.

(p. 49) One of 200 scripts submitted . . . : George Currie, "*Too Many Thumbs* at Cherry Lane Turns Out to Be Monkey Business," *Brooklyn Eagle,* 7/28/49.

(p. 49) "The play had its weaknesses . . .": Int. with Nehemiah Persoff, 1/25/02.

(p. 49) "I was stage-managing it . . .": Int. with Tony Franciosa, 5/1/02.

(p. 49) "I don't think she took care . . .": Int. with Merle Debuskey, 7/14/02.

(p. 50) "The rehearsals started the demise . . .": Int. with Tony Franciosa, 5/1/02.

(p. 50) Persoff . . . brought [Conway] in . . . : Int. with Nehemiah Persoff, 1/25/02.

(p. 50) "I first became aware of Kim . . .": Robert Wahls, "Kim Stanley's War With Success," *NYDN,* 4/5/59, 101.

(p. 50) "We got to the end of the play . . .": Int. with Nehemiah Persoff, 1/25/02.

(p. 50) "Curt was asked to look . . .": Int. with Tony Franciosa, 5/1/02.

(p. 50) "Soon all the people of our time . . .": Robert Hivnor, *Too Many Thumbs: A Three-Act Play* (Minneapolis: University of Minnesota Press, 1949), 84.

(p. 51) "We thought that was wonderful . . .": John Corry, "Kim Stanley Returns, Directing Ensemble Troupe," *NYT,* 9/20/79, C-15.

(p. 51) "It has the rare gift . . .": Richard Watts Jr., "Of Apes and Men in a New Comedy," *NYP,* 8/3/49.

(p. 51) it started weakly, although it built . . . : "Too Many Thumbs," *WV,* 8/3/49.

(p. 51) It was confusing . . . : "Too Many Ideas in *Too Many Thumbs,*" *Daily Compass,* 7/29/49.

(p. 51) it was cluttered with . . . : "Too Many Thumbs," *Women's Wear Daily,* 8/2/49.

(p. 51) "He took a shine to Kim . . .": Int. with Nehemiah Persoff, 1/25/02.

(p. 51) "There was a lot of sexual intrigue . . .": Int. with Tony Franciosa, 5/1/02.

(p. 51) "She later told me that . . .": Wahls, 4/5/59.

(p. 51) "The first day in class . . .": Int. with Jack Klugman, 1/5/03.

(p. 52) Network radio was at its peak . . . : Harry Castleman and Walter J. Podrazik, *Watching TV: Four Decades of American Television* (New York: McGraw-Hill Book Company, 1982), 24.

(p. 52) Only 225 television sets were produced: Ibid., 27.

(p. 52) Kim appeared on *Hollywood Screen Test . . . The Bigelow Show . . . Boris Karloff Mystery Playhouse:* See Kim's listing from the 1950 *Player's Guide.*

(p. 52) "She really didn't like confrontation . . .": Int. with Jack Klugman, 1/5/03.

(p. 53) "She was wonderful. She was developing . . ." Ibid.

(p. 53) "I've seen many Saint Joans . . .": Int. with Walt Witcover, 9/20/03.

(p. 53) "Sometimes it was uncomfortable . . .": Ibid.

(p. 53) He knew he would never be half as good . . . : Wahls, 4/5/59.

(p. 53) producer Kermit Bloomgarden saw her . . . : Arthur Gelb, "Actress Minus Frills," *NYT,* 4/3/55, Sec. 2, 1.

CHAPTER 4

(p. 54) But Kim gave that as a reason for not signing . . . : Int. with PZ, 11/6/02.

(p. 55) "The little Indian girl who goes . . .": Kobal, 694.

(p. 55) "'There goes Willy' . . .": Louis Calta, "Bemelmans Story Set as Stage Show," *NYT,* 11/5/49, 10.

(p. 55) "Lillian Hellman . . . has found a play . . .": John Chapman, "*Montserrat* A Brutal Melodrama," *NYDN,* 10/31/49.

(p. 55) "after a dozen curtain calls . . .": William Hawkins, "*Montserrat* Hits Like 'Quake," *NYWT,* 10/31/49.

(p. 55) "In view of the harrowing theme . . .": BA, "*Montserrat* Adapted from the French of Emmanuel Robles by Lillian Hellman," *NYT,* 10/31/49.

(p. 56) "This enormously powerful British actor . . .": Richard Watts Jr., "*Montserrat,* Tragic Play," *NYP,* 10/31/49.

(p. 56) Lillian Hellman . . . admitted she felt . . . : Lillian Hellman, *Pentimento* (Boston: Little, Brown and Co., 1973), 198.

(p. 56) Kim . . . stood in the wrong place . . . : Int. with Wayne Sabato, 3/24/03.

(p. 56) "She had a terrific sense of humor . . .": Int. with Vivian Nathan, 12/24/01.

(p. 56) "She was a more vulnerable person . . .": Ibid.

(p. 56) Kim married . . . under the hybrid name . . . : Marriage certificate of Patricia Kimberly Stanley and Curt Conway; in possession of JK.

(p. 57) After Elia Kazan "named names" . . . Conway crossed the street . . . : Elia Kazan, *Elia Kazan: A Life* (New York: Da Capo Press, 1997), 467.

(p. 57) "He quit the Actors Studio . . .": Int. with Lonny Chapman, 1/11/02.

(p. 57) More than 2,000 performers auditioned . . . : Garfield, 90.

(p. 57) the Studio was a place where . . . actors could pursue . . . : Harold Clurman, "The Famous Method" in *The Collected Works of Harold Clurman* (New York: Applause Books, 1994), 370.

(p. 58) Studio actors would become known . . . : Garfield, 158.

(p. 58) "quite sane about their activities . . . ": Harold Clurman, "The Famous Method," 370.

(p. 58) "It was like coming home . . .": Ross, 59.

(p. 58) "a jeweler's eye": Ibid., 82.

(p. 58) "Along with Stanislavski and Brecht . . .": Foster Hirsch, *A Method to Their Madness: The History of the Actors Studio* (New York: W.W. Norton & Company, 1984), 150.

(p. 58) "James Dean did a scene . . .": Joe Morella and Edward Z. Epstein, *Paul and Joanne* (New York: Delacorte Press, 1988), 27.

(p. 59) "Good night, Lee": Susan Strasberg, *Bittersweet* (New York: G.P. Putnam's Sons, 1980), 153.

(p. 59) She worked . . . *Red Peppers* . . . and . . . *The Importance* . . . : Garfield, 150.

(p. 59) Kazan oversaw the staging of three different versions . . . : Ibid., 84.

(p. 59) "Wearing a leather jacket . . .": Ross, 59.

(p. 59) "The purpose of the . . . Method": Clurman, "The Famous Method," 370.

(p. 60) "Since the Method is a technique . . .": Clurman, "The Famous Method," 370.

(p. 60) "the Method is useful only . . .": Robert Lewis, *Method—Or Madness?* (New York: Samuel French, Inc., 1958), 4.

(p. 60) "[Elia] Kazan . . . had always had . . .": Garfield, 79.

(p. 60) "the most powerful tool . . .": Shelley Winters, *Shelley: Also Known as Shirley* (William Morrow and Company, Inc., 1980), 208.

(p. 60) "Strasberg is the greatest man . . .": Ross, 59.

(p. 60) "the First Lady of the Studio": Hirsch, 327. (On page 318, Hirsh lists eighteen important actresses who came out of the Studio. Kim is first on the list, which is not alphabetical.)

(p. 60) "Like Brando, the ultimate actor's actor . . .": Ibid., 322.

(p. 60) Arthur Penn would call her . . .": Ibid., 326.

(p. 61) "She was kind and warm to me . . . : Jada Rowland e-mail to JK, 12/9/02.

(p. 61) "I'll never forget Kim's preparation": Sylvia Davis ltr. to JK, 10/16/02.

(p. 61) "The production was ordinary . . .": Int. with JP Miller, 9/20/01.

(p. 61) "Breadth, eloquence . . . ": Howard Barnes, "Baleful Tragedy, *NYHT,* 1/8/51.

(p. 62) "This little dandy is from . . .": John Chapman, "ANTA's *House of Bernarda Alba* Makes Playgoing a Serious Task," *NYDN.*

(p. 62) "[It's] primarily for students . . .": Robert Coleman, "*House of Bernarda Alba* Grim Study of Five Women," *DM,* 1/8/51.

(p. 62) "she dispels such force of character . . .": William Hawkins, "Lorca Play Pivots on Love and Hate," *NYWT,* 1/8/51.

(p. 62) "there is something about her highly mannered style . . .": Richard Watts Jr., "The Grim Home of Bernarda Alba," *NYP,* 1/8/51.

(p. 62) "Oh honey . . . she was chewing up . . .": Int. with Bob Traweek, 3/26/03.

(p. 62) "Kim Stanley makes a frightening . . .": Barnes, "Baleful Tragedy," *NYHT,* 1/8/51.

(p. 62) "Miss Stanley is particularly outstanding . . .": Coleman, "'House of Bernarda Alba' Grim Study of 5 Women," DM, 1/8/51.

(p. 62) "She took a look at her . . .": Int. with Anne Jackson, 10/23/01.

(p. 63) "She hadn't seen her father since . . .": Int. with Arthur Laurents, 1/5/02.

(p. 63) "I'd never seen Kim . . .": Int. with HF, 12/10/01.

(p. 64) "[A]t night . . . there is the quietness . . .": HF, "Richmond, U.S.A," *NYT,* 4/13/52.

(p. 64) "She was just marvelous . . .": Int. with Lonny Chapman, 1/11/02.

(p. 64) "She was extraordinary in it . . .": Int. with HF, 12/10/01.

(p. 64) "It remains for a young actress . . .": R.E.P. Sensenderfer, "*The Chase,* Melodrama, Opens at Locust," *PB,* 4/1/52.

(p. 65) "a psychological western . . . I enjoyed and admired . . ." John Chapman, "John Hodiak an Admirable Sheriff in a Well-Staged *The Chase,*" *NYDN,* 4/16/52.

(p. 65) "[I]t's a real arouser! . . .": Jim O'Connor, "Violence Highlights Drama of Suspense," *JM,* 4/16/52.

(p. 65) "*The Chase* suffers from the tendency . . .": Richard Watts Jr., "A Manhunt in a Texas Community," *NYP,* 4/16/52.

(p. 65) "Mr. Ferrer's direction is self-conscious . . .": BA, "HF's Texan Drama, *The Chase,* Staged at the Playhouse by Ferrer," *NYT,* 4/16/52.

(p. 65) "In the small role of the killer's . . . wife": Watts, "A Manhunt in a Texas Community," *NYP,* 4/16/52.

(p. 65) "Outstanding in a small role . . .": O'Connor, "Violence Highlights Drama of Suspense," *JM,* 4/16/52.

(p. 65) Kim was not in the cast when it closed . . . : Louis Calta, "*Shuffle Along* Quickens Pace," *NYT,* 5/3/52, 18.

(p. 65) "She was bright and just marvelous . . .": Int. with HF, 12/10/01.

(p. 66) "She would always take . . .": Int. with Eileen Heckart, 11/16/01.

(p. 67) "The regular Broadway actors . . .": Int. with Porter Van Zandt, 9/21/01.

(p. 67) "I have to pee": Told by Elaine Stritch at Actors Studio memorial service for KS, 10/12/01.

(p. 67) "I never think anybody's watching": Entry for KS in *Current Biography,* 1955.

(p. 68) "The family would gather around . . .": Int. with Ray Hankamer Jr., 12/31/02.

(p. 68) "I remember thinking how fragile she was . . .": Int. with Ann Holmes, 2/12/03.

(p. 68) "When Vivien Leigh's Blanche gets off . . .": Int. with Bob Traweek, 2/13/03.

(p. 68) "When she finished that scene . . . : Ibid.

(p. 69) "It was a terrible situation . . .": Ibid.

CHAPTER 5

(p. 70) "For Millie, an unknown actress . . .": Henry Hewes, "Goon Girl," *SR,* 4/11/53, 53.

(p. 70) "lush, blonde and womanly": Robert Wahls, "Kim Still Perfecting That French Touch," *NYDN,* 11/22/59.

(p. 70) she wrapped a diaper . . . : Hewes, 4/11/53.

(p. 71) "I remember Josh telling her . . .": Int. with Elizabeth Wilson, 3/13/02.

(p. 72) "I haven't moralized . . . : William Inge, "*Picnic:* Of Women," *NYT,* 2/15/53, Sec. 2, 3.

(p. 72) "During rehearsals, Janice Rule . . .": Hewes, 4/11/53.

(p. 72) "When I know and understand . . .": Laura Lee, "Kim Stanley Borrows Texas Drawl for Role," *PB,* 2/20/55.

(p. 72) "Kim went into characters . . .": Int. with Anne Jackson, 10/23/01.

(p. 73) "Janice respected Kim . . .": Int. with Ben Gazzara, 7/19/02.

(p. 73) "You dance well . . .": Joshua Logan, *Movie Stars, Real People and Me* (New York: Delacorte Press, 1978), 7.

(p. 73) "This thrilling creation . . .": James G. Crossley, "Columbus Audience Gets First Look at New Play, *Picnic,*" *Columbus Citizen,* 1/16/53, 6.

(p. 73) The *St. Louis County Medical Bulletin* blasted . . . : "*Picnic* Rapped by St. Loo Medico on Line That 'Sabotages' Legit," *Variety,* 2/4/53, 57.

(p. 74) "For this improvement . . .": Elliot Norton, "On the Stage," *Boston Post,* 2/12/53.

(p. 74) "You gave a charming performance . . .": "Broadway's Little Mother," n/p, n/d. In KS bio file at NYPL.

(p. 74) "Except for Williams, Miller, and a few others . . .": BA, *Broadway* (New York: Limelight Editions, 1990), 415.

(p. 74) "There was a real theater world . . .": Int. with Ellen Adler, 3/5/02.

(p. 75) "[It] is one of those rare plays . . .": William Hawkins, "Inge Again Vivifies Little People's Souls," *NYWT*, 2/20/53.

(p. 75) "Memorable though . . .": BA, "At the Theatre," *NYT*, 2/20/53.

(p. 75) "It revealed power . . .": Richard Watts Jr., *NYP*, 2/20/53.

(p. 75) Walter Kerr . . . questioning why . . .": Walter Kerr, "Picnic," *NYHT*, 2/20/53.

(p. 75) lyric realism in the sound 1920s tradition . . . : Harold Clurman, *Picnic* review, *The Nation*, 3/7/53.

(p. 75) "As a tomboy with brains . . .": BA, "At the Theatre," *NYT*, 2/20/53.

(p. 75) "Kim Stanley gives a stunning . . .": BA, "Inge's *Picnic*," *NYT*, 3/1/53, Sec. 2, 1.

(p. 75) one of the play's most touching moments . . . : William Hawkins, "Inge Again Vivifies Little People's Souls," NYWT, 2/20/53.

(p. 75) "Kim Stanley has . . . added her name . . . : Hewes, 4/11/53.

(p. 76) "She has amazing control . . .": Ibid.

(p. 76) "Since Marlon Brando last appeared . . .": Walter Kerr, "Picnic," *NYHT*, 2/20/53.

(p. 76) "The adolescent sister who . . .": Harold Clurman, *Picnic* review, *The Nation*, 3/7/53.

(p. 76) an explanation the amused Clurman said . . . : Minoff, 2/11/56.

(p. 76) "Her dressing room was jammed": Int. with Dorothy L. Fitzgerald, 6/25/02.

(p. 76) "Sometimes Kim was friendly . . .": Katherine Norris e-mail to JK, 1/28/03.

(p. 77) most of the actors had gone dead, Rule thought . . . : Ross and Ross, 398.

(p. 77) "She didn't like to act . . .": Int. with Eileen Heckart, 11/16/01.

(p. 78) Kim and Brooks got together . . . : JC e-mail to JK, 11/10/02.

(p. 78) "I became emotionally unhinged . . .": Patricia Bosworth, *Montgomery Clift* (New York: Bantam Books, 1979), 229.

(p. 78) "For Brooks, the relationship . . .": Int. with Patricia Bosworth, 2/26/02.

(p. 80) "She was one of the great actresses . . .": Int. with Delbert Mann, 9/15/01.

(p. 80) "She had the guts of a thief . . .": Int. with RH, 8/24/01.

(p. 80) "The show was rather ludicrous . . .": Int. with Sidney Lumet, 2/13/02.

(p. 80) "She was absolutely brilliant . . .": Ibid.

(p. 81) "I'll rent out rooms and sit on the front porch . . .": HF, *Harrison, Texas* (New York: Harcourt, Brace and Co., 1956), 14.

(p. 81) "She was an incredible person . . .": Int. with RH, 8/21/01.

(p. 81) "a personal triumph . . .": "Tele Follow-Up Comment," *Variety*, 4/8/53.

(p. 81) "All the eccentricities . . .": Int. with Delbert Mann, 9/27/02.

(p. 82) she had come closer . . . : Agronsky int. with KS on *Look Here*, 11/17/57.

(p. 82) they were looking forward to watching it: "Professor's Daughter to Be Seen on TV Here," *AJ*, 4/1/53.

(p. 82) "They did not have anything near . . .": Int. with JR, 5/16/02.

(p. 82) "Florence was just lovely . . .": Int. with RZ, 1/19/02.

(p. 83) "A friend of mine said . . .": "The Girl on Your Set," *Newsweek*, 6/17/57, 106.

(p. 83) "Kim Stanley pulled off . . .": "Tele Follow-Up Comment," *Variety*, 12/2/53.

(p. 84) "There was a sort of explosion . . .": Int. with Leslie Nielsen, 8/16/02.

(p. 84) she would express gratitude . . . : KS profile in *Traveling Lady Playbill.*

(p. 84) "usually crazy girls . . .": William Glover, "Kim Stanley Not Pleased by Time She's 'Wasted,'" *AJ*, 11/14/54.

(p. 84) "She was fiercely loyal . . .": Int. with JP Miller, 9/20/01.

(p. 85) "She liked to toss off . . .": Ibid.

(p. 85) "Miss Stanley, always in character . . .": Ronald Muchnick, "*Trip to Bountiful* Called Miss Gish's 'Masterpiece,'" *Ann Arbor News,* 5/8/54.

(p. 86) "Their marriage was stormy . . .": Int. with Lonnie Chapman, 1/11/02.

(p. 86) "I asked several big stars . . .": Int. with Nehemiah Persoff, 1/25/02.

(p. 86) "This is to certify . . .": Dr. Sewall Pastor "to whom it may concern" ltr., 7/15/54. In correspondence 1952–61 folders, Box 665, LK/LOC.

(p. 87) "She was a great champion . . .": Int. with HF, 12/10/01.

(p. 87) "She liked to work into the role . . .": Int. with Lonnie Chapman, 1/11/02.

(p. 87) "Out of town, you couldn't unwind . . .": Ibid.

(p. 88) "The heroine is supposed to be . . .": "The Traveling Lady," *Variety,* 10/13/54.

(p. 88) "[it] moves like a tired turtle . . .": Henry Humphreys, "Aisle Say," *Cincinnati Times-Star,* 10/12/54.

(p. 88) "Between acts of . . .": Edward Carberry, "Theater, Flesh and Shadow, *Cincinnati Post,* 10/12/54.

(p. 88) "a moody and often richly human . . .": Arthur Spaeth, "Showtime," *Cleveland News,* 10/19/54.

(p. 88) "There's that dove again": Omar Ranney, "Stage & Screen," *Cleveland Press,* 10/19/54.

(p. 89) "We had to hold the curtain . . .": Int. with HF, 12/10/01.

(p. 89) "She was very kind to me . . .": Int. with Brook Seawell Ashley, 6/19/02.

(p. 89) "In our opening scene . . .": Ibid.

(p. 89) "Kim gave my arm a jerk . . .": Ibid.

(p. 90) "In the old days of the Palace . . .": John Chapman, "*Traveling Lady* Rueful but Slim," *NYDN,* 10/28/54.

(p. 90) "It is a series of minor . . .": BA, "Theatre: Texas Drama," *NYT,* 10/28/54.

(p. 90) "The author has . . . been true to life . . .": Walter Kerr, "The Traveling Lady," *NYHT,* 10/28/54.

(p. 90) "Georgette is an inarticulate . . .": BA, "Theatre: Texas Drama, *NYT,* 10/28/54.

(p. 90) "Toward the end of the evening . . .": Kerr, "The Traveling Lady," *NYHT,* 10/28/54.

(p. 91) Kim Stanley is the youngest addition . . .": Harold Clurman, *The Traveling Lady* review, *The Nation,* 11/13/54.

(p. 91) she was occasionally very affecting . . . : William Hawkins, "*The Traveling Lady* Unpacks at Playhouse," *NYWT,* 10/28/54.

(p. 91) members of the Playwrights Company . . . voted . . . : "Kim Stanley Elevated to Stardom in *The Traveling Lady,*" Playwrights Company press release, n/d, in KS bio file at NYPL.

(p. 91) "Roger Stevens called me . . .": Int. with HF, 12/10/01.

(p. 91) "She had enormous instincts . . .": Ibid.

(p. 91) "We certainly are proud . . .": "Former Albuquerquean Stars in Broadway Play," *AT,* 10/29/54.

(p. 92) "William Fields thinks Texas . . .": John Rosenfield, "Kim Stanley of Southwest," *Dallas Morning News,* 11/6/54, 6.

(p. 92) "Miss Stanley, who majored in psychology . . .": Lee, "Kim Stanley Borrows Texas Drawl for Role," PB, 2/20/55.

(p. 92) "significant public records . . .": *Aware Bulletin #12,* 12/27/54. In KS bio file at NYPL.

(p. 93) "economic anarchy . . . not susceptible..: Atkinson, 434.

(p. 93) "Curt is delighted she's starring . . .": Virginia Wiatt, untitled International News Service article, 12/13/54. In KS bio file at NYPL.

(p. 93) "She is a wonderful mother . . .": Wahls, 4/5/59.

(p. 94) "It developed into a rather tawdry . . .": Barbara L. Wilson, "Inge Play Lesson in Humility," *PI,* 2/13/55.

(p. 95) "I don't think I ever thought . . . : Int. with RW, 11/27/01.

(p. 95) "I don't know anyone . . .": "Dramatic Actress," n/p, n/d. In KS bio file at NYPL.

(p. 95) "Kim Stanley's idealistic thirst . . . : Harold Clurman, *All People Are Famous* (New York and London: Harcourt Brace Jovanovich), 245.

(p. 95) "I haven't had a call . . .": Ibid., 117.

(p. 95) his script . . . almost word for word: Walter Wager, ed., *The Playwrights Speak* (New York: Delacorte Press, 1967), 119.

(p. 95) "I hardened it a little . . .": Lee, 2/20/55.

(p. 95) "The naive expression on her face . . .": Undated two-inch clipping beginning "Kim Stanley, who stops the show . . ." In KS biographical file at NYPL.

(p. 96) "Although Inge says Cherie . . .": Lee, 2/20/55.

(p. 97) "If I ask you, 'Is it cold . . .'": Constantin Stanislavski, *An Actor Prepares* (New York: Theatre Arts, Inc., 1936), 67.

(p. 97) "I said to her, 'You're off . . .'": Int. with RW, 11/27/01.

(p. 97) "I never knew how Whitehead . . .": Wahls, 4/5/59.

(p. 97) she looked like a helpless little girl . . . : Marion Kelley, "Kim Asks Critics to be Gentle," *PI,* 2/13/55.

(p. 97) "She constantly did things . . .": Int. with RW, 11/27/01.

(p. 98) a moving and richly rewarding play . . . : R.E.P. Sensenderfer, "William Inge's *Bus Stop* Goes on View at Walnut," *PB,* 2/15/55.

(p. 98) "You know before she has said . . .": Lee, "Kim Stanley Borrows Texas Drawl for Role," *PB*, 2/20/55.

(p. 98) a letdown . . . sprawling . . . : Henry T. Murdock, "Walnut Presents Inge's *Bus Stop*," *PI*, 2/15/55.

(p. 98) "We did not mean to say . . .": "*Bus Stop* B'way Click Has Philly on a Limb; Columnist Swears Off," *Variety*, 3/16/55.

(p. 98) "A single major fault . . .": *Bus Stop* review, *Variety*, 2/16/55, 24.

(p. 99) "It just wasn't working out . . .": Int. with Terry Fay, 6/20/02.

(p. 99) "I thought she would be shaken . . . : Int. with RW, 1/25/02.

(p. 99) a key to the success . . . : Int. with Elaine Stritch, 5/10/02.

(p. 99) Rubyann was shocked . . . : Lee, 2/20/55.

(p. 99) "Cherie just isn't . . .": Gelb, 4/3/55.

(p. 99) "That's not commercial . . .": Wilson, 3/13/55.

(p. 99) she had set a precedent . . . : Gelb, 4/3/55.

(p. 99) "I'm sure I never offered her . . .": Int. with RW, 1/25/02.

(p. 100) "I would think she would be . . .": Int. with Terry Fay, 6/20/02.

(p. 100) "She expected her dress . . .": Int. with Elaine Stritch, 5/10/02.

(p. 100) "When she came to the theater . . .": Int. with Phyllis Love (Osanna Gooding), 3/24/02.

(p. 101) "Having written a wonderful . . .": BA, "Theatre: *Bus Stop*," *NYT*, 3/3/55.

(p. 101) "It has heart, compassion . . . : Robert Coleman, "*Bus Stop*, Loaded With Laughs, A Sure Hit," *DM*, 3/3/55.

(p. 101) "*Bus Stop* has the same irresistible glow . . .": William Hawkins, "*Bus Stop*—All Out for Laughs," *NYWT*, 3/3/55.

(p. 101) "I just couldn't get myself . . .": John Chapman, "New Inge Comedy, *Bus Stop*, Well Acted, but It's Sketchily Written," *NYDN*, 3/3/55.

(p. 101) "Sullenness isn't normally . . .": Walter Kerr, "Theater: *Bus Stop*," *NYHT*, 3/3/55.

(p. 101) "Earlier this season, Miss Kim Stanley . . .": Ibid.

(p. 102) "As the nightclub singer . . .": BA, "Theatre: *Bus Stop*," *NYT*, 3/3/55.

(p. 102) "She now stands as one . . .": "Best Comedy of the Season," *Life*, 3/28/55, 77.

(p. 102) "She owns a perfectly amazing . . .": Maurice Zolotow, "The Season On and Off Broadway: *Bus Stop*," *TA*, May 1955.

(p. 102) "Show-stopping routines in musicals, . . .": Louis Calta, "Canadian Troupe Postpones *Joan*," *NYT*, 3/5/55, 10.

(p. 102) "Even as she's ducking . . .": Kerr, "Theater: *Bus Stop*," *NYHT*, 3/3/55.

(p. 102) "Most of my part in *Bus Stop* . . .": Int. with Elaine Stritch, 5/10/02.

(p. 102) she suspected much of it . . . : Minoff, 2/11/56.

(p. 102) she was making $1300 a week . . . : LK 4/5/55 ltr. to KS. In correspondence 1952–61 folders, Box 665, LK/LOC.

(p. 103) "We met at Downey's . . .": Int. with Ben Gazzara, 7/19/02.

(p. 103) Kim dated Cliff Robertson . . . : Int. with Cliff Robertson, 11/18/01.

(p. 103) "Kim was very restless . . .": Int. with JP Miller, 9/20/01.

(p. 103) Kim also had an affair with Clurman . . . : Int. with Ellen Adler, 3/4/02.

(p. 103) "I wouldn't be surprised . . .": Int. with RW, 3/22/02.

(p. 103) "No! No. Ooh . . .": Int. with Phyllis Love (Osanna Gooding), 3/24/02.

(p. 103) "She was very proud . . .": Int. with Ellen Adler, 3/5/02.

(p. 103) Curt Conway was often around. But . . . : Int. with Phyllis Love, 3/24/02.

(p. 104) very gentle and cultured . . . : Int. with Pat Hingle, 3/24/02.

(p. 104) he was a good match for Kim . . . : Int. with Phyllis Love, 3/24/02.

(p. 104) "He was tense. Extremely tense . . .": Int. with Ellen Adler, 3/27/02.

(p. 104) By October of 1955 . . . Kim was living with Alfred at 54 Riverside Drive: KS 10/8/55 ltr. to RW. In correspondence 1952–61 folders, Box 665, LK/LOC.

(p. 104) recent spread with glamor photos . . . : "Kim for Success," *Vogue*, 4/1/55, 108.

(p. 104) "Miss Stanley showed up . . .": Gelb, 4/3/55.

(p. 104) "Kim Stanley . . . is the first . . . : "Leads a Double Life," *NY Mirror*, 6/19/55.

(p. 105) "When we sold the movie rights . . .": Int. with RW, 11/27/01.

(p. 105) "Anyone who had any largeness . . .": Kobal, 699.

(p. 105) "She simply keeled over . . . : Int. with Ken Pressman, 1/15/02.

(p. 105) "I remember watching Kim . . .": Int. with Tammy Grimes, 8/17/02.

(p. 106) "I didn't realize . . .": Ibid.

(p. 106) seven performances . . . vacationed . . . became ill . . . out of the show . . . : Stage manager's record from *Bus Stop* as reported in Wahls, 4/5/59.

(p. 106) "Kim fell apart . . .": Int. with RW, 11/27/01.

(p. 106) Kim was suffering from paroxysmal tachycardia . . . : Dr. William N. Zahm 10/27/55 ltr. in correspondence 1952–61 folders, Box 665, LK/LOC.

(p. 107) "let's skip that Actors Studio stuff . . .": Lukas, 65.

(p. 107) "I'd never have said . . .": Int. with Elaine Stritch, 5/10/02.

(p. 107) "Once you pushed Kim . . .": Int. with RW, 11/27/01.

(p. 107) Phyllis Love's first husband suffered: Int. with Phyllis Love, 3/24/02.

(p. 107) "a bunch of fatheads": Minoff, 2/11/56.

(p. 108) What is quite obviously chewing . . . : John McClain, "Labels Critics Fatheads," *JM,* 2/20/56, 17.

(p. 108) "It is almost impossible . . .": Whitney Bolton, "Miss Stanley Has Full Right to Statement," *Morning Telegraph,* n/d. In KS bio file at NYPL.

(p. 109) "He was a good, solid movie actor . . .": Int. with TM, 12/28/01.

(p. 109) "With only seconds to go . . .": Minoff, 2/11/56.

(p. 109) "For about the first ten minutes . . .": "Tele Follow-Up Comment," *Variety,* 12/28/53.

(p. 110) "She can take a line . . .": John Crosby, "Some Superb Acting in a Low-Key Drama," *NYHT,* 3/30/56.

(p. 110) "inarticulate drama in which . . .": Ibid.

(p. 111) the movies didn't really want her . . . : Int. with JP Miller, 9/20/01.

(p. 111) "The Donna Reed girl! . . .": Kobal, 692.

(p. 111) "Staring right at me . . .": Ibid., 693.

(p. 111) he's never heard the story . . ." Int. with Eli Wallach, 6/3/02.

(p. 111) "I am calling your attention . . .": LK 11/12/52 ltr. to Jerry Wald in correspondence 1952–61 folders, Box 665, LK/LOC.

(p. 111) Cohn would undoubtedly see Kim: Jerry Walk 11/15/52 ltr. to LK. In correspondence 1952–61 folders, Box 665, LK/LOC.

(p. 111) Cohn wanted . . . Donna Reed . . . because: Bob Thomas, *King Cohn* (New York: G.P. Putnam's Son, 1967), 311.

(p. 112) Lucy Kroll wrote to Harold Hecht . . . : LK 10/19/53 ltr. to Harold Hecht. In correspondence 1952–61 folders, Box 665, LK/LOC.

(p. 112) director Delbert Mann had returned . . ." LK 7/30/54 ltr. to KS. In correspondence 1952–61 folders, Box 665, LK/LOC.

(p. 112) Kroll told Wallis that Kim . . . : LK 11/10/55 ltr. to Hal Wallis. In Hal Wallis papers at AMPAS Library.

(p. 112) "I saw Kim Stanley last night . . .": Paul Nathan memo dated only "Wednesday." In Hal Wallis papers at AMPAS Library.

(p. 112) he was pleased she had agreed . . . : Hal Wallis 12/29/55 ltr. to KS. In Hal Wallis papers at AMPAS Library.

(p. 112) Kim said she was going to make . . . : "Kim Stanley, in City for Visit, Looking Forward to Movie Roles," *AT,* 1/11/56.

(p. 113) a copious and non-negotiable list . . . : Joseph Hazen 1/6/56 memo to Hal Wallis. In Hal Wallis papers at AMPAS Library.

(p. 113) obtaining a Mexican divorce on April 3: Alfred Albelli and Neal Patterson, "Kim Stanley Names Her Daughter's Dad," *NYDN,* 12/30/58.

CHAPTER 6

(p. 114) Mary Tahmin recalls Ryder as . . . : Int. with Mary Tahmin, 5/12/03.

(p. 114) "Alfred was a skyrocket . . .": Int. with JR, 1/16/02.

(p. 114) Laurie Rachel . . . was delivered through Caesarean . . .: LK 4/24/56 note in "Clearing in the Woods/Miscellany" file, Box 662/File 17, LK/LOC.

(p. 115) her name was listed as "Laurie Rachel Conway": "Daddy Emerges: Actor Admits Paternity of Girl, 2," *Newark Evening News,* 12/30/58.

(p. 115) "My answer is that . . . :" Int. with RZ, 1/19/02.

(p. 115) About 1955, Arthur Laurents had a vision: Int. with Arthur Laurents, 1/5/02.

(p. 115) "I'll tell you who else flirted with it . . .": Ibid.

(p. 116) she made it plain that she would not do the film . . . : Joseph Hazen 1/6/56 memo to Hal Wallis re: Kim Stanley in Hal Wallis papers at AMPAS Library.

(p. 116) "You just went in . . .": Int. with Robert Culp, 4/13/02.

(p. 116) "a truly heroic actres . . .": Lukas, 65.

(p. 117) "Concentration is one of the real secrets . . .": Int. with Arthur Laurents, 1/5/02.

(p. 117) "Her laugh is inimitable . . .": Laurents quoted in Roddy McDowall, *Double Exposure* (New York: Delacorte Press, 1966), 92.

(p. 117) "It was a big laugh . . .": Int. with Arthur Laurents, 1/5/02.

(p. 117) She knew there was humor . . . : Laurents in *Double Exposure.*

(p. 117) "She said, 'Kim can lick you all . . .'": Int. with Arthur Laurents, 1/5/02.

(p. 117) "Kim balked . . .": Ibid.

(p. 118) "the method that playwright Laurents . . .": William Peper, "Kim Stanley Again Stars in *Clearing,*" *NYWT,* 1/5/57, 9.

(p. 118) "While the acting is often brilliant . . .": R.E.P. Sensenderfer, "*A Clearing in the Woods* Has Premiere at Walnut," *PB,* 12/27/56.

(p. 118) "Miss Stanley has always had . . .": Jerry Gaghan, "*Clearing* a Foray Into Mental Wonderland," *Philadelphia News,* 12/27/56.

(p. 118) "beguiling and stimulating": Henry T. Murdock, "Walnut Offers World Premiere of Laurents Play," *PI,* 12/27/56.

(p. 118) "All plays . . . that resort . . .": "A Clearing in the Woods," *Variety,* 1/2/57.

(p. 118) "In a flabby season . . .": "New Play in Manhattan," *Time,* 1/21/57.

(p. 118) "Virginia is not an interesting woman": BA, "Theatre: Heroic Attempt," *NYT,* 1/11/57.

(p. 118) "written with grace by a man . . .": BA, *American Drama,* Vol. 12, Nos. 1 and 2 (2003), 19.

(p. 119) "Something tells me I'm going to have . . ." Tom Donnelly, "I Found a Light in the Clearing," *NYWT,* 1/11/57.

(p. 119) "I can only guess . . . :" John Chapman, "*Clearing in the Woods* Fraught With Freud or Something Else," *NYDN,* 1/11/57.

(p. 119) "I am Virginia!": Robert Coleman, "*Clearing in Woods* Is Bore . . . ," *DM,* 1/11/57.

(p. 119) "personally beautiful, plastic in its flow . . .": BA, "Theatre: Heroic Attempt," *NYT,* 1/11/57.

(p. 119) "[The play] is never monotonous": BA, "The Haunted Lady," *NYT,* 1/20/57.

(p. 119) "Kim Stanley wrestles . . .": Coleman, "*Clearing in Woods* Is Bore . . . ," *DM,* 1/11/57.

(p. 119) "Miss Stanley keeps tossing . . .": Chapman, "*Clearing in the Woods* Fraught with Freud or Something Else," *NYDN,* 1/11/57.

(p. 120) "I don't think Miss Stanley . . .": John McClain, "Critics Aren't Her Dish," *JM,* 2/8/57.

(p. 120) "a sort of field-and-stream . . .": "New Play in Manhattan," *Time,* 1/21/57.

(p. 120) *Saturday Review* praised . . .": Review of *A Clearing in Woods,* *SR,* 1/26/57.

(p. 120) "It was a very dysfunctional cast": Int. with Tom Hatcher, 1/18/02.

(p. 120) Kim had a crush on [Onslow Stevens] . . . : Arthur Laurents in *American Drama,* Vol. 12, Nos. 1 and 2 (2003), 82.

(p. 120) "At first, she was wonderful . . .": Int. with Arthur Laurents, 1/5/02.

(p. 120) "He went after her with an axe . . .": Ibid.

(p. 120) minus the salient detail . . . : Int. with Tom Hatcher, 1/18/02.

(p. 121) "There was some bad blood . . .": Int. with Robert Culp, 4/13/02.

(p. 121) "Onslow Stevens was probably wishing": Coleman, "*Clearing in Woods* Is Bore . . . ," *DM,* 1/11/57.

(p. 121) "I'm notoriously bad at guessing . . .": Frances Herridge, "Kim Stanley Fights for *Clearing,*" *NYP,* 1/18/57.

(p. 121) "Alfred Ryder was sitting with her . . .": Int. with Robert Culp, 4/13/02.

(p. 122) "In the short, flickering history . . .": "The Girl on Your Set," *Newsweek,* 6/17/57, 106.

(p. 122) "Kim Stanley . . . is the greatest . . .": "NY Critics Laud Ex-Albuquerquean," *AT,* 6/14/57.

(p. 122) "I've never understood . . .": "The Girl on Your Set," *Newsweek,* 6/17/57, 106.

(p. 122) "It deserved a better fate . . .": William Ewald, "Kim Stanley Speaks Out," UPI article in KS biographical file at NYPL, n/d.

(p. 123) "magnificently controlled and moving": "The Glass Wall," *NYT,* 5/16/57.

(p. 123) "restrained pathos": Sid Shalit, "Sid Caesar Quits NBC," *NYDN* 5/17/57, 57.

(p. 123) "Following Kim Stanley's sensitive portrayal . . .": Marie Torre, "Lawyers Seeking a Fair Shake," *NYHT,* 5/17/57, Sec. 2, 12.

(p. 124) "I didn't think the show . . .": Int. with RH, 8/24/01.

(p. 124) "I said to the director . . .": Int. with Jack Klugman, 1/5/03.

(p. 124) Kim was sent a form in which she was to certify . . . : "Consolidated List of Organizations and Groups Designated Totalitarian, etc." In "Playhouse 90/Clash by Night" file, Box 670, LK/LOC.

(p. 125) "Certainly no one is going to confuse me . . .": Hal Humphrey, "Kim Finally Breaks Down," *Los Angeles Mirror-News,* 6/10/57.

(p. 126) "He moved unobtrusively": "Clifford Odets Dies," *NYT,* 8/16/63, 27.

(p. 126) "We had a great chat . . .": Int. with Lamont Johnson, 6/7/02.

(p. 126) "Clifford was the one I didn't marry . . .": Kobal, 693.

(p. 126) "Clifford had cruelty in him": Ibid., 698.

(p. 126) "I think it was very brief . . ." Int. with Dr. Walt Odets, 4/13/02.

(p. 126) "They had one of the biggest brawls": Int. with Martin Landau, 7/17/03.

(p. 126) "Curt was crazy about Jamie . . ." Ibid.

(p. 127) "There's just one in a generation . . .": Richard C. Wald, "New Chayefsky Screen Play Is Filmed Locally," *NYHT,* n/d. In KS bio file at NYPL.

(p. 127) "Who the hell do you think . . .": LK notes of 5/22/57 conv. with Paddy Chayefsky, Box 664, File 6, LK/LOC.

(p. 127) "Columbia . . . they lied . . .": LK notes of conv. with KS, attached to LK 6/26/57 note of conv. with Lee Moselle, Box 664, File 6, LK/LOC.

(p. 127) "an actress of size": LK notes of 4/29/57 conv. with Paddy Chayefsky, Box 664, File 6, LK/LOC.

(p. 127) Cromwell . . . would not do the movie with Kim . . . : LK notes of 6/27/57 conv. with KS, Box 664, File 6, LK/LOC.

(p. 128) Milton Perlman . . . said she promised to lose weight . . . : Shaun Considine, *Mad As Hell* (New York: Random House, 1994), 131.

(p. 128) "She did not ask for . . . 15 lbs.": LK notes of 6/27/57 conv. with KS, Box 664, File 6, LK/LOC.

(p. 128) Chayefsky had told her the part was hers . . . : LK notes of 7/1/57 conv. with KS, Box 664, File 6, LK/LOC.

(p. 129) "The heat was pushed into the background . . .": Wald, "New Chayefsky Screen Play Is Filmed Locally," NYHT, n/d, in KS bio file at NYPL.

(p. 129) "As the Cadillac was bounced up and down . . .": Ibid.

(p. 129) the most elderly-looking teenager . . . : "Chayevsky's *Goddess,*" *SR,* 5/10/58.

(p. 129) "I've tried to write *The Goddess* as . . .": Richard W. Mason, "Glimpse of a *Goddess,*" *NYT,* 8/18/57.

(p. 129) "Didn't you ask Paddy . . . ?": Ibid.

(p. 130) "They don't care about quality acting . . .": Int. with Gerald Hiken, 1/13/03.

(p. 130) "I was shocked to learn . . .": Joe Hyams, "Kim Stanley Unhappy in Film Debut," *NYHT,* 9/20/57.

(p. 130) Making films . . . like playing poker in the dark: Cecil Smith, "Far Country Puts Freud on the Couch," *LAT,* 11/26/61.

(p. 130) "Kim needed a strong hand . . .": Int. with Martin Landau, 7/17/03.

(p. 131) "The religious conversion scene is . . . : Int. with Betty Lou Holland, 2/26/02.

(p. 131) "What's the movies coming to . . .": Sidney Skolsky column beginning "Watching them make pictures . . ." In KS bio file at NYPL, n/d.

(p. 131) "I felt like an amateur . . .": Hyams, "Kim Stanley Unhappy in Film Debut," *NYHT,* 9/20/57.

(p. 131) "Hollywood is like a Hollywood movie . . .": Ibid.

(p. 132) Joanne Woodward . . . said she . . . did the best Kim Stanley . . . : Arthur Laurents, *Original Story By* (New York: Alfred A. Knopf, 2000), 336.

(p. 132) She had majored in psychology at the University of Texas: Miriam Teichner, "Kim Stanley Had Struggle to Attain Top as Actress," *AT,* 9/3/57.

(p. 132) "Acting, she said, isn't as taxing . . .": "Actress Kim Stanley Is Intelligent, Poised," *AT,* 11/18/57.

(p. 132) "She's the greatest . . .": Irene Thirer, "*The Goddess* Does a Turnabout," *NYP,* 8/27/57.

(p. 132) "Now remember, there should be . . ." Considine, 138.

(p. 132) "Paddy told me she banished him . . . : Int. with Arthur Laurents, 1/5/02.

(p. 132) "We had about twenty extras . . .": Int. with Johnny Friedkin, 3/21/02.

(p. 133) "She cried through the whole thing . . .": Ibid.

(p. 133) Milton Perlman thought she was unhappy because . . . : Considine, 142.

(p. 133) "she was beginning to be . . .": Int. with Elizabeth Wilson, 3/16/02.

(p. 133) the rider to her contract . . . : Milton Perlman 6/10/57 ltr. to LK, in "The Goddess: Contracts and Correspondence" file, Box 664, LK/LOC.

(p. 133) "Kim Stanley told Columbia Pictures . . . : Walter Winchell column beginning "*Marriage Go Round* starring Claudette Colbert . . ." in KS bio file at NYPL.

(p. 133) the film looked like it was in . . . : Considine, 142.

(p. 133) "She doesn't give a damn . . .": Wahls, 4/5/59.

(p. 134) "You have some ideas that you discard . . .": KS interviewed by Martin Agronsky on *Look Here*, 11/18/57.

(p. 135) "Reclining on a couch . . .": *Look Here* review, *Variety*, 11/20/57.

(p. 135) She refused, saying . . . : LK 12/12/57 ltr. to Milton Perlman, in "The Goddess: Contracts and Correspondence" file, Box 664, LK/LOC.

(p. 135) Chayefsky had an attorney send Kim . . . : Lee Moselle 12/12/57 telegram to LK, in "The Goddess: Contracts and Correspondence" file, Box 664, LK/LOC.

(p. 135) she . . . responded with a letter . . . : KS 12/13/57 ltr. to Lee Moselle, in "The Goddess: Contracts and Correspondence" file, Box 664, LK/LOC.

(p. 135) "There was a big piece in the *Telegraph* . . .": Int. with JWR, 4/22/02.

(p. 136) "Tennessee Williams was very keen . . .": Int. with Sir Peter Hall, 5/28/02.

(p. 137) "The Lord Chamberlain was the head of . . .": Ibid.

(p. 137) "I don't know what the fuss . . .": "School Bars Girl Actress," *Daily Telegraph*, 1/25/58, 7.

(p. 138) "I had to violate my own intuition . . .": Tennessee Williams, *Memoirs* (Garden City, N.Y.: Doubleday & Company, Inc., 1975), 169.

(p. 138) "I thought the third act was by far the weakest . . .": Kazan, 543.

(p. 138) Crawford always asked him not to order . . . : Cheryl Crawford, *One Naked Individual* (Indianapolis/New York: Bobbs-Merrill Company, Inc., 1977), 216.

(p. 138) "one third of a world premiere": Cecil Wilson, "Like a Whiplash Across the Face for London," *Daily Mail*, 1/31/58.

(p. 138) "I am happier with the third act . . .": J.C. Trewin, Review of *Cat on a Hot Tin Roof*, *Illustrated London News*, 2/15/58.

(p. 139) "I still prefer the author's third act . . .": Kenneth Tynan, Review of *Cat on a Hot Tin Roof*, *The Observer*, 2/2/58.

(p. 139) "When [Big Daddy] is on stage . . .": W.A. Darlington, "Violence and Brilliance," *Daily Mail*, 1/31/58.

(p. 139) "it struck London last night . . .": Wilson, "Like a Whiplash Across the Face," *Daily Mail*, 1/31/58.

(p. 139) "an evening of many powerful moments . . .": Philip Hope-Wallace, *MG*, 2/1/58.

(p. 139) "In *Cat on a Hot Tin Roof*, there is no . . .": Harold Hobson, "Speak Out, Please," *Sunday Times*, 2/2/58.

(p. 139) the characters behaved with such animal ferocity . . . : "London Sees *Cat*; Opinion Is Divided, *NYT*, 1/31/58.

(p. 139) "a[n] hysterical erotic hotpot . . .": Article in *Cat on a Hot Tin Roof* file in London's Theatre Museum at Covent Garden beginning, "When I saw *Cat on a Hot Tin Roof* in Paris," n/p, n/d.

(p. 139) "pretty good, but does nothing to modify . . .": W.A. Darlington, "London Letter," *NYT*, 2/9/58.

(p. 139) "Only Kim Stanley is exactly right": Review of *Cat on a Hot Tin Roof*, *Harpers and Queen*, 2/18/58.

(p. 139) "Miss Kim Stanley, the gifted Broadway actress . . .": Anthony Cookman, "Neuroses of the South," *Tatler and Bystander*, 2/12/58, 276.

(p. 139) "an artificial, tricksy performance": Derek Monsey, "Even Tennessee Can't Shock Us Now," *Sunday Express*, 2/2/58.

(p. 139) "I feel I ought to be on hand . . .": Tennessee Williams, *Five O'Clock Angel* (New York: Alfred A. Knopf, 1990), 154.

(p. 140) "Barbara Bel Geddes was excellent . . .": Int. with Sir Peter Hall, 5/28/02.

(p. 140) "She was charming": Kobal, 701.

(p. 140) "Most horrendous time . . .": LK notes of 3/20/59 conv. with Helen Hayes, in "A Touch of the Poet: Notes" file, Box 672, LK/LOC.

(p. 140) "It was difficult for the panel of judges . . .": LK 1/17/58 ltr. to KS, Box 665, File 1, LK/LOC.

(p. 140) "I have passed on your love to Nathan . . .": LK 1/10/58 ltr. to KS, Box 665, File 1, LK/LOC.

(p. 140) "I suspect she'll be presented to the Queen . . .": LK 2/5/58 ltr. to KS, in "Cat on a Hot Tin Roof: Contracts and Correspondence" file, Box 662, LK/LOC.

(p. 140) "I was at the opening of Beckett's *Endgame* . . .": Ibid.

(p. 141) "They talk to you as a character . . .": Kobal, 696.

(p. 141) Kim sent Lucy Kroll an anxious telegram . . . : KS 4/25/58 telegram to LK, in "The Goddess: Contracts and Correspondence" file, Box 664, LK/LOC.

(p. 142) "Very few times does the camera cut away from her . . .": Michael Morrison 12/21/02 e-mail to JK.

(p. 142) Kim asked Marie Kenny . . . where her hands . . . : Considine, 134.

(p. 142) "Get set for heartbreak . . .": Bosley Crowther, Review of *The Goddess, NYT,* 6/25/58.

(p. 142) "a morbid drama unrelieved . . .": Wanda Hale, "55th. St. Playhouse Shows *The Goddess,*" *NYDN,* in KS bio file at NYPL, n/d.

(p. 143) it could have been about a "harassed heroine" . . . : Rose Pelswick, "Chayefsky Film Uneven," *JM,* 6/25/58.

(p. 143) the character delineation was like Eugene O'Neill . . . : Wald, "New Chayefsky Screen Play Is Filmed Locally," *NYHT,* in KS bio file NYPL, n/d.

(p. 143) she expressed disappointment that . . .": Frances Herridge, "Kim Stanley: Hard-to-Please Critic," *NYP,* 12/1/58.

(p. 143) "It was a great script . . .": Ross, 10/21/61.

(p. 143) "Kim Stanley . . . gives a frenzied portrayal . . .": Wanda Hale, "55th. St. Playhouse Shows *The Goddess,*" *NYDN,* in KS bio file at NYPL, n/d.

(p. 144) "Every time I play Georgette . . .": Cecilie Leslie, profile of KS to accompany article on *The Travelling Lady,* n/p, in KS bio file in London's Theatre Museum at Covent Garden.

(p. 144) "At first, my part in *Traveling Lady*": Leslie, "The Travelling Lady," n/p, in Kim Stanley bio file in London's Theatre Museum at Covent Garden.

(p. 144) "Are you interested?" Clurman asked . . . : "Kim Stanley" press release beginning "Only four lines of dialogue . . ." in KS bio file at NYPL.

(p. 145) As Clurman later recalled . . . : Clurman, 269.

(p. 145) "Bob [Whitehead] was really jubilant . . .": LK 5/22/58 ltr. to KS, Box 672, File 10, LK/LOC.

(p. 145) both Hayes and Portman did make financial concessions . . . : LK telegram to KS beginning "Unsuccessful phoning you" in "A Touch of the Poet: Contracts and Correspondence" file, Box 672, LK/LOC.

(p. 146) "I don't recall ever being inside . . .": Int. with RZ, 1/22/03.

(p. 146) "She came up to me and said . . .": Int. with Betty Lou Holland, 2/26/02.

(p. 146) "He talked too much . . .": Helen Hayes and Katherine Hatch, *My Life in Three Acts* (New York: Harcourt Brace Jovanovich, 1990), 199.

(p. 146) Eric Portman . . . refused to accept direction from Clurman . . . : "*Poet* An Unpleasant Overture; Stanley: 'Mr. Portman, I Presume,'" *Variety,* 3/25/59, 1.

(p. 147) Kim . . . "drove herself mercilessly . . .": Hayes and Hatch, 200.

(p. 147) "Bob Whitehead . . . promised me out of town . . .": Kobal, 702.

(p. 147) "A brilliant cast was recalled . . .": Peggy Doyle, "Boston Wildly Cheers *A Touch of the Poet,*" *Boston American,* 9/16/58.

(p. 147) "a production long to be remembered . . .": A. Maloney, "*Touch of the Poet* Outstanding," *Boston Traveler,* 9/16/58.

(p. 147) Portman was not enunciating his lines . . . : Untitled brief beginning "Helen Hayes reportedly complained . . ." in KS bio file NYPL.

(p. 147) "Whatever happens in New York . . .": Elliot Norton, "Kim Stanley Emerges as True Artist in *Poet,*" *Boston Daily Record,* 9/30/58.

(p. 148) "When we first opened . . .": Frances Herridge, "Kim Stanley: Hard-to-Please Critic," *NYP,* 12/1/58.

(p. 148) "The effect . . . is electric . . .": BA, "Theatre: Eugene O'Neill's *A Touch of the Poet,*" *NYT,* 10/3/58.

(p. 148) "magnificent," "a masterpiece" . . . : Robert Coleman, "*Touch of Poet* Magnificent," *DM,* 10/3/58.

(p. 148) the play was not great O'Neill . . . : John Chapman, "Portman, Hayes and Stanley Magnificent in *Touch of Poet,*" *NYDN,* 10/3/58.

(p. 148) it was one of O'Neill's mastodonic dramas . . . : Richard Watts, "Eugene O'Neill's *Touch of the Poet,*" *NYP,* 10/3/58.

(p. 148) Con Melody an impossible fake and a bore . . . : John McClain, "O'Neill Again Proves He's Incomparable," *JM,* 10/3/58.

(p. 148) "the core of the production": Herbert Whittaker, "A Touch of the Poet," *NYHT,* 10/3/58.

(p. 148) *A Touch of the Poet* brings us the two finest actresses . . .": BA, "Theatre: *A Touch of the Poet,*" *NYT,* 10/3/58.

(p. 149) "Although not of Irish parentage . . .": Edward L. Brennan, "O'Neill's *Touch of the Poet*," *Irish Echo,* 12/20/58.

(p. 149) "I gave three performances . . .": Don Ross, "Kim Stanley Says Her Role is 'Difficult But Not Painful,'" *NYHT,* 1/11/59.

(p. 149) "You tell Jamie and me . . .": Int. with Lisa Conway, 9/9/01.

(p. 150) "Kim Stanley, whose high-voltage emoting . . .": "Kim Stanley Names Daughter's Father," *Daily Mirror,* 12/30/58, 4.

(p. 150) Kim asked the court to approve the issuance . . . : "Daddy Emerges: Actor Admits Paternity of Girl, 2," *Newark Evening News,* 12/30/58.

(p. 150) Ryder acknowledged paternity in an affidavit . . . : Ibid.

(p. 150) "It was the only honest thing to do . . .": Wahls, 4/5/59.

(p. 150) because of a bad cold, Kim had played the last five weeks . . . : LK 11/25/5 ltr. to RW, Box 672, LK/LOC.

(p. 150) she felt the onset of her virus just before her big scene . . . : Bob Williams and Edward Kossner, "Kim Stanley's Exit: A Touch of Mystery," *NYP,* 3/21/59.

(p. 150) Kim . . . out of the show thirty-one times: Wahls, 4/5/59.

(p. 151) "Feeling better?": Sidney Fields, "No Touch of the Poet in Kim Vs. Eric," *DM,* 4/7/59.

(p. 151) "Eric Portman was very difficult . . .": Int. with RW, 1/25/02.

(p. 151) "He wasn't a darling companion . . .": Ibid.

(p. 151) "He accused her of drinking . . .": Int. with RW, 11/27/01.

(p. 151) Kim keeping a pint-size silver flask . . . : Int. with Patricia Frye, 2/6/04.

(p. 151) her income . . . : KS income for 1955–57 from KS "income tax" file, Box 667, LK/LOC.

(p. 151) Whitehead told Lucy Kroll he would accept . . . : LK notes of 3/12/59 meeting with KS and RW, in "A Touch of the Poet: Notes" file, Box 672, LK/LOC.

(p. 151) Kim decided she would not accept illness . . . : LK note of convs. with Barry Hymes and Kim in "A Touch of the Poet: Notes" file, Box 672, LK/LOC.

(p. 152) It would be difficult to protect Kim . . . : LK 3/13/59 note beginning "I called Bob for mechanics . . ." in "A Touch of the Poet: Notes" file, Box 672, LK/LOC.

(p. 152) "a goddamn shame": LK 3/13/59 note of conv. with RW beginning "Sympathetic . . . to Kim . . ." in "A Touch of the Poet: Notes" file, Box 672, LK/LOC.

(p. 152) Calta felt Kim's remarks . . . : LK 3/20/59 note beginning "Kim and Bob talked and Kim . . ." in "A Touch of the Poet: Notes" file, Box 672, LK/LOC.

(p. 152) "Shubert Alley's most puzzling mystery . . . : Arthur Gelb, "Portman Named by Kim Stanley," *NYT,* 3/23/59.

(p. 152) "Mr. Portman's behavior had annoyed me . . .": Joseph McNamara, "Kim Dislikes Eric's Touch in the *Poet,*" *JM,* 3/23/59.

(p. 152) "There's one scene where he . . .": Sidney Fields, "Part One: She Who Got Slapped," *DM,* 4/6/59.

(p. 153) "He possibly did . . .": Int. with RW, 11/27/01.

(p. 153) "I am very sorry for Miss Stanley . . .": McNamara, "Kim Dislikes Eric's Touch in the *Poet,*" *JM,* 3/23/59.

(p. 153) "I don't go bashing people . . .": Fields, "No Touch of the Poet in Kim Vs. Eric," *DM,* 4/7/59.

(p. 153) "Broadway's most spectacular feline feud . . . : "One Touch of . . .," *Time,* 4/6/59, 45.

(p. 153) "There have never been any differences . . .": Gelb, "Portman Named by Kim Stanley," *NYT,* 3/23/59.

(p. 154) "Portman was just a red herring . . .": "One Touch of . . .," *Time,* 4/6/59, 45.

(p. 154) Kim . . . couldn't stand opening her eyes . . . : "*Poet* An Unpleasant Overture," *Variety,* 3/25/59, 1.

(p. 154) "Probably there were a few evenings . . .": Int. with RW, 1/25/02.

(p. 154) "Cover-up for Kim . . . vicious woman . . .": LK 3/21/59 note of conv. with Helen Hayes in "A Touch of the Poet: Notes" file, Box 672, LK/LOC.

(p. 154) "Frankly I am in a rage . . .": Nathan Kroll 3/21/59 ltr. to Helen Hayes, Box 672, File 10, LK/LOC.

(p. 154) "She blamed me for not keeping order . . .": Int. with RW, 1/25/02.

(p. 154) "Nothing will wipe out the memory . . . : "Helen Hayes Has Own Slant on Kim Stanley," *Variety,* 4/22/59, 1.

(p. 155) "I would never want to go back . . .": Frances Herridge, "Kim Stanley is Winning the Battle," *NYP,* 10/30/59.

(p. 155) "Is Kim deliberately trying . . .": Wahls, 4/5/59.

(p. 155) "Miss Stanley stomped out . . .": John Watson, "Lioness in April Purrs in October," *JM*, 10/25/59.

(p. 155) "I think the offer . . .": Arthur Gelb, "Understudy Quits KS Role," *NYT*, 3/27/59.

(p. 155) "Actors have been mistreated . . .": Ibid.

(p. 155) "Nancy not a genius": LK notes of 3/27/59 conv. with RW in "A Touch of the Poet: Notes" file, Box 672, LK/LOC.

(p. 156) Lewis had a sure touch . . . : Int. with Eli Wallach, 4/3/03.

(p. 156) "opulent . . . no toothpick . . .": Watson, "Lioness in April Purrs in October," *JM*, 10/25/59.

(p. 156) "After the show, we went back . . .": Int. with Flo Miller Shields, 12/13/02.

(p. 156) "I actually got feelings from it . . .": Ross, 10/21/61, 59.

(p. 157) "I think it should come from within . . .": Short captioned "Illusion," *NYT*, 9/20/59.

(p. 157) "Every day, another Lea peeled off her . . .": Gilbert Millstein, "Theatre Arts Gallery: Kim Stanley," *TA*, November 1958, 14.

(p. 157) "Colette, in her book . . .": Int. with TM, 9/18/01.

(p. 157) "Think Bwy. will like": R. Coe telegram to S. Zolotow in "Cheri" file at NYPL.

(p. 157) "With *Lady Chatterley's Lover* . . .": "Cheri," *Variety*, 9/23/59, 76.

(p. 158) "that upper area where a woman's . . .": Watson, "Lioness in April Purrs in October," *JM*, 10/25/59.

(p. 158) "The atmosphere surrounding this play . . .": Ross, "Kim Stanley Says Her Role Is 'Difficult but Not Painful,'" NYHT, 1/11/59.

(p. 158) "There's a quality in [Lea] . . .": Kenneth Tynan, "Eros Misconstrued," NY, 10/24/59, 91.

(p. 158) "[a] startlingly dull, prosaic . . .": Richard Watts Jr., "Sad Fate of Two Colette Novels," *NYP*, 10/13/59.

(p. 158) it could be made into a French musical . . . : John Chapman, "*Cheri* a Sex-Packed Romance That Belasco Would Have Loved," *NYDN*, 10/13/59.

(p. 158) "as far as we're concerned . . .": Robert Coleman, "Loos' Luck Runs Out in *Cheri*," *DM*, 10/13/59.

(p. 158) "Colette would have thought of you . . .": Herridge, "Kim Stanley Is Winning the Battle," *NYP*, 10/30/59.

(p. 158) "as French as corn flakes": Ibid.

(p. 158) "Miss Stanley mops up . . .": Review of *Cheri*, *Variety*, 10/14/59, 56.

(p. 158) "Kim Stanley is magnificent . . .": Frank Aston, "*Cheri* Makes Entrance at Morosco Theater," *NYWT*, 10/13/59.

(p. 159) "Everyone knows by now . . .": Richard Watts Jr., "Sad Fate of Two Colette Novels," *NYP*, 10/13/59.

(p. 159) "The evening requires that . . .": Walter Kerr, "Cheri," *NYHT*, 10/13/59.

(p. 159) "I said *Private Lives* . . .": Int. with Arthur Laurents, 1/5/02.

(p. 159) "Unless she went into a frenzy . . .": Int. with Anne Jackson, 10/23/01.

(p. 160) Alfred Ryder filed a petition . . . : "Inside Stuff—Legit," *Variety*, 11/4/59, 78.

(p. 160) After he paid about $8,000 . . . : "In the Matter of Alfred Ryder," Bankruptcy Docket of John E. Joyce #94489, U.S. District Court of Manhattan, 10/23/59.

(p. 160) "Howard had a serious . . .": Int. with Lucille Reid Brock, 6/14/02.

(p. 160) Kim would tell her children that he had lost . . . : Int. with RZ, 1/19/02.

(p. 161) Kim . . . would abandon acting: "Kim Stanley to Quit for Year," *NYT*, 12/1/59, 47.

(p. 161) she didn't intend to stir from her . . . apartment . . . : Gael Greene, "Kim Stanley Taking Stage Recess for Role of Mother and Citizen," *NYP*, 12/2/59.

(p. 162) "She was in a very good mood . . .": Int. with HF, 7/2/03.

(p. 162) "Car chases are the polyester suits . . .": JK, *The Man in the Shadows* (Rutgers University Press, 1997), 181.

(p. 162) "There was always something strange and new . . .": Int. with JC, 11/16/01.

(p. 163) "Every actress must choose . . .": Steve Richards, "She Knows What She Wants," *Sunday News*, 12/7/58.

(p. 163) "I don't think that she functioned . . .": Int. with RW, 11/27/01.

(p. 163) "I have three children. I want . . .": Ross, "Kim Stanley Says Here Role is 'Difficult but Not Painful," NYHT, 1/11/59.

(p. 163) "She sat at the front table . . .": Int. with RH, 8/21/01.

(p. 164) In November of 1956 . . . Fred Coe sent the script to Kim: Fred Coe 11/20/56 ltr. to LK, Box 673, File 6, LK/LOC.

(p. 164) "She was so much a shikse . . .": Int. with William Gibson, 1/8/02.

(p. 164) "I wanted to kill her . . .": Alan Schneider, *Entrances: An American Director's Journey* (New York: Viking, 1986), 279.

(p. 164) "After one rehearsal . . .": Int. with Kevin McCarthy, 4/5/02.

(p. 164) Kim . . . had a miscarriage: Int. with Mary Tahmin, 5/12/03.

(p. 164) Newspaper reports . . . support Tahmin's version: See, for example, "Recovering," *NYDN*, 3/24/60, 81, and "Kim Stanley Leaves Hospital," *NYT*, 3/25/60.

(p. 164) Kim worried everyone would say . . .": LK 3/17/60 note beginning "Kim not up for three days . . . Can't do it," Box 673, File 7, LK/LOC.

CHAPTER 7

(p. 192) "When we would get to the part . . .": Int. with Anna Marie Barlow, 9/3/03.

(p. 192) "Both Lucy Kroll and Audrey Wood . . .": A.M. Barlow ltr. to JK, 1/12/04.

(p. 192) "There were no costumes . . .": Int. with Lou Gossett Jr., 9/26/03.

(p. 193) Davis . . . remembers watching . . . : Sylvia Davis ltr. to JK, 10/16/02.

(p. 193) "When we started run-throughs . . .": Int. with Michael Tolan, 3/6/02.

(p. 193) "I considered her to be . . .": Int. with James Earl Jones, 10/2/03.

(p. 193) "She would be more sensitive . . .": Int. with Lou Gossett Jr., 9/26/03.

(p. 193) $50,000 of the play's $125,000 capitalization . . . : Stuart Little, "*Taffy* Seeks New Producer, Suspends for Lack of Money," *NYHT*, 10/21/60.

(p. 194) "something that was quite common . . .": Int. with James Earl Jones, 10/2/03.

(p. 194) "My father was very intense, very intellectual . . .": Int. with RZ, 11/3/01.

(p. 194) "All children should be raised . . .": Int. with RZ, 1/19/02.

(p. 194) Lillian Ross . . . remembers Kim preparing . . . : Int. with Lillian Ross, 4/22/02.

(p. 194) "Kim was not a good cook . . .": Int. with RZ, 11/3/01.

(p. 194) "She wanted to be a housewife . . .": Int. with HD, 11/9/01.

(p. 195) Real-estate mogul Roger Stevens was . . . dubious of the benefits . . . : Don Ross, "The First Play About Freud," article, Box 664, file 1, LK/LOC.

(p. 195) "Lynn Austin was the production supervisor . . .": Int. with HD, 11/9/01.

(p. 195) "She is an extremely sensitive instrument . . .": "A Switch: He Tells Wife What to Do," article in Alfred Ryder file at AMPAS Library.

(p. 195) "I find . . . it's a great advantage . . .": Ross, "The First Play about Freud," article, Box 664, File 1, LK/LOC.

(p. 195) "What transpired between the star and her husband . . .": Remarks read by HD at KS memorial service at Actors Studio, 10/12/01.

(p. 195) "I hated that couch": Robert Wahls, "Blonde, Lush Kim . . . ," *NYDN*, 7/9/61.

(p. 195) "During my hatred . . .": Ibid.

(p. 196) "a many-faceted, hard jewel . . .": Ross, 10/21/61.

(p. 196) "burst[ing] through the surface . . .": Richard P. Cooke, "Freud's Breakthrough," *Wall Street Journal*, 4/6/61.

(p. 196) "like a pistol shot in a silent tomb": Whitney Bolton, "Theatre," *NY Morning Telegraph*, 4/11/61.

(p. 196) "In order to do the scream . . .": Erica Munk, *Stanislavski and America: An Anthology from the Tulane Drama Review* (1966), 167.

(p. 196) "Kim says Steve is completely withdrawn . . ." LK 3/21/61 ltr. to HF, Box 663, File 6, LK/LOC.

(p. 197) "He would mumble his way . . . : Int. with HD, 11/9/01.

(p. 197) "Having spent all her time at the Actors Studio . . .": HD remarks at KS memorial service at Actors Studio, 10/12/01.

(p. 197) "Kim was a star in the true sense . . .": Ibid.

(p. 197) "Certain of the lines . . . she delivered . . .": HD, *The Actress* (New York: Simon and Schuster, 1978), 252

(p. 197) "lovely, loveable, alcoholic, psychotic, darling Kit": Ibid., 230.

(p. 198) "She would be doing this 'floating' thing . . .": Int. with Salome Jens, 10/8/03.

(p. 198) "At one of those performances . . .": Ibid.

(p. 198) "Even though officially they pretended . . .": Int. with Robert Ball, 6/8/03.

(p. 199) The four-year-old picked up a makeup pencil . . . : Int. with RZ, 1/19/02.

(p. 199) "[T]autly written play about Dr. Sigmund Freud . . .": Robert Coleman, "*Country* Tense Play on Freud," *New York Mirror,* 4/5/61.

(p. 199) "Mr. Denker has captured . . .": Howard Taubman, "Theatre: Freud Is Key Figure in Gripping Drama," *NYT,* 4/5/61.

(p. 199) "Henry Denker's *A Far Country* is a psychiatric detective story . . .": Frank Ashton, "Far Country Roams Stage of Music Box," *NYWT,* 4/5/61.

(p. 199) "It has some difficulties": Walter Kerr, "First Night Report," *NYHT,* 4/5/61.

(p. 199) "What Miss Stanley does that is most stunning . . .": Ibid.

(p. 200) "Kim Stanley is as gifted . . .": John McClain, "Kim Stanley at Gifted Best," *JM,* 4/5/61.

(p. 200) "Miss Stanley plays to perfection . . .": "First into the Depths," *Newsweek,* 4/17/61, 69.

(p. 200) "Sitting in the front row of the theater . . .": Larry Moss, *The Intent to Live: Achieving Your True Potential as an Actor* (New York: Bantam Books, 2005), 2.

(p. 201) "My colleagues . . . seem to believe . . .": Bolton, "Theatre," *NY Morning Telegraph,* 4/11/61.

(p. 201) "has a figure out of Titian or Rubens": Review of *A Far Country, Cue,* 4/15/61.

(p. 201) "illuminates the stage with her buxom fragility": Stanley Eichelbaum, "Magnificent Kim Stanley Transcends Freudian Slips," Box 664, File 1, LK papers at LOC.

(p. 201) "Kim paced her dressing room": Wahls, "Blonde, Lush Kim . . . ," *NYDN,* 7/9/61.

(p. 201) he rarely looked at the script and finished . . . to solid applause: Stuart W. Little, "Director of *A Far Country* Substitutes for Ailing Star," *NYHT,* 4/13/61.

(p. 202) "They talk as if they are a little bit angry . . .": William Glover, "Two Stage Sides," *Newark Evening News,* 5/21/61.

(p. 202) "I hate you . . .": William Peper, "Kim Stanley Critical of Own Work," *NYWT,* 6/12/61.

(p. 202) she found herself short $200 . . . : Eva Weith ltr. to Weissberger & Frosch, 4/14/61, Box 663, File 6, LK/LOC.

(p. 202) she would be short $4,000 on the closing costs . . . : Anonymous 10/19/62 memo to LK, Box 661, File 11, LK/LOC.

(p. 202) "She missed thirty-eight performances . . .": Int. with HD, 11/9/01.

(p. 203) "It was an impossible part to play . . .": Int. with Michael Tolan, 3/6/02.

(p. 204) "The curtain did not rise . . .": HD remarks at KS memorial service at Actors Studio, 10/12/01.

(p. 204) "The evening concluded after midnight . . .": James Powers, Review of *A Far Country, HR,* 12/1/61.

(p. 204) "Did [Kim] shine that night . . .": HD remarks at KS memorial service at Actors Studio, 10/12/01.

(p. 204) "We see Freud driving to a new frontier . . .": Patterson Greene, "Long Wait for Curtain at Hartford Well Worthwhile," Box 664, File 1, LK/LOC.

(p. 204) "Miss Stanley is worth waiting any length of time . . . : Harrison Carroll, *Herald-Express,* 11/30/61.

(p. 204) "Just to watch the delicate nuances . . .": Dick Williams, "A Far Country Absorbing Play of Freud Case," *LA Mirror,* 11/30/61.

(p. 204) "She was a very attractive, warm, smart . . .": Int. with Lillian Ross, 4/22/02.

(p. 205) "Unlike other artists, the actor . . .": Lillian Ross, *Here but Not Here* (Washington, DC: Counterpoint, 1998), 65.

(p. 205) she said she had received a B.A. in psychology . . . : Ross, 10/21/61.

(p. 205) "My father always thought acting was very silly . . .": Ibid.

(p. 206) she talked about playing Ophelia . . . : Whitney Bolton, "The Theatre: Kim Stanley Sticks by Critics Quote," *NY Morning Telegraph,* 11/4/58.

(p. 206) she held out the possibility of playing Gertrude . . . : Robert Wahls, "Kim Still Perfecting That 'French Touch,'" *NYDN,* 11/22/59.

(p. 206) she was back to Ophelia . . . : Ross, 10/21/61.

(p. 206) "She was just terrible to Buddy Ebsen . . .": Int. with Patricia Neal, 6/15/02.

(p. 206) "He played all his scenes . . .": Int. with TM, 2/14/04.

(p. 206) "Pat Neal called me from the airport . . .": Int. with TM, 9/18/01.

(p. 207) She apparently did it to get money . . . : Walt Odets message on JK's answering machine, 12/14/03.

(p. 207) "The producer and director have asked . . .": LK 10/9/62 ltr. to KS, Box 661, File 10, LK/LOC.

(p. 207) "Kim asked me to [say] . . .": 10/10/62 LK ltr. to John Bennett, Box 661, File 10, LK/LOC.

(p. 207) "Vince behaved like the perfect angel . . .": Paul Robert Coyle, "*Ben Casey:* High Medical Melodrama," *Emmy Magazine,* March/April 1984, 38.

(p. 207) "She called me 'Mr. Pollack' . . .": Int. with Sydney Pollack, 8/16/02.

(p. 208) "I knew right away what the problem was . . .": Ibid.

(p. 209) "Kim Stanley [was] outstanding . . .": *Ben Casey* review, HR, 1/23/63.

(p. 209) "Miss Stanley . . . pull[ed] out . . .": *Ben Casey* review, *Variety*, 1/23/63.

(p. 209) Horton Foote says it was Alan Pakula's idea: "The Song of the Mockingbird," mini-documentary on *To Kill a Mockingbird* videocassette.

(p. 210) "She was not very commercial . . .": Int. with HF, 12/10/01.

(p. 210) Pakula-Mulligan Productions paid her $500: LK 11/20/62 note, Box 672, File 4, LK/LOC.

(p. 210) Jamie remembered wandering through . . . : Int. with JC, 11/16/01.

(p. 210) "It was a suburban area . . .": Int. with RZ, 11/3/01.

(p. 211) "the world's greatest mother": Lukas, 65.

(p. 211) "She was funny and cheerful . . . : Int. with RZ, 11/3/01.

(p. 211) "She was somewhat opinionated . . .": Int. with JC, 11/16/01.

(p. 211) "I was told her son . . .": Int. with Patricia Neal, 6/15/02.

(p. 211) "Jamie has felt separate . . .": Int. with JR, 10/9/01.

(p. 211) "The children go to the local public school . . .": Lukas, 65.

(p. 211) "Kim would read all the parts . . .": Int. with Walt Odets, 4/13/02.

(p. 211) one night she led Alfred and several friends . . . : RZ 1/25/02 e-mail to JK.

(p. 212) "eclectic Kim": Int. with RZ, 1/19/02.

(p. 212) "As was Kim's . . .": Ibid.

(p. 212) "a really strong person . . .": Int. with JC, 11/16/01.

(p. 212) "a little Texas firecracker . . .": Int. with RZ, 11/3/01.

(p. 212) "We had a small tomato garden . . .": JC 11/6/02 e-mail to JK.

(p. 213) "We really had one hell of a childhood . . .": Int. with JC, 11/16/01.

(p. 213) "All these people were really . . .": Int. with RZ, 11/3/01.

(p. 213) "I do remember some screaming fights . . .": Ibid.

(p. 214) It took a personal pilgrimage to Congers . . . : Tony Richardson, *The Long-Distance Runner* (New York: William Morrow and Company, Inc., 1993), 172.

(p. 214) Stevens . . . was not so keen on the play but was keen on Kim . . . : Ibid.

(p. 214) "never, before or since, have I worked with someone . . .": Ibid., 173.

(p. 215) "Kim would make me cry . . ." : Int. with Mitch Erickson, 9/22/01.

(p. 215) "She drove Audrey Wood . . . ": Int. with Mitch Erickson, 12/27/03.

(p. 215) Richardson found [Inge] inert and passive . . . : Richardson 175.

(p. 215) "a slightly catatonic young actor . . .": Ibid., 173.

(p. 215) "go out there willing to fail . . .": Int. with Bonnie Bartlett, 6/25/02.

(p. 215) "We had to place her with a family . . .": Ibid.

(p. 216) "I start to philosophize . . .": Int. with Tom Bosley, 7/26/02.

(p. 216) "Kim had a couple of drinks . . .": Ibid.

(p. 216) Inge's best play yet . . . : Richard L. Coe, "Inge Returns in Rare Form," *Washington Post*, 1/17/63.

(p. 216) "This . . . is a family that could startle . . .": Jay Carmody, "It's Pitch Black Now up Those Inge Stairs," *Washington Star*, 1/17/63, A-16.

(p. 216) "These people just haven't got the stuff . . .": Tom Donnelly, "Another Inge Binge," *NYDN*, 1/17/63, 48.

(p. 217) "This could have been a strikingly good . . .": Norman Nadel, *Natural Affection* review, *NYWT*, 2/1/63.

(p. 217) "a baneful bouquet of human unhappiness . . .": Richard Cooke, "Unnatural Affection," *Wall Street Journal*, 2/4/63.

(p. 217) "*Natural Affection* has the roiling, quivering hysteria . . .": "Oedipus Hex," *Time*, 2/8/63.

(p. 217) "At the climax, [a] neighbor wanders in . . .": Int. with Tom Bosley, 7/26/02.

(p. 218) "The only way to account for *Natural Affection*: Michael Smith, "Inge and Others," *Village Voice*, 2/7/63.

(p. 218) "Kim Stanley is an actress . . .": "Natural Affliction," *Newsweek*, 2/11/63.

(p. 218) "In this appallingly difficult part . . .": Anthony West, "The Best Actress, and Others," *Show*, May 1963, 20.

(p. 218) "For a woman who has shown so little interest . . .": Lukas, 65.

(p. 220) "Alfred was drunk all the time . . .": Int. with Joanna Frank, 10/11/02.

(p. 220) "She had a bad father problem . . .": Int. with RH, 8/24/01.

(p. 220) "I just don't think she was very stable": Int. with Anne Jackson, 10/23/01.

(p. 220) "I don't think Kim could live . . .": Int. with Bonnie Bartlett, 6/25/02.

(p. 220) "No matter what you do in a film . . .": Ross, 10/21/61.

(p. 221) "We offered it to a number of people . . .": Int. with BF, 1/16/02.

(p. 221) "The complexity of dramatic impression . . .": Int. with Sir Richard Attenborough, 1/23/02.

(p. 221) "taking up 99 percent . . . ": Richard Attenborough ltr. to LK, 6/25/63, Box 670, File 9, LK/LOC.

(p. 221) "I'm out of my head to see . . .": KS ltr. to LK, rec'd. 7/2/63, Box 670, File 1, LK/LOC.

(p. 222) "Who was this impostor . . .": Remarks by RZ at KS memorial service at College of Santa Fe, 9/9/01.

(p. 222) Joe Siegel . . . went to England several times to visit Kim . . . : Int. with Sally Radin, 9/15/02.

(p. 222) "I can't tell anything . . .": KS ltr. to LK, rec'd. 7/2/63, Box 670, File 1, LK/LOC.

(p. 222) "That figures . . . the last owner . . .": Int. with BF, 1/16/02.

(p. 222) "When we built a replica of the seance room . . .": Ibid.

(p. 222) "She always went beyond the evidence . . .": BF remarks read at KS memorial service at the Actors Studio, 10/12/01.

(p. 223) "She was an extraordinary actress . . .": Int. with Sir Richard Attenborough, 1/23/02.

(p. 223) "It was quite complicated when I put my actor's hat on . . ." Ibid.

(p. 223) "There was one notable occasion . . .": Int. with BF, 1/16/02.

(p. 224) "I can't recall, apart from the problems she gave herself . . .": Ibid.

(p. 224) "She would leave the set . . .": Int. with Sir Richard Attenborough, 1/23/02.

(p. 224) "On one occasion I asked the wardrobe mistress . . .": Int. with BF, 1/16/02.

(p. 224) "I was sitting at home one night . . .": Ibid.

(p. 224) "Another myth that Miss Stanley is quick to destroy . . .": Stephen Watts, "On Camera Again," *NYT,* 9/8/63.

(p. 225) "The men never cease . . .": KS ltr. to LK, rec'd. 7/2/63, Box 670, File 1, LK/LOC.

(p. 225) unaware that a movie was being made, several prominent Londoners . . . : *Seance on a Wet Afternoon* review, *Variety,* 6/10/64.

(p. 226) As Newsweek astutely noted . . . : "Dust in the Eye," *Newsweek,* 11/16/64.

(p. 226) "I am trying to finalize . . .": BF 10/24/63 ltr. to LK, Box 670, File 10, LK/LOC.

(p. 226) "a superbly atmospheric film": Michael Thornton, "Attenborough Can Do No Wrong," *London Express,* 6/7/64.

(p. 226) "an original, intensely exciting film . . .": Philip Oakes, "Fear in the Afternoon," *Sunday Telegraph,* 6/7/64.

(p. 226) "With her ravaged beauty . . .": "British—That's the Spirit," *Evening News and Star,* 6/4/64.

(p. 226) "[The] lady medium [is] lambently played: Oakes, "Fear in the Afternoon," *Sunday Telegraph,* 6/7/64.

(p. 226) "Kim Stanley's performance as the half-mad wife . . . : Ernest Betts, "It's All in the Mind . . .," *The People,* 6/7/64.

(p. 226) "Kim Stanley does it horribly well . . .": Penelope Gilliatt, "The Malevolent Medium," *Observer,* 6/7/64.

(p. 227) the Berlin Film Festival refused to accept . . . : Leonard Mosley, "Studies in Obsession: This Is Something to Cherish," *Daily Express,* 6/3/64.

(p. 227) "Attendance figures everywhere . . .": BF 8/4/64 ltr. to LK, Box 670, File 11, LK/LOC.

(p. 227) An account [Kim] had . . . was overdrawn: LK 6/27/63 ltr. to KS, Box 670, File 9, LK/LOC.

(p. 227) "as to your Congers bank account . . .": LK 7/3/63 ltr. to KS, Box 670, File 10, LK/LOC.

(p. 227) "the perfect psychological suspense thriller . . .": Judith Crist, "A Suspenseful Seance on a Wet Afternoon," *NYHT,* 11/6/64.

(p. 227) "It isn't often you see . . .": Bosley Crowther, Seance on a Wet Afternoon review, *NYT,* 11/6/64.

(p. 227) "Miss Stanley gives a horrifying . . .": *Seance on a Wet Afternoon* review, *HR,* 12/4/64.

(p. 228) "With a seraphic smile . . .": Roald Dahl, "The Painful Pleasure of Suspense," *Life,* 12/18/64.

(p. 228) "In all but the best actress category . . .": A.H. Weiler, "Film Critics Name *My Fair Lady* the Fairest of Them All . . .," *NYT,* 12/29/64, 20.

(p. 228) Marilyn Murphy . . . was in the class, and J.T. invited her . . . : Int. with Marilyn Murphy, 10/18/02.

(p. 229) Lucy Kroll cabled her . . . : LK cable to KS, 9/11/63, Box 664, File 1, LK/LOC.

(p. 229) Kim . . . was interested in doing a stage version of Othello: LK notes of 4/16/64 conv. with KS, Box 664, File 11, LK/LOC.

(p. 229) she had signed a contract . . . : Contract in Box 670, File 1, LK/LOC.

(p. 229) Philip Rose . . . believes they had problems . . . : Philip Rose, *You Can't Do That on Broadway!* (New York: Limelight Editions, 2001), 192.

(p. 229) On July 2, 1963, Stanley Prager . . . : LK 7/3/63 ltr. to KS, Box 670, File 1, LK/LOC.

(p. 229) Lucy Kroll felt . . . Prager was afraid of working with Kim . . . : Ibid.

(p. 229) "Josh Logan loves *The Owl* . . . : LK 7/11/63 ltr. to KS, Box 670, File 1, LK/LOC.

(p. 229) "Logan said play . . . ": LK notes of 7/13/63 conv. with Alexander Cohen, Box 670, File 2, LK/LOC.

(p. 231) "The arch villain in last night's presentation . . .": Lewis Funke, "Theater: *Hamlet* in Park," *NYT,* 6/17/64.

(p. 231) "He entertained beautifully . . .": Int. with Sally Radin, 9/15/02.

(p. 231) "[He was] a highly dependent-type person . . . : Int. with JR, 1/16/02.

(p. 232) "When we were in Germany . . . : Int. with Mel Juffe, 11/26/01.

(p. 232) "He almost immediately began playing us . . . : Int. with RZ, 1/19/02.

(p. 232) "I thought the marriage was bizarre . . .": Int. with RH, 11/5/01.

(p. 232) "the extraordinary ingenuity . . .": Int. with Robert Lasky, 9/16/03.

(p. 233) "I remember his telling me once . . .": Int. with Robert Matson, 6/6/03.

(p. 233) he came into their office bloodied . . . : Int. with Robert Lasky, 9/16/03.

(p. 233) "Joe was very much a believer . . .": Ibid.

(p. 234) "No, no, darling. I play Masha . . .": Hirsch, 269.

(p. 234) Kim had withdrawn from the show: "Kim Stanley Is out of Sisters," *Variety,* n/d, in "Three Sisters" file at NYPL.

(p. 234) "Kim Stanley, who withdrew several weeks ago . . .": "Kim Stanley in Studio's *Sisters;* Swap Strasbergs," *Variety,* 4/8/64.

(p. 234) "Kim feels that Susan Strasberg . . .": Typed 10/11/63 note by unknown LK assistant "Re: Kim Stanley & 'Three Sisters,'" Box 672, File 2, LK/LOC.

(p. 234) "She was a very loving woman . . .": Int. with Shirley Knight, 3/1/02.

(p. 234) "I have a scar on my right hand . . .": Ibid.

(p. 235) "her alcoholism frightened me . . .": Ibid.

(p. 235) "There was a pillow on that chaise . . .": Int. with Robert Loggia, 7/16/02.

(p. 235) According to . . . Martin Fried, Marlon Brando was offered . . . : Garfield, 235.

(p. 235) "It was as though she wanted . . .": Int. with Kevin McCarthy, 4/5/02.

(p. 236) Strasberg told her one day at lunch . . . : Garfield, 235–236.

(p. 236) "Because Tony says so": Int. with Kevin McCarthy, 4/5/02.

(p. 236) "I thought, 'What the hell's going on . . .'": Ibid.

(p. 236) "What's this?" he asked Strasberg . . . : Garfield, 237.

(p. 236) "Kim said, 'You know, Lee . . .'": Int. with Gerald Hiken, 1/13/03.

(p. 237) "I love your translation . . .": Garfield, 239.

(p. 237) "There were those who pointed out . . .": Ibid.

(p. 237) "I thought Kim had really broken loose . . .": Richard Schechner, "The Bottomless Cup: An Int. with Geraldine Page," *Tulane Drama Review* "Stanislavsky in America" issue (1966), 255.

(p. 237) "It is gallant of the Actors Studio . . .": Howard Taubman, "Theater: A Tender *Three Sisters,*" *NYT,* 6/23/64.

(p. 237) hardly the sort of entertainment . . . : "The Three Sisters," *Variety,* 7/1/64, 66.

(p. 237) "It was a rare and enchanted . . .": Emory Lewis, "Cheers for Chekhov," *Cue,* 7/4/64.

(p. 237) "The Actors Studio talks a good deal . . .": Jerry Tallmer, "Truth, Chekhov, Strasberg," *NYP,* 6/23/64.

(p. 237) "[T]here is a diffusion of character . . .": Judith Crist, "Chekhov on Broadway Illumed by Kim Stanley," *NYHT,* 6/23/64.

(p. 238) "In the gaping interstices . . .": John Simon, *Uneasy Stages: A Chronicle of the New York Theater, 1963–1973* (New York: Random House, 1975), 57.

(p. 238) Robert Loggia and several other cast members . . . would go down . . . : Int. with Robert Loggia, 7/16/02.

(p. 238) "She had a moment that tore . . .": Int. with Ben Gazzara, 7/19/02.

(p. 238) "Miss Stanley's Masha is . . .": Crist, "Chekhov on Broadway Illumed by Kim Stanley," *NYHT,* 6/23/64.

(p. 238) "Kim Stanley's portrayal of Masha is astonishing . . .": Michael Smith, "Strasberg's Chekhov," *Village Voice,* 7/2/64.

(p. 238) "one of our national art treasures": Lewis, "Cheers for Chekhov," *Cue,* 7/4/64.

(p. 238) "In Mr. Strasberg's production, the sisters . . .": Nathan Cohen, "Three Sad Sisters," *Toronto Daily Star,* 7/28/64.

(p. 238) "She was totally ill-disciplined . . ." : Int. with Sir Richard Attenborough, 1/23/02.

(p. 238) "a solid, ample figure in black": Crist, "Chekhov on Broadway Illumed by Kim Stanley," *NYHT,* 6/23/64.

(p. 238) she had the look of a vegetating hausfrau: Norman Nadel, "Actors Studio Superb in Chekov Finale," *NYWT,* 6/23/64.

(p. 239) "Under Lee Strasberg's direction . . .": Taubman, "Theater: A Tender Three Sisters," *NYT,* 6/23/64.

(p. 239) "Lee Strasberg proved . . . that he could direct . . .": Tallmer, "Truth, Chekhov, Strasberg," *NYP,* 6/23/64.

(p. 239) "the strangely disjointed minuet . . .": Crist, "Chekhov on Broadway Illumed by Kim Stanley," *NYHT,* 6/23/64.

(p. 239) "his direction is halting . . .": Jack Thompson, "Strasberg Slips," *JM,* 6/23/64.

(p. 239) "When Kim was at the theater, he would go out . . .": Int. with Sally Radin, 9/15/02.

(p. 239) "When you walk into Sardi's . . .": Ibid.

(p. 239) "Patty and her husband had a party . . .": Int. with Lucile Reid Brock, 6/11/02.

(p. 240) "Terrific. Just fine . . .": Int. with Kevin McCarthy, 4/5/02.

(p. 240) "Kim quit the next day . . .": Ibid.

(p. 240) "The box office response . . .": "Kim Stanley out of *Sisters,*" *Variety,* 9/2/64.

(p. 240) "The men were wonderful . . .": Int. with Paul Bogart, 3/21/02.

(p. 241) "She was a very intense woman . . .": Ibid.

(p. 241) "Shelley has many, uh, intonations of New York . . . : Ibid.

(p. 242) "Great actresses are rare . . .": Eugene Archer, "Kim Stanley on a Snowy Afternoon," *NYT,* 1/31/65.

(p. 242) "I don't want to say I don't want to act again . . .": Ibid.

(p. 243) Paul Newman got Pan Am . . . : Crawford, 239–240.

(p. 243) "To get her to say 'yes' to the London appearance . . .": Robert Lewis, *Slings and Arrows: Theater in My Life* (New York: Stein and Day, 1984), 261. [Later references as "Lewis 2."]

(p. 243) "He tells me that unless a visiting company . . .": LK 3/11/65 ltr. to Joseph Siegel, Box 672, File 1, LK/LOC.

(p. 244) "I am very pleased, flattered . . .": Stuart W. Little, "Actors Studio Theater Company off with Two Plays . . . ," *NYHT,* n/d, Box 672, File 3, LK/LOC.

(p. 244) "My God, what are you doing . . .": Hirsch, 247.

(p. 244) "He browbeat some people if he felt . . . : Int. with Robert Loggia, 7/16/02.

(p. 244) Kim's first choice . . . was Montgomery Clift: Garfield, 243.

(p. 244) Kim . . . said he did it as a favor to her: Kobal, 695.

(p. 244) Scott had an ulterior motive . . . : Int. with Robert Loggia, 7/16/02.

(p. 244) (I)t was Kazan's theory that Strasberg envisioned . . . : Kazan, 709.

(p. 245) "It's partly Baldwin's . . .": James Feron, "*Charlie* Scored by London Critics," *NYT,* 5/4/65.

(p. 245) Strasberg's harsh criticism offended the British audience . . . : Lewis 2, 261.

(p. 245) "We had no rehearsal space . . .": Hirsch, 288–89.

(p. 245) "It was like a ski run . . .": Int. with Robert Loggia, 7/16/02.

(p. 245) "It was as big as the set . . .": Int. with Gerald Hiken, 1/13/03.

(p. 245) George C. Scott . . . was busy over at the Savoy Hotel: Hirsch, 289.

(p. 246) "On the afternoon of the opening, I went to watch . . .": Crawford, 241.

(p. 246) "The audience was quite used to . . .": Int. with Gerald Hiken, 1/13/03.

(p. 246) the men in the production talked . . . : "The Three Sisters," *Sunday Times,* 5/16/65.

(p. 246) "Nobody called us to places . . .": Int. with Gerald Hiken, 1/13/03.

(p. 246) "Yankees, go home!" . . . : Lewis 2, 262.

(p. 246) "At the curtain call, we were hooted . . .": Int. with Robert Loggia, 7/16/02.

(p. 246) "The stage manager, to whom the Studio was God . . .": Kobal, 695.

(p. 246) "Kim was wonderful at the curtain call . . .": Int. with Gerald Hiken, 1/13/03.

(p. 246) "when Ava Gardner attend . . .": Int. with Robert Loggia, 7/16/02.

(p. 247) Laurence Olivier . . . ". . . helped cushion the blow . . .": Peter Hay, *Theatrical Anecdotes* (New York: Oxford University Press, 1987), 345.

(p. 247) "This is not only the last production of the season . . .": Bernard Levin, "So Much Promise Fades into Such a Lot of Gloom," *Daily Mail,* 5/14/65.

(p. 247) "After the fire of *Blues for Mister Charlie* . . .": Colin Frame, "Too Much—This Chit-Chat . . . ," Box 672, File 3, LK/LOC.

(p. 247) "an occasion to have raised Stanislavsky's ghost . . .": *The Three Sisters* review, *Illustrated London News,* 5/29/65.

(p. 247) "The admirable World Theatre's dismal task . . .": Crawford, 241.

(p. 247) "This production did not . . . deserve the disgraceful . . .": Milton Shulman, "Isn't It Time to Ban the First-Night Gallery?" *Evening Standard,* 5/14/65.

(p. 247) "Masha and Irina are ludicrous and painful": *The Three Sisters* review, *Sunday Times,* 5/16/65.

(p. 247) "Kim Stanley flashed a whole battery . . .": Philip Hope-Wallace, *The Three Sisters* review, *MG,* 5/14/65.

(p. 247) "Outside of a school for stammerers . . .": Shulman, "Isn't It Time to Ban the First-Night Gallery?" *Evening Standard,* 5/14/65.

(p. 247) "They gave an unbelievable, self-indulgent . . .": Crawford, 241.

(p. 248) "Kim Stanley's Masha was a marvelously timed . . .": Frame, "Too Much—This Chit-Chat Over the Samovar," Box 672, File 3, LK/LOC.

(p. 248) "Kim Stanley's Masha is . . .": "Chekhov the Method Way," *Times of London,* 5/14/65.

(p. 248) "Irina (Miss Sandy Dennis) has one trick . . .": Levin, "So Much Promise Fades into Such a Lot of Gloom," *Daily Mail,* 5/14/65.

(p. 248) "Scott, who always referred to Strasberg . . .": Lewis 2, 262.

(p. 248) "Mr. Strasberg, you called us together . . .": Garfield, 245.

(p. 248) "George was fueled with anger . . .": Int. with Robert Loggia, 7/16/02.

(p. 248) Kim and five other[s] . . . were interviewed on the BBC . . . : Videotape of 6/13/65 BBC-2 interview; in possession of JK.

(p. 249) Gerald Hiken would recall Dallas . . . : Int. with Gerald Hiken, 1/13/03.

(p. 249) "the mercurial Russian temperament . . .": Frances Wyndham, "Actors Studio Ambushed," Box 672, File 3, LK/LOC.

(p. 249) Robert Lewis later speculated . . . : Lewis 2, 262.

(p. 249) she felt betrayed by Strasberg . . . : Garfield, 245.

(p. 249) "She waddled on the stage . . .": Hay, 345.

(p. 249) Daniel Petrie had risked his participation . . . : Int. with Daniel Petrie, 9/29/03.

(p. 250) "When I saw her, I almost blurted out . . .": Ibid.

(p. 250) "After all, I have to be . . .": Ibid.

(p. 250) [O]n June 28, Edward R. Morse . . . wrote a deal memo . . . : Edward R. Morse 6/28/65 ltr. to LK, Box 664, File 9, LK/LOC.

(p. 250) Notes [Kroll] made from the conversation indicate that Kim . . . : The relevant passage of LK's note is: "regarding her pregnancy—to bring to her attention this fact which is illegal to withhold—he [presumably Joe Siegel] will talk to her.": LK 6/29/65 notes of conv. with Joe Siegel, Box 664, File 10, LK/LOC.

(p. 250) "She had three or four abortions": Int. with Lynn White, 9/7/02.

(p. 250) "Kim is on the boat . . .": LK 8/13/65 ltr. to Mr. and Mrs. Daniel Petrie, Box 664, File 9, LK/LOC.

(p. 250) "All he saw was the vodka . . .": Int. with Dorothea Petrie, 10/1/03.

(p. 250) Dan Petrie called from London . . . Kim not doing picture . . . : LK 8/23/65 notes of conv. with Daniel Petrie, Box 664, File 10, LK/LOC.

(p. 251) "the bottle scars of four marriages, 11 psychiatrists and 10,000 puce-colored hangovers": Daniel Petrie, "Directed by Jack Phelan." Copy in possession of JK.

(p. 251) "You really had the feeling . . .": Int. with Dorothea Petrie, 10/1/03.

(p. 252) several friends of Kim's . . . had . . . gone up to Congers: Int. with Daniel Petrie, 9/29/03.

CHAPTER 8

(p. 254) "a devilishly adroit mind . . .": Denker, 23.

(p. 254) "She was drinking, drinking, drinking . . .": Int. with Ben Gazzara, 7/19/02.

(p. 255) "She always had a sardonic sense . . .": Ibid.

(p. 255) "Roddy McDowall took her . . .": Int. with Patricia Frye, 1/30/04.

(p. 255) William Gibson . . . says it was Chestnut Lodge: Int. with William Gibson, 2/25/02.

(p. 255) Patricia Frye says Chestnut Hill . . . : Int. with Patricia Frye, 1/30/04.

(p. 255) Kim's daughter Rachel says Silver Hill: Int. with RZ, 1/19/02.

(p. 255) "Kim became so difficult . . .": Int. with HF, 12/10/01.

(p. 256) "She was such a consummate actress . . .": *American Drama,* "Special Double Issue 2003: Arthur Laurents," 83.

(p. 256) "Her brother the psychiatrist . . .": Int. with Sally Radin, 9/15/02.

(p. 256) "People would laugh so hard . . .": Int. with Eli Wallach, 10/23/01.

(p. 257) "To arrive at true realism . . .": Int. with PZ, 11/6/02.

(p. 258) "Lasky kind of leaned on him . . .": Int. with Robert Matson, 6/6/03.

(p. 258) Kim . . . was hemorrhaging: Int. with Alice Hirson, 8/31/01.

(p. 258) "Vivian made a frantic call . . .": Int. with Elissa Myers, 11/12/01.

(p. 259) "He wants you desperately": LK 3/30/67 ltr. to KS, Box 664, File 3, LK/LOC.

(p. 259) Penn advanced her the money: LK 5/16/67 ltr. to KS, Box 664, File 3, LK/LOC.

(p. 259) "The lady is a bitch . . .": LK notes of 4/4/67 talk with KS, Box 664, File 4, LK/LOC.

(p. 259) Laurie Rachel . . . would help cue her mother . . . : Int. with RZ, 1/22/03.

(p. 260) "Arthur is to tell her the bad news . . .": LK 7/22/67 note beginning "Dr. Gibson . . . ghastly," Box 664, File 4, LK/LOC.

(p. 260) "Arthur Penn said, 'I don't want . . .'": Int. with Phil Hymes, 12/15/02.

(p. 260) "Her performance was brilliant . . .": Int. with William Hanley, 4/8/03.

(p. 260) "Sometimes she would step out . . .": Int. with Warren Clymer, 9/8/02.

(p. 260) "The problem with tape . . .": Int. with Phil Hymes, 12/15/02.

(p. 261) "Rarely have so many . . .": Harriet Van Horne, "High-Priced Suds," *NYP,* 1/27/68.

(p. 261) "a dreary two hours . . .": *Flesh and Blood* review, *Variety,* 1/31/68.

(p. 261) "His tax accountant must be . . . : Jack Gould, "Hanley's Short Cut to Easy Street," *NYT,* 1/27/68.

(p. 261) "two hours of unrelieved . . . ": *Flesh and Blood* review, *HR,* 1/29/68.

(p. 261) "Here at last is a play . . .": Rex Reed, *Big Screen, Little Screen* (New York: MacMillan, 1971), 4.

(p. 261) If for no other reason . . . : Ibid., 5.

(p. 262) she had not made her last two house payments . . . : Jerome Handler 1/26/68 ltr. to KS, in "CBS Playhouse: Secrets" file, LK/LOC.

(p. 262) "hounded by the tax man": LK 2/13/68 notes of talk with Jerome Handler, in "CBS Playhouse: Secrets" file, LK/LOC.

(p. 262) "It had a wonderful scene in the middle . . .": Int. with Paul Bogart, 3/21/02.

(p. 262) she wanted a drawing room . . . : 2/21/68 ltr. to KS by anonymous LK assistant, in "CBS Playhouse: Secrets" file, LK/LOC.

(p. 262) CBS put out a statement . . . : "C.B.S. Mosel Drama Loses Kim Stanley," *NYT,* 3/9/68.

(p. 263) "She said, 'A community theater? . . .'": Joan Turner (aka Joan Turetzky) 9/30/02 ltr. to JK.

(p. 263) "I am trying to do what I can . . .": LK 2/14/68 ltr. to KS in "CBS Playhouse: Secrets" file, LK/LOC.

(p. 263) "She would call me at two . . .": Int. with Shirley Knight, 3/1/02.

(p. 263) "I talked to her on the phone . . .": Int. with Dorothy Land Fitzgerald, 6/25/02.

(p. 263) "Peter Witt Associates Inc. has signed . . .": "Artists & Agents," *HR,* 7/24/68.

(p. 264) "She was full of fun . . .": Int. with Betsy Norton Barrios, 8/22/02.

(p. 264) "I can hear her laugh . . .": Ibid.

(p. 264) "She did seem to take . . .": JC 3/30/02 e-mail to JK.

(p. 264) "We were not allowed . . .": Int. with RZ, 1/22/03.

(p. 264) "an artist, a cool guy, gorgeous": Int. with Betsy Norton Barrios, 8/22/02.

(p. 264) "She was a straight-A student . . . .": Ibid.

(p. 265) "I think it was just carried on too long . . .": Int. with JC, 11/16/01.

(p. 265) "I kind of knew school wasn't for me . . .": Ibid.

(p. 265) "Jamie was running around on communes . . .": Int. with PZ, 11/6/02.

(p. 265) 'When I was making a film . . .': Lewis 2, 262.

(p. 266) Kim had just come out of . . . : Int. with George Morrison, 1/19/02.

(p. 266) "We did a reading with Ron Leibman . . .": Ibid.

(p. 267) "She had a great sweetness . . .": Ibid.

(p. 267) "When the production didn't materialize . . .": S. Sondheim 7/23/02 ltr. to JK.

(p. 268) "Although it shapes up as no big winner . . .": Review of *UMC, Variety,* 4/23/69.

(p. 268) a brief item ran in the *Albuquerque Tribune:* 8/14/69 item in *AT* beginning, "I just found out Kim Stanley is a New Mexico native . . ."

(p. 268) "Kim Stanley was having emotional problems . . ." Diana Douglas Darrid, *In the Wings: A Memoir* (New York: Barricade Books, 1999), 265–266.

(p. 268) "It just seemed to me that Kim was . . .": Int. with PZ, 11/6/02.

(p. 269) "I knew I was in an adventure . . .": Ibid.

(p. 269) "She would speak two different ways to me . . .": Ibid.

(p. 270) "Her hair is dramatic . . .": PZ, *Ladies at the Alamo* (New York: Dramatists Play Service Inc., 1977), 21–22.

(p. 271) "The house looked sort of dark . . .": Int. with Ashley Feinstein, 2/26/02.

(p. 271) "When I came in, she said, 'You must be freezing . . .'": Ibid.

(p. 271) "It could have been brilliant for her . . .": Ibid.

(p. 272) "They had to bring in extra coaches . . .": Int. with PZ, 11/6/02.

(p. 272) "Miss Stanley's performing was . . .": *Dragon Country* review, *Variety*, 12/9/70, 40.

(p. 273) "Kim asked me, 'So Elissa, what do you want to be?'": Int. with Elissa Myers, 11/12/01.

CHAPTER 9

(p. 274) That summer, Jamie drove Kim back . . . : JC 1/13/02 e-mail to JK.

(p. 274) She rented an apartment in a large house . . . : Int. with R.C. Gorman, 4/26/03.

(p. 275) "She had the most beautiful hands . . .": Ibid.

(p. 275) "I always thought she was rather exuberant . . .": Int. with Virginia Dooley, 4/26/03.

(p. 276) "Gradually she started to act, not read . . .": Richardson, 280–81.

(p. 276) Hepburn announced she was withdrawing . . . : Ibid.

(p. 276) "Hepburn worked from the top . . .": Int. with Bonnie Bartlett, 6/25/02.

(p. 276) "How sad that Kim Stanley . . .": "Broadway Ballyhoo," *HR*, 11/14/72.

(p. 277) "Wasn't she supposed to surpass . . . ?": Robin Adams Sloan column, *NYDN*, 12/19/72, Sec. 3, 2.

(p. 277) "Is it true Kim Stanley will never act . . . ?": Robin Adams Sloan column, *NYDN*, 10/9/73, 59.

(p. 277) "It was scary—she drove about . . .": Int. with Betsy Norton Barrios, 8/22/02.

(p. 277) "I've been married four times . . .": Kobal, 701.

(p. 278) "When I came out of the spin": Ibid., 705.

(p. 278) she did not want to live in the ugly city of Albuquerque . . . : KS 12/5/74 ltr. to Edward Purrington; in possession of JK.

(p. 278) she said she had also done *Yerma* . . . : KS résumé; in possession of JK.

(p. 278) "She didn't come in with the teaching credentials . . .": Int. with JW, 4/22/03.

(p. 278) "I was ecstatic, because . . .": Int. with JW, 3/2/02.

(p. 279) "I'm no actor," Peck said . . .: JW remarks at KS memorial service at College of Santa Fe, 9/9/01.

(p. 279) "My initial impressions . . .": Int. with Meredith Alexander, 3/26/03.

(p. 279) "She was unpredictable . . .": Int. with Sue Ann Carpenter, 3/25/03.

(p. 279) "She listened unbelievably . . .": Int. with Katharine Lee, 3/13/02.

(p. 279) "One of the things I got from her . . .": Int. with Stephen Reynolds, 7/30/02.

(p. 280) "I wanted to move into scene work . . .": Ibid.

(p. 280) "Her work was intense . . .": Int. with Wayne Sabato, 3/24/03.

(p. 280) "I can almost pinpoint when I thought . . .": Int. with JW, 3/2/02.

(p. 281) "I always wanted to do that play . . .": Ibid.

(p. 281) "She was born with a duplicate kidney . . .": Int. with RZ, 1/22/03.

(p. 281) "She was deathly ill . . .": Int. with JW, 3/2/02.

(p. 281) paid for by the indigent fund . . . : Int. with JW, 4/22/03.

(p. 282) "It was like she haunted me . . .": Int. with Sue Ann Carpenter, 3/25/03.

(p. 282) After Kim told Weckesser . . . : JW 6/15/76 ltr. to KS; in possession of JK.

(p. 282) he suggested other ways Kim could maintain . . . : Ibid.

(p. 282) as Kim was fond of pointing out . . . : Int. with Katharine Lee, 3/13/02.

(p. 282) "This is an unusual play, but Kim says . . .": Anne Hillerman, "Maureen Stapleton [sic] opens SF rehearsals," *Santa Fe New Mexican*, 10/22/76, A-8.

(p. 282) "I called Maureen and said . . .": Barbara Mackay, "Kim Stanley Is Radiant in New Setting," *Denver Post*, 12/19/76.

(p. 282) Sue Goodson . . . noted how Kim enjoyed a good laugh . . . : Sue Goodson remarks, read at KS memorial service at College of Santa Fe, 9/9/01.

(p. 283) "He's not an actor, he's a child . . .": Mackay, "Kim Stanley Is Radiant in New Setting," *Denver Post*, 12/19/76.

(p. 283) "The opening night of *Godot*, Kim was plastered . . .": Int. with JW, 3/2/02.

(p. 283) "He sat right behind me . . .": Int. with Sue Ann Carpenter, 3/25/03.

(p. 283) "After the play, Marlon wanted to take over . . .": Cecil Dawkins, ed. *A Woman of the Century: Frances Minerva Nunnery* (Albuquerque: University of New Mexico Press, 2002), 138.

(p. 283) "She was quite heavy . . .": Int. with Edward Balcomb, 12/14/02.

(p. 283) "She was exceedingly mean and abusive . . .": Int. with JW, 3/2/02.

(p. 284) "That produced a great deal of resentment . . .": Ibid.

(p. 284) "frequently you had been drinking . . .": JW 1/7/77 ltr. to KS; in possession of JK.

(p. 284) "You treated your fellow artists . . .": Ibid.

(p. 284) Weckesser . . . got a call that something was . . . : Int. with JW, 3/2/02.

(p. 285) one drink was too many and a hundred not enough . . . : Charles Jackson, *The Lost Weekend* (Syracuse, NY: Syracuse University Press, 1996), 222.

(p. 285) the academic dean . . . wrote to Kim . . . : E.F. Ferneau ltr. to KS, 2/25/77; in possession of JK.

(p. 285) "We took a trip to the country . . .": Judy Klemesrud, "A Star-Studded Party Honors Harold Clurman," *NYT*, 5/7/79.

(p. 285) "I just adored actress Kim Stanley . . .": Robin Adams Sloan column, *NYDN*, 10/26/76, 43.

(p. 285) Carol White . . . started dating other men—and women: Int. with Lynn White, 9/7/02.

(p. 285) "Kim Stanley . . . ran away from Broadway . . .": Liz Smith, "A New Crisis for Brando?" *Chicago Tribune*, 3/27/77, Sec. 5, 2.

(p. 286) "Woody was a great admirer of hers . . .": Int. with Juliet Taylor, 2/3/03.

(p. 286) "Kim Stanley, who has been living in New Mexico . . .": John Corry, "Woman in Red Rides Uptown with Mamet's *Water Engine*," *NYT*, 1/20/78, C-2.

(p. 286) "Laurie is a name that I had always disliked . . .": Int. with RZ, 11/3/01.

(p. 286) "They were kicked out of Joe Allen's . . .": Int. with Bill Schelble, 7/4/02.

(p. 286) "were really big name-droppers . . .": Int. with Larry Gold, 10/8/02.

(p. 287) "She was big on working with props . . .": Ibid.

(p. 287) "We ran over to help her . . .": Ibid.

(p. 287) "George Scott . . . knew more about Stanislavsky's theories . . . : Paul Rosenfield, "Kim Stanley Plays with a Full Deck," *LAT*, 1/10/82, Calendar sec., 20.

(p. 287) "Miss Stanley is one of the most extraordinary talents . . .": John Springer, "Stanley and the Studio," *LAT*, 1/17/82, Calendar sec.

(p. 287) "Mo will call up and say, 'You lonesome?' . . .": Rosenfield, "Kim Stanley Plays With a Full Deck," *LAT*, 1/10/82, Calendar sec., 20.

(p. 288) "pretend we were on a train . . .": Matthew Armstrong 4/18/05 e-mail to JK.

(p. 288) a class at the Met . . . : Int. with Jackson McGarry, 9/4/02.

(p. 288) "She would teach for six weeks or so . . .": Ibid.

(p. 288) "She passed a paper bag around . . .": Int. with John Tyrrell, 6/12/03.

(p. 288) "We kind of just sat . . .": Int. with Jackson McGarry, 9/4/02.

(p. 289) "Instead of the classic animal improvisation . . .": Int. with Robert Ellerman, 9/14/03.

(p. 289) Kim . . . was talking about the importance of evoking . . . : Katharine Lee remarks at KS memorial service at College of Santa Fe, 9/9/01.

(p. 289) "What I learned from Kim . . .": Int. with Jackson McGarry, 9/4/02.

(p. 289) "need" was Kim's word for "objective": Int. with Robert Ellerman, 9/14/03.

(p. 290) "Kim did not like Lee Strasberg . . . : Int. with Jackson McGarry, 9/4/02.

(p. 290) "Class would start around 7 P.M . . . .": Jackson McGarry posting on thespiannet.com, since removed; in possession of JK.

(p. 290) "These modern acting classes . . .": Int. with Robert Ellerman, 9/14/03.

(p. 290) "One by one, the actors came in . . .": Int. with Carl Palusci, 1/2/03.

(p. 290) "As far as I'm concerned, Kim could not . . .": Ibid.

(p. 290) "You want to know about emotion?": Victor Slezak remarks at KS memorial service at the Actors Studio, 10/12/01.

(p. 291) "I've got some very, very bad news . . .": Ibid.

(p. 291) "Oh, you've gotten this far": Ibid.

(p. 291) "He was doing a scene from a play . . .": Int. with Arthur Laurents, 1/5/02.

(p. 291) "Fortunately, it missed her . . .": Int. with Carl Palusci, 1/2/03.

(p. 291) "something extremely authentic . . .": Int. with John Tyrrell, 6/12/03.

(p. 292) "The place was very, very dirty . . .": Int. with Carl Palusci, 1/2/03.

(p. 292) "the real attraction is a rare . . .": Rex Reed column, *NYDN*, 4/4/79, 26.

(p. 292) "I've been working quietly—from within": "Missing Ingredient," *Women's Wear Daily*, 5/8/79, 4.

(p. 292) "I loved her . . . and when I saw her . . .": Int. with RW, 11/27/01.

(p. 293) Kim . . . attend[ed] the opening of . . . *The Price*: "Kim Stanley Stars at an Opening," *NYDN*, 6/21/79, 9.

(p. 293) J.T.'s ninetieth birthday party . . . : Tape of event in possession of JK.

(p. 293) [Justin] stood at the edge of a cliff . . . : Interviews with JR, 8/10/02 and 4/25/03.

(p. 293) "She was in a Greenwich Village restaurant . . .": John Corry, "Kim Stanley Returns, Directing Ensemble Troupe," *NYT,* 9/20/79, C-15.

(p. 294) "It's what I want to do with the rest . . .": Ibid.

(p. 294) "We have to have her": John Guare remarks at KS memorial service at the Actors Studio, 10/12/01.

(p. 294) "You can send the script, but . . .": Ibid.

(p. 295) "Kim was attempting to carry on . . .": Int. with Robert Ellerman, 9/14/03.

(p. 295) "I think Kim, because of her alcoholism . . .": Int. with Carl Palusci, 1/2/03.

(p. 295) Gregory Peck was sending her money . . . : Ibid.

(p. 295) Paul Newman and Lauren Hutton helped to pay . . . : Int. with Jackson McGarry, 9/4/02.

(p. 295) the scene had an odd feeling to Palusci . . . : Int. with Carl Palusci, 1/2/03.

(p. 296) "He was livid, pacing back and forth . . .": Ibid.

(p. 296) "Geraldine Page was trying to get Kim . . .": Ibid.

(p. 296) "I'm quite sure Kim viewed the 'heist' . . .": RZ 5/14/03 e-mail to JK.

CHAPTER 10

(p. 297) "We had met with the usual suspects . . .": Int. with Jonathan Sanger, 6/28/04.

(p. 298) "When I got to L.A . . .": Ibid.

(p. 298) "It was typically eccentric . . .": Int. with Graeme Clifford, 7/5/04.

(p. 298) A slew of Hollywood stars was reportedly interested . . . : Dale Pollock, "Screen Biography of Actress Frances Farmer Scheduled," *LAT,* 4/21/81.

(p. 299) "a family tinged with brilliance . . .": William Arnold, *Shadowland: The Search for Frances Farmer* (New York: McGraw-Hill, 1978), 23.

(p. 299) "incapable of dissembling" . . ."could not abide dishonesty": Ibid, 26–27.

(p. 299) "I remember Kim telling me . . .": Int. with RZ, 1/19/02.

(p. 299) "It was very inspiring . . .": Int. with Graeme Clifford, 7/5/04.

(p. 299) "It helped Jessica an awful lot . . .": Ibid.

(p. 300) "Having someone as solid . . .": Int. with Jonathan Sanger, 6/28/04.

(p. 300) "If I had a problem, ever . . .": Ibid.

(p. 300) "They just went at each other . . .": Int. with Graeme Clifford, 7/5/04.

(p. 300) "Kim was probably the most perceptive . . .": Ibid.

(p. 300) "Whether it was her age or what . . .": Int. with Bonnie Bartlett, 6/25/02.

(p. 301) "She didn't look like herself . . .": Int. with Dorothy Land Fitzgerald, 6/25/02.

(p. 301) "Now 61 and many kilos overweight . . .": Rex Reed, "Laureling Stanley's Driving Acting Force," *GQ*, 1/83.

(p. 301) "she was so critical of herself . . .": Int. with Graeme Clifford, 7/5/04.

(p. 301) "Kim Stanley, who was a theater figure of importance . . .": Stanley Kauffman, Review of *Frances, The New Republic*, 2/7/83, 24.

(p. 302) Kim [said] Clifford had to cut . . . : Kobal, 686.

(p. 302) "Universal wanted Jonathan and me to cut . . .": Int. with Graeme Clifford, 7/5/04.

(p. 302) "Unfortunately, all of the trims . . .": Ibid.

(p. 303) "Retrospective? . . . I've only done two": Paul Rosenfield, "Kim Stanley Plays with a Full Deck," *LAT,* 1/10/82, Calendar sec., 20.

(p. 303) "We had a nice visit . . .": Ollie Reed Jr., "KS Goes Public," *AT,* 3/12/82.

(p. 304) "She moved in on my wife and me . . .": Int. with PZ, 11/6/02.

(p. 304) "She was sleepy, so she curled up . . .": Int. with Bonnie Zindel, 6/25/03.

(p. 304) "At that time, we had a big Great Dane . . .": Ibid.

(p. 304) "Oh my God, you don't have flowers . . .": Ibid.

(p. 305) "This was one of those occasions . . .": Int. with PZ, 11/6/02.

(p. 305) "There she was, ordering me about . . .": Ibid.

(p. 305) "I'm really for Men's Lib..": Kobal, 697.

(p. 305) creation of the . . . Hollywood Opera and Theatre Ensemble Theatre. . . : "Kim Stanley New Director of H'wood Ensemble," *Variety*, 3/24/82.

(p. 306) "To prove Kim is really back on track . . .": Liz Smith, "Virtues of Love with a Younger Woman," *NYDN*, 5/10/82.

(p. 306) Joseph Siegel . . . died of a heart attack: Death notice for Joseph Siegel, *NYT*, 7/13/82, A-22.

(p. 306) "Kim begg[ed] off due to a . . . dental abscess . . .": RZ e-mail to JK, 5/14/03.

(p. 307) "Kim was very moved by her mother's death . . .": Int. with JR, 5/16/02.

(p. 307) Rachel . . . didn't even learn . . . J.T. had died . . . : RZ e-mail to JK, 1/6/02.

(p. 308) "From where? I hadn't gone anywhere . . .": Kobal, 697.

(p. 308) "I can't tell you how many plays . . .": Ibid.

(p. 309) "I want to do the big shows . . .": "Dialogue on Film: Kim Stanley," *American Film*, 6/83, 26.

(p. 309) "I heard she was in town . . .": Int. with Jack Klugman, 1/5/03.

(p. 309) "I sent a limo for her . . .": Ibid.

(p. 310) "He would get upset from time to time . . .": Int. with Phylis Geller, 7/1/04.

(p. 310) "Kim was kind of an anchor . . .": Ibid.

(p. 311) "less than compelling": "Views and Previews," *TV Guide*, 6/22/85, A-4.

(p. 311) "Miss Stanley . . . retains the practical shrewdness . . .": John J. O'Connor, "From Cable to the Air, *Cat on a Hot Tin Roof*," *NYT*, 6/24/85, C-14.

(p. 311) "I was saying goodbye and thanking her . . .": Int. with Phylis Geller, 7/1/04.

(p. 311) "I saw myself as the playwright . . .": Chuck Blasius e-mail to JK, 8/2/02.

(p. 312) "We knew Kim was out here teaching . . .": Int. with Erma Dean Chapman, 1/28/02.

(p. 312) [Brooks Clift] and Kim often spoke . . . : Michael Morrison e-mail to JK, 11/4/02.

(p. 312) "She was very heavy, so she dressed in caftans . . .": Int. with RZ, 1/19/03.

(p. 312) Michael Morrison . . . believes Kim had her teeth pulled . . . : Michael Morrison e-mail to JK, 11/4/02.

(p. 312) "She had pretty decent dentures . . .": RZ e-mail to JK, 5/14/03.

(p. 312) "When she spoke to you, she might say . . .": Int. with Alan Rachins, 10/11/02.

(p. 313) "In every moment of being with her . . .": Int. with Joanna Frank, 10/11/02.

(p. 313) "We were animals in the forest . . . : Int. with Alan Rachins, 10/11/02.

(p. 313) "She was excited by danger . . .": Int. with Joanna Frank, 10/11/02.

(p. 313) "However long this class was . . .": Int. with Alan Rachins, 10/11/02.

(p. 314) "It was like being in the presence . . .": Int. with Anna Gunn, 1/18/02.

(p. 314) "Did you ever go into your mother's closet . . .": Ibid.

(p. 314) saw [Kim] being held at gunpoint: Int. with Rochelle Tetrault, 5/5/02.

(p. 315) "The students were completely petrified . . .": Anna Gunn remarks at Kim Stanley memorial service at the College of Santa Fe, 9/9/01.

(p. 315) "Her voice was almost like a whisper . . .": Int. with Rochelle Tetrault, 5/5/02.

(p. 315) "I found out that her favorite thing . . .": Int. with Randy Bennett, 1/5/03.

(p. 316) "Her bedroom was directly above ours..": Ibid.

(p. 316) "She opened the door and returned to bed . . .": Int. with Craig Strong, 1/5/03.

(p. 316) she didn't drink after 1988 or '89: Ibid.

(p. 316) "she never left the house": Int. with Rochelle Tetrault, 5/5/02.

(p. 316) Kim wouldn't let the paramedics in . . . : Int. with Rochelle Tetrault, 5/5/02.

(p. 316) Bennett and Strong think Kim's impaired mobility . . . : Int. with Randy Bennett and Craig Strong, 1/5/03.

(p. 317) "She was terrified of death . . .": Int. with RZ, 1/22/03.

(p. 317) "And drinking! We were more scared of them . . .": Int. with Randy Bennett, 1/5/03.

(p. 317) "We talked several times and would go up . . .": Int. with Craig Strong, 1/5/03.

(p. 317) "She was crying . . . She was so afraid . . .": Int. with Randy Bennett, 1/5/03.

(p. 318) "Those apartments were not particularly warm . . .": Int. with Craig Strong, 1/5/03.

(p. 318) If no students showed up . . . she would teach the prairie dogs . . . : KS ltr. to Betsy Norton Barrios, 11/15/95.

(p. 319) "I almost felt like she was acting . . .": Int. with Solea Reid, 9/20/03.

(p. 319) The later part of her life was characterized by . . . : Int. with Marilyn Murphy, 10/18/02.

(p. 319) her body so decomposed . . . : Int. with Lynn White, 9/7/02.

(p. 319) "We were beginning to put together . . .": Int. with Wayne Sabato, 4/23/03.
(p. 319) "I mentioned it to Kim . . .": Ibid.
(p. 319) "We were going to do the piece . . .": Int. with Hilton Als, 7/24/02.
(p. 320) "I talked with Kim about a year before . . .": Int. with Rietta Netter Oppenheim, 6/19/02.
(p. 320) she told Betsy she was still teaching . . . : Int. with Betsy N. Barrios, 8/22/02.
(p. 320) "So I told her I had a play . . .": Int. with Arthur Laurents, 1/5/02.
(p. 320) "We had to hold her down . . .": Interviews with Patricia Burger, 4/25/03 and 6/10/03.
(p. 320) she'd much rather go see a performance . . . : KS ltr. to Lillian Ross, 3/18/01.
(p. 320) "She was leaving for the hospital . . .": Int. with Lillian Ross, 4/1/02.
(p. 321) "She was sent to a recovery-rehab type of place . . .": Int. with Wayne Sabato, 4/23/03.
(p. 321) "Oh, well . . . that doesn't matter . . . : Jean Moss remarks at Kim Stanley memorial service at the College of Santa Fe, 9/9/01.
(p. 321) she noticed brother and sister steering away . . . : Int. with Paula Reid, 10/4/03.
(p. 321) "When I came back, she couldn't open her eyes . . .": Interviews with JR, 10/9/01 and 4/25/03.
(p. 321) Some time after Kim's hysterectomy . . . : Most of the information in this paragraph comes from Kim's death certificate; in possession of JK.
(p. 321) a legendary brilliant raw wound . . . : Int. with Mark Rydell, 8/29/03.
(p. 322) "[Kim's] infrequent but luminous stage portraits . . .": Robert Berkvist, "Kim Stanley, Reluctant but Gripping Broadway and Hollywood Actress, Dies at 76," *NYT,* 8/21/01, C-14.
(p. 322) many of the riddles in her own life went unsolved: "Transition: Stage Presence," *Newsweek,* 9/3/01, 9.
(p. 322) "one of the legendary fiascos": "Obituaries: Kim Stanley," *The Independent* (U.K.), 8/22/01.
(p. 322) "Although the film was based . . .": "Obituaries: Kim Stanley," *MG,* 8/24/01, 24.
(p. 322) "The reporter from the *L.A. Times* called . . .": Int. with RZ, 11/3/01.
(p. 323) "Lisa called me . . .": Int. with JW, 4/22/03.
(p. 323) "like a Nazi visiting": Rex Reed remarks at KS memorial service at the Actors Studio, 10/22/01.
(p. 323) "Something disappointing had happened . . .": John Guare remarks at KS memorial service at the Actors Studio, 10/22/01.
(p. 323) "Acting . . . requires integrity, judgment, and, above all . . .": Sir Peter Hall ltr. read at KS memorial service at the Actors Studio, 10/22/01.
(p. 324) "Kim had a passion for the truth . . .": BF ltr. read at KS memorial service at the Actors Studio, 10/22/01.
(p. 324) "The thing that matters most . . .": Int. with Meredith Alexander, 3/26/03.
(p. 325) "The easy answer is yes . . .": Int. with RZ, 1/19/02.
(p. 325) "Clearly, it wasn't because her clothes . . .": Ibid.

INDEX